# A HISTORY OF
# MODERN GREEK LITERATURE

LINOS POLITIS

# A HISTORY OF
# MODERN GREEK
# LITERATURE

OXFORD
AT THE CLARENDON PRESS
1973

*Oxford University Press, Ely House, London W. 1*

GLASGOW  NEW YORK  TORONTO  MELBOURNE  WELLINGTON
CAPE TOWN  IBADAN  NAIROBI  DAR ES SALAAM  LUSAKA  ADDIS ABABA
DELHI  BOMBAY  CALCUTTA  MADRAS  KARACHI  LAHORE  DACCA
KUALA LUMPUR  SINGAPORE  HONG KONG  TOKYO

PRINTED IN GREAT BRITAIN
AT THE UNIVERSITY PRESS, OXFORD
BY VIVIAN RIDLER
PRINTER TO THE UNIVERSITY

# Preface

IT IS NOT, I think, mere chance that the first attempts at a history of modern Greek literature should have been written in other languages. The first, by the Phanariot J. Rizos Neroulòs, was in French, published in Geneva in 1827, while the War of Independence was still in progress, and Europe wished to know something of what lay at the bottom of the Greek struggle for freedom. The same intention lay behind the later two-volume history by A. R. Rangavìs, first published in French (1877) and later in German, with the collaboration of A. Sanders (1884). At the end of the last century and the beginning of this, many foreigners also wrote histories or studies of modern Greek literature: R. Nicolai (1876), Juliette Lamber (1881), K. Dieterich (1902), D. C. Hesseling (1920). The work by the last-named, first published in Dutch and later translated into French (1924), is the first that is essentially modern. Later came the short works by A. Mirambel (1953) and Br. Lavagnini (1955; 3rd edn., 1969) and the lengthier work by B. Knös (1962, preceded by a shorter version in Swedish, 1952). It is strange that there has been nothing in English. In 1925 we have the first book on modern Greek literature in Greek by a Greek, A. Kambanis, which is rather short. (The works of G. Zaviras, 1872, and K. N. Sathas, 1868, were merly collections of biographies of authors.) The works of E. Voutieridis (1933) and J. M. Panagiotopoulos (1938) followed, also short, particularly the second, and in 1948 the compendious history by K. Th. Dimaràs (4th edn., 1968), which is the fullest and most responsible presentation to date.[1]

The present book owes much to those mentioned above, and above all to that of K. Th. Dimaràs; my friendship with the author is close and of long standing, and our views on many points are similar. I have tried to indicate clearly each occasion

---

[1] For further bibliographical information see the Selected Bibliography at the end of the book.

on which I have made use of his ideas or means of expression (particularly in the chapters on Enlightenment and Romanticism, subjects which he has studied exhaustively). Nevertheless there must be places where one cannot easily draw the line between similarity of view and an unconscious debt or reminiscence.

Much in this book is due to the monographs and research of others, especially in those chapters which deal with subjects outside my own particular field of work. I have already spoken of K. Th. Dimaràs. In the chapter on the demotic songs I have relied above all on the work of J. Apostolakis, St. Kyriakidis, and S. Baud-Bovy; for Kavafis on the books of T. Malanos, S. Tsirkas, F. M. Pontani, and G. P. Savvidis; for Kazantzakis mainly on that of P. Prevelakis. For the last chapters, which deal with contemporary literature, I have thought it best to rely on the views of the most authoritative critics. Thus, apart from the books by J. M. Panagiotopoulos, A. Karantonis, G. Chatzinis, and M. Vitti, I have read all the criticism for the last few years in literary periodicals, especially *Nea Estia*, *Kritikì*, and *Epochès* (criticism of A. Karantonis for poetry, of G. Chatzinis, A. Sachinis, and others for prose, and of M. Anagnostakis, N. Anagnostaki, and T. Sinopoulos for post-war poetry). Sometimes I have not hesitated to quote an appropriate phrase, as my intention was to render accurately the critic's point of view. In the Excursus I have been particularly helped by the books of G. Themelis, K. Stergiopoulos, M. Vitti, A. Sachinis, and D. Raftopoulos. In the Introduction the treatment of all that concerns the language is based on the *Short History* of G. N. Chatzidakis, the *Historical Introduction* of M. Triantafyllidis, and the *Bericht* of S. G. Kapsomenos.

The aim of this book is to provide a synoptic and objective account of the history of modern Greek literature, from its early beginnings in the Middle Ages until our time. But history can be objective only up to a certain point; indeed I would say that an absolutely objective account, even if it could be written, would be without interest. The fact that the writer of the book is a Greek perhaps deprives it of an element of objectivity—even though he believes himself to be free from all chauvinism (and particularly literary chauvinism). Moreover the author is a *demoticist*, and must naturally look at the historical development of literature from that point of view. The fact that this point of view is shared by the whole literary and practically the whole intellectual world of Greece removes the danger of subjectivity or one-sidedness—at least to the extent that the facts are seen from the historical–humanist standpoint rather than (for example) a Marxist one.

The book is addressed to the educated English-speaking reader —which means that it is assumed that the Greek world and the ancient language and literature of Greece are not totally unknown to him. To him particularly are addressed the pages of the Introduction relating to the modern language, with details of its similarity to and difference from the ancient language, which might to others seem superfluous. For the same reason passages of poetry quoted in translation in the body of the text are given in the original in the Appendix. Naturally a classical education is not a pre-requisite for the reader.

It gives me particular pleasure that the publication of this book has been undertaken by the Clarendon Press, for one of my main aims is to make modern Greek literature known to as many educated English-speaking people as possible. I am grateful to Zannetos Tofallis, who was among the first to urge me to write the book and who first tried to get it published. My wife has unfailingly provided me with moral support and practical assistance throughout the writing of it. I owe particular thanks to my colleague G. P. Savvidis, not only for useful advice on many points, but also for his help in ensuring the accurate rendering of delicate points of Greek phraseology. Mrs. M. Fatouros, Mrs. Chr. Kliridis, and Mr. A. L. Vincent have also earned my gratitude for looking over the English version. I am deeply grateful to Mr. Robert Liddell, who undertook the heavy burden of translating the Greek text; he is one of the few men who combine a literary knowledge of modern Greek with the sensibility of a trained writer. Each chapter is the result of careful collaboration between us and the checking of every detail. His previous experience in translating modern Greek verse enabled him to enrich the text with poetical extracts, always rendered in the original metre.

L. P.

# Contents

Part Two

# Note on Transcription

UNFORTUNATELY there is no accepted system for the transcription of Greek names into foreign languages, so we often find two versions, e.g. Calbo or Kalvos, Hadji or Chatzis, Yannopulo or Jannopoulos, Rhigas or Rigas, etc. I have proceeded on the double principle that transcription ought first of all to render the modern pronunciation and not the historical spelling (Politis not Polites), but at the same time that it should preserve the image of the word. This system (which can be applied to all European languages) is here carried out only with regard to proper names. (I ignore other transcriptions of the writers themselves, e.g. Calbo, Coray, Cavafy.) For Christian names it was not necessary to follow the same system, though here too I have generally preferred the forms nearest to the Greek: e.g. Andreas (not Andrew), Dionysios (not Denis). For geographical names I have kept the usual English forms: Athens, Corfu, Rhodes.

I transcribe letters which do not correspond exactly in the Greek and Latin alphabets as follows: $\beta:v$, $\gamma:g$ (neither $gh$, nor $y$, nor $j$), $\delta:d$, $\zeta:z$, $\eta:i$ (not $e$), $\theta:th$, $\kappa:k$ (never $c$), $\rho:r$ (not $rh$ even at the beginning of the word), $\sigma:s$ (also between two vowels), $v:y$, $\phi:f$ (not $ph$), $\chi:ch$ (not $h$ nor $kh$), $\omega:o$. The diphthongs $\epsilon\iota$ and $o\iota:i$, $\alpha\iota:ai$, $ov:ou$; the double consonants $\mu\pi:mb$, $\gamma\gamma$, $\gamma\kappa:ng$, $v\tau:nt$ (at the beginning of a word—or wherever else it is so pronounced—$b$, $g$, $d$), $\tau\sigma:ts$, $\tau\zeta:tz$. As for the accent, since the greater number of Greek names are accentuated on the penultimate, I put an accent only in the rarer cases where the name is accentuated on the last syllable. I do not particularly favour accents, but I thought it necessary, in order to avoid misreadings such as Palámas or Sikeliános. However, I thought it unnecessary for names accentuated on the antepenultimate, which are even more rare: such is the case especially for all names ending in -opoulos.

Examples: Vikelas, Digenìs, Giannopoulos, Makrygiannis, Drosinis, Kavafis, Koraìs, Rigas, Roidis, Vasiliadis, Vizyinòs, Fotiadis, Chatzopoulos, Soutsos, Embirikos, Rangavìs, Antoniou, Papadiamantis, Beratis, Gatsos, Tsatsos, Kazantzakis, Solomòs, Palamàs.

# Note on Transcription

# Introduction

MODERN HELLENISM has the enviable but invidious fate of descending from a civilization so glorious as that of ancient Greece. But it descends more directly from another civilization also, that of Byzantium, less glorious indeed but one whose significance in shaping the Europe of today has been fully acknowledged. This weighty double heritage has often been a motive for lofty actions, but it has sometimes led to an unrealistic romanticism or to groundless boasting. And foreigners, in their exclusive devotion to the famous past, have often been unfair to the new nation and to its cultural contribution.

Ancient Greek literature is thoroughly well known and well studied; it is one of the summits, if not the very peak, of the European spirit. Byzantium, with its history, its unrivalled art and its literature, has also interested scholars and men of letters; it is studied in universities, and special periodicals are devoted to it. As for modern Greek literature, it is so commonly associated with the Byzantine that the one term recalls the other, as if they constituted an undivided whole. Latterly in certain circles abroad (particularly in England) a lively interest has been shown in contemporary Greek literature, which revolves round a few outstanding poets whose work has had wide appreciation: Kavafis, Sikelianòs, Seferis, Kazantzakis. But these poets could not have existed in isolation; they must have roots, and a tradition behind them. What that tradition was, when it began, and how it developed through the years—that is the subject of this book.

## THE BEGINNING: PERIODS

When can we say that modern Greek literature began, and when did modern Greek civilization in general attain an existence of its own that differentiates it from that of Byzantium? An artificial division is, of course, 1453. With the fall of Constantinople and the annihilation of the Byzantine state, we may say that Byzantine civilization came to an end. But in history, and particularly in cultural history, there are no such abrupt and arbitrary breaks. The Rumanian historian Jorga spoke of 'Byzance après Byzance',[1] and scholars often employ the term 'post-Byzantine'. This occurs always in transitional periods: the old coexists with the new—or on the contrary, we might say, the new has already made an appearance alongside the old. This, we shall see, is the case with Greek literature. I prefer not to use the term 'post-Byzantine' for literature after the fall of Constantinople. In contrast to what may have occurred in other cultural spheres, the Byzantine elements surviving in literature are of the slightest. Rather, in the last centuries of Byzantium certain elements of a marked character appeared, which we can without hesitation call 'modern Greek'. When Constantinople fell, the people lamented its fall in a song in which we already find the technique and modes of expression that we shall later meet in the klephtic songs of the eighteenth century. We find the same characteristics in earlier songs which certainly belong to the Byzantine period, such as those of the Akritic cycle. The same phenomenon can be seen in learned poetry: the *Erotopaignia*, for example, written about 1450, have much in common with earlier Byzantine poetry, and at the same time pave the way for the poetry of the second half of the fifteenth century. From *Digenìs* to *Erotokritos* there is a unity and an organic development that is unbroken, so that to make a division at 1453 into 'Byzantine' and 'post-Byzantine' literature would be an arbitrary falsification of reality. Krumbacher, acknowledging the continuity, reckoned Byzantine *Vulgärliteratur*[2] as existing until the fall of Crete in 1669. Other scholars have tried to classify things by speaking of 'post-medieval' or 'Proto-neohellenic' literature.[3] It is more natural, and more in accordance with the facts, to admit that the modern Greek element appears underneath the literary veneer in Byzantine times, and to consider the *Vulgärliteratur* of the last Byzantine period—the

[1] N. Jorga, *Byzance après Byzance*, Bucharest, 1935.
[2] K. Krumbacher, *Geschichte der byzantinischen Literatur*, 2nd edn., Munich, 1897, §§ 328 ff., pp. 787 ff.
[3] E. Kriaràs, 'Η μεσαιωνική ελληνική γραμματεία (Τὰ ὅρια, μερικὰ χαρακτηριστικά) [Athens, 1950]. (Reprinted from Ἀγγλοελληνικὴ Ἐπιθεώρηση, 5 (1950–2), 92–6.)

most vital part of Byzantine literature, with the elements of future development in it—as the beginning of genuine modern Greek literature.

On this critical point, language should be the decisive argument. In fact, in *Digenìs*, and to a larger extent in the chivalric romances of the fourteenth century, we shall find the first attempts at a literary use of the spoken, common, i.e. modern Greek language. But the testimony of language has not as much weight as in the literature of other European nations. First because the Greek language is by nature conservative, and slow in its development (which prevents clear distinctions from being drawn), but chiefly (as we shall see) because Byzantium was dominated by a linguistic archaism which put difficulties in the way of an unadulterated use of the spoken language even in works of popular literature. For this reason the above-mentioned elements (such as the manner of expression of the demotic songs), genuinely modern Greek elements, are more conclusive than the testimony of language alone.

Thus while some of the older and some of the more recent histories of modern Greek literature begin in 1453 (sometimes later still, with Cretan literature), most scholars are now agreed that the birth of modern Greek literature should be identified with the Epic of *Digenìs Akritas*,[1] probably written in the first half of the eleventh century, which is the first literary text in which the modern Greek language is used (though not quite purely). This poem moreover flows from the Akritan demotic songs of the same epic cycle and is in the same epic spirit that prevailed at that time both in the East and the West, and shows the same stirring of a new national consciousness.

We need not in this introduction describe the periods into which the history of modern Greek literature is divided. The chapters of this book give the reader a sufficiently clear idea of this. But summarily we may say that there was a first phase which ends organically not (as we said) with the fall of Constantinople, but with that of Crete in 1669. The eighteenth century, as in the West an unpoetical age, was characterized more by strong intellectual activity and the development of

---

[1] All the later histories of modern Greek literature begin with *Digenìs Akritas*, e.g. K. Dimaràs (1948), A. Mirambel (1953), Br. Lavagnini (1955), B. Knös (1962).

education, particularly under the influence of European Enlightenment. The centre was now the Danubian provinces under their Greek princes. A new epoch begins in the last decades of the eighteenth century, with the development of education and the national orientation towards unity and liberation from the Turkish yoke. The revolution of 1821 and the creation of the new Greek state was a decisive point. For many years more, however, literature was to be divided between two separate streams or schools. In the Ionian Islands (under British occupation till 1866) the literary school cultivated the demotic language, taking up the broken thread of Cretan literature, and (further back) of the Byzantine *Vulgärliteratur*. In the free Greek state and the capital (Athens) the Phanariot learned tradition of the Turkish period survived, and the poets (romantic in mode) wrote in katharevousa. About 1880 a new generation (that of Palamàs and Psycharis) firmly introduced the demotic into literature and united the two traditions. These were the years of progress, often halted by reactionary forces or by political developments (the Balkan wars, the First World War, the Asia Minor disaster of 1922). The writers of the 1930 generation (Seferis among them) introduced a new period which, with the reinforcement of a younger post-war generation, continues to this day.

### THE MODERN GREEK LANGUAGE

If in literature there is no clear break between the medieval and the modern Greek periods, the same is even more true in the case of the language. Already Koraïs, and more definitely the great Greek linguist G. N. Chatzidakis, have declared the unity of the Greek language and its continued development through the centuries. Particularly from the end of the fourth century B.C., when a unity of the Greek world was caused by the conquests of Alexander the Great, the Greek language, previously split into many dialects (Attic, Doric, Ionic, etc.), was united in the Koine (see below). In all this long period of 2,300 years (from 300 B.C. until today) linguists regard the Greek language as an organic whole, distinguishing two or three periods within it : the Hellenistic Koine (300 B.C.–A.D. 550), the medieval (550–1453), and the modern Greek language (from 1453 on). The dividing line between the last two is most difficult to draw, and many reckon

them as a single period. Others date the division between the
Koine and the medieval language to A.D. 330.

The great age of Greek literature in the fifth and fourth centuries B.C. had already made the Attic dialect a common Greek
language. The loss of autonomy of the ancient Greek cities, the
Macedonian and later the Roman domination, the creation of
great urban centres in the Hellenized East, and other factors
contributed to the formation of a single Greek language with the
Attic dialect as its base, which linguists call the Hellenistic Koine.
It is the language in which the New Testament is written, and
that from which the medieval and later the modern Greek
language stems.

According to G. N. Chatzidakis—the first to refute the earlier
unscientific opinions and prejudices, and to put forward this
theory—the ancient dialects altogether disappeared on account
of the prevalence of Attic, and the Koine was formed on an Attic
base, with the admixture of many Ionic elements (for which
reason it is also called Attic–Ionian Koine).[1] Of the ancient
dialects the only one to survive was the Laconian, which is preserved in the Tsakonian of today (in a limited region of the
south-east Peloponnese, between Parnon and the sea). Meanwhile later linguistic research has brought to light the existence
of Doric remains in many modern Greek dialects, and arrived at
the conclusion that at the time of the Koine some Doric elements
—especially in the southern region—offered resistance to the
encroachments of the new speech. The last refuge of this resistance was the region of Tsakonia.

Characteristics of the Koine (which indeed did not all show
themselves at the same time) are as follows. In phonetics, the distinction between long and short vowels disappears; the diphthongs
$\alpha\iota$, $o\iota$, and $\epsilon\iota$ become monophthongs ($\alpha\iota > e$, and $o\iota$, $\epsilon\iota > i$); the $\eta$
is equivalent to $\iota$; $\upsilon$ in the diphthongs $\alpha\upsilon$ and $\epsilon\upsilon$ is heard as $f$
or $v$; both voiced ($\beta$, $\gamma$, $\delta$) and aspirated ($\phi$, $\theta$, $\chi$) plosives lose
their ancient pronunciation ($b$, $g$, $d$, $ph$, etc.) becoming spirants,
as they still are ($v$, $gh$, $ð$, $f$, etc.). In accidence, many forms are
simplified by analogy; the third declension tends to disappear,
the dual number becomes extinct, and the optative mood falls
into desuetude; verbs in -$\mu\iota$ give way to verbs in -$\omega$, and in

[1] G. N. Chatzidakis, *Einleitung in die neugriechische Grammatik*, Leipzig, 1892. Id.,
Μεσαιωνικὰ καὶ νέα ἑλληνικά, 2 vols., Athens, 1905–7.

general many irregularities are smoothed out and the language becomes easier. Syntax becomes more analytic and the vocabulary is greatly enriched, many words change their meanings (especially under the influence of Christianity, e.g. ἐκκλησία, ἄγγελος), and others are replaced by their diminutives (οὖς> ὠτίον) ; at the same time many foreign words, particularly from Latin and Hebrew, are introduced. Thus the Koine became 'far more like our modern language than the ancient. . . . The change of Attic into the Koine may in a way be considered as a simultaneous change from the ancient language to the modern.'[1]

The Koine was a spoken and written language (translation of the Septuagint, New Testament, and numerous papyri). But at the time of Christ one may observe a strange tendency to halt this natural development as men of letters began to write according to ancient Attic rules. This phenomenon, known as Atticism,[2] created the first split between the written and spoken language. Here, we may say, began the fateful bilingualism (the *diglossia* or διγλωσσία), which was to do so much harm in all its subsequent development.

The principal theoretician of Atticism was Phrynichus of Bithynia (second century A.D.), but the man who made it more of a reality was the rhetorician and sophist Aelius Aristides, a pupil of Herodes Atticus. A characteristic symptom is the condemnation of certain words and phrases, denounced by Phrynichus as 'barbarian', 'unacceptable', or 'illiterate', although we find them in the N.T.: σκίμπους λέγε ἀλλὰ μὴ κράββατος ∼ ἆρον τὸν κράββατόν σου (John); ἔμελλον γράψαι, ἐσχάτως βάρβαρος ἡ σύνταξις ∼ τῆς γυναικὸς τῆς μελλούσης τεκεῖν (Apocal.); γρηγορῶ· τῶν ἀμαθῶν, γράφε ἐγρήγορα ∼ μείνατε ὧδε καὶ γρηγορεῖτε (Mark).[3]

The Byzantine empire was a continuation of that of Rome, and its official language for all state purposes was in the first centuries Latin. Therefore Latin exercised the greatest influence

---

[1] G. N. Chatzidakis, Σύντομος ἱστορία τῆς ἑλληνικῆς γλώσσης, Athens, 1913, p. 71.

[2] The most important book about Atticism is *Der Attizismus in seinen Hauptvertretern* by W. Schmid, 4 vols., Stuttgart, 1887–97. See also M. Triantafyllidis, Τὰ Εὐαγγέλια καὶ ὁ Ἀττικισμός (1913), now in Ἅπαντα, vol. 4, pp. 111–18.

[3] Many such examples, mainly from Phrynichus, along with the parallel quotations from the N.T., are collected by M. Triantafyllidis, op. cit., pp. 114–15; cf. id., Νεοελληνικὴ γραμματική, Ἱστορικὴ Εἰσαγωγή, Athens, 1939, pp. 405–18.

on the formation of the new language (and Greeks in later years were called Romaioi and Romioi). But already from the time of Justinian (527–65) Greek was introduced into legislation (the *Novellae* of Justinian, written 'in the Greek and common tongue'), and in a few centuries the linguistic and cultural Hellenization of the state was thoroughly established. Throughout the whole medieval period of more than a thousand years, however, the phenomenon of the *diglossia* can be observed. The written language of the learned was closely attached to the Attic dialect, and with the centralization of the Byzantine state Constantinople became the centre of linguistic archaism and 'Attic' culture. At the same time there was the living spoken language which also, owing to the existence of this centre in the capital, developed into a common spoken language.

This spoken (Constantinopolitan) Koine has naturally disappeared; few traces of it were preserved under the thick layer of Atticism. Such are, for example, some satirical verses of the people (from the sixth to the eleventh century) and some linguistically more popular texts such as the *Chronicle* of Malalas, the author of which was a Hellenized Syrian (sixth century), some lives of saints, the works written at the instigation of Constantine VII Porphyrogenitus (tenth century), the *Strategicon* of Cecaumenos (eleventh century), and some other works. From the eleventh and twelfth centuries works written in the vernacular abound, and the spoken language is used with purely literary intentions. They are the texts of the *Vulgärliteratur*, which, as we said, are the beginning of modern Greek literature. It is not without significance that the literary use of the spoken language increases in the period of Frankish rule, and flourishes particularly in Frankish-occupied areas, far from the linguistic influence of the capital.

On the other hand, during the Comnenian and Palaeologian periods (eleventh to fifteenth centuries) we notice in the written language an intensification of archaism which is not unconnected (especially in Palaeologian times) with the cultivation of humanist letters. Anna Comnena (twelfth century) wrote a pure Attic language and Laonicus Chalcocondyles (fifteenth century) took Thucydides as his model for style and language. Often Byzantine writing is harsher and more difficult than that of the ancients.

The modern Greek language was already perfectly formed in the last Byzantine centuries, in the texts of the *Vulgärliteratur.* Thenceforward, separated from the medieval Koine, modern Greek dialects have been formed (see below). Subsequent development has been slow and the *Florios,* for example, or the *Achilleid,* of the time shortly preceding the fall, differ little linguistically from a modern demotic song.

The modern Greek language is characterized by the following features, which distinguish it from the ancient (and medieval) language: phonetically, there is a simplification of many consonant groups, the change of κτ, φθ, σχ, etc. into χτ, φτ, φκ, etc.; the final ν is dropped (ξύλο), and new diphthongs appear (νεράιδα). In accidence the declension of nouns is simplified, there are only four cases, and there is a tendency to drop the genitive too (especially in the plural), and for the other cases to coincide. There are only two voices in the verb, active and passive, and only two verb stems, the present and the aorist. The future, the perfect, and the pluperfect are formed periphrastically, the infinitive no longer exists, the participle, in most cases, has become indeclinable, and the augment, when not accented, has disappeared. Many prepositions have gone, and those remaining govern only the accusative.

The vocabulary of modern Greek derives in great part from the ancient language: some words have remained almost unchanged (γάλα, ξύλο, γράφω), most have changed in sound and form (πατήρ>πατέρας, παῖς>παιδί). Contact with other peoples has enriched the language with many foreign words; as we remarked, the Hellenistic Koine already contained Latin and Hebrew words, and later many Italian and Turkish words were introduced from the language of the conquerors; there are very few Slav, Albanian, and Vlach words. In the nineteenth century, with the establishment of the independent state, many of the Turkish words fell out of use or became obsolete, while many learned words and scientific terms were introduced and (from the many contacts with Western Europe) a new range of foreign words came in (especially technical terms and words from an intellectual environment).

In general, modern Greek is simple in its phonetics, having no aspirated consonants (such as *sh, ch, dj*), nor closed vowels (like the French *u, eu,* etc. or the English *o, ow,* etc.). There is also no difference between long and short vowels, the pronunciation is homogeneous and clear, there are many polysyllabic words, and every word has a definite accent on one syllable (which makes this syllable somewhat longer).

If we examine the development of the language in its entirety we find that Greek is essentially conservative. The pronunciation is certainly very different from that of classical times, but not very different from that of the Koine. Accidence has known no radical innovation, while vocabulary, in spite of all the new elements it has assimilated, has retained its ancient heritage. Statistics show that out of some 4,900 words of the New Testament, almost half are employed in the modern spoken language. 'The expression "daughter of the ancient language" is a metaphor inappropriate and false as applied to the modern language. It is the same language that has been spoken without a break by the Greek nation for thousands of years, passing from mouth to mouth and father to son, changing with speech . . . until it took the present form of the mother tongue, which will be a beginning for further development.'[1]

As we noticed, the ancient dialects have disappeared (apart from that of Tsakonia) since the time of the Koine. But perhaps at the end of the Middle Ages certain dialects began to be distinguished—some conserved more ancient elements. Linguists have attempted to classify modern Greek dialects;[2] some, taking as a starting-point their particular characteristics, have distinguished six basic dialects (Chatzidakis), others have seen more or fewer. We may distinguish some more compact groups, e.g. a western and an eastern group, or, using other criteria, a northern and a southern. Another distinction is between (*a*) a central body of dialects closely connected (mainland Greece, the Peloponnese, and the surrounding islands), the basis of modern Greek (whether spoken or literary), and (*b*) some dialects from outlying regions, with their own individualities. Such are the dialects of the Greeks of Asia Minor (Pontus and Cappadocia) and the Greek spoken in southern Italy (Otranto and Bova). We may also add Tsakonian. The differences in the central dialects are mainly lexical; in syntax, phonetics, and morphology

---

[1] M. Triantafyllidis, *Νεοελληνικὴ γραμματική, Ἱστορικὴ Εἰσαγωγή*, p. 56.
[2] For a good bibliography on modern Greek dialects see G. Kapsomenos, *Die griechische Sprache zwischen Koine und Neugriechisch*, Munich, 1958, pp. 16–19.

they are not great, and from that point of view the Greek language has great continuity.

In the literary texts up till the fifteenth century it is difficult to distinguish dialectical elements underneath the prevailing language. But already in Cyprus the local dialect was employed in writing (*Assises*, fourteenth century, Machairàs, fifteenth century), and in the sixteenth century it was used with complete success in the Cypriot love-poems. Dodecanesian (Rhodian) elements are found in poems of the fifteenth century (probably in the *Erotopaignia*, certainly in Georgillàs), but it was in Crete that a local dialect was fully established for the first time as a literary medium, and was written with unadulterated purity in the great works of Cretan literature (sixteenth and seventeenth centuries). Later the school of the Ionian Islands based itself to a great extent upon the local dialect; and in the early years of demoticism (late nineteenth century) some prose writers used dialect forms from mainland Greece in their stories. The great development of creative literature at the beginning of this century brought about a unification of the written literary language, excepting only the peripheral regions, where some Cypriot poets have written in their local dialect, and some Greeks from Pontus (in Athens or Thessaloniki) have produced theatrical works in their dialect. But these are exceptions.

### THE LANGUAGE QUESTION

The history of modern Greek literature, along with other aspects of intellectual and even political life in modern Greece, is incomprehensible in its significance and consequences without a clear understanding of what is called 'the language question'. In all civilized nations there is some difference between the written and spoken language. Other countries have to face the problem of the coexistence of two or more national languages, and European literature at the end of the Middle Ages passed through the stage where there was competition between the vernacular and Latin. Yet the Greek language question—still unsolved and acute in our own day—is not like any other. In Greece today there are two languages (or let us say rather two linguistic branches) that differ from each other in all points that form the structure of a language: vocabulary, phonetics, accidence, syntax. One branch is the common modern Greek language, the demotic, spoken by all Greeks and written by most of them; it is also the established language of literature. The other is the katharevousa, which is spoken by no one (at least in ordinary talk), but is the official language of the state; it was the common written language until fifty or sixty years ago, and is still used as a written language in a few quarters. It is odd and even comic that today, while anyone would at once be laughed at if he spoke in katharevousa in a circle of friends, it is thought perfectly natural that a public speech or university lecture should be in katharevousa; it would be equally ridiculous to write a friendly or family letter in katharevousa, while this would not be so in the case of a letter to be published in a newspaper, or of a scientific book or article. This strange *diglossia*, which is not easily comprehensible to a foreigner (or to any reasonable man), is due to particular historical and national circumstances, and has played a decisive role in the whole development of modern Hellenism. Its effect on education in particular, and more generally on intellectual and even on political life, has always been and still is extremely important. If the *diglossia* is not to blame for all our misfortunes (as the first demoticists were simple enough to say) it is not, however, innocent of the disastrous upshot that a student who has finished at secondary school is not able to write his own language or to express himself in it clearly (whether it be demotic or katharevousa). And the fact that all the liberal and democratic governments (from Venizelos in 1917 to G. Papandreou in 1964) have supported the demotic (and its introduction in education) while all the conservative and reactionary governments (with the single exception of that of Metaxàs) have been hostile to it, shows the deeper political and social significance of the question.

We have seen that this dualism in the language originated in the phenomenon of Atticism, and lasted through the whole Byzantine period for a thousand years. But it would be an error to say that the Byzantines had a 'language question'.[1] The first to be aware of the problem and to realize the general significance of the development of the popular language was the learned humanist N. Sofianòs at the beginning of the sixteenth century;

[1] On this subject see E. Kriaràs, *Diglossie des derniers siècles de Byzance: Naissance de la littérature néo-hellénique*, Oxford, 1966 (Thirteenth International Congress of Byzantine Studies, Main Papers, 9).

his preaching, however, was in vain. Throughout the Turkish period the learned wrote in ancient Greek, as their Byzantine forebears had done. Demotic was confined to literature (following an independent tradition), to books for the people, and to church sermons.

The problem was posed again in the last decades of the eighteenth century when, influenced by the Enlightenment, the Greeks made an attempt to awake and educate the people and to bring to the country the new ideas and the scientific progress of Western Europe. Conservatives thought the ancient language, already formed and established, was the right vehicle for this purpose; a small group of progressive intellectuals, on the other hand, thought that this could be better achieved by developing the common language. Between the 'archaicists' and the 'demoticists', A. Koraïs (1804) sought a *via media*: a language based on popular speech, but 'corrected' and 'embellished' on the model of the ancient. He was thus the creator of the katharevousa. Arguments and disputes lasted for some thirty years (1789–1821). Finally the compromise and the realism of Koraïs prevailed. Perhaps it was still too early for the definite triumph of demotic (on the side of which the poets unhesitatingly ranged themselves: Christopoulos, Vilaràs, and above all Solomòs). It was so much to the good that the 'archaicists' were altogether put aside.

With the creation of the Greek state the katharevousa of Koraïs was used by writers (with the exception of the Heptanesian school) and established as the language of the state and of all aspects of intellectual life. Its domination was universal; the lively discussions during the three decades before the revolution were now over. In any case, the general spirit now dominant was that of archaism, and the dream of a return to ancient glory. Thus the moderate and elegant katharevousa of Koraïs was gradually transformed—contrary to the theory behind that system—to an increasingly pure form of linguistic archaism which reached its height about 1880 (K. Kontos).

This exaggeration, however, produced fruitful reactions; in the ten years between 1876 and 1886 the language problem again became acute and topical, and it took a decisive turn with the appearance of Psycharis (see Chapter XI). Demotic again claimed its rights, and demoticism as a wider ideological movement extended greatly, thereby dominating all subsequent cultural history. After the initial reactions the movement spread to wider circles (no doubt Psycharis's fighting spirit had a lot to do with this); the years till 1917 have been called those of 'militant demoticism'. Psycharis's followers at home—the leader lived in Paris where he wrote his ardent articles and passionate pamphlets —carried on publishing their own periodical, the *Noumàs*, and founding societies. The most important step was the foundation of the 'Educational Society' (1910) which linked the language question with the educational problem ('educational demoticism'). Meanwhile the followers of the katharevousa also organized themselves, students caused riots in the streets of Athens, and in 1911 an article in the new constitution established the katharevousa as the official state language.

Demotic won a significant victory in the educational reform of 1917 which, for the first time, introduced the mother tongue into the three lowest classes of the elementary school. In the fifty-five years that have since gone by, demoticism, as a progressive movement (particularly in education), has known many ups and downs and internal crises. Successive governments have taken different sides over the question, and these switches have of course not been helpful to education. Besides, the (fatal) interference of politics, and particularly the wicked confusion of demoticism with communism, have held up natural development. The constitution of 1952 retained the anachronistic article of 1911. The last constitution, that of 1968, added that the katharevousa is the official language also of education. The educational reform of 1964 established the equality in education of the katharevousa and the demotic; the Emergency Law 129 of 1967 is a pitiful regression: the katharevousa was ordained as the exclusive medium of oral and written expression for teachers and pupils from the fourth class in the elementary school until the high school.

It is unfortunate that such reactions have so often interrupted natural development, which, as facts show, can only be towards the final triumph of demotic. The demotic (even after the recent unnatural revival of the katharevousa) is still the medium of expression for the greater part of everyday life; that is, it has been unofficially established, thus forcing a solution. But this solution does not appear to be near at hand.

## PRONUNCIATION AND SPELLING

That the ancient Greeks did not pronounce Greek like the Greeks of today is a scientific truth, known from the time of Erasmus (1528). In the long period of time between antiquity and today, the sounds of the language changed every so often by a natural development. The more essential differences were already established by the time of the Koine (see pp. 5 f.). Most typical is the phenomenon of iotacism, i.e. the pronunciation of the ancient vowels η, υ, ι, and the diphthongs ει, οι, υι as iota (*i*). But though the pronunciation changed, the spelling remained the same; from being phonetic it became historical, with all the weight of a long history. Modern Greeks, for example, write ποικίλη, φιλειρηνικοί, and say 'pikíli', 'filiriniki'. This creates unimaginable difficulties, to which may be added those of accents and breathings, which the ancients did not have, and which Alexandrian grammarians invented to mark the musical pronunciation (which had then been lost). Today accents and breathings have only a historical (or decorative) value. The printers, however, are compelled to use twenty-four alphas, children at elementary school are tormented with learning 'words with rough breathings', and the most educated (for in Greece education is more or less identified with correct spelling) consult their dictionary to make sure about the accent of κρίνος or the breathing of ἁδρός.

It should be mentioned, however, that while Greek employs a multitude of different letters to render the same sounds (as in the case of *i*), certainly many more than any other European language, yet only one sound corresponds to any one letter; we do not have the phenomenon (so exaggerated in English) of the same letter being pronounced in different ways. (The sole exceptions are σ, which in front of certain consonants is heard as *z*: σβήνω—zvino, and υ in the diphthongs αυ and ευ, sometimes heard as *f* and sometimes as *v*: αὐτός—aftós, αὔρα—ávra.)

In 1814 Vilarás wrote a book in phonetic spelling, and Solomòs in his own writings adopted a kind of phoneticism. Previously, in the seventeenth century, it was common in Venetian-occupied places to write Greek in Latin characters; the system was used also in papal propaganda addressed to Greek Catholics in the islands ('Frangochiotika')[1]—as recently in the Soviet Union in the case of the Greeks of the Caucasus. Such extreme solutions, however, are neither desirable nor practically feasible. Simplification of spelling, but within the historical framework, is an urgent necessity, particularly for purposes of education. Such simplifications were introduced by 'educational demoticism', and they have been codified in the *Modern Greek Grammar* (1941) of M. Triantafyllidis. On the basis of the easily used rules of this Grammar we could do away with most difficulties, and bring order out of the orthographical chaos. But Greeks are individualists and in spelling each has his personal preferences.

One of the difficulties would be overcome by a decisive diacritic reform, that is, by getting rid of the breathings, and retaining only one of the three accents (which is indispensable). Such a reform would not alter the visual appearance of words, it would be painless, and it could be applied immediately. But it seems that these diabolical little marks of the Alexandrian grammarians have become a sort of fetish, and no one dare take the decisive step. A leading Greek scholar, Professor J. Kakridis,[2] was censured by the disciplinary council of the University of Athens (during the German occupation) because he had published a book without accents, and essentially on this ground lost his position at that University.

### MODERN GREEK PROSODY

Modern Greek prosody—like that of most modern languages—is based on strong accentuation. Regular alternation of accent determines rhythm and metre. The two basic metres are the iambic (with the accent on the second syllable of the foot) and the trochaic (with the accent on the first). These are the only metres of demotic poetry. Learned poetry, influenced by foreign or ancient metrics, uses the anapaest, the dactyl, and the amphibrach. In the iambic and trochaic, syllables due for accentuation are not always accented; since most words in the Greek language are polysyllabic, this is quite usual; however, if more than four syllables together remain unaccented there is a kind

---

[1] See Eug. Dallegio, 'Bibliographie analytique d'ouvrages religieux en grec imprimés avec des caractères latins', Μικρασιατικὰ Χρονικά, 9 (1961), 385–499.

[2] See " Ἡ δίκη τῶν τόνων" (Ἡ πειθαρχικὴ δίωξις τοῦ καθηγητοῦ κ. Ι. Θ. Κακριδῆ), Athens, [1942]. Cf. Ἡ ἀντιδικία τῶν τόνων (ἐκ τῶν συνεδριῶν τῆς Φιλοσοφικῆς Σχολῆς τοῦ Πανεπιστημίου Ἀθηνῶν), Athens, 1944.

of slackening of the metre, and often there is reversion of stress.
Naturally only the accents that are heard are reckoned, and not
all that are written (for some of these, especially on the articles,
are merely symbols).

Examples:

βαριὰ βροντοῦν, πικρὰ βαροῦν
◡ ΄,  ◡ ΄ ,  ◡ ΄, ◡ ΄          (iambic)

στὸ ρημοκλήσι τοῦ Δηροῦ
◡ ◡, ◡ ΄, ◡ ◡, ◡ ΄          (iambic)

φύσα βοριά, φύσα θρακιά
΄ ◡, ◡ ΄ , ΄ ◡, ◡ ΄          (iambic)

Λευθεριά, γιὰ λίγο πάψε
◡ ◡, ΄ ◡, ΄ ◡, ΄ ◡          (trochaic)

τώρα σίμωσε καὶ κλάψε
΄ ◡, ΄ ◡, ◡ ◡, ΄ ◡          (trochaic)

τὰ τραγούδια μου τά 'λεγες ὅλα
◡ ◡ ΄ , ◡ ◡ ΄, ◡ ◡ ΄, ◡      (anapaest)

Ἡ Δόξα δεξιὰ συντροφεύει
◡ ΄ ◡, ◡ ΄ ◡, ◡ ΄ ◡          (amphibrach)

ξέρω μιὰ λύρ' ἀκριβότατη
΄ ◡ ◡ , ΄ ◡ ◡, ΄ ◡ ◡          (dactyl)

A very common phenomenon, particularly characteristic of
modern Greek prosody, is synizesis, that is, the single pronunciation in a verse of two vowels belonging to adjacent words: ἡ αὐγή,
νύχτά ἦταν. The modern (not ancient) diphthongs are pronounced in the same way (ὀιμέ, νεράιδα; also πιάνω, ποιός). e.g.:

Τοῦ πατέρα σου ὅταν ἔλθης          ◡◡, ΄◡, ΄◡, ΄◡
δὲ θὰ ἰδῆς παρὰ τὸν τάφο,          ΄◡, ΄◡, ◡◡, ΄◡
εἶμαι ὀμπρός του καὶ σοῦ γράφω     ΄◡, ΄◡, ◡◡, ΄◡
μέρα πρώτη τοῦ Μαγιοῦ.            ΄◡, ΄◡, ◡◡, ΄
                      (Solomòs)

The commonest modern Greek line is the iambic decapentesyllable (of fifteen syllables). With a regular caesura after the
eighth syllable, it is like two hemistichs of eight and seven
syllables.

Σημαίνει ὁ Θιός, σημαίνει ἡ γῆς, ‖ σημαίνουν τὰ ἐπουράνια. (a) (demotic)
Τοῦ κύκλου τὰ γυρίσματα ‖ π' ἀνεβοκατεβαίνουν.     (b) (*Erotokritos*)

The first hemistich may be oxytone (a) or proparoxytone (b).

The decapentesyllable is the usual verse of demotic song; with few exceptions all the poetry before and after the fall of Constantinople was written in it. After the mid fifteenth century (when rhyme came in) it is usually written in the form of couplets, and the fifteen-syllable couplet is the main verse form of Cretan literature. It is an adaptable line and capable of taking a variety of forms; in the hands of clumsy versifiers it becomes boring and monotonous, but the greatest Greek poets have given it depth and music. Solomòs particularly cultivated it, especially in the great compositions of his mature period. Palamàs tried to introduce rhythmic innovations in the form, and it knew its last creative use in the lines of Sikelianòs and Seferis.

The hendecasyllable came into Greek prosody through Italian influence; we first see it in the Cypriot love-poems of the sixteenth century, and later in Cretan poetry (the *Voskopoula*, and choruses from the Cretan drama). In later times it has been cultivated by poets brought up on Italian poetry, such as Solomòs (in the *Lambros*) and Mavilis. They knew how to use the stress (or 'discord') on the third or seventh syllable (Dantesco), which breaks the iambic rhythm, but creates a particular tension. For example:

*Καθαρότατον ἤλιο ἐπρομηνοῦσε.* (Solomòs)
ᵕᵕ ′ᵕ ᵕ ′ ᵕ ᵕᵕ ′ᵕ

*Φυσάει τ' ἀεράκι μ' ἀνάλαφρη φόρα.* (Mavilis)
ᵕ ′ ᵕ ′ᵕ ᵕ′ᵕ ᵕ ′ᵕ

Of other iambic lines the octosyllable is frequent (also in demotic song); in literary verse it is often used in combination with the seven- (or rarer) nine-syllable line. The short and pliable five-syllable line was used by the Phanariot poets (Christopoulos, Vilaràs) and by Solomòs; Palamàs also used it skilfully in his collection *The Five-syllables*:

*Πουλάκι ξένο*
*ξενιτεμένο.* (Vilaràs)

The trochaic octosyllable seems to be very old. We find it in satirical Byzantine popular songs, and in one longer poem (*Ptocholeon*). In later times it has been used by the Phanariots and Solomòs, particularly in combination with seven-syllable lines:

Σὲ γνωρίζω ἀπὸ τὴν κόψη
τοῦ σπαθιοῦ τὴν τρομερή.  (Solomòs)

The romantics of the Athenian school made a sort of unwieldy sixteen-syllable line out of two octosyllables:

θόλωσε καὶ μαύρη τρέχει ‖ ʿΟδοιπόρε ἡ ζωή σου.  (P. Soutsos)
ʹ◡,◡ ◡, ʹ◡, ʹ◡, ‖ ◡ ◡,ʹ◡,◡ ◡,ʹ◡

Solomòs used the anapaestic decasyllable, under the influence of Italian prosody, particularly in elegiac poems (e.g. *The Farmakomeni*), and also the amphibrachic nine-syllable line:

ʿΗ Δόξα δεξιὰ συντροφεύει.  ◡ʹ◡,◡ʹ◡,◡ʹ◡

The amphibrachic metre was preferred by many poets because of its rocking rhythm. The dactyl, however, is not easily adaptable to the modern Greek language, and therefore those who have tried to import the Homeric hexameter have not met with success. The principal impediment is the lack of long syllables in the modern language, and therefore the impossibility of using the spondee.

Kalvos employed a prosody of his own; his odes are all written on a plan of five-line stanzas, with four seven-syllable lines and a final five-syllable line. Kalvos, the pupil of Italian classicists, was thus trying to imitate Sapphic or Alcaic stanzas.

ʿΆς μὴ βρέξῃ ποτὲ             ◡◡ʹ◡◡ʹ]
τὸ σύννεφον, καὶ ὁ ἄνεμος    ◡ʹ◡◡◡ʹ]◡◡
σκληρὸς ἃς μὴ σκορπίσῃ       ◡ʹ◡ʹ◡ʹ]◡
τὸ χῶμα τὸ μακάριον          ◡ʹ◡◡◡ʹ]◡◡
ποὺ σᾶς σκεπάζει.            ◡◡◡ʹ◡

Kalvos always has a firm accent on the penultimate (sixth) syllable, and like his Italian models places his other accents indifferently on the first or second syllables of each foot. Moreover (except for his final five-syllable line) his lines are indifferently oxytone, paroxytone, or proparoxytone (of six, seven, or eight syllables).

# Part One

FROM THE BEGINNING
TO THE
EIGHTEENTH CENTURY

# I

## LITERATURE BEFORE THE FALL
## OF CONSTANTINOPLE
## (ELEVENTH TO FIFTEENTH
## CENTURIES)

THE YEARS BEFORE 1000 were the centre and climax of medieval history, both in the eastern and western world. Byzantium was at its glorious zenith under the Macedonian dynasty, especially under its three great emperors, Nicephorus Phocas, John Tzimiskes, and Basil II. Nicephorus was crowned emperor in 963 (after driving the Arabs out of Crete, and founding the monastery of Grand Lavra on Mount Athos), a year after the coronation of Otto I as Holy Roman Emperor. In 1071 the eastern empire suffered two mortal blows; it finally lost its eastern provinces in Asia Minor after the defeat at Manzikert, and it lost control of Italy after the victories of Robert Guiscard— just five years after the battle of Hastings. The East and West went their parallel ways. With the first crusade, at the end of the eleventh century, the two worlds were to come into conflict, but also into closer touch.

It was a critical time, a time of readjustment, of conflict between peoples, and of the creation of national consciousness; it was also the peak period of the medieval spirit, of the age of faith and chivalry. It is true that an Ottonian church is very different from Daphni or the Nea Moni of Chios, and a Frankish knight does not find his parallel in a Byzantine warrior, but the religious and militant spirit is the same. We know how this spirit, especially when brought into competition with foreign peoples, could give birth to legends centring upon outstanding characters, whether real or imaginary, and that these legends gradually turned into the material for epic, and later to definite poetical creation—

this occurred, for instance, in Spain with the epic of the Cid and of Roland.

At the other end of the western world (for Byzantium is also 'the West'), the Byzantines had to face the same dangerous enemy, the Arabs. There, at the eastern frontiers of the empire (which were not always stable, and from the eighth to the tenth century fluctuated between Cappadocia and the Euphrates), the external flank of the state was guarded by *akrites* (frontier guards). They were not a special military body; the central administration gave them property and thus in this border territory a strong military feudalism grew up, comparable with that of the wardens of the marches in the West. The akrites fought the Arabs, particularly the local rulers, the emirs, but they also fought the *apelates*, who as bandits and outlaws were famous for their prowess and seem to have had the same military tactics and the same ethical code as the akrites.

Various legends began early to form round the akrites' achievements, and there developed a cycle of popular songs (ballads) of an epic nature; a scholion by Arethas, the learned pupil of Photius (at the beginning of the tenth century), gives us definite information, that singers from Pontus and Cappadocia ('accursed Paphlagonians') sang of the akrites' prowess 'for money'.[1] This epic cycle, the 'akritic' popular songs, was preserved in the frontier districts (Pontus and Cappadocia), and also in Cyprus, Crete, and elsewhere, by oral tradition, and is still sung, (or was until very recently). It told of the daring, of the almost supernatural strength of the akrites, of the heroic deeds of Andronicus, Armouris, and Skleropoulos. We shall talk about these songs in another chapter (see Chapter V).

Drawing principally on these songs and legends, but also (as we shall see) on other more literary sources, a poet composed a lengthy poem, *The Epic of Digenìs Akritas*, the first text of modern Greek literature. We have shown in the Introduction why the beginning of modern Greek literature (that written in the spoken, popular, and therefore *modern* Greek language) must be placed so far back in time, in the heyday of the world of Byzantium.

---

[1] Τοὺς ἀγείροντας λέγει, ἤτοι ἀγύρτας, ὧν νῦν δεῖγμα οἱ κατάρατοι Παφλαγόνες ᾠδάς τινας συμπλάσαντες πάθη περιεχούσας ἐνδόξων ἀνδρῶν καὶ πρὸς ὀβολὸν ᾄδοντες καθ' ἑκάστην οἰκίαν, Commentary by Arethas on Philostratus' *Vita Apollonii*, see S. Kougeas, "Αἱ ἐν τοῖς σχολίοις τοῦ Ἀρέθα λαογραφικαὶ εἰδήσεις", Λαογραφία, 4 (1914), 239.

But the *Digenìs* is not only 'modern Greek' in its language, but—like other epic poems of the East and West—it is the expression of the appearance of a new national consciousness, which we may call modern Greek.

## THE EPIC OF DIGENÌS AKRITAS

Until 1875 nothing was known about *Digenìs Akritas*. In that year two scholars, K. N. Sathas and E. Legrand, published a first version of the epic from a manuscript at Trebizond. It was as if a signal had been given; three other versions were discovered in the following five years (in Andros; in Grottaferrata, the monastery of the Greek rite near Rome; and in Oxford). And *c.* 1900 two others were added to the list: one at the Escorial, and another (in prose) again in Andros. There is another recension in Russian. We shall presently see what is the relation between these versions.

The central hero is Basil Digenìs Akritas. The first three books (the poem has eight or ten parts, as the case may be) relate the story of his father, the Syrian emir Mousour: his capture of the daughter of a Greek general, his pursuit by her five brothers, his duel with the youngest, his defeat, his conversion to Christianity, and his marriage with her. The son of that marriage (Digenìs, i.e. of two races, Arab and Greek) is the hero of the epic, and the remaining books relate his achievements: his hunting of wild beasts, his love story (an elopement, with the girl's cooperation), his retirement to the frontier where he became an akrite, and finally his death. In accordance with the old technique of epic, the hero's own account of his achievements has a central place (Bks. v and vi in the Grottaferrata version, and vi and vii in the others): his battles with the leaders of the apelates, and above all his duel with the amazon Maximò—one of the finest episodes in the whole epic.

An early text such as this, based on tradition and historical fact, open to many influences, and coming down to us in so many variant versions, inevitably raises a number of problems. Literary research, though vigorously pursued, has not yet given a final answer to most of them. In 1930–40 the attractive and bold, though really improbable, theories of Grégoire[1] broadened

---

[1] He gave a synopsis of his theories in his book '*O Διγενὴς Ἀκρίτας*, New York, 1942 (see Selected Bibliography).

the horizon of the research, but went beyond the permissible limits. On the other hand, by contrast with the more historical and folklorist research of earlier scholars, the sober and strictly literary examination of the problems by John Mavrogordato (1956) has, in my opinion, yielded more satisfactory results.

It is certain that none of the versions gives us the original text of the epic, which Grégoire dated between 928 and 944, basing his argument upon historical events, reflected (in his view) in the work. This date is undoubtedly rather premature. Mavrogordato places the original text in the peaceful years of Constantine IX Monomachus (1042–54), the last ruler of the 'legendary' Macedonian dynasty. This is perhaps too late. The middle of the eleventh century is a firm *terminus ante quem*; then the new power of the Seljuks displaced the Byzantines in their turn from the eastern frontiers of the empire, and delivered the final blow at Manzikert (1071). Perhaps the most probable date is the end of the tenth and the beginning of the eleventh centuries, the peak period of the Macedonian dynasty and a time of perpetual warfare on every front, years so suitable for epic treatment.

However, as we have said, the original text has not come down to us. What then is the relationship of the different versions to the original text, and to each other? The Grottaferrata manuscript has many more learned and archaic elements in its language, and provides the most satisfactory text; Trebizond and Andros derive evidently from Grottaferrata, while the Escorial version is in a class quite by itself: its text is the worst and severely abridged, its language the most demotic. Earlier scholars thought that it preserved the original text; this, they believed, was written in the demotic and was later 'translated' into a more archaic language, as preserved in the other versions. Recent investigation seems to prove the contrary: the Grottaferrata version is closest to the original; its language, although essentially archaistic, is very near the spoken language of the time, with, naturally, many learned elements; later revisers continually adapted their language towards that of later times; the popular elements of the Escorial version (which so much attracted scholars) are only due to the reviser's familiarity with the popular poetry of his time.

The opinions of scholars are also divided on the subject of the relation between the written epic and the demotic songs of the akritic cycle. It must be regarded as certain that these songs existed before the epic, and that they were one of its most important sources. On the other hand we must not exclude the possibility that the epic, becoming widely known, gave rise to its own series of songs. To this group must certainly belong those which refer to the hero by name; they are not numerous, they celebrate his death, and chiefly originate in Cyprus and Crete, where there are many popular traditions connected with Digenìs.

These akritic songs often attain a true poetic quality. This caused earlier scholars to underrate the written epic, and to consider it the redaction of some pedantic monk. They were wrong. If the poet of *Digenìs* is not as great as the poet of the *Chanson de Roland*, his work is not without poetical qualities, and it faithfully renders the heroic spirit of the age and the environment in which it was born. His indubitable learning and his tendency to edifying exhortations (which may be due to a later recension) must not make us overlook the genuinely epic scenes of the first three books, for example, or the fights with the apelates and with Maximò. The composition is often purely descriptive or simply narrative; but the whole is neither a romance nor a court epic. It is a heroic epic, like its contemporary equivalents in the East and West. Perhaps its epic character was more manifest in its first recension. And there is something else that we ought not to forget: this unknown poet who lived far from the literary world of the capital, near the akrites and their army life, in Pontus or in Cappadocia, was the first to use the popular language for a poetical creation. To him we owe the first text in the popular (i.e. the modern Greek) language.

## THE COMNENIAN COURT

We meet the group of poems which we are now to examine in quite a different atmosphere: in the capital, at the court of the Comneni, about the middle of the twelfth century. The most important poems are the *Prodromika*, thus named after Theodore Prodromos, to whom the manuscripts attribute them. However, everything persuades us to believe that these poems, written in a forceful contemporary popular language, have no connection with the well-known learned and prolific writer. They are a form of petition to the emperor, either John or his son Manuel

Comnenus, or to other members of the imperial family, asking their help. As Theodore Prodromos was well known for petitionary poems of that sort, the unknown writer or writers place their words in his mouth.

In the first of the four poems (according to the numeration of the latest editors, Hesseling and Pernot) the 'poor Prodromos' complains of his poverty and of the way his wife grumbles about it; in the second he relates all the responsibilities which he has to face on account of his large family (thirteen in number). The third is rather different, a kind of poem popular in the Middle Ages: it is a satire against abbots, and their luxurious food, and the soaked beans and the ptisan of cumin that they give to others. The last is the eternal complaint of the 'clerk', or the teacher, against the poverty that torments him, and his lament that he would have fared far better had he learned any other trade. One line has become proverbial:

A curse upon all learning, Christ, and cursèd he who wants it!

Is one or more poet hidden behind the pseudonym of the 'poor Prodromos'? Until now the poems have mainly been studied from the point of view of linguistics or folklore (until the discovery of the akritic epic they were the oldest known text in modern Greek); they have been less studied from a literary angle. Like the *Carmina Burana* or the poems of François Villon (with which they have been compared)[1] they give a picture of the society of the time with much clarity and humour, and with a satirical bent. The theme makes the poet use words from everyday life and lively expressions, all of which give an intensity and vigour to the work. Sometimes (though we do not know if this was intentional) he approaches social satire.

The other two poems which are directly connected with the Comnenian court are not of comparable importance with the *Prodromika*. The *Spaneas*, modelled on Theognis, consists of advice addressed by an elderly courtier, possibly a member of the imperial house, to a young prince—it is an outline of court morals and etiquette. In its original form it may have been written by Alexios, the son of the emperor John Comnenos, who

---

[1] Sofia Antoniadi, "Πτωχοπροδρομικά", in *Mélanges offerts à Octave et Melpo Merlier*, vol. 1, Athens, 1953, pp. 13–23.

died before his father in 1142; the young prince to whom it is addressed may be the son of his sister, and of the Sicilian 'Caesar', John Roger. The original core was soon encrusted with additional advice added by successive transcribers. From the middle of the sixteenth century it circulated as a printed pamphlet.

We know the author of the other poem: he was Michael Glykàs, a well-known man of letters of the Comnenian age, who has given us theological works, a chronicle, and other writing (naturally written in the archaic language of Byzantine writers). It is in a mixed language with many demotic elements. In this, his only demotic poem, Glykàs addresses Manuel I Comnenus from the prison where (so he says) a neighbour's slanders have cast him. The poem was perhaps written in 1159; in its better moments the energy of the style brings it near to the *Prodromika*. The language often gains in demotic colour from the popular proverbs that Glykàs delights to insert in his work. Among his learned works moreover there is a collection of popular proverbs, with their theological interpretation.

## THE FRANKISH OCCUPATION: ROMANCES

In 1204 the Frankish crusaders occupied Constantinople and dissolved the Byzantine state. They were only to remain in the capital till 1261, but the various small principates which they founded and organized after the western feudal manner were to have a longer life; most of them were to exist until the second fall of the city in 1453, and many were to survive even longer. The Frankish conquerors naturally came into violent conflict with the local population, and many were the battles in which they engaged, especially after the restoration of the Byzantine state in 1261. But there were also peaceful and civil contacts, which were remarkably fruitful, as two peoples with great and very different traditions got to know each other more intimately. The West in the early thirteenth century was at a stage of remarkable creativity (this was when the cathedral of Chartres was built, and the national literatures were producing a flourishing poetry), its civilization was younger and more vigorous. Byzantium had passed the zenith, but the outstanding charm and delicacy of the art of the Palaeologi still retained much of the former glory. The Franks gave much, but what they took was not little. The gothic churches at Andravida and in Crete, the sculptural decoration in the Byzantine church of the Parigoritissa in Arta still bear witness to the exchange between civilizations. Strong Western influence is also seen in the literary texts of the thirteenth and of the two following centuries.

Many of the Franks who settled permanently in Greece were linguistically integrated, particularly in the second or third generation. Some of these were *gasmules*, i.e. sons of Franks by Greek mothers. One of the Greek-speaking Franks (not necessarily a gasmule) wrote *c.* 1300 in some 10,000 Greek decapentesyllables the *Chronicle of the Morea*. It is a narrative, from the conquerors' point of view, and definitely anti-Greek and anti-Orthodox, of the occupation of the Peloponnese (the Morea) by the Franks, and of its rule under various lords or princes. The greater part is given up to the story of what happened under the rule of Guillaume II Villehardouin (1246–78), whom the writer admired and presented as the epitome of chivalric virtue. The story continues until 1292.

The work has been preserved to us in several Greek manuscripts and in three foreign recensions, one French, one Italian, and one Aragonese. This—and other valuable observations— brought the editor John Schmitt (1904) to the conclusion that the original was in Greek, and that the foreign versions derived from it. His views have recently been questioned, and it has been maintained that the original version was written in French.[1] This theory is open to doubt. The work is a historical, geographical, and also linguistic monument of the first importance, as this Hellenized Frank is entirely uninfluenced by the Greek ecclesiastical and classical tradition, and writes more purely the spoken language of his time. We must not, of course, expect literary or poetic qualities; but they are not the only things that make interesting an early piece of writing.

The *Chronicle of the Morea* belongs indeed to the history of modern Greek literature. It is written in Greek (and in verse, as was natural for a Greek but inconceivable for a Frenchman); but it expresses nothing of the new Greeks pirit, as it was first expressed in the epic of *Digenìs*. We shall find the sequel to

---

[1] See G. Spadaro, 'Studi introduttivi alla Cronaca di Morea', *Siculorum Gymnasium*, 1959–61. H. Lurier, *Crusaders and Conquerors*, New York and London, 1964.

this in a maturer and later phase, in which we also discern the strong influence of the western spirit, in a series of romances written in the last two centuries of Byzantium: the mid thirteenth to mid fifteenth centuries. We rightly call them romances of love and chivalry. They are love tales, because they are always the story of two lovers who are parted (generally after their union) and who suffer trials and adventures until they come happily together again. They are tales of chivalry, for western medieval chivalry has a marked influence on them, with the man a vassal to Love, with their single combats and tournaments, and the love of adventure in distant countries. At the same time we find in these romances the element of legend, of the supernatural and the magical (magic palaces, monsters who guard captive princesses, magic rings, etc.).

In contrast with *The Epic of Digenìs*, the romances represent a more lyrical and romantic orientation in modern Greek. The hero does not fight against Saracens or apelates, but against the monster who is tormenting the princess, or the foreign king who has stolen his wife. Fantasy, adventure, and descriptive narrative have taken the place of epic conflicts. The love element is everywhere dominant, with its melancholy and oppression, but also with its sensual fulfilment. It is a charming and different world, like that represented in the French *roman courtois* and in the ballads of the Arthurian cycle.

It was not only Frankish influence that was behind these medieval romances, though this was undoubtedly the dominant element. But also a strong eastern influence must be acknowledged, which is expressed in the love of wandering and adventure and in fairy-tale motifs used profusedly. Hellenism did not abruptly turn its face from the East to the West, and research has found at many points the influence of *The Thousand and One Nights* (for example), or of modern Greek fairy-tales. A third element, sufficiently marked in some of the stories, is the influence of the Byzantine literary tradition: they might write in the popular language of the time, and they might be influenced by the corresponding romances of western chivalry, but the creators of these works were still Byzantines, and under Byzantine literary influence. They knew (as the author of *Digenìs* knew) the romances of the second sophistic age, they also certainly knew the Byzantine literary novels, scholastic and insipid works that flourished in a strange way in the middle of the twelfth century. They have in common with them the *ekphraseis* (ἐκφράσεις): the lengthy rhetorical descriptions of a castle, a work of art, a garden, or even a person. Finally, there is a fourth most important component, or perhaps we should call it the soil upon which other influences worked creatively: this is the modern Greek element, the genuine, popular, demotic feeling, which we meet again here, further developed since the time of *Digenìs*. In some romances we find *katalogia* (καταλόγια), apparently independent demotic songs of the time.

Of the romances of love and chivalry proper, five have come down to us. The longest and most characteristic, and certainly that which was most popular (it has come down to us in five manuscripts), is *Libistros and Rodamne*. The story is very involved. The whole romance is related by a youth called Klitovòs to his friend Myrtane. Once going for a walk, and feeling sad, he met another young man; this was Libistros, a Latin nobleman, prince of the land of Libandros. Libistros in his turn tells his story; after an allegorical dream he left his country and came to Argyro-kastron, where he fell in love with the daughter of the king, Rodamne. Much of the narration is taken up with the messages that Libistros sent her, shooting them on arrows up to the terrace of the castle. Finally the two young people were married, but after a short time Berderichos, king of Egypt, stole away Rodamne with the help of a witch, and Libistros went round the world to find her. At this point he met Klitovòs. The two friends continued the search together, they found the witch who had assisted the kidnapping, she gave them magic horses, they crossed the sea with them, found Rodamne, and returned happily to their country.

The other romances develop in a similar way. In *Libistros* the narration flows on easily, as it should in a fairy-tale, without ever becoming tedious. Moreover the complicated technique (the two pairs of lovers, the partial narration of the hero's adventures by himself to his friend, and by the latter to the woman with whom he is in love) shows an expert hand. The romance has also many poetical qualities, a pure lyric feeling and even a Mediterranean (or Oriental) feeling for nature, for the countryside, and for song: e.g. the songs sung by Rodamne and her attendants when they go out at night on to the castle terrace:

And late that evening when it shone and when the moon arose,
There went out on the terrace the handmaidens of the lady,
And there they stood, and they began to sing, my friend, a song:
'There was a youth, the slave of love, who left his parents' home,
And then he came and pitched his tent upon a lovely meadow;
The daybreak never gave him sleep, nor did the night-time tire
him . . .'

The language and verse are more demotic and more like
modern Greek; there is a quality and warmth that we have not
met before. It is a significant work, by no mean poet, and it
expresses more definitely that advance of modern Greek feeling
of which we were speaking. Naturally we know nothing at all
about the poet. In general, the date of the romances has not yet
been accurately established. Some indications place the work in
the fourteenth century, but it is still uncertain in which half of
that century. My personal opinion is in favour of the first half.
Nor have we any evidence as to where the works were written.
Certainly it was somewhere where Frankish influence was strong,
and had been long established; Crete and Cyprus have been
suggested. We receive no help from the language, a primitive
but common demotic (the text also is in a bad state).

In *Kallimachos and Chrysorrhoe* there are even more abundant
legendary elements. The Frankish influence is less pronounced,
and the language is somewhat more literary. This has made some
people think this romance earlier, perhaps of the thirteenth century. But the archaisms in a Byzantine work cannot be decisive
for its dating. Indirect evidence leads us to the most probable
conclusion that the writer was Andronicus Palaeologus, son of
the Sebastocrator Constantine, and first cousin of Andronicus II.[1]
This would place the work between 1310 and 1340, and would
explain the literary character of the language.

The work is half as long as the *Libistros*, and has come down to
us in only one manuscript. It is doubtful if it was widely known.
Still shorter (1,350 lines), and also surviving in one manuscript,
is the *Belthandros and Chrysantza*. It has many likenesses and motifs
in common with the others (e.g. the castle of Love), but also
a number of differences; for example, here there are no supernatural elements as in folk-tales, and love has a more sensual tone,

[1] See recently Börje Knös, 'Qui est l'auteur du roman de Callimaque et de
Chrysorrhoè?', Ἑλληνικά, 17 (1962), 274–95.

connected with the feeling of nature and of night, as in the *Libistros*. The language and verse appear to be an advance towards demotic and modern Greek. Other indications lead us to give it a late date, perhaps in the first half of the fifteenth century.

The two other romances of love and chivalry are clearly adaptations (if not actually translations) of well-known and popular western originals. *Imperios and Margarona* is a version of the French *Pierre de Provence et la belle Maguelone*, whose first recension dates from the end of the twelfth century. In many of its details the story reminds us of the genuine Byzantine romances (the acquaintance with the princess of Anapoli, and the duel with the German); but the element of legend is lacking, and so are the Byzantine *ekphraseis*. The narration is sober, and the central episode (the eagle which takes the amulet from the sleeping Margarona) in its realism is a step from the romance towards the prose tale (the *novellistica* which was later to flourish in Italy). It seems that this work was much appreciated by the Greek people, and had a wide circulation. It has come down to us in four manuscripts; later it was put into rhyme (like many others, as we shall see), and from the middle of the sixteenth century it circulated in popular editions printed in Venice.

*Florios and Platziaflora* is also a recension of a French romance, *Floire et Blanchefleur* (whose first form dates from the twelfth century). The Greek adapter draws directly on a metrical Tuscan version (in *ottave*) of the early fourteenth century, *Il cantare di Florio e Biancifiore*. Many medieval commonplaces are to be found (the duel symbolizing divine judgement, the foreign king who holds the princess prisoner, and the adventures of the separated lovers until their reunion). But there are a number of elements that herald a new spirit. There is a closer spiritual affinity between the hero and heroine, their love is youthful and pure. Florios does not only move us by his courage, but also by his nobility and his devotion to the girl whom he loves. The Greek adapter has overburdened the simple narration with 'lyrical' expressions borrowed from the demotic songs, which give a somewhat empty effect. Here also we are certainly at a late period, perhaps a little before the middle of the fifteenth century.

A love of romance and adventure, and the exploitation of foreign originals, are characteristic features of other romances of this period besides those of love and chivalry. Thus the *Tale of Apollonius of Tyre* is an adaptation of a western romance: the one surviving manuscript states clearly that it is a 'translation from the Latin [i.e. Frankish] into Romaic'. The earlier prototype, however, was a Greek sophistic novel (of the third or fourth century A.D.), now lost, which was early translated into Latin, and had a wide circulation in the West throughout the Middle Ages (the *Historia Apollonii Regis Tyrii*).[1] The subject has nothing in common with the tales of love and chivalry, and is very reminiscent of the romances of Xenophon of Ephesus or of Achilles Tatius. Apollonius, his wife, and his daughter undergo various adventures, are parted, believe each other dead, and at the end are happily reunited. The action takes place in the Greek regions of the East, in Antioch, Cyrenaica, Ephesus, Tarsus, and Mytilene. It may be this that moved the Greek adapter to 'translate it from the Latin'.

The *Trojan War*, a translation of the *Roman de Troie* of Benoît de Sainte-Maure (twelfth century), is of great length, and clumsy in its expression. It survives in many manuscripts, which indicates a large circulation. No scholar has yet had the courage to edit it.[2] The *Old Knight* (which, on the contrary, survives in only one manuscript) is a short, dry version in literary language of the French romance *Gyron le Courtois*.

Krumbacher's term 'romances with a national subject' is not, as we shall see, organic, but it is convenient enough for use in referring to another class of writing. These romances are very unlike each other. The *Life of Alexander* is a metrical version, in the Byzantine literary language and dated 1388, of the well-known Hellenistic romance of Pseudo-Callisthenes; it derived directly from the ancient text. It is hard to bring this within the same rubric as the works we are examining. But later we have a rhymed version in the now usual demotic language, which was often printed from 1529 onwards by the Venetian presses. We have also a prose version, from the same or slightly earlier period (about 1500), in different redactions, transmitted by many manuscripts; and later on a prose version, more demotic in

[1] Edited by A. Riese, 2nd edn., Leipzig, 1893 (Bibliotheca Teubneriana). See E. Rhode, *Der griechische Roman und seine Vorläufer*, 3rd edn., Leipzig, 1914, pp. 435–53.
[2] An edition is being prepared by Mrs. E. M. Jeffreys of Cambridge and Professor M. Papathomopoulos of Janina.

form and language, the famous 'Chap-book' (*Phyllada*) of Alexander the Great, a popular work, which circulated in cheap editions from about 1680 onwards until our own day; the Macedonian king is carried into the sphere of popular mythology and collects a number of strange and marvellous stories around his personality.

The *Tale of Belisarius* also gathers legends and fantastic stories round a historical personage, Justinian's general Belisarius. It appears that these legends were of early invention. The *Tale* makes him the object of the courtiers' envy, and they persuade the emperor to imprison him and finally to blind him. (The English reader may be amused to read that Belisarius, after his first release from prison, leads the army to make war on England, subjugates it, and returns to Constantinople in triumph, bringing with him the English king as captive.) The first recension cannot be earlier than the fifteenth century; there is another version by Georgillàs of Rhodes (see p. 39), and yet another in rhyme. (The well-known western versions of the tale of Belisarius by Rotrou and Marmontel are independent of the Byzantine work.)

The *Tale of Achilles* or the *Achilleid*, also of the fifteenth century, has quite another character. It is a love romance, on the lines of those which we have seen; the poet has simply taken the mythical Achilles for his hero. His Achilles is indeed son of the king of the Myrmidons and has a friend called Pandrouklos; but he has no further connection with the hero of the *Iliad*, and it may be doubted if the writer was acquainted with it. His Achilles is dressed like a Frank and is the hero of a love story, like Belthandros or Imperios. There are many correspondences between this and the other two romances, but one thing is of significance, the close dependence of this romance on *Digenìs Akritas*. Achilles, like Digenìs and like his father Mousour, runs away with the woman he loves, is pursued by her five brothers, and ends up in reconciliation and marriage. Perhaps this dependence gives the romance a purer Greek colour. There is not so exclusive an influence of western prototypes; it must date from the last age of Byzantium, shortly before the middle of the fifteenth century.

### ALLEGORIES

Allegorical and didactic poetry was always very popular in the Middle Ages, the greatest example being the famous *Roman de la Rose*. One example of this genre is the relatively short poem (756 lines) entitled *A Tale of Consolation about Good and Bad Fortune*. A young man afflicted by Bad Fortune walks towards her castle. On the road he meets Time; he enters the castle of Bad Fortune and thence is led to that of her sister, Good Fortune, where a *pittakion* (a charter properly sealed and signed) releases him from his troubles. The personifications have certainly something artificial about them; nevertheless the whole narration (which is all in the first person) is not without interest. The work is clearly influenced by the romances of which we have been speaking, and perhaps it follows one of them (the *Libistros*) fairly closely. It belongs to the fourteenth century.

Equally early, and perhaps earlier (it probably dates from before the Frankish occupation), is the *Story of Ptocholeon*. The verse form, in the less common trochaic octosyllables, may well be a mark of early date. Behind it is an oriental (perhaps Indian) story. A rich, wise old man loses all his property in a raid by corsairs and is himself sold as a slave into a palace where he has many opportunities of displaying his wisdom—he even reveals the illegitimate origins of the king. We find the same motif in the *Eracle* (the Byzantine emperor Heraclius) of Gautier d'Arras (twelfth century), in the Russian song of Ivan, and in a Turkish legend.

There are other lesser poems of varied character, and of undetermined date. The few lines of the *Sinner's Prayer* are genuinely moving. The short *Drunkard's Philosophy* is satirical (of the type of the *Prodromika*). And (in its better parts) the poem on *Exile* is very near to the popular feeling about absence from home; linguistic elements allow us to place it in Crete in the fifteenth century. At the same time Leonardos Dellaportas (c. 1350–1410/20) was writing at Chandax in Crete; a man of many activities, he was a lawyer at home, and acted as ambassador for Venice on various missions. In his old age he was sent to prison, where he wrote a long poem in the form of a dialogue between the poet and Truth, with many autobiographical elements, but strongly influenced by the romances, above all by

*Libistros*. He is the one poet of the age whom we know by name, and the fact that he was a Cretan links him with the Cretan literature which followed the fall of Constantinople, and particularly with Stefanos Sachlikis, not much his junior, who like him was a lawyer and also suffered imprisonment.

From Aesop to La Fontaine animal stories have been widely enjoyed, whether in the form of popular amusing tales, or in a more literary form with a didactic and edifying character. The *Paidiophrastos Tale about Quadrupeds* (the title means 'playful' or 'witty'; but in some manuscripts the work is entitled *Pezophrastos*, i.e. written in popular speech) is a work of some length (1,000 lines and more), and certainly dated to 1364. A meeting of all the animals, harmless and bloodthirsty, at the invitation of their king, the lion, is related with much humour. After they have sworn mutual friendship, each animal speaks separately, and relates his merits and the faults of one of the others. At the end the lion suddenly decides to dissolve the friendship, and the meeting turns into a Homeric battle in which the beasts eat one another. There is no doubt that there is some didacticism at the beginning, and perhaps the writer meant to try to write a popular handbook of zoology. But the 'war of words' among the beasts goes far beyond this intention; it has vigour and genuine humour, and sometimes is piquant and very free. Humour and wit dominate the descriptive and didactic elements.

The *Poulologos*, a poem corresponding to the *Tale about Quadrupeds* but about birds, also has great quality. It does not necessarily derive from the latter work; indeed it is probable that the dependence is the other way round. Here the eagle, 'the great king of all the birds', invites them to the marriage of his son. The birds appear two by two, and (like the quadrupeds) speak their own praise while disparaging the others. Finally the eagle tells them to leave off their quarrel and to eat and drink at his feast. Here we find the humour of the tale at its best; the descriptions of the creatures and their insults are most apt, and the satire very much to the point; the language is more demotic and vigorous. Here, for example, is the address of the dove to the crow:

> Tell me, you evil-visaged crow, what is it you are saying?
> With raucous voice and ugly face and very little sense,
> You're an Egyptian in your cloak, an old witch in your mantle.

demotic songs or conscious works of art. Some manuscripts preserve such collections of love songs. In expression they are very
near to the demotic love songs (composed at the same time and
in the same places), though we cannot call them genuine
demotic songs; some of them have the same atmosphere as the
late medieval *katalogia*, while in others we perceive the new freshness of the Italian Renaissance. The earliest and most remarkable
collection is that in a British Museum manuscript (known by the
name *Erotopaignia*, given to it by editors). It may be a collection
of entirely demotic lines or, more probably, the original works of
a learned poet. But the learned poet is so near to the people that
he does not hesitate to borrow whole demotic lines to express
his own sentiments, without allowing their guileless demotic
charm to fade. In the second collection (a Vienna manuscript)
we reach the end of the fifteenth or even the beginning of the
sixteenth century. What is new is here in a more advanced state,
and rhyme makes its appearance, while the half-way position
between demotic song and learned writing is preserved.

From the end of the fifteenth century onwards we must mention several poets, of lesser or greater importance, whose names
we know, and who were active in the islands or in Italy.
Emmanuel Georgillàs of Rhodes (which was to remain in the
hands of the Knights of St. John until 1522) wrote a metrical
chronicle of the plague which attacked that island in 1498. The
verses are mediocre; but they warm up when he speaks of the
great ladies of Rhodes and gives a detailed description of their
dress. A similar disaster, the great earthquake of 1508, is described
by the Cretan Manolis Sklavos, while another Cretan, George
Choumnos, composed in simple verse a popular Old Testament
narrative of Genesis and Exodus. The *Mourning for Death* of
Gioustos Glykỳs, from the Venetian-held Korone, has a religious
and edifying character, and follows the lines of similar medieval
work; it is one of the first literary works printed in Venice (1524).
An uneven work, it had, however, a wide circulation and echoes
of it are heard in *Erofili* and *Erotokritos*. The Corfiot Jakovos
Trivolis, who lived in Venice, published two very dissimilar
works there about the middle of the sixteenth century. One is
a panegyric of the Venetian admiral Tagiapiera, in short,
demotic, eight-syllable lines; the other, *The History of the King
of Scotland and the Queen of England* has nothing to do with any

Scottish king or English queen, in spite of its title; it is a rather scandalous tale taken from Boccaccio (or one of his imitators). The rhymed fifteen-syllable lines here flow with greater ease; for all its imperfections, the poem is not without interest.

## RENAISSANCE POETRY IN CRETE

From now on, however, the island which offers the most promising signs of a flourishing literature is Crete. The Venetians occupied the island immediately after the Fourth Crusade; their rule was already established there in 1211 and lasted until 1669, more than 450 years; throughout this long period Crete was a basic centre of Venetian colonialism, and in time experienced considerable commercial and economic development. In the first two centuries of Venetian domination, the Greek inhabitants made frequent attempts to shake off the Venetian yoke by bloodstained risings, but in the fifteenth century, and particularly after 1453, circumstances led to the peaceful coexistence of the two elements and in consequence to a deeper infiltration of western civilization—now the civilization of the Renaissance. At the same time many Byzantine scholars fled to Crete, where we find a humanist development which often unites the last flourishing in Byzantium with the development of ancient Greek scholarship in the West.

Before the fall of Constantinople we met with Leonardos Dellaportas in Crete, and we saw that some of the last Byzantine poems were perhaps Cretan (see p. 35); in the period with which we are concerned (late fifteenth and early sixteenth century) we have already spoken of Choumnos and of Manolis Sklavos. A far more interesting personality is their contemporary, Stefanos Sachlikis. Many of his poems have an autobiographical character, so we learn many details of his prodigal life: how he passed some time in prison after quarrels with the courtesan Koutagiotaina, how later he lived on his property in the country, or as a lawyer in the capital (Kastro or Chandax). Though the expression is still uncouth, the verse has nerve and humour, both in the purely autobiographical parts (*Strange Story*), and where he satirizes the courtesans and gives a very piquant account of their conversation, and finally when he advises a young friend of his not to roam about at night, not to play dice, and, above all, not to associate with the courtesans—things which he had learnt from experience. In his poems we feel something of the turbulent life of the world and of the underworld of a great harbour, a distant colony of Venice. He is charming when he describes his boorish jailer, and quotes his Venetian speech; but he is at his best when he speaks of courtesans; something between Villon and Aretino.

The poems of another poet, Marinos Falieros, are set in another world. He has no connection with the ill-famed Doge of Venice of the same name, nor do we know exactly when he lived (but it must have been about the time that we are now studying). Of the five poems that have come down to us under his name, two are admonitory or consolatory (a parallel to those of Sachlikis); another falls quite outside the normal categories: it is short, and is a kind of dramatization of the Crucifixion (an elementary mystery play). His two erotic poems, closely akin to each other, have much greater importance. The poet sees in his dreams (one of the poems is entitled *History and Dream*) his beloved together with Destiny and Pothoula (the personification of love). The strong and sometimes realistic erotic element, together with the allegorical mood and the dream narration, give something quite original and most pleasing to these poems. But much concerning this poet is still obscure and we have as yet no satisfactory edition of his work.

A dream is also the basic material of the *Apokopos* of Bergadìs, though the theme is entirely different. Its curious title is due to the first line (*Μιὰν ἀπὸ κόπου ἐνύσταξα*—'Once I grew sleepy after toil'), and we know nothing of the poet, not even his Christian name; we only know that the poem was first printed in Venice in 1519, and was the first modern Greek literary work to be in print. The poet (or rather, the narrator) has a strange dream: he is hunting a doe, and suddenly finds himself up a tree, and finally in Hades. The dead ask him how he comes there 'all alive and living', and two young men come into the foreground and eagerly ask him for news of the world above:

> And are there trees and gardens still, and are there birds that sing?
> And do the mountains still smell sweet, do trees flower in the spring?
> And are the meadows still so cool, and does the sweet breeze blow?
> And do the stars in heaven shine, and does the day-star glow?

They are anxious to know whether the living remember the
dead, but get no answer. Asked in turn by the poet, the youths
relate their story, their noble origin, every detail of the equipping
of a ship for a journey, the shipwreck which cost them their
lives, and their meeting in Hades with their sister, who died at
the same hour.

The poet set out to write a didactic, admonitory poem, a
*memento mori* in accordance with the custom of the time. But his
tone has undergone a strange alteration, and instead of speaking
of the darkness of Hades he speaks of the joy of life; his lines are
full of light and spring. And instead of wasting time on counsels
and edifying admonitions he concentrates on one point, giving
the strange story of the two youths with its inexplicable charm;
his love of detail, and the warm, golden tones of his description
remind us of pictures of the early Renaissance (e.g. of Benozzo
Gozzoli or of Melozzo da Forlì). The *Apokopos* (together with the
Cypriot love-poems) is the most poetical work of the sixteenth
century. It was much read and loved by the people, as is shown
by the many editions, right into the nineteenth century. In Crete
many of its lines passed into folk poetry, and are still sung as
laments for the dead.

In contrast, Joannis Pikatoros of Rethymno, though dealing
with the same theme, a descent into hell, and perhaps imitating
the *Apokopos*, has none of the latter's virtues. It appears, moreover, that the work did not have a large circulation as it is
preserved in only one manuscript. It has a strong religious
and exhortatory character and, unlike the *Apokopos*, the tone is
gloomy. The lines seldom attain more than mediocrity.

We are in a more lyrical atmosphere with the *Rimada of the
Girl and the Youth* (which Legrand called *La Séduction de la
jouvencelle*). The song is distinguished by its narrative skill and
its genuinely demotic expression and also a sensual realism which
never loses its freshness and grace, and which is paralleled in
some demotic love songs. Some critics, perhaps for this reason,
have mistakenly thought it a demotic song.

Literary quality shows itself in another work, which also had
a wide circulation and was first printed (also in Venice) twenty
years after the *Apokopos*, in 1539. It is *The Delightful Tale of the
Donkey, the Wolf and the Fox*, or (as it was popularly called) *The
Chap-book of the Donkey*. It belongs to the very much appreciated

type of tales about animals, and its immediate prototype is the late Byzantine *Synaxarion of the Estimable Donkey* (see p. 37). The poet arranges his prototype in the rhymed lines that are now the fashion of the time; this he does in a masterly way, and rhyme, which is such an encumbrance to other adaptors, becomes in his hands an instrument of poetic expression:

> νὰ φᾶς τὸ μαρουλόφυλλον ἐκεῖνο χώρις ξίδι—
> καὶ πῶς δὲν ἐπνιγήκαμε σὲ τοῦτο τὸ ταξίδι!¹

The plot is the adventure of the wolf and the fox (they had become friends and gossips), who wanted to take in the donkey and eat him, but in the end he was the victor. It is a purely popular poem, with popular wisdom and a humour that is not afraid of coarseness or impropriety (though it is always wholesome). This, and the symbolism of the guileless donkey who is victor in the end, (together with its superior literary quality), explains why it has been such a favourite.

All the above-mentioned works, whether from Crete or elsewhere, belong to the first half of the sixteenth century. In the second half, and towards the end of it, we reach the period when literature most flourished in Crete, as it continued to do until 1669, the year when the island fell to the Turks (see the following chapter). In the years between we have nothing of significance. We shall only make brief mention of a verse chronicle, which in 20 chapters and 2,500 lines describes the siege of Malta by the Turks in 1565, when the island was held by the Knights of St. John, driven out of Rhodes in 1522. Writen by Antonios Achelis of Rethymno, it was published in Venice in 1571, and is merely a version of the French chronicle by Pierre Gentil de Vendôme (which first circulated in Italian in 1565). The original chronicle was of course in prose; the metrical version of the Italian shows that verse continued to be the most natural form of expression in modern Greek literature.

### PETRARCHISM IN CYPRUS

At the same period in Cyprus, and in particular just before its fall to the Turks in 1571, we have a series of love-poems which are certainly among the most beautiful lyrics of early modern

---

¹ Did you really eat that lettuce-leaf with no vinegar?
It is a miracle that we have not been drowned in this our voyage!

Greek literature. They are written in the markedly characteristic local idiom of the island, and not in the conventional popular decapentesyllable, but in the Italian hendecasyllable and in a variety of forms familiar to the Renaissance: sonnets, octaves, terzinas, even canzones, sestinas, ballades, barzelettas, etc. The Italian influence on these poems is marked; some are direct imitations of Petrarch or of his followers (such as J. Sannazaro and P. Bembo); while others, which cannot be imitation, are in the full spirit of Petrarchism. The poet brings into Greek (into the local idiom, which he raises to the level of a literary language) the language, the forms of expression, the metrical forms of the Petrarchan originals, and moves with ease in the same poetical world. His diction has not yet become a burden, and the poet takes delight in playing with it, in an artificially constructed dialectic; words give rise to correspondences or antitheses, as in the music and dances of the time. Of all the prosodic forms, it is perhaps in the octaves that we find the most successful blending of the foreign influence with what is personal to the poet; in this limited form there is a freer semantic play, whether on one word or on two which are opposed or brought into connection (as here, *flame*, *heat*, *cold*, and *snow*).

> Nature it is that gives its heat to fire,
> Nature it is that makes snow cold and white;
> And makes one flame spring from another pyre,
> And with the snow makes sharper winter's bite.
> Quenched by the snow, the flame must needs retire,
> Before the flame the cold must vanish quite.
> Me only never doth consume a flame
> That rises from a fair but frozen dame.

The love-poems of Cyprus are one of the highest points of Renaissance literature in Greece, in its purest form. Unfortunately they had no sequel after the fall of the island to the Turks.

### INTELLECTUAL LIFE IN THE DIASPORA AND IN TURKISH-OCCUPIED GREECE: DEMOTIC PROSE

After the fall of Constantinople the retention of the Patriarchate and ecclesiastical hierarchy was of great importance to Hellenism, especially the Hellenism under Turkish rule, which was thus strengthened in its faith and nationalism. But in those parts of

Greece occupied by the Turks one cannot speak of the existence of literature or of any intellectual life for at least a hundred years. Literary activities were confined to the regions held by the Franks, and came to their zenith in Crete and Cyprus. We have explained the reasons for this.

The third section of Hellenism, that of the diaspora, was not a fruitful field for creative literature; nevertheless some intellectual activity is there to be observed, especially in Italy, where many scholars had taken refuge, some before the fall of Constantinople, many more after it. It was there that the early humanism was concentrated, which had shown itself so richly in the last years of Byzantium. The contribution of the Greek scholars to the Italian Renaissance is well known. It is not that they created this intellectual movement (the contrary is the case: it was because this movement was in existence that scholars fled there rather than elsewhere). But these Byzantine refugees had something of inestimable value to reveal to the West, which was now discovering ancient Greece: the knowledge of ancient Greek and the writings of the ancients, which—unknown to the West— they had preserved through all the centuries, and knew how to interpret.

Therefore most of them worked, in the foreign land that gladly received them, either as editors of classical texts, or as teachers of the Greek language. Many received great honour among learned humanists and cultivated rulers; they obtained high positions, and undertook diplomatic missions. In the first years many were moved by the hope of organizing a crusade for the liberation of their enslaved nation.

Perhaps the most important of the intellectuals abroad was Bessarion. He was born in Trebizond towards the end of the fourteenth century, and studied with Gemistos Plethon in the Peloponnese, but went early in life to Constantinople, where he distinguished himself in church circles. In 1437–9 he was with the emperor and a large mission at the councils of Ferrara and Florence (which declared the union of the Eastern and Western Churches), and pronounced himself on the side of union. He settled in Italy, where the Pope gave him the rank of cardinal, and gathered round him many pupils, both Greek and foreign (such as Filelfo). He also collected a fine library which on his death (in 1472 in Ravenna) he left to the Marciana at Venice.

Janos Laskaris (1445–1535) was a pupil of Bessarion, and his career was almost equally important. He lived and taught in Florence under Lorenzo Medici, also in Rome, and in France under Louis XII and François I. A pupil of his was the Cretan Markos Mousouros (1470–1517), professor at Padua and collaborator with Aldus Manutius. Many ancient texts were edited by him, notably the Aldine edition of Plato (1513), preceded by an inspired ode (naturally in ancient Greek) to Plato, in which he begs the Pope, Leo X, to liberate Greece. Such poems (more often epigrams in elegiacs) were a common literary exercise among Greek scholars (as they were among the humanists of the Renaissance); it is not without interest that Laskaris (for example) composed a similar epigram on the death of Raphael (1520), and the Cretan Frankiskos Portos on that of Calvin (1564).[1]

Among these Renaissance humanists who in the first half of the sixteenth century wrote in the ancient language, a special place belongs to Nikolaos Sofianòs of Corfu. While he indubitably belongs to the same group of learned humanists, and was brought up on the classical ideal, at the same time he shows (for the first time) an interest in the modern Greek tongue and the education of the subjugated people. Working in Venice, he wrote a grammar of the modern Greek language (which was not printed at the time)[2] and—still more remarkable—with an educational aim (for the enlightenment of the people) he endeavoured to translate ancient authors into the modern language. In 1544, at the press he had himself founded in Venice, he issued, under the title *Pedagogue*, a translation of the Pseudo-Plutarchan treatise on the *Education of Children*. Apart from pedagogics, he showed his modern and enlightened spirit in his interest in geography and the natural sciences; he wrote a commentary on the *Geography* of Ptolemy and printed a study (in ancient Greek) *on the ringed astrolabe*, which he dedicated to Pope Paul III.

In Venice it seems that a small intellectual circle united by the same interests had gathered round Sofianòs (he himself mentions, for example, Jakovos Trivolis, whom we know as a poet). Perhaps it is no accident that it is in Venice at this time that we

---

[1] The collected epigrams of Janos Laskaris were edited in one volume in 1527. The two epigrams mentioned above appear in L. Politis, Ποιητικὴ Ἀνθολογία, vol. 2, pp. 140 and 148.

[2] It was edited for the first time by É. Legrand, Paris, 1870. A second edition in É. Legrand, *Collection des monuments*, Nouvelle série, vol. 2, Paris, 1874.

meet with the first prose works written in the popular language. It is the first time that we encounter a demotic, modern Greek prose. During the whole Byzantine period prose remained exclusively the territory of learned archaistic literature, even when the works were of a 'popular' nature, e.g. the tale of *Barlaam and Josaphat* and *Syntipas the Philosopher*. It was only on the periphery, and in quite particular circumstances, that the popular language was used for prose during the Byzantine period.

Such places on the periphery were above all southern Italy and Cyprus. From southern Italy we have only charters in the popular language, but from Cyprus we have documents of greater interest: first of all the *Assises*, i.e. the jurisprudence of the kingdom of Cyprus, which early needed to be translated into the Cypriot dialect, to be understood by the people. The text preserved to us is of the fourteenth century. It is strange that the first extensive document in modern Greek prose should be a legal text.

In the Cypriot dialect (which we saw become in the second half of the sixteenth century a vehicle for the expressive poetry of the unknown author of the Cypriot love-poems) Leontios Machairàs wrote his Chronicle, *The Tale of the Sweet Land of Cyprus*, in the first half of the fifteenth century. He had a post at the court of the Lusignan kings, and wrote the history of his island and of his times. Unlike the Byzantine historians, his contemporaries, who tried to imitate the language of Herodotus and Thucydides, the Cypriot chronicler wrote in simple language and in a plain, paratactic style, providing always a careful and accurate relation of the events. The fact that he wrote in prose and not—like so many other similar chronicles—in verse, is not perhaps unconnected with the great tradition of the French chroniclers, which could not be unknown in French-occupied Cyprus. Chronologically Machairàs comes between Froissart and Commines.

This, however, was an isolated instance. The popular language really began to be used in prose for the first time at Venice, in the first half of the sixteenth century, and this was definitely connected with Sofianòs's educational efforts. The first works were not indeed literary, they were written in the popular language because they were addressed to the people, and are mainly theological (popularization of Christian teaching, and sermons), or practical. Thus the Corfiot Joannikios Kartanos (fellow-countryman and contemporary of Sofianòs) published in 1536 at Venice the *Flower and Essence of the Old and New Testament*. A cleric, and later a bishop, and closely connected with the patriarchate, Damaskinòs Stouditis, published, under the title of *Thesaurus*, ecclesiastical homilies in a very simple language and style, and he translated the *Physiologus* into modern Greek. Alexios Rartouros, another Corfiot, followed Damaskinòs in his attempt at popular preaching (*Sermons*, 1560), while yet another Corfiot, Nikandros Noukios, translated Aesop's *Fables* (1543). We must at the same time mention the *Calculus* (1568) of the Chiot Emmanuel Glyzonios—a popular work of practical arithmetic. All these, of course, were printed at the presses of Venice, where there was now intense activity.

Many of these works have already brought us into the second half of the century. The subjugated nation was now gradually beginning to recover from its intellectual lethargy; foreigners, particularly German protestants, began to take an interest in modern Hellenism, in its language and education. The patriarchate, headed by an admirable prelate, Jeremias II ('the Great', 1572–95) established contact with them, under pressure from many opposing forces, particularly Catholic propaganda. Martin Crusius, professor at Tübingen, corresponded with two learned men at the Patriarchate, Joannis Zygomalàs and his son Theodosios, who sent him abundant information, and even manuscripts of works in the modern language. Crusius incorporated this material in the eight books of his *Turcograecia* (Basel, 1584).

The personality of Sofianòs was reflected in many directions—most importantly, perhaps, in education. From his works it is clear he had conceived a wide programme of language and education, which aimed at the instruction of the subjugated people, and began with the study of the popular language and the translation of the classics, 'since our once happy nation of the Greeks has fallen into such an evil state, that one can scarcely find a teacher able to teach the young even the art of grammar . . .'.[1] The words of Sofianòs are no exaggeration. It is true that immediately after the fall the patriarchate took care to found a kind of elementary school near it, for the education of the clergy, but in the rest of the subjugated country, at least for

---

[1] From the epilogue of the Grammar, Legrand, *Collection*, p. 84a.

the first hundred years, there were almost no schools, and only occasionally priests taught children to read and write out of church books (hence the later legends of 'secret schools').

The first attempts at modern Greek education began again in the West. At the instigation of Janos Laskaris Pope Leo X founded a Greek Gymnasium in Rome, and brought boys from Greece to study there. The school was short-lived, from 1513 to 1521 (when Leo died). But its career was distinguished, and it seems that the intentions of its founder, the last pope of the Renaissance, were generous and disinterested. On the other hand Gregory XIII's foundation (by a bull of 1577) of the Greek College of St. Athanasius (still functioning in Via del Babuino) had an obviously proselytizing character. Nevertheless many Greek clerics and learned men were educated here; they were indeed devoted to the Catholic Church, but they were distinguished in letters, and in their way contributed to the enlightenment of the nation.

The Chiot Leon Allatios (1588–1669) was a multifarious writer, with an entirely western education, but always with an interest in Greek matters; the role of the learned humanist of the Renaissance was more fully expressed by the Athenian Leonardos Filaràs (d. 1673), who was active at the side of Richelieu, and is known for his friendship with Milton, whom he knew personally in London (the latter's letter to him of 1654 is the most authentic source of information about his blindness). He also wrote many epigrams in the ancient language; we are more moved by four lines of modern Greek, which he sent to his mother with his portrait, in clothes of the fashion of Louis XIII's time.[1]

It was natural that there should be a reaction against Catholic influence. In 1593 the Greek community of Venice founded a Greek school, which was not to last long. Venice was an important centre of Hellenism. There from the end of the fifteenth century an important Greek colony had been formed, with its own quarter and its church, San Giorgio dei Greci. The domination of Venice in most of the Greek islands and its well-known religious toleration enabled the commercial and intellectual life of this community to develop. We have already spoken of the learned circle of Aldus Manutius, of Sofianòs and his friends,

---

[1] On Filaràs see É. Legrand, *Bibliographie hellénique du XVIIᵉ siècle*, vol. 3, pp. 407–16. Milton's letters to him, ibid., pp. 412–15.

and of the popular books issued from the presses. In 1648 the Corfiot lawyer Thomas Flanginis bequeathed money to found a Greek school (and seminary) for Greek boys, clearly in rivalry with the College at Rome. Another scholar, Joannis Kottounios (d. 1658) did the same thing at Padua, where he had been professor. The Flanginianòn Hellenomuseion worked without interruption till 1797 and played an important role through all this long space of time (in the baroque building which now houses the Greek Institute of Byzantine and Post-Byzantine Studies).

## THE SEVENTEENTH CENTURY

Even in Turkish-occupied Greece a ray of enlightenment began to dawn from the middle or end of the sixteenth century. The Church played an important role, for, being attacked on many sides, it struggled to keep nationalism and orthodoxy alive, and sought to strengthen the nation by education: a 'religious humanism', as it has been well defined. We spoke of the important personality of the Patriarch Jeremias II. Another outstanding character was Maximos Margounios (1530–1602), a Cretan who studied at Padua and had an active career in Venice. His work includes theological books in the ancient language; but it is no less worthy of mention that he translated lives of the saints and wrote sermons in the popular language. His friend and fellow countryman Meletios Pigàs (1535–1602) was one of the most enlightened clerics produced by the Orthodox Church at the time. He also studied at Padua; most of his active career was spent in Greece, in Crete, and in Constantinople, and in 1590 he became Patriarch of Alexandria. As well as writings in the ancient language he wrote sermons in a lively demotic. This cultivation of a demotic rhetoric, which began with Stouditis and Rartouros, was, as we shall see, to have an important development; in the case of Margounios and Pigàs the parallel cultivation of demotic language and poetry in Crete must have had some influence (both were contemporaries of Chortatsis).

The pupil and friend of them both, especially of Pigàs, was Kyrillos Loukaris (1572–1638), the most striking personality of this 'religious humanism'. He also was a Cretan and had studied at Padua. He succeeded Pigàs on the patriarchal throne of Alexandria, and in 1620 he was ordained patriarch at Constantinople. The times were troubled; Loukaris was to hold the patriarchate three times, with intervals between them, till he was executed by the Turks in 1638. He was the first patriarch to suffer that fate. He was an energetic champion of Orthodoxy, but his activities produced a violent reaction, particularly in his relations with the Protestants, which ended in the signing of a 'confession' (whose authenticity was formerly doubted, though, as it appears, for no cogent reasons). But Loukaris's main interest was to guard Orthodoxy against its most dangerous enemy, Catholicism. In this he was successful. After Loukaris, Catholic propagandists abandoned the scheme of a mass proselytism of the Greeks, and limited themselves to individual cases.

Loukaris was progressive; he founded a printing press at the patriarchate (the first in the subjugated Greek world), he encouraged a translation of the Gospels into demotic (1638), and modernized the Patriarchate School, wishing to make it a school for more advanced studies. He therefore summoned there as a teacher the most important philosopher of the age, Theophilos Korydaleus (1560–1645), the chief representative in Greece of the Aristotelianism of the school of Padua, where he was educated. His work consists almost exclusively of commentaries on the works of Aristotle, which were the most important school-books throughout the Turkish occupation (some were printed, but most of them were in manuscript). Korydaleus taught in many of the schools that were now being founded in a number of Greek cities and were already vying with each other. They were to increase in number in the following century, the century of 'enlightenment'.

'Korydalism', with its philosophy and also its undoubted pedantry, exercised a great influence. The commentaries on Aristotle had many imitators. Nikolaos Koursoulas of Zakynthos, a contemporary of Korydaleus, wrote commentaries on almost the same selection of Aristotle's works, in competition with him; so later did Alexandros Mavrokordatos and George Sougdourìs (of Janina); many manuscripts of their commentaries exist in libraries.

Eugenios Giannoulis of Aetolia is a pleasing personality among the pupils of Korydaleus; he too was closely attached to Loukaris and combines the scientific spirit of Korydalism with Orthodox piety and a disposition towards asceticism. After the

death of Loukaris he retired to his own province and taught
in the small village of Vranianà. His letters, often written in
demotic, are important, and 'one admires the simplicity, the
sweetness combined with a natural dignity, and an ascetic hard-
ness and inflexibility'.[1] Eugenios took a lively interest in the
foundation of schools in the country. Under his inspiration a rich
fur merchant of Kastorià, a typical character of the changing
times called Manolakis Kastorianòs, gave generously towards
the founding of schools.

The works of Korydaleus are naturally written in the ancient
language; and the revived education was to remain in that
language. The linguistic interpretation of the ancients (by the
oddly called 'psychagogic' method of scholastic juxtaposition of
synonyms) was its main objective. Nevertheless at the same time,
on the fringe, as it were, the popular language continued to be
used—not always so purely as by Sofianòs—in works addressed
to the people.

In 1631 the first edition of the *Historical Book* appeared in
Venice; this was a patchwork chronicle made up of various
Byzantine and post-Byzantine chronicles, beginning with the
creation of the world and going down to somewhere about the
end of the sixteenth century. The language is fairly simple, not
pure demotic; the writer is said to be Dorotheos, Bishop of
Monemvasia, a non-existent personage. The chronicle of pseudo-
Dorotheos had a wide circulation among the people, for it
satisfied their desire for marvellous stories as well as for historical
knowledge. Recent research has listed among the sources of these
chronicles some Italian works, e.g. those of Paolo Giovio.[2] We
have another Italian work in Greek translation, the *Annali
Turcheschi* of Sansovino, in a manuscript of the late sixteenth
century;[3] the anonymous translator writes in a pleasing and
unadulterated popular idiom; this is one of the best specimens
of early demotic prose.

---

[1] K. Dimaràs, Ἱστορία τῆς νεοελληνικῆς λογοτεχνίας, 4th edn., Athens, 1968,
p. 62.

[2] Elizabeth Zachariadou, "Μία ἰταλικὴ πηγὴ τοῦ ψευδο-Δωροθέου γιὰ τὴν ἱστορία
τῶν 'Οθωμανῶν", Πελοποννησιακά, 5 (1962), 46–59.

[3] Edited by G. Zoras, Χρονικὸν περὶ τῶν Τούρκων σουλτάνων κατὰ τὸν Βαρβερινὸν
ἑλληνικὸν κώδικα III, Athens, 1958. See Elizabeth Zachariadou, Τὸ Χρονικὸν τῶν
Τούρκων σουλτάνων καὶ τὸ ἰταλικό του πρότυπο, Thessaloniki, 1960 ('Ελληνικά,
Supplement 14).

As well as history (in the form of the popular chronicle), popular religious literature also used the demotic. The work of the Cretan priest Joannis Morezinos was until recently not sufficiently known; about 1595 he wrote, also in excellent demotic, a very extensive work, much read in his time (we have a large number of manuscripts); it includes theoretical chapters devoted to the praise of the Blessed Virgin Mary, each one followed by an account of a miracle (the latest happened in his own time). Morezinos also derives from western sources, from various books of miracles of the late Middle Ages and the sixteenth century. Much better known is a similar work, the *Salvation of Sinners* by Agapios Landos, first published in 1641, a Cretan who was a monk on Athos, and who, as it clearly appears, relied upon Morezinos and also on Italian sources. His language is simple, despite a tendency towards the literary form, while his narration is unaffected and natural. This work was much loved by the people, and made edifying reading up to our own times. We have other religious works by the same writer, and a charming *Agriculture* (1643), a sort of popular handbook to that subject.

As was natural, the popular language was also used for propaganda by the Catholic Church. Among such writing the work of Neofytos Rodinòs of Cyprus (*c.* 1570–1659) is noteworthy. He was first an Orthodox monk (and an assistant to Margounios); later in life he went to the College in Rome and undertook many missions to the East (for example, to Poland and Russia), where his fanatical zeal often caused violent opposition. He was a very prolific writer, and his many works were issued from the office of the Propaganda in Rome: *Spiritual Armour, Spiritual Exercise,* etc. His language is completely popular, without any admixture of literary elements, as Rodinòs remained entirely uninfluenced by the tradition of the Orthodox Church.

# III

## THE GREAT AGE OF
## CRETAN LITERATURE
### (1570–1669)

AFTER CYPRUS also had fallen to the Turks (1570)—and we know what that loss meant to all Europe—almost the only Greek lands left under Venetian domination were Crete and the Ionian Islands. Both were to play an important role in literature, Crete at once, the Ionian Islands later. In Crete, in the century between 1570 and 1669 (when it too fell to the Turks), that great age of literature (which we saw beginning in the previous period) was to develop and to reach a high degree of excellence. Cretan literature of the late sixteenth and of the seventeenth centuries is a golden period in the history of modern Greek literature.

### THE THEATRE

This is also the zenith of Renaissance literature in Greece. Its principal characteristic is that, apart from the early *Voskopoula* (Shepherdess) and the more mature *Erotokritos*, all the works of this period are dramatic. This is of fundamental importance; for as the drama is the most social of all forms of literature, addressed to and necessarily presupposing an audience, this development of the theatre in Crete means that the social conditions which obtained at that time lent themselves to such a phenomenon.

Drama, which reached its climax in fifth-century Athens, declined and gradually became extinct in later antiquity. For all that has been written, the art of the theatre never existed in Byzantine times. Nor did it exist in the West during the Middle Ages (apart from the peculiar form of the 'mysteries' or *sacre rappresentazioni* at the end of the period). The theatre presupposes the clash of characters, the Aeschylean 'suffering and knowledge' (πάθος and μάθος); it presupposes the free individual, liberated from myth or dogma. Such was not the human type of the seventh century B.C., or of the Middle Ages. Only the return to the same ideals at the Renaissance could bring the theatre back to Europe. First, naturally, it came to Italy—though it did not there achieve the development that we might have expected; Petrarch, Ariosto, and Tasso were none of them concerned with the theatre, except very occasionally. Yet, setting out from Italy, the theatre was to reach its peak in other countries of Europe, in France, Spain, and England—and finally in Greece, at least in that part of Greece that had not yet fallen into Asiatic hands. George Chortatsis, who introduced the theatre into Crete, was more or less contemporary with Shakespeare.

We must emphasize another feature of the Cretan literature of the seventeenth century: the pure and elevated literary language. The poets of this period use the spoken Cretan dialect, entirely purified of medieval residue and of other learned elements; the local idiom is elevated into an elegant literary language, adequate to render the finer shades of the poet's thought, a language formed by the artist's will. Perhaps demotic has never been written with such purity and consistency at any other period in Greek literature.

The poetic personality at the beginning of this development, the man who introduced the theatre to Crete and, with his superior poetical consciousness, unquestionably transformed and elevated the local idiom into a literary language, was George Chortatsis. Contemporary, as we have said, with Shakespeare, he was also the contemporary of another great genius from his own island: Domenico Theotokopoulos (El Greco). Today, after recent discoveries, we are in a position to know rather more about the life and work of Chortatsis. Coming from a noble family of Rethymno (the small aristocratic town between Kastro and Chania), he must have been born about the middle of the century, and must have gone in youth to Italy to study, as did so many of his fellow countrymen. We are unable to say whether he studied at the famous University of Padua, but from his work it appears that he had received no mean education; he knew the ancient (particularly the Latin) authors, and shows great familiarity with contemporary Italian literature (especially the theatre). We now know definitely that he wrote three dramatic works: *Erofili*, *Katzourbos*, and *Gyparis*. He wrote them *c.* 1585–1600 at the height of his maturity, when he was between thirty-five and fifty years of age. The fact that these works are examples of three different types of drama, of tragedy, comedy, and pastoral (precisely the three kinds of play then written in Italy) surely cannot be an accident. Chortatsis is a dramatic writer and poet of the first rank. His verse is distinguished by its delicacy and refinement; yet at the same time there is a certain artificial coldness. In spite of the completely demotic language, the fifteen-syllable lines do not have the same internal rhythm as those of the demotic song, and make too much use, for example, of metrical enjambment, which is unknown to demotic poetry. In the choruses of *Erofili* he also makes use of the hendecasyllable, in the form of the Dantesque *terzina*, a thing which further removes him from demotic verse, and brings him nearer to the poet of the Cypriot songs.

His masterpiece is *Erofili*, a classical tragedy on Italian lines. The immediate prototype is the *Orbecche* of Giambattista Giraldi (1547), the first Italian classical tragedy. The poet follows the general lines of the plot, but handles his material with complete originality, and has also removed from his work many of those elements of blood and thunder in which the tragedy of that age delighted. The three pseudo-Aristotelian unities are of course preserved. The chief characters are Erofili, daughter of King Philogonos, and the brave general Panaretos; they have been secretly married, and when the king learns this he lets his wrath flow at this unsuitable marriage; he will kill Panaretos by a cruel death and (pretending to forgive her) he will present his daughter with her lover's severed limbs in a golden bowl, for a wedding gift; Erofili laments and commits suicide, but finally the chorus of girls kill the heartless king. Charos (a popular personification of Death) speaks the prologue, and the ghost of the king's brother—whom he killed in order to seize the throne—appears on the scene as an instrument of divine justice.

The merits of this work are many: first, among its purely literary virtues, are its elevated language, skilled versification, and a literary competence which is far above the ordinary level of the works of the first half of the century. Nor are its purely theatrical virtues few, if we ignore the defects common to all tragedies of this time. The poet knows how to create fantasy, and as the action advances, the interest grows. The great scene of the fourth act, in which Erofili and her father face each other, brings the two different worlds of this work into collision and is full of strong dramatic pathos. In other scenes (e.g. in the laments of Erofili or the nurse) a higher lyric feeling dominates. In this connection, we must give a special place to the wonderfully polished Dantesque *terzinas* of the four choruses.

Between the acts are four intermezzi, with an entirely different theme: a dramatization of the episode of Rinaldo and Armida from the *Gerusalemme Liberata* of Torquato Tasso. Here is a highly skilled and completely successful blending of poetry, music, and dance, which gives rise to a peculiar enchantment (in the original sense of that word, like the enchantment by which the Oriental witch enticed the brave knight). It is the work of a masterly hand, and there is no doubt that the intermezzi are by Chortatsis himself. Moreover we know two other sets of four intermezzi, certainly written by him, and very probably for his other two dramatic works. These, however, cannot attain to the quality of the intermezzi of the *Erofili*.

The other two tragedies that have come down to us, are later than *Erofili*, and inferior in poetic worth. *King Rodolinos* was written by Joannes Andreas Troilos of Rethymno, and printed in Venice in 1647. Its original is *Il Re Torrismondo*, the late dramatic work of Tasso (1587), and its theme is its hero's conflict between love and friendship. The tragedy has some of the merits of *Erofili* (by which it is obviously influenced), particularly in the handling of the language and the verse. The choruses are worth mention; two of them are written in sonnet form.

It is doubtful whether the third tragedy, *Zenon*, should be thought Cretan. A young scholar who is also a theatrical director, Mr. Sp. Evangelatos, has recently argued persuasively that the work was written and performed in Zakynthos in 1682–3.[1] But it remains to be shown whether the unknown poet was a Zakynthian (as is more probable) or a Cretan. It is an imitation of the Latin tragedy of the same name by the English Jesuit Joseph Simeon, printed in Rome in 1648, and it follows the rules laid down for

[1] Sp. A. Evangelatos, "Χρονολόγηση, τόπος συγγραφῆς τοῦ 'Ζήνωνος' καὶ ἔρευνα γιὰ τὸν ποιητή του", Θησαυρίσματα (Venice), 5 (1968), 177–203.

the dramatic works of the Jesuits, written to be played in their seminaries. Its plot is concerned with the intrigues of Zenon, the Byzantine emperor of the fifth century, and of his cousin Longinus, to get the throne, and their final punishment. The tragedy, like its prototype, is a gloomy work, a typical tragedy of blood and thunder, without any relief, and in a clerical and fanatical tone—in fact it is a work of propaganda. Such merits as it has are the perfection of the verse-writing, some lyrical passages, and the knowledge of theatrical practice and scenery design shown by the author at certain points.

Chortatsis also wrote the best of the three comedies of the Cretan theatre that have come down to us: *Katzourbos* (or perhaps *Katzarapos*) which is certainly dated between 1595 and 1600 and is his most mature work. The three comedies have similar plots, revolving round a theme very common at that time, the recognition of lost children. In *Katzourbos* two young people, Nikolòs and Kassandra, are in love, but the girl's foster-mother (Poulissena) wants to give her to the old man Armenis to get money from him. Finally it appears that Kassandra is his daughter, who had been carried away by the Turks, and the comedy ends with the marriage of the two young people. But apart from this thin plot, the stage is filled with a number of comic types who give the play its special colour: the braggart Koustoulieris (the *miles gloriosus*), courtesans, bawds, the schoolmaster who mixes up Greek, Italian, and Latin, and produces a number of misunderstandings, and different slaves, one of whom is a glutton (the type of the parasite), another a cunning thief, and another a clown (*ridicoloso* as he is called in the dramatis personae).

Anyone at all familiar with the Italian theatre of the Renaissance will have no difficulty in recognizing that this comedy has its origins in the Italian comedies of the sixteenth century, particularly in the type known as *commedia erudita*. This is the source not only of the main theme, the recognition of the lost children, but also of the stock comic characters. The second type of Italian comedy, that which was to be so widely performed and to have so much success in the seventeenth century, the *commedia dell'arte*, seems unknown in Crete; its essential elements, masks and extemporization, are lacking. However, Chortatsis, as we have seen, was in all probability in Venice as a young man, precisely at a time when three talented poets (who

were also actors) Ruzzante, Calmo, and Giancarli, were renew-
ing and reviving the conventional *commedia erudita*. He thus did
not merely use its old form in his comedy, but was able to lay
claim also to many of the new elements.

*Katzourbos* is, like *Erofili*, a masterpiece; it has swift action and
comic invention and a real sense of the humorous, and creates
a living theatrical atmosphere; it has a fine, nervous verse and a
cultivated poetical language which never becomes feeble—both
literary and theatrical merits of a high order.

As for other Cretan comedies, we do not know who was the
author of *Stathis*, nor can we say exactly when he wrote it; our
only certainty is that it was written before 1648 (the year when
the great siege of Kastro began). The main plot is more or less
the same, only we have here two pairs of lovers whose love is
somewhat strange: Phaedra loves the youth Chrysippos, who in
turn loves Lambrousa, while Pamfilos loves Phaedra. Here again
is the old man Dottore, a lawyer, and at the end there will be
the recognition of the lost child, and the double marriage of the
young lovers. Much of the development is difficult to follow, for,
as it would seem, we have not the original work but a later
adaptation (and abridgement) in three acts. If we had the whole
work, it might be on a level with *Katzourbos*.

We have *Fortounatos*, the third Cretan comedy, in the autograph manuscript of its author, Markos Antonios Foskolos. The
poet, who had an important position in the Cretan community,
died (as has recently been shown)[1] in 1662; the comedy should be
dated shortly before. It is clearly indebted to *Katzourbos*, which
it imitates both in its general structure and more directly in
individual scenes. The basic plot is the same: there is the pair of
young lovers, the old fool, who here combines that function with
that of the comic doctor, and the recognition of the lost child
at the end. Foskolos seems less literary than the other writers,
and his comedy is the most bawdy, though (strangely) the
least dissolute. He may have wished to escape from the influence
of Italian comedy, and to give a more faithful picture of the
society of his time. Had he been a gifted poet this might have
led to a new development of comedy.

[1] A. L. Vincent, "῾Ο ποιητὴς τοῦ ῾Φορτουνάτου᾽", Θησαυρίσματα, 4 (1967),
53–84. Id., "Νέα στοιχεῖα γιὰ τὸ Μάρκο Ἀντώνιο Φώσκολο", ibid. 5 (1968),
119–76.

### PASTORAL POETRY

Apart from one tragedy and one comedy, Chortatsis, as we have said, also wrote a work of the third dramatic kind, a pastoral play, *Gyparis* (or *Panoria*). It appears to be his earliest work, written *c.* 1585–90. We have also another example of pastoral from Crete, *The Voskopoula* (Shepherdess). We do not know the name of the author, nor its exact date. When it was first printed in 1627 it appears already to have been quite well known; perhaps it is of the same date as *Gyparis* or more probably a little earlier. It is not a play, but a short narrative poem. The story is simple, even naïve: a shepherd sees a shepherdess and is so much smitten by her beauty that he faints. They go together into the cave where she lives, and pass happy days and nights of love. The shepherd has to go away, and promises to return within a month, but he falls ill and cannot keep his promise; when he returns he learns from the father of his beloved that she has died of grief. The style and the narration are as simple as the plot; the verse is not the well-tried popular fifteen-syllable line, but a simple hendecasyllable fitted to the rhyming couplet. The language and style are of a clumsiness which, by its very genuineness, gives a simple charm to the poem.

At one time it was believed that *Voskopoula* was based on a true story; this is an error. There is no doubt that it has a prototype among the innumerable Italian 'idylls' of the Renaissance. The simple Cretan shepherdess must there be a nymph, and the shepherd a hero with divine ancestry, and the action must surely have been set in ancient Arcadia. The cave where the shepherdess lives is certainly borrowed from the original; and similarly the days and nights full of love are not consonant with the traditional life of the Cretan countryside in the sixteenth century. It is obvious that the Italian prototype has suffered a radical change.

We see all this more clearly in the case of *Gyparis*. The theme follows the typical pattern of Italian *tragicommedie pastorali*, with the characteristic peculiarity that we have two pairs of shepherds: Gyparis loves Panoria and Alexis, Athousa: the shepherdesses, however, do not accept their love and wish to live without ties, hunting in the woods and in the mountains. Old Giannoulis, the father of Panoria, and the elderly woman Frosyni, both comic characters, try in vain to change the obstinate mood of the young shepherdesses. Finally the shepherds supplicate the goddess Aphrodite, and her son Eros shoots the girls with his bow and thus brings about a favourable solution.

In contrast with that of the *Voskopoula*, the immediate prototype of *Gyparis* has (in all probability) been established;[1] it is *La Calisto*, 'nova favola pastorale di Luigi Groto Cieco d'Adria', a poet forgotten today, but known and esteemed in his time. *La Calisto* was first published in Venice in 1583. The whole subject is taken from ancient mythology (from the *Metamorphoses* of Ovid). Calisto is the daughter of Lycaon; Zeus falls in love with her and takes the form of Artemis in order to obtain her, he takes Hermes with him, metamorphosed into a nymph. Many comic misunderstandings arise between the metamorphosed gods, the nymphs, and the two shepherds who love them (Gemulo and Silvio). The gods, cunning as they are, lose no time in obtaining what they will from the nymphs (Calisto and her companion Selvaggia), while the shepherds believe that the change in the nymphs (who make a virtue of necessity, and yield to their love after this experience) is due to their prayers to Aphrodite. The same basic theme is discerned in the two works (with the uncommon motifs of the two pairs of shepherds and the invocation of Aphrodite). But there are also radical differences. The chief of these is the total disappearance in *Gyparis* (as in *Voskopoula*) of the mythological setting: there are no metamorphosed gods, no nymphs, and no Arcadia. The nymphs have become simple Cretan shepherdesses and have even lost their conventional ancient names, and have received popular Cretan names instead. The action takes place in Crete. Inevitably, the only ancient motif remaining is the goddess Aphrodite and the invocation to her.

There is a particular significance in this. Pastoral poetry in Italy, born of classical imitation, cared little about a faithful rendering of the countryside and the real life of shepherds. It was rather an escape from reality into an idyllic dream-world, Arcadia, where sophisticated gods and heroes moved about in an archaistic setting. The far-fetched poetical style corresponded to the tastes of a most select society in the courts of Ferrara or Mantua. The Cretan public, however, was entirely different; the countryside and the shepherds of Ida were far too near and

---

[1] Linos Politis, 'La poésie pastorale en Crète, etc.' (see Bibliography).

far too real to become mere conventional patterns. Thus the Cretan pastorals, both the simple *Voskopoula* and the more elaborate *Gyparis*, though they imitate Italian originals, free them from their mythological setting, and bring into this far-fetched conventional genre a new and unexpected freshness and simplicity. The nymph of the Italian 'idyll' would certainly never stir our sympathy as much as the guileless simplicity of the Cretan shepherdess; and the intervention of Aphrodite, which is only a simple pretence in the Italian work, really brings about the happy ending in the Greek work and makes the shepherdesses of Chortatsis far more human and lovable than their counterparts in the work of Groto.

## *THE SACRIFICE OF ABRAHAM* AND *EROTOKRITOS*

In the Cretan theatre a quite unique position is held by *The Sacrifice of Abraham*, a dramatization of the well-known Old Testament episode. The action begins with the appearance of the angel to the sleeping Abraham, there follow dramatic dialogues with Sarah, the journey to the sacrifice, and the happy ending. The work, first published in 1696, must have been written in 1635, and has always been favourite reading amongst the people, as the succession of editions proves.

The poet has exploited most advantageously the drama of the story; and he has convincingly portrayed the human characters: the father, the mother, and the son, and the warm love that unites them, and also the violent conflicts into which they are brought by inexorable fate. Isaac's gentle disposition is wonderfully rendered, and the minor personages (menservants and maidservants) are complete characters. Some passages, such as Sarah's laments or Isaac's waking, are infused with moving tender lyricism.

For all its dramatic plot, and its conflict, the *Sacrifice* cannot properly be called a tragedy because of its happy ending. Nor is it really a 'mystery play', as it used to be called (and perhaps still is by some); this work, so full of dramatic tension, has nothing in common with those static representations of episodes from Holy Writ. The *Sacrifice* is indubitably drama, a religious drama. We know its immediate prototype, *Lo Isach* by the same Luigi

Groto[1] of whom we have been speaking. The Greek work is in every respect superior to the insignificant Italian original. But the difference is not only in quality. The *Sacrifice* has peculiarities which place it apart not only from its original but also from all other Cretan dramatic works. For instance, it is not divided into acts and scenes, and does not observe the conventional unities: the action begins in Abraham's house, the personages set out and walk for three whole days before they reach the mountain of sacrifice, and then they go back to Abraham's house again. Nor are there choric passages, as in the other Cretan works (and as in the original by Luigi Groto).

Formerly the failure of the *Sacrifice* to conform to the sanctioned conventions was put down to its primitive character; now that we are better informed—and know its original—we cannot accept that explanation. It is not a primitive work; on the contrary, it is obvious that we have something quite new, a bold and individual poetic personality who seeks 'new wine-skins' for his message, and therefore does not hesitate to disregard every theatrical convention (even those that are necessary). Thus his personages acquire a greater human warmth, and seem nearer to us. Panaretos and Panoria, for all their genuineness, were still dramatic types; the footlights are between them and us. In the *Sacrifice* there are no footlights and Isaac and Sarah move us by their entirely human appearance. *Erofili* was more conventional theatre, the *Sacrifice* more human drama.

There is a warmth not only about the characters but also about the language, a warm and more popular spirit. While (as we saw) Chortatsis is more aristocratic and learned, the poet of the *Sacrifice* comes nearer to real folk verse. Metrical enjambment is severely restricted, and the laments of Sarah are exactly like demotic laments or *mirologia* (μοιρολόγια):

> For nine long months I carried you, my precious little one,
> Within this dark, unlucky womb of mine, my only son. . . .
>
> And tell me now, what pleasure you will give to me, my dear?
> Like thunder and like lightning you are going to disappear.

The same warmth of verse and language are paralleled in the greatest work of Cretan literature, the *Erotokritos*. That is not the

---

[1] The first to identify it was John Mavrogordato, *Journal of Hellenic Studies*, 48 (1928), 243 (A Postscript)—see Bibliography.

only thing the two works have in common; they use similar modes of expression, and we find lines repeated from one work to the other. Scholars have from early days noticed these resemblances, and have concluded that the poet of the *Sacrifice* is the author of *Erotokritos*, Vitsentzos Kornaros.[1] The dramatic work was written in his youth, and thus its bold and revolutionary character is explained. *Erotokritos* is the poem of his maturity.

'A love-poem', its first editor calls it. Some later scholars, looking simply at its length, have called it, somewhat thoughtlessly, an epic. We shall do better to call it a narrative poem, or a verse romance. In his introduction the poet tells us that he is going to speak of 'the power of love' and 'the troubles of arms'. The poem turns on these two favourite and eternal themes, love and valour, and relates (in five parts and more than 10,000 lines) the love story of Erotokritos and Aretousa, their toils and troubles until the final happy ending. As a man of the Renaissance, and also a Greek, the poet sets his story in antiquity, and in Athens. Aretousa is the only daughter of the king, Herakles, and Erotokritos the son of his counsellor. Erotokritos feels a strange love for Aretousa, which is unsuitable (on account of their difference in rank), and in the first part we watch the same feeling slowly ripening in her as well. The poet, who is particularly sympathetic to his heroine (who is thirteen or fourteen years old, Juliet's age), shows us in a wonderful way the blossoming and gradual transformation of the innocent child into a woman who is entirely obsessed by her passion. The second part consists of the description of a tournament organized by the king for his daughter's amusement. Youths from all parts of Greece come to take part in this savage game. Of course Erotokritos is the victor; but the son of the King of Byzantium, the prince of Cyprus, and the Cretan are also given a distinguished place. We must particularly mention the later added episode of the duel between the Cretan and the Karamanitis (Oriental) 'who with the isle of Crete was long at enmity'. In the third part the two lovers manage to meet at midnight by the iron window of the palace,

---

[1] Stefanos Xanthoudidis was the first to arrive at this conclusion in the Introduction to his edition of *Erotokritos* (1915). See Linos Politis, " 'Ο 'Ερωτόκριτος καὶ ἡ Θυσία τοῦ Βιτσέντζου Κορνάρου", in Ἀφιέρωμα στὴ μνήμη τοῦ Μανόλη Τριανταφυλλίδη, Athens, 1960, pp. 357–71.

he outside and she within. When the king finds out, he is furious, and sends Erotokritos into exile and shuts Aretousa up in prison. Meanwhile war has broken out between the Athenians and the Vlachs; Erotokritos, blackened in face and rendered unrecognizable by a magic philtre, comes to the help of the king, and is finally victorious in a decisive single combat with Aristos, nephew of the Vlach king (fourth part). The end is now at hand. King Herakles gives his daughter and his kingdom to the unknown warrior who has saved him, and the hero at last reveals his true identity.

The poet is first of all an excellent story-teller. He takes his subject, as we shall see, from a French romance of chivalry, and relates it with an ease that fascinates with its spacious flow and at the same time with an accuracy of description and an insistence on the concrete. He further delights us with repetitions which take up the same theme in a series of parallels with inexhaustible inventive fantasy. And this throughout the whole work; open the book at random, and you need never fear to light upon a boring or even a less interesting passage; the poet always conserves his highest powers, which spring from a rich source. Besides, he has the skill not to confine himself to simple narration, but (influenced perhaps by the drama) to bring to life the dialogues of his personages, who in this way show more clearly their passions and sentiments. He knows also how to introduce frequently proverbs or gnomic sayings drawn from his experience of life, and how to address his characters: 'Vain were it, Erotokritos, to act in such a way . . .', or 'Frosyni, thou unhappy one . . .'. This narrative ease is accompanied by absolute surety in language and expression. Seferis observes:[1] 'There is no trace of linguistic inflation, or of any sort of rhetoric.' The verses are among the most melodious decapentesyllables in modern Greek literature, and have a lyrical colouring which is never sentimental. He is an artist in words, with complete consciousness of his powers, a fact which we can read between these lines:

> Of all that man has good on earth, 'tis words that have the power
> To give to every human heart their comfort in its hour;
> And he who has the gift to speak with knowledge and with style
> Can make the eyes of other men to weep, and make them smile.
>
> (i. 885–8)

[1] G. Seferis, " '*Ερωτόκριτος*", in *Δοκιμές*, 2nd edn., Athens, 1962, p. 219.

The fine epilogue reveals who the poet is: 'Vitsentzos is the poet's name, his family's Kornaros . . .', and that he is from Sitia in eastern Crete. Yet we know nothing about him but his bare name. The attempts of scholars to identify him with this or that member of the aristocratic Venetian family of that name (Cornaro, Corner) have been without any real success. It is unlikely that this poem, so full of genuine Greek feeling, could have been written by a foreigner, and we hear of many Greeks with the names Vitsentzos or Kornaros (e.g. the man who wrote his name in 1677 on the wall of a chapel at Mochlos near Sitia— may he not have been the poet?). Nor are we sure of the date; most probably it was written between 1640 and 1660. Possibly the poet wrote a first draft at Sitia and completed it at Kastro, after the beginning of the Turco-Venetian war and the siege of the city (1645–69). The added episode of the Oriental as a foe of the Cretan is indicative here.

Much research has also been done into the question of sources; most scholars (as was natural) sought for a prototype in Ariosto or Tasso. But the prototype has now been established as the medieval French romance by Pierre de la Cypède, *Paris et Vienne*.[1] The Greek poet, who must certainly have got it from an Italian translation, follows the basic development of the plot but makes radical alterations at critical moments (all the war between Athens and the Vlachs is his own invention). More important, almost nothing of the world of the French medieval romance is left; the Greek work breathes the air of the Renaissance, with its ease, its nobility, and its human dignity. If the plot is that of Pierre de la Cypède, the spirit is surely that of Ariosto.

And combined with it is the spirit of Greek popular mythology. In speaking of the *Sacrifice of Abraham*, which has been shown to be a work of Kornaros's youth, we said how close the poet was to the folk spirit, close in prosody and in expression to the demotic song. We find here the same elements in his work, but to a more marked degree. He has now mastered his mode of expression, and advances with a longer, easier stride. He has now experience of life, and wisdom, and follows the doings of his

---

[1] The identification was established by N. Cartojan, 'Poema cretană Erotocrit', Bucharest, 1935 (Academia Română, Memor. Sect. liter., 3rd Ser. vol. 7, mem. 4). Id., 'Le modèle français de l'Erotocritos', *Revue de littérature comparée*, 1936. Cf. E. Kriaràs, Μελετήματα περὶ τὰς πηγὰς τοῦ 'Ερωτοκρίτου, Athens, 1938.

youthful hero and heroine with the sympathy of a mature man 'knowing what sort of temper possesseth man'[1] and optimistically believes in the happy ending. *Erotokritos* is the masterpiece of Cretan literature; it is also a high point in all modern Greek poetry, a milestone. It marks the end of the first phase of modern Greek poetry, which (as we have seen) begins in Byzantine times with *Digenìs*. Thereafter there is a decline in poetry for a century and a half.

'Habent sua fata libelli.' The fall of Crete delayed the publication of this work; the first edition was printed in Venice in 1713. From then on, however, there were frequent editions and it quickly became a popular book. Until the beginning of our century, the pedlar, going round the villages, used to sell *Erotokritos* with his other stock-in-trade. Naturally the poem had its widest circulation in Crete, where the people learned whole passages by heart, and collected in the evenings to recite it, or rather to sing it (as they still do) in a sort of recitative which slightly changes from one region to another. It is an example of a work of conscious art being assimilated by a popular audience, and almost becoming a demotic song.

[1] Archilochus, frag. 67a Diehl.

# IV

## THE EIGHTEENTH CENTURY
## MODERN GREEK ENLIGHTENMENT

THE OCCUPATION of Crete by the Turks in 1669, after a twenty-two-year siege of Chandax, marks the end of Cretan literature. It was one of the most vital breaks in the history of modern Greek literature. After the brilliant flowering of Cretan literature we find ourselves, in 1669, in a poetical desert. But also from a more general point of view, 1669 is an important moment in history. A new order of things had come about in the Greek world in the two centuries that followed the fall of Constantinople. Essentially the people remained disunited nationally, and divided into three distinct groups (the Turkish-occupied, the Frankish-occupied, and the Greeks of the diaspora). But now the Frankish (i.e. Venetian) territory (after the fall of Cyprus and Crete) was limited to the Ionian Islands (apart from a short period of Venetian rule in the Peloponnese from 1684 to 1714), and the Turkish occupation had spread all over Greece. Moreover these groups were no longer to have the mutual independence that they had in the first centuries. Between Venice (the most important centre of the Greeks of the diaspora) and the Ionian Islands there was more contact than before, so that they may almost be considered as one group. The type of Greek who emigrated was now also very different; in the fifteenth century Greeks went to the West to teach, now they went to be taught. The universities of Italy (especially Padua) were educating a number of young men, not only from the Venetian-occupied area, but also from the rest of Greece; these returned home to teach what they had learned. We have seen that schools began to be founded in different towns in Greece even before 1669; now education was much more extensive, and intellectual life was secured by a firmer foundation. This lively movement in the

Greek regions had its centre in Constantinople, in the circle of the Patriarchate and the Phanariots; it was later to be transferred to the Danubian principates, to the courts of the Greek princes. These were critical and decisive years for Hellenism, which at first by gradual and later by firmer steps was advancing towards a synthesis of its scattered members and the re-establishment which was finally achieved by the rising of 1821.

With this as our guiding line, we may divide the 150 years between 1669 and 1821 into two main periods, the division coming *c.* 1770–80. About that time the situation altered radically; the Russo-Turkish treaty of Kutchuk Kainardji of 1774 gave special privileges to the Greeks in the Turkish empire, and thus ensured the rise of a new urban class, and material prosperity. In all fields during the following fifty years, and naturally in the intellectual life too, a new energy was manifested, which was leading rapidly to a climax.

### FIRST PERIOD: 1669 TO 1770–80

As we have seen, Cretan literature abruptly ceased to flourish with the fall of Crete. Possibly that historical event was not the only reason for this. Cretan literature had run its course: the *Erotokritos*, its peak, was also an end (see p. 67). The same thing has happened in other European literatures, with which Greek has made parallel progress. There too poetry has had an early phase, beginning with an epic cycle and ending with the great works at the end of the sixteenth or in the seventeenth century— we may think of Torquato Tasso, of Racine and Molière, of the Elizabethans and Milton. What follows in poetry is a decline. All over Europe the eighteenth century is anti-poetical. Lyricism will not revive until the end of that century or the beginning of the nineteenth, and then a lyricism altogether different from that of the earlier poetical period, more subjective, and isolated in individual sensitivity, more personal and introspective. We think of Hölderlin, Keats, and Shelley. The development in Greece was not dissimilar. Solomòs is the first genuine representative of the new lyricism; Vitsentzos Kornaros was the last representative of the first phase of poetry.

A refugee wave followed the events of 1669, like that which followed those of 1453. Although the Venetians had been foreigners, the Cretans felt the Turkish occupation as a real enslavement; they fought bravely on the side of the Venetians, and many fled with them to Venice after the disaster, or to the Ionian Islands. With them they brought their literary tradition and something more tangible, the manuscripts of the poetical works. In 1713 the *Erotokritos* was first printed at Venice, 'an ancient poem much praised and honoured in the islands of the Adriatic', as the publisher wrote. In 1725 Edward Harley, second Earl of Oxford, bought in Corfu the one known manuscript of the *Erotokritos*, written by a Heptanesian fifteen years earlier.[1]

Thus the tradition of Cretan literature was transplanted to the Ionian Islands after 1669. There it was preserved, but not continued. First it was in the hands of the Cretan refugees, and then it passed into those of the Heptanesians. In 1681 Marinos Tzanes Bounialis of Rethymno published a long metrical chronicle of the war and fall of Crete; the curious thing is that he copies the chronicle of a Cephalonian, Anthimos Diakrousis.

As a verse-writer, Marinos is clumsy, as is shown by another pamphlet of his with religious verses (Venice, 1684). His brother Emmanuel Tzanes, priest in charge of San Giorgio dei Greci at Venice, was also a clumsy verse-writer, but one of the most remarkable hagiographers of the 'Cretan school'.

Even before 1669 there had been close contact between Crete and the Ionian Islands. In 1646 Theodore Montseleze, from Zakynthos, published a strange and rather awkward theatrical work, *Eugena*, clearly influenced by the Cretan dramas, and in 1658 another Zakynthian, Michael Soummakis, translated the *Pastor Fido* of G. B. Guarini, into decapentesyllabic verse, which has much of the quality of the Cretan poems. The same work had been translated at the beginning of the century by an unknown Cretan who seems to have lived in Venice, isolated from the literary activity of his island. His translation remained unpublished until recently.[2] In all probability the author of the *Zenon*, played in Zakynthos (see p. 57) in 1682–3, was also a Zakynthian.

The Cephallonian Petros Katsaïtis was also nourished by the crumbs that fell from the Cretan table. He was a late descendant,

---

[1] British Museum, MS. Harleian 5644. In the beginning: Ἀρχὴ τοῦ Ρωτόκριτου; *1710*.

[2] P. Ioannou, 'Ο πιστικὸς βοσκός, Berlin, 1962—see Selected Bibliography.

of doubtful value. His work is preserved in only one manuscript; it is a metrical chronicle, in rhymed hendecasyllables, about the fall of the Peloponnese to the Turks in 1715, after the second Venetian occupation (*Lament of the Peloponnese*, 1716), and two tragedies, *Iphigeneia* and *Thyestes*, poor reflections of the *Erofili*. The editor, E. Kriaràs, has proved that they are direct imitation of tragedies of the same title by Lodovico Dolce. A curious element, which does not occur in the original, is the use of comic personages and situations in the last act of the *Iphigeneia*, which transform the work into a tragicomedy.

An isolated work, without cohesion or continuity, is the *Flowers of Piety* ('poured out for the glorious transmigration of Mary, the Mother of God'), a little pamphlet issued in 1708 by the students of the Flanginis's School of Venice. It is a school album, with epigrams in ancient Greek and in Latin, Sapphic odes, and Italian sonnets, but also prose and verse compositions in modern Greek. Far from the learned tradition of the Phanariots, the students of the school of Venice, under the supervision of their teachers, also wrote rhetorical and poetical compositions in the modern language. It is worth special mention that four of the poems are sonnets—the third collection we have met with, after the Cypriot love-poems and the choruses of *Rodolinos*. Naturally there is no question of influence or continuity; it is the Italian tradition working independently in three different places and at three different times: in Cyprus in 1570, in Crete in 1647, and in Venice in 1708.

Though poetry is so wretchedly represented in the Ionian Islands and among the Greeks of the diaspora, nevertheless a new thing was to develop there after 1669: literary prose in the demotic language. We meet with the first prose works in demotic even before 1669 (see pp. 52–3); but there was no question of literary prose. They were works destined for the people (the *Historical Book* or the *Salvation of Sinners*), and therefore written in simple and easily comprehensible language. But now the language is employed as a vehicle of literary expression, and not for the popular chronicle or the theological work of edification, but in a higher form, that of ecclesiastical rhetoric.

We saw the beginning of this earlier, in Venice and in Crete, with the sermons of Margounios and of Pigàs. Two Cretans, a little later in date, Gerasimos Vlachos (who became 'Metropolitan of Philadelphia' in Venice in 1679) and Athanasios Varouchas (d. 1708) who fled to the Ionian Islands after the fall of Crete, as well as their theological works in the ancient language, wrote 'Sermons' in a polished popular idiom. So also did another Cretan, Gerasimos Palladàs, who was patriarch of Alexandria (1677–99).

But the man who above all developed ecclesiastical rhetoric, in whose hands the language could equal the highest demands of the literary rhetorical speech, was Frankiskos Skoufos (1644–97). He was a child one year old when the Turks took Chania in 1645, and his parents fled with him to Italy. He studied at the College at Rome, and was active in Italy and the Ionian Islands, always devoted to the Catholic Church. In 1670 he published a 'panegyric' on the birth of St. John the Baptist, in Venice. His chief work is the *Art of Rhetoric* (1681), a manual, that is, in which one by one all the rhetorical devices are given with examples of each (drawn from his own work). Skoufos is an artist, with the highest artistic conscience. He learned his art in Italy (certainly his first lessons were at the College in Rome), where especially in Catholic circles ecclesiastical rhetoric was particularly cultivated. (The most important representative of it, the Jesuit Paolo Segneri, was almost contemporary with Skoufos.) Skoufos's style is elaborate and flowery, like that of his Italian masters; in his case we may speak of the modern Greek 'baroque'. But this style, adapted to a language used for the first time for literary prose, has neither the worn-out quality nor the exaggeration of the Italian *seicento*. It is much fresher, as we observed in the case of pastoral poetry. It is the freshness of a simple language, which is not destroyed by the artificial style.

The Heptanesian Elias Miniatis followed the line set by Skoufos. He was born in 1669 at Lixouri in Cephalonia; his father was a priest, and he studied at the Flanginianòn Hellenomouseion; his career was spent in the Ionian Islands and Venice, and also in Constantinople, where he was appointed by the patriarch as 'preacher of the Great Church'. He was the Orthodox counterpart of Skoufos. Towards the end of his life we find him in the Venetian-occupied Peloponnese, where he became a bishop in 1711; he died, comparatively young, at Patras in 1714.

Miniatis acquired great fame during his lifetime. Even the Venetians went to hear him at Nauplia; and a later writer tells us that in his birthplace 'many people recite by heart many parts' of his speeches.[1] Though Skoufos was not actually his teacher, Miniatis can certainly be described as his pupil. In a youthful speech in 1688, when still a scholar at the Flanginianòn, he ends with a moving apostrophe to the Mother of God, praying for the deliverance of the Greek people, an apostrophe which we find word for word in the (then already printed) *Rhetoric* of Skoufos. Plagiarism? Or rather a deliberate manifestation of influence and admiration? We cannot know. On the other hand the style of Miniatis is the same as that of Skoufos, though even more baroque in spirit, more artificial and carefully calculated. The language is always demotic, but warmer and more vigorous than that of Skoufos. The warmth of the speech is indeed the chief characteristic of his sermons, and the secret of his charm. Beneath the artificial construction, skilfully established and articulated, there is yet a warmth of language, which reflects the warmth of his faith, a faith both moral and religious.

The cultivation of demotic as literary prose did not have a sequel. In Turkish-occupied Greece the cultural atmosphere favoured a more literary language. But in the Ionian Islands the tradition of Skoufos and Miniatis never entirely died out. In 1718 the Corfiot Petros Kasimatis published *Most Useful Thoughts for Acquiring the Fear of God*, and the sermons preached in Corfu and Venice in 1745–55 by the archimandrite Spyridon Milias, also a Corfiot, follow the lines of Miniatis. A Peloponnesian painter, Panagiotis Doxaràs, who lived and worked in Zakynthos (1670–1729), translated the *Art of Painting* by Leonardo da Vinci, and wrote an original work *On Painting* in a simple and fluent demotic. And the Cephalonian Vikentios Damodòs (1700–52), who had studied at the Flanginianòn and at Padua, tried to break the influence of 'Korydalism' (though he himself wrote a commentary on Aristotle) and wrote his philosophical handbooks in simple demotic language.

Already from the end of the sixteenth century there was, as we saw in a previous chapter, some intellectual activity in

---

[1] Anthimos Mazarakis, Ἠλία Μηνιάτη Διδαχαί, 2nd edn., Venice, 1870, Introduction, p. κα'.

Constantinople round the Patriarchate, reaching its peak with
Kyrillos Loukaris. At about that time (1603) the Patriarchate
was established deep in the Golden Horn, in the quarter of the
Phanar, where it is still to this day. There gathered the clergy in
the services of the Patriarchate, and laymen to whom it gave
titles and offices. These 'Phanariots' were now to play a most
important role both in political and in intellectual life. They
began to become prominent and to receive important titles and
posts from the Sublime Porte, particularly that of Great Interpreter (who was almost in control of foreign affairs). Much has
been said for and against this class, and in it we find examples
both of nobility and baseness, brave actions and contemptible
intrigues. It is hard for us today to understand the mentality
and the strange position of these people, who, though slaves,
had held such powerful posts, being always in danger of losing
their heads at the conqueror's nod. It was a peculiar world that
set its seal on the whole of the eighteenth century—which has
well been named 'the century of the Phanariots'.

The first Greek to receive the office of Great Interpreter was
Panagiotis Nikousios (he was at the side of the Capudan-pasha
when the Venetians surrendered Crete to him). He was succeeded by Alexandros Mavrokordatos of Chios (1641–1709),
the progenitor of the greatest Phanariot family. He had taught
at the Patriarchal Academy, where he succeeded Korydaleus,
and had himself written commentaries on Aristotle. His son
Nikolaos (1670–1730) was the first Greek prince in the Danubian
principates of Wallachia and Moldavia—whither the Phanariot
activity was transferred, and where for a hundred years (till
1821) the courts of the Greek princes became centres of Greek
education and enlightenment.

The Phanariot climate was erudite, and in favour of the ancient
language, unconnected with that of Venice and the Ionian
Islands. The Mavrokordati wrote their works in the official
language, and their interests revolved round their new political
experience: *Political Thoughts* and *Political Theatre*. Students
of this age pick out the *Parerga of Philotheos* by Nikolaos Mavrokordatos (written in 1718, but not printed until 1800), a sort
of novel where the progressive European spirit of the time,
which had reached these enlightened princes through France
and the French language (now widespread and influential), is

faithfully reflected. This is the beginning of Greek enlightenment.

Mr. K. Dimaràs, the most authoritative student of the modern Greek Enlightenment, divides the movement into three periods, corresponding to those of the French Enlightenment.[1] The first, which is preliminary, is that of the period we are now examining (up to 1774), and is principally dominated by the influence of Voltaire. The chief proponent of this spirit was the Corfiot Eugenios Voulgaris, who passed his long and troubled life (1716–1806) in the subjugated Greek area, and after 1770 at the court of Catherine II of Russia. In his youth he was a progressive and an admirer of Voltaire and then turned towards the conservatism that characterized the intellectual development of that time, particularly the years that followed the French Revolution.

The eighteenth century is the age of thought, of intellectual change and development. The part played by literature is small. In the Phanariot region the poetic desolation is even more disheartening than in the Ionian Islands. There is not even the recollection of the Cretan tradition, which, with its cultivated language, gave some freshness to the Ionian poetical exercises. In the Phanar the language has not passed through this phase of cultivation; it is either colder and more learned, or flat-footed and uncultivated in the realm of popular speech, where it often has an admixture of Turkish words which had come into common use.

Naturally the content is not different; neither the relatively short *Stoicheiomachia* (1746) of Joannis Rizos Manès, nor the lengthy *Bosporomachia* influenced by it (the latter is by Momars, the doctor and interpreter of the Austrian ambassador at Constantinople), is of any value as poetry or as anything else. More interesting is Konstantinos Dapontes (Kaisarios as monk) from Skopelos, who joined the monastery of Xeropotamou on Mount Athos in 1757 and died there in 1784. A singularly voluminous writer, his output is amazing. He put all he heard or saw or read into thousands of careless, prosaic lines. Many of his works were printed in his lifetime, and loved and admired by his contemporaries (The *Mirror of Women*, 1766, the *Chrestoetheia*, 1770, the *Spiritual Table*, 1770), others were published after his death

[1] K. Dimaràs, 'Ιστορία etc., part 4, pp. 143 ff. Id., 'Ο ελληνικός διαφωτισμός, Athens, 1964, pp. 23–5.

(the *Garden of Graces*, 1881), and others remain still unpublished. It is of course not poetry, nor has it even the most elementary literary polish. Nevertheless, in this endless flow of verses we are sometimes made to pause by a sharp observation or an accurate description, and more often by a genuine sense of humour and a wit that is frequently apt, for example in the parodies of ecclesiastical hymns. It is not without surprise that we read, beautifully engraved on the great marble fountain that Dapontes brought from Chios and placed in the severe court of his Athonite monastery, these very unmonastic lines of his:

> I am a Chian girl, a Chian, Father, why ask me?
> And that is why, good Father, I am pretty, as you see.

Prose, in the sense of a cultured literary language (as we found in the Ionian Islands and among the diaspora) is almost non-existent in Greece proper. The learned wrote in the ancient language, as in the case of the Mavrokordati. Certainly preachers must have used a simpler language in the pulpit; in libraries we find many manuscripts of such sermons, anonymous for the most part. They have no connection with the tradition of Skoufos and Miniatis; if they may be compared with anything it is rather with the uncultivated and more popular style of Dapontes.

This uncultivated popular style, when genuine and unadulterated, can sometimes have a special interest. Such a case is the *Chronicle of Galaxidi*. Galaxidi is a small village in Roumeli on the Corinthian gulf where shipping once flourished. In 1703 a monk called Euthymios wrote the chronicle of his village in simple, popular language. He had little education, and his language is popular demotic. His intention is purely historical: he says he has studied 'old vellum manuscripts, and authentic patriarchal and imperial letters' which he had found in his monastery, and there is no reason to disbelieve him. But in his simple imagination historical events have become mixed up with legends, miracles, and fantastic tales that he narrates with the same attention to detail, and the same faith in their reality. 'Then St. Euthymios appeared to them and comforted them and said . . .'. We are in the world of popular mythology.

Towards the end of this period another man leads us into this same world. He is not uneducated, like the monk Euthymios, nor has he the same credulity, though he has the same faith. This is Kosmàs the Aetolian. He was born in 1714 in a village in Aetolia; he seems to have been a pupil of Voulgaris, and from 1760 he started going all round Greece preaching. We find him principally in Roumeli and Macedonia, but also in Epirus, the Ionian Islands, and Thrace. Memoranda in old books and manuscripts testify to the astonishing impression that he left among the simple people whom he addressed. Those were difficult years for the Greek people, especially for those who lived in the country in remote and mountainous regions, where many were forcibly converted to Islam. Kosmàs the Aetolian strengthened these people in their Christian faith, and encouraged them to found schools. He seems not to have written his sermons but to have improvised them; they were later written down from memory by his devoted followers; they have therefore the spontaneous and unstudied character of spoken speech, without literary or rhetorical ornament; there is a roughness and directness which is both Doric and Roumeliot, and which conceals a surprising force. Kosmàs combines in the highest form the spirit of education and enlightenment with religious faith and national consciousness. He may be considered as one of the precursors of the awakenment of the nation, like Rigas. They met with the same fate; in 1779 the Turkish authorities arrested Kosmàs and executed him.

Kosmàs the Aetolian and the *Chronicle of Galaxidi* bring us into another world, far from the learned world of the Phanariots and the literary culture of the Ionian Islands; it is the world of the countryside, the backbone of Hellenism. Without education or other culture it created its own world, which was so wonderfully expressed by the demotic song. At this time, and particularly on the mainland, demotic poetry finds a new stimulus in the 'klephtic song'. We shall speak of this, and of the demotic song in general, in the next chapter. But first we must follow the further development of modern Greek Enlightenment.

### SECOND PERIOD: 1770–1820

Greek Enlightenment, according to the distinction we have already made (p. 75), after a first introductory phase, entered into its peak period in the last decades of the eighteenth century.

It was decisively influenced by French culture, and particularly by the circle of the *Encyclopédistes*. We note a greater intellectual maturity, which will lead gradually and firmly towards union and rehabilitation.

Josephus Moisiodax (*c.* 1730–90) was a pupil of Voulgaris, but he also studied abroad and taught in the schools of the princes at Bucharest and Jassy. He was distinguished for his progressive ideas, especially in relation to the language; he spoke of a 'common style' which he thought, if suitably cultivated, would be suitable for any subject. He was interested in mathematics and the sciences, and also in ancient literature; but special mention must be made of his concern for educational problems. His *Education*, printed in Venice in 1779, is directly dependent on *Thoughts Concerning Education* by John Locke.

The increase of intellectual interests, the lively movement of ideas, and the ever growing circulation of books that characterized this period naturally raised the language question again. What language should be the vehicle for the 'enlightenment of the nation'? The established idea (that of Voulgaris and his followers) was that it should be the ancient language; Moisiodax proposed 'the common style'. In 1789 two learned men at Bucharest, one the headmaster of the Academy and the other a High Court judge, exchanged a correspondence on the subject, taking diametrically opposite sides.[1] The headmaster, Lambros Fotiadis, was the archaist, and the demoticist was Dimitrios Katartzìs. For three decades, until 1821, the language struggle was kept up with intensity.

Katartzìs (*c.* 1720/5–1807) has a central place in the debate, and indeed through this whole period of the Enlightenment. Those who came after forgot his teaching, or allowed it to become forgotten. Most of his work remained unprinted; one of his works was printed after 'translation' into the learned language. Later research (particularly that of K. Th. Dimaràs)[2] reveals him as a distinguished personality, one of the most remarkable of the years preceding the revolution. On the language question his

[1] The letters have been printed by N. Doukas, Ἡ κατ᾽ ἐπιτομὴν γραμματικὴ Τερψιθέα, 3rd edn., Vienna, 1812, pp. 53–84, and reprinted by K. N. Sathas, Νεοελληνικῆς Φιλολογίας Παράρτημα, Athens, 1870, pp. 154–76. Extracts: A. E. Megas, Ἱστορία τοῦ γλωσσικοῦ ζητήματος, vol. 2, Athens, 1927, pp. 23–33.

[2] He has written many monographs about Katartzìs, and has recently edited his Εὑρισκόμενα—see Selected Bibliography.

views were radical and sensible; he was also a man of deep reflection and progressive vision, a representative example of the beneficial effect of the Enlightenment on education and the awakening of the people. He exposed his philosophical system in the *Know Thyself*. Katartzìs wrote in the popular language (as it was spoken in Constantinopolitan circles) without any compromise with the learned tradition, and in an individual and personal way; and he wrote it systematically and with persistence. Perhaps he was ahead of his time; eight years later he was obliged to accept a mixed, 'selected' language, rather than the 'natural' language he had written up till then. This was really a tactical retreat and not a defeat. At all events his main aim was a higher one: 'to help the nation'.

Though forgotten by those who came after, Katartzìs exercised a significant influence upon his contemporaries. Many people who were to be important in other fields came from his immediate circle and were influenced by his ideas. Of these, the most distinguished was, without doubt, Rigas. We have clear evidence that Katartzìs was fascinated by the qualities of the young Rigas, loved him like a father, and helped him with his wisdom and his knowledge of politics. In 1791 two scholars from Thessaly, G. Konstantàs and Daniel Filippidis, published a *Modern Geography* in which the influence of Katartzìs is obvious not only in the demotic language but also in the general spirit, the realistic facing of problems and the desire for knowledge of the immediate environment. Athanasios Christopoulos also came from the close circle of Katartzìs. We shall examine his place in modern Greek poetry in another chapter; his contribution to the language problem was significant. In 1805 (five years before the publication of his *Lyrics*) he placed himself on the side of the champions of the demotic with his *Grammar of Aeolo-Doric* ('or the Greek language now spoken'). His theory was that the modern Greek language was one of the dialects of ancient Greek, a mixture of Aeolic and Doric; it had therefore as noble an origin as the Attic which the archaists wished to write. This theory was altogether mistaken and unscientific, but it strengthened the side of the 'demoticists' and for a long time 'Aeolo-Doric' was used as a synonym for modern Greek (or 'Romaic' as it used to be called). Later, together with the *Lyrics*, a prose work was printed, the *Dream*, a sort of dialogue between the writer and two ugly painted women, who are the 'Mixed Barbarian Language' and 'Orthography'. The work, a satire on the theories of Koraïs for the most part, is written in warm, lively language and has considerable literary quality; it is not by Christopoulos, as many people thought, but must have some connection with his circle. Other similar literary or satirical works that take sides in the sharp linguistic dispute of the thirty years before the revolution are *The Most Learned Traveller* of Vilaràs,[1] and the comedy *Korakistika* (1813) by the Phanariot Jakovakis Rizos Neroulòs, which is written with wit and feeling for the theatre; in the latter there is satire obviously directed against Koraïs.

The name of Adamantios Koraïs has been mentioned in the foregoing pages. He only entered the linguistic dispute in 1805, when he put forward his theory in the preface to one of his books;[2] its appearance at once gave another turn to the contention. Koraïs proposed a *via media* to the two parties, the 'demoticists' (or the 'vulgarizers' as they were contemptuously called) and the 'archaists'; and he drew the fire of both sides.

Koraïs lived eighty-five years, holds a large and important place in the history of Greek culture, and marks the third phase of modern Greek Enlightenment, in the two decades before the revolution (1800–20). He was of Chian descent, born in 1748 in Smyrna where he received his elementary education; after a few years in Amsterdam, where he helped his father in a commercial enterprise, he went to France, studied medicine at Montpellier, and after 1788 settled definitely in Paris. He lived through the French Revolution and accepted its liberal ideas, he took a keen interest in the liberation of his country, and published anonymous pamphlets with political tendencies (1798–1803); but at the same time he devoted himself to his main work which was his philological studies and the editing of ancient writers. The Revolution found him at the advanced age of seventy-three, and though he was not in complete agreement with the outbreak of the movement, he followed the fortunes of his country with a warm and youthful ardour, and never ceased to give counsel till his death in 1833.

Koraïs is first of all a philologist, the first Greek philologist of

---

[1] Edited posthumously, in the 1st edn. of his works, Corfu, 1827.

[2] Πρόδρομος Ἑλληνικῆς Βιβλιοθήκης, Paris, 1805.

European authority, completely part of that great advance in classical scholarship and in the study of antiquity which characterized the Europe of his time, a friend of Villoison and other European savants. He published editions of, and commentaries on ancient writers and studied the modern language which he rightly saw as the last phase in the history of the same language, from ancient times until today. But the significance of Koraïs in modern Greek civilization is not limited to this. With his powerful personality and his great authority he influenced a whole age of modern Greek letters. On the way towards unity which modern Hellenism was then treading, Koraïs marks the first step.

It would be a mistake to regard him as a savant, isolated in his study; we have seen how closely and intensely he shared in all the movements of his time. Fundamentally he was ardent and enthusiastic, but his classical education, his experience of life, and his liberal and democratic ideas led him towards moderation and intellectual balance. The *via media*, the solution which he proposed for the language question, was also a democratic solution, in accordance with his ideas. To depart too far from common speech was 'tyrannical', while to 'vulgarize' was 'demagogic'. Between oligarchy and ochlocracy, Koraïs stood for democracy in its true sense. All members of the nation ought to share in the language with 'democratic equality'.

Therefore he takes the common spoken language as the basis of the written language; but he says that nations can only be called enlightened when 'they bring their language to perfection'. This is brought about by the 'beautifying', the 'tidying and the adorning of the language'. Up to this point, no one will disagree with him; all of the second part of Solomòs's famous *Dialogue* develops this theory of the beautification and cultivation of the language. But a poet approaches language differently from a savant, no matter how profound or how vital he may be. While Solomòs desired an interior deepening and enrichment of the language, the end desired by Koraïs was merely grammatical and limited to the re-establishment of ancient forms of popular words (μάτι—ὀμμάτιον, ψάρι—ὀψάριον, etc.). Nevertheless, the language of Koraïs remained much closer to common speech, and those whom he most attacked and who most attacked him were the 'mixed barbarian' archaists. The katharevousa of the first years of the Greek state was modelled on the language of

Koraïs. But Koraïs's 'solution' did not lead to a real solution. Its basis was artificial and grammatical; and apart from this, the learned writers of the liberated nation more and more abandoned his moderate principles as the years went by, and returned towards archaism.

# V

## THE DEMOTIC SONG

THE DEMOTIC SONG has a place of its own in modern Greek
literature and, more generally, in the intellectual life of
modern Greece. This not only on account of its undoubted
poetical quality, which places it much higher than the usual
popular song of the village or town, but also because it always
remained near to learned and personal poetry, had a strong
influence upon it, and often determined its modes of expression.
We have seen how *The Epic of Digenìs Akritas*, the first monument
of modern Greek literature, was closely connected with the
'Akritic' demotic songs; we have followed the constant presence
of the demotic songs in the romances of chivalry or the *katalogia*, and we have emphasized the demotic character of Cretan
poetry, in the sense that in verse and expression it was close to
the established modes of the demotic song (Chortatsis was less so,
Kornaros more). Solomòs was to give a new urge to his poetry,
because of what he learned from the demotic songs, and we
may follow its continuous presence and influence up to the poets
of our own time. It is not too much to say, that the advance
of the poets towards complete expression in modern Greek is
a continuous and constantly revised adaptation to the modes of
expression of the demotic song.

The demotic song is also without doubt the means by which
the people gave the most authoritative expression to its world and
to its personality. What we call the soul of a people, its griefs,
and its desires, and even its historical adventures are to be found
crystallized in the poetical expression of the song. It is natural
that it should invite the enthusiasm of all who have approached
it, from Fauriel, who first made it known to the western world,
until our own days. Goethe in a letter to his son in 1815 speaks
of the modern Greek demotic song as 'the finest that we know,

from the point of view of lyric, dramatic, and epic poetry'.[1] He
also translated one of the finest:

> Olympus and Mount Kissavos, those mountains were at
> strife . . .

The demotic song, then, is something that appears parallel
with other poetry throughout the ages, and cannot be classed
with the works of any determinate period. Certain songs, such
as the Akritica, are older than the first monument of learned
literature; the roots of the demotic song perhaps go back
even further; and yet the songs are still performed. However,
although the demotic song still survives and is sung, it is a survival, kept up as a 'tradition', in the folklore sense of the word. It
is still sung at weddings and village feasts and on other occasions
of social life, mainly in remote districts and in small provincial
towns (how long this will go on, and how far it will remain
genuine and unchanged by foreign influence or by tourism is
another question); but it does not live creatively, and new songs
are not composed (apart from odd couplets in the islands and
elsewhere). The demotic song flourished for the last time with
the 'klephtic song' of the eighteenth century and the years
immediately preceding the War of Independence, and chiefly in
mainland Greece, where we have found the *Chronicle of Galaxidi*
and Kosmàs the Aetolian (see pp. 76–7).

For this reason it has seemed better to treat the demotic song
in its entirety at this point. It rises to its height after a long
development and expresses the robust and warlike spirit of the
mountain dwellers of Epirus and of mainland Greece who as
'klephts' or *armatolì* were generally under arms and were perhaps
the most significant element in the struggle for unification and
the re-establishment of Hellenism. It is indeed true that the
learning of Koraïs and the political experience of the Phanariots
and many other elements united to produce the happy result,
but the burden of the war fell on these hardy and warlike
mountaineers who sang and were sung of in the klephtic
songs: Kolokotronis, Makrygiannis, Karaïskakis. Makrygiannis,

---

[1] In a letter to his son, August, 5 July 1815: 'Ein Freund der Neugriechen war
bei mir, der Lieder dieses Volkes mit sich führt, das Köstlichste in dem Sinne
der lyrisch-dramatisch-epischen Poesie, was wir kennen.' For his translations see
K. Dieterich, 'Goethe und die neugriechische Volksdichtung', *Hellas-Jahrbuch* 1929,
pp. 61–81 (cf. S. Kougeas, *Néa 'Εστία*, 11 (1932), 621 ff.).

besieged on the Acropolis, gave expression to his grief by improvising a klephtic song:

> The sun is set—friend Greek, it's set—
> the moon is lost to sight,
> And the clear morning star that seeks the Pleiades,
> The four are talking secretly . . .[1]

Not all the songs are of this high quality. Folklorists have rightly divided the songs into two main categories, the 'songs proper' which 'accompany all the expressions of people living a natural or a civilized life', and the narrative songs or 'ballads', which 'presuppose considerable poetical preparation, maturity, tradition, and art'.[2] The people call the latter *paralogès* (παραλογές) and they are more perfect from a literary point of view, and more interesting.

The simplest of the 'songs proper'[3] are the work songs, those which maintain the rhythm of some human task, for instance rowing, and those which accompany various feasts or popular customs, for instance the *kalanda* (carols). The swallow songs are interesting; they are sung on 1 March by small children from door to door, holding a toy swallow in their hands. The custom has come down from antiquity; a 'swallow song' by Athenaeus is like those sung today:

| | |
|---|---|
| The swallow is here | The swallow is here, |
| Bringing good seasons | And the nightingale dear; |
| Bringing good years. | She sat and gave tongue, |
| | And sweet was her song. |
| (Athenaeus viii. 60) | (A. Passow, *Τραγούδια* |
| | *Ρωμαίικα*, no. cccvii) |

Another large class is that of children's songs, whether to be sung by children themselves or to them by their elders; such are the ταχταρίσματα (sung by mothers when they rock the baby in their arms) and the cradle songs or lullabies; some of them are remarkable for their lyrical quality:

---

[1] General Makrygiannis, *Ἀπομνημονεύματα*, ed. J. Vlachogiannis, 2nd edn., Athens, 1947, vol. 1, p. 285. *The Memoirs of General Makriyannis*, edited and translated by H. A. Lidderdale, London, 1966, p. 111.

[2] St. Kyriakidis, *Ἑλληνικὴ Λαογραφία*, vol. 1, *Τὰ μνημεῖα τοῦ λόγου*, 2nd edn. Athens, 1965, pp. 48–9.

[3] For the division of the 'songs proper' see ibid., pp. 52–99.

O sleep my star, o sleep my dawn, o sleep my small new moon,
Sleep to make glad the eyes of him who'll take you for his own.
I've sent unto the City for the gold you are to wear,
To Venice for your gown, and for the diamonds for your hair.[1]

Among the 'songs proper' are grouped those that are bound up with the most significant events in a man's life, love, marriage, and death, and exile, which the Greek people have always felt to be a great misfortune. The marriage songs are more closely connected with ritual, but in the love songs a pure lyricism wells out freely, which surprises us with its freshness and grace. They are often confined to distichs, *lianotrágouda* or *amanedes*, *patinades* or *mantinades*, but many are longer and more consciously composed, differing little from the ballads.

The songs of death are of a higher lyricism; these are the *mirologia* (the word is Byzantine), according to Fauriel 'the richest vein of modern Greek popular poetry'.[2] This sort of lament is customary among all peoples. We find it widespread in ancient Greece; in the *Iliad* (xxiv. 719) some 'minstrels, leaders of mourning', come and sit near the corpse of Hector, and women accompany their songs with wailing, something in the manner of the professional mourners of today. The people have preserved the ancient Greek feeling in their laments, quite uninfluenced by Christian eschatology. There is no distinction between heaven and hell; the dead go to the 'underworld' which is black and decaying, and no longer rejoice in the 'world above' with its grace and beauty; many of the *mirologia*, while lamenting the dead, hymn the beauties of nature and the spring:

It did not fit, it did not suit you to be laid in earth,
A garden in the month of May is what was meant for you,
Between two apple trees to lie, between three orange trees,
That blossom might fall over you, and apples at your feet,
And round your throat carnations dark and crimson should
be growing.[3]

Like this is the laconic distich, that Athanasios Diakos is said to have sung as he was led to his martyrdom:

See what a time Death chose for you, to take you to your doom,
Just when the earth grows green again, and branches are in bloom.[4]

---

[1] N. G. Politis, Ἐκλογαί, no. 153.
[2] C. Fauriel, *Chants populaires de la Grèce moderne*, vol. 1, Paris, 1824, Introduction p. cxxxv.     [3] Politis, Ἐκλογαί, no. 196.     [4] Ibid., no. 212.

A particular class of *mirologia*, called those 'of the Under-world and Charos', revolves round Charos, the tragic personifica-tion of Death created by popular thought out of Charon, the ancient ferryman of the Styx. He is commonly imagined as gigantic in height, invincible, generally clad in black, a horseman who pulls the dead on to his horse, and sheds terror all around:

Why are the mountains all so black, why do they stand in tears?
Is it the wind that beats on them, is it the rain that lashes?
'Tis not the wind that beats on them, 'tis not the rain that lashes,
But it is Charos that goes by, with his dead passengers,
He puts the young in front of him, he puts the old behind him,
The tender little babes he takes, he puts upon his saddle.[1]

He is deaf and unrelenting to the prayers of the living. Popular imagination represents him dining with his wife, the Charontissa, and a young girl entertaining them; it also gave him a mother, who is sorry for the dead, and in vain beseeches her son to have pity on them. One of the most beautiful and most widely known songs about the slender girl who 'boasted that she had no fear of Charos', attains the perfection of the ballads and a really tragic profundity: Charos, as representative of inexorable fate, punishes the *hybris* of the young woman.[2]

The *mirologi* was particularly cultivated in the Mani (southern Peloponnese), where it acquired a character of its own. It is sung by professional mourners, following a strict convention; the verse is not the common decapentesyllable, but a shorter, eight-syllable line. The Mani, that wild, isolated, warlike region, re-tained a character of its own and an austerity in its social and family life, which springs from its customs (and from the practice of the vendetta). The Maniot *mirologia* have not the character of relief for sorrow which is found in other Greek laments; they are heavy and oppressive and hardly go beyond relating the circumstances. 'What distinguishes the Maniot *mirologi* [writes J. Apostolakis][3] is the flood of sentiment and the lack of imagina-tion. The Maniot faces life with its events naked and unadorned, and his bare, almost materialistic expression of them is a physical relief to him.' A peculiar region, with an interest all its own.

---

[1] Passow 409; Politis 218.
[2] A very popular song, with many variations: Passow 413–19; Politis 217.
[3] J. Apostolakis, *Τὸ κλέφτικο τραγούδι*, Athens, 1950, p. 103.

There are many things in common between the *mirologia* and the klephtic songs. Often a klephtic song is a *mirologi*, and vice versa; they are both the most lyrical form of the demotic song. We shall speak of the klephtic songs later on. Of the other non-ballad songs we must mention the satirical songs (often charming on account of their popular humour), the gnomic songs, and above all the historical songs. These, too, often come near to the *mirologia* in expression (as in the famous 'St. Sophia' song about the fall of Constantinople); others recount events along more or less formal lines. The most ancient are of Byzantine times, about events in Pontus at the beginning of the twelfth century, about the sack of Adrianople in 1361, and a whole series celebrates the conflicts of the Suliots against Ali Pasha; these are the last that are of interest. The songs about the War of Independence are insignificant, and those later are much inferior. Sometimes the song broadens into a sort of metrical chronicle, half demotic and half learned, especially in Cyprus and Crete, where a class of poets still exists, the *piitarides* (ποιητάρηδες). Such a song, by the Cretan Pantzeliòs, relates the actions and the violent death of Daskalogiannis, leader of a revolution in Crete after the Orloff rising (1771); we are on the frontier line between popular and personal poetry.

We placed the narrative songs at the topmost rung of demotic poetry. We can divide these also into categories, into the Akritica and the narrative songs proper—those which are popularly called *paralogès*. S. P. Kyriakidis[1] produced strong reasons for finding their origins in the last period of the ancient world. The very word *tragoudi* (τραγούδι = song) takes us back to antiquity, and we know that by the first century A.D. the word *tragodia* (τραγῳδία = tragedy) meant song. But the word *paralogì* (and the medieval *katalogi*) also has an ancient origin. At the end of the ancient world its highest literary creation, tragedy, had become dissolved into its component elements; the actors produced the dialogue only, and not all of it, others sang only the choral parts. ('To sing a tragedy' or τραγῳδεῖν came simply to mean 'to sing'). Apart from this division between the sung and spoken part, another division grew up between singing and acting. The actor was gradually displaced by the gesticulator, who

---

[1] In his excellent study: *Αἱ ἱστορικαὶ ἀρχαὶ τῆς δημώδους νεοελληνικῆς ποιήσεως*, Thessaloniki, 1934; 2nd edn., 1954.

expressed himself only by mime. In the later centuries such silent performances were widespread; this was the 'tragic pantomime', whose subject was most often taken from mythology. The performance was accompanied by a song specially written, and adapted to the requirements of the pantomime, and naturally it related or 'sang' (ἐτραγῴδει) the events of the myth. These songs and dances became very popular and were sung (as Libanius tells us in the fourth century A.D.)[1] by children or young servants going along the streets to do the shopping, while the dancers were invited to private houses, to banquets, and weddings, for which St. John Chrysostom severely castigates the Christians. These songs and dances are the remote origin of the *paralogès* according to Kyriakidis's theory. It is not without interest that until quite recently the *paralogès* were sung by the people, especially at weddings, as dance songs.

Some of the narrative songs sung by the people are distinguished by their tragic myth, and thus give further support to Kyriakidis's theory. But the question is when they really took the shape in which they have been handed down to us by tradition. It would be of extreme interest if the time and place at which each song took form for the first time could be ascertained, and the way in which it spread across the country. The Swiss scholar Samuel Baud-Bovy attempted this in his admirable study *La Chanson populaire grecque du Dodecanèse* (1936), and his conclusions are convincing and enlightening.

Thus the earliest narrative songs that have been preserved must be considered to be the well-known Akritica. They are immediately recognized for their antiquity by their mention of Arabs and Saracens and above all by their heroic and epic content. We are in a world of single combat and personal bravery, and what is outstanding is the courage and physical strength of the heroes, which attain a supernatural degree:

> He slew a thousand as he went, two thousand as he came,
> And at his joyful coming back there was not any left.[2]

The supernatural element is everywhere present. The warrior converses with his horse, and the horses (the warrior's companions) are also exalted to a noble and heroic level. The songs

---

[1] Libanius, *Oratio lxiv pro saltatoribus*, ed. Foerster, vol. 4, p. 493 (Teubner).
[2] Politis, Ἐκλογαί, no. 70, vv. 37–8.

were created among men whose sole occupation was war; the same world as that of the *Iliad*. There is no softer note in their rough life. Love plays no part; the woman belongs to the same warlike environment, sometimes she is 'the slender heroine', like Maximò of the epic. The songs must have come to birth in the heroic age of Byzantium, in the ninth and tenth centuries, and in Asia Minor, whence they spread all over Greece and into the neighbouring Slav countries. The best-known are those of *Armouris*, of the *Sons of Andronicus*, of *Porfyris*, of the *Castle of the Fair Lady* (this in dodecasyllables), and the cycle of songs about the death of Digenìs (these last seem to have taken on their final form in Cyprus).

Baud-Bovy places in the same period and place (Asia Minor) two of the ballads most widely known in all Greece, *The Bridge of Arta* and *The Dead Brother*.[1] Here the same manly and inexorable world dominates as in the Akritica, with an admixture of supernatural and also of tragic elements, and the appearance of an implacable fate. It is of no significance that the first song is best known as *The Bridge of Arta*; the most authentic versions, in fact, call it *The Hair Bridge* and come from Asia Minor. It is the tragic story of the master-builder's wife who must be sacrificed to make the bridge stand firm. The song of the *Dead Brother* is even more startling in its tragedy; it is the ghostly story of 'The Mother with nine sons of hers, and with her only daughter', and the dead brother raised from the grave by the mother's curse to fulfil his promise and bring back her daughter who has been married in foreign parts—a theme similar to that of the well-known *Ballad of Leonora*. This song spread from Asia Minor, where it was composed, all over Greece and, as research has shown, passed later into the Slav countries and elsewhere.

Another well-known and widespread ballad, that of *Chartzianìs* (or the *Sun-born Maiden*)[2] is inspired by a different spirit. Here the erotic element makes its first appearance, connected with that of fraud; the hero dresses as a woman and presents himself to the woman he loves as her cousin, in order to obtain her. No version of it has come to us from Asia Minor. Baud-Bovy places it in the Dodecanese in the twelfth century.

[1] S. Baud-Bovy, *La Chanson grecque*, pp. 163–74. Politis, nos. 92 and 89.
[2] "*Τῆς Διογέννητης*", Politis no. 74.

Here, in the Dodecanese, and more generally in the islands of
the Aegean, a whole series of songs had its origin; they are very
different in spirit from those we have previously mentioned. They
are mainly love-songs, with a young girl as the central figure and
love as the main sentiment: *The Abandoned One, The Bridesmaid
Who Became a Bride*, etc.[1] They belong to the time of the Frankish
occupation, from the thirteenth to the fifteenth century, the age
of the romances of love and chivalry, among which we found
many *katalogia* of the same sort. Here the Frankish influence is
strong and easily discernible, the tone is mainly lyrical, and
there is a sweetness which fits well with the climate of the islands
and the character of the people—the same tone which is reflected
in the *Erotopaignia*.

Among the love-songs, Baud-Bovy distinguishes a group in
which the central figure is a girl, not the typical virgin, but the
mistress or the unfaithful wife. These songs show a relaxation
in morals and an environment like that which we meet in
the poems of Sachlikis; their origin must be Crete, from the
thirteenth and fourteenth centuries (the earliest songs) to the
sixteenth. Others again, including the few nautical songs (*Kyr
Voriàs* and *The Travelling Girl*),[2] come from islands which obtained
a nautical pre-eminence in the seventeenth and eighteenth centuries. There is a strange shifting of the centres of the demotic
song from east to west; finally several ballads, such as the most
tragic *Murderous Mother*[3] (older than the sixteenth century) may
be placed in mainland Greece. But it was here, mainly in the
eighteenth century, that an outstanding type of demotic song
developed, which was also the last stage of its creative evolution:
the klephtic song.

Throughout the Turkish occupation the loss of liberty and the
misery, particularly of the mountain people, impelled the inhabitants of Greece to acts of resistance against the occupiers.
Thus the 'klephts' came into existence; the word simply means
a thief, but the original depreciatory meaning was lost and the
klepht came to mean the man who never submitted and the
combatant for liberty.

---

[1] "*Τῆς Ἀπολησμονημένης*", "*Τῆς κουμπάρας πόγινε νύφη*", Politis nos. 82, 83.

[2] "*Τοῦ κὺρ Βοριᾶ*", Politis no. 88; "*Κόρη ταξιδεύτρια*", Fauriel, vol. 2, 95,
Passow 476 (cf. Baud-Bovy, *La Chanson grecque*, pp. 266, 258).

[3] Passow 462, 463; Politis 41.

Against these dangerous guerillas the Turkish authority organized the *armatolì*, a regular body, often composed of former
klephts, who were responsible for order in each district. Even
before the fall of Constantinople the Sultan Murad II had been
obliged to form the first headquarters of *armatolì* in Agrapha, the
dangerous mountain region in the west of mainland Greece. The
next seems to have been that on Olympus, the highest mountain
in Greece, which became the chief home and refuge of the
klephts, and is frequently named in klephtic songs. Klephts and
*armatolì*, though opposed, were both warriors, lived the same
rough life, and created a wild, heroic world of their own, whence
sprang the klephtic song.

In some respects, the conditions now obtaining were like those
in which the akritic songs came to birth. But the klephtic song
is, in spirit and in form, quite different from that of the akrites.
It is not a narrative song, but belongs to the category of 'songs
proper'. It does not relate events, nor do the klephts perform
supernatural or improbable actions. If the akrites were distinguished by their bodily strength, the klephts are distinguished
by their brave spirit, as the most authoritative student of the
klephtic song, J. Apostolakis, has well observed: 'The demotic
poet does not base his song on the data of time and place and
psychology, so much as on the outstanding spirit of the hero,
and still more upon his conception of Man.'[1] Formed during a
period of preparation for liberty, the klephtic song is 'the robust
pattern of a new type of Greek',[2] that which was to be brought
to birth by the revolution of 1821. According to Apostolakis we
are not to seek the successor of the klephtic song among the
insignificant historical songs of the War of Independence, but
in Solomòs's *Hymn to Liberty*.[3]

In its most genuine form the klephtic song is, therefore, lyrical.
'A deep emotion lies behind the conception of the song',[4] and
this emotion takes lyric form. A common device is the dialogue
between the chief characters themselves or with other persons,
purposeless questions, or situations in which mountains, clouds,
and birds speak, and contribute to the moral tone:

> What ails the mounts of Zichna that they stand so bare and sad?
> Is it the hail that beats on them, is it the stormy winter?

---

[1] *Τὸ κλέφτικο τραγούδι*, p. 106.     [2] Ibid., p. 96.
[3] Ibid., p. 145.                      [4] Ibid., p. 111.

The hail it does not beat on them, nor does the stormy winter,
It's Nikotsaras who is fighting with three vilayets.[1]

Or

Thus says the cuckoo on the branch, the partridge on the hill
And thus the women of Plagià say in their black lament.[2]

An entirely individual motif, a most genuinely lyrical invention
which became the formal beginning of most klephtic songs, is
the three birds which ask after the klepht or lament him:

Three little birds were sitting on the ridge, the hiding-place;
And one looked towards Almyròs, the other towards Valtos,
The third one and the best of them spake this lament and said . . .[3]

The music of the klephtic songs is of the same sort, in lyrical
stanzas with an entirely free rhythm; they are therefore sung
seated (they are 'songs of the table') and never danced.

By and large we may divide the klephtic songs into two main
categories: those which refer to one person (to a klepht, such as
Zidros, Stournaris, or Gyftakis) or to one event, and those which
speak generally of the life of the klephts with its joys and difficulties. Apostolakis[4] only considered the first group genuine, in
the sense that it was composed at the time of and with a lively
feeling for the events; the later group was composed at a subsequent period when the life of the klephts was no longer a
reality, but something distant which was idealized by men who
were no longer themselves heroic.

## THE TECHNIQUE

The most usual form of verse in the demotic song is the
decapentesyllable, which we have seen is used almost without
exception even in personal poetry. There is no rhyme in the
demotic song, with rare exceptions, and these are generally
much later. Rhyme was used only in one genre, and was the
cause of its creation: the distichs or *lianotrágouda*, widespread
throughout all Greece, but especially in Crete and the islands,
where they are living till this day and are still a creative form.
In their terse form they express their meaning succinctly: some
are gnomic, but most of them are erotic:

He who is young and does not fly with clouds when they are driven
By the north wind, one wonders why life to him has been given.

[1] Passow 78–9; Politis 61 B.    [2] Passow 120, etc.
[3] Fauriel, vol. 1, p. 4; Politis no. 49.    [4] Op. cit., pp. 88 ff.

Ah wert thou but the lemon tree and I the mountain snow,
That I might melt and over your cool branches I might flow.

You left me and you went away and now my poor heart grieves,
Just like an abandoned church, in a city sacked by thieves.[1]

The age-old tradition and cultivation of the demotic song
created some conventional motifs, certain forms of expression, i.e.
a special language with its own rules. One of the most fundamental is the isometrical or symmetrical correspondence of form
and content (Kyriakidis),[2] a principle obtaining in all forms of
popular art: every unit of sense corresponds to a unit of form.
Metrical enjambment is a thing unknown in the demotic song.
And as the decapentesyllable, the usual form of verse, is divided
into two half-lines of eight and seven syllables, the principle of
isometry also determines the relations of the two half-lines to each
other; we have a kind of balance between them:

In the night the armatolì, and at the dawn the klephts—

O ye trees blossom if you will, or wither if you will.

In many lines we have a further division in the first hemistich
into two four-syllable parts, and thus the line is divided into
three:

O mother mad, mother insane, and mother without wit—

Strikes on the right, strikes on the left, and strikes before and aft.

Often this balance between the half-lines is completed by a third
unit of meaning which occupies a whole line, and thus re-
establishes the equilibrium of metre and meaning:

He takes the deer still living, and he takes the wild beasts tamed,
He takes a tiny little fawn bound tightly to his saddle.

O take the sun to be your face, the moon to be your breast,
And take the black crow's wing to be the ribbon of your brow.

In this case another principle of folk literature is also at work, the
well-known 'rule of three'.

Often in the second hemistich we have a simple completion of
the line which adds nothing, but generally this addition enlarges
the picture and leads us nearer to the poetical centre:

It was dawning in the east, and reddening in the west;

[1] Politis nos. 233γ′, 135 μς′, νβ′.

[2] S. Kyriakidis, Ἡ γένεσις τοῦ διστίχου καὶ ἡ ἀρχὴ τῆς ἰσομετρίας, Thessaloniki,
1947.

or we have a gradual increase in intensity:

> On a feast day, on a Sunday, on a holiday;

or in clarity:

> They fired three gun-shots after him, the one after the other,
> The first one hit him in the side, the second in the head,
> The third and the most deadly hit him right between the eyes.

Sometimes the heightening of power comes with a change of tense (aorist to present):

> And they lamented and they spake, and they lament and speak.

The language of the demotic song is remarkable for its expressive force and its clarity, the phrase is 'simple, nervous, and matter-of-fact'.[1] Apostolakis well observes that it is based on the noun and verb, that is, on the solid world of facts, and not on the fancy represented by the adjective. 'The nature of the actual thing, and its changes, which the adjective conveys absolutely and timelessly, is expressed by the demotic poet definitely by the verb and in time.'[2]

The demotic song, we must never forget, is not 'mere poetry' but is inextricably joined with music, and is always sung. This is not the place to speak of the special characteristics of Greek popular music, and its difference from that of western Europe and from that which is typically Oriental, though it indeed belongs to the Oriental family. Although there are vital differences between, for example, a Roumeliot, an insular, and a Cretan song, there are some features common to all Greek music. The musical *modes* are not restricted to the Western major and minor, and the scales make use of intervals slightly greater and smaller than a semitone. For this reason there is no greater falsification of the popular music than its accompaniment on a piano. In this respect popular music resembles that of Byzantium, which also inherited elements from ancient Greek music. The rhythms also are different: they are not the usual forms of western music (2/4, 3/4, 6/8, etc.); in this, too, they are individual and 'irrational' (5/8, 7/8). The 7/8 rhythm (that of the *Syrtòs-Kalamatianòs*) is the most common and the most widespread throughout Greece; it is a triple rhythm punctuated thus

---

[1] C. Fauriel, op. cit., vol. i, p. cxxxii.
[2] J. Apostolakis, op. cit., p. 171.

♩. ♩ ♩ or – ◡ ◡, but the long first note is equivalent not to two short but to one and a half. Thr. Georgiadis[1] has demonstrated that, according to ancient musical theory, this was the rhythm of the Homeric hexameter and that the relation of the long to the two short syllables was there also 'irrational', i.e. not 2:2 but $1\frac{1}{2}$:2.

Most of the songs are not only sung but also danced. Few are never danced, and among these, as we saw, are the klephtic songs. The klephtic songs are sung according to a peculiar strophic system, 'the klephtic strophe':[2] the singer sings the first (fifteen-syllable) line, and proceeds to the first hemistich of the second; then he repeats all of the second line and the first hemistich of the third, and so on, each time singing a line and a half as a unit. In other songs the singer often breaks the line or inserts small units called *gyrismata* (γυρίσματα) or *tsakismata* (τσακίσματα), which give great variety and elasticity to the song.

As with the songs, there is great variety in the dances. Among the most common, as we saw, is the *Syrtòs-Kalamatianòs*. The admirable *tsámikos* is heavy, Doric, and manly, with its triple rhythm, which corresponds to the ancient iambus. The dances of Macedonia and the Morea have a special nobility, while the island dances have a feminine charm and delicacy; those of Crete are particularly distinguished by a wonderful elegance and swiftness, while those of Asia Minor and Pontus (in which weapons often figure) are astonishingly dynamic. Greek dances are *syrtoi*, that is, they are danced in line, and not in couples, with the foremost dancer 'dragging' the rest. The term is ancient; in an inscription of the first century A.D. from Boeotia there is mention of a landowner who 'piously performed the traditional dance of the *syrtoi*'.[3] It is only in the islands that knew Frankish influence that some dances (for instance, the *ballos*) are exceptionally danced by couples.

### THE COLLECTIONS

It was during the Greek War of Independence that, from a spirit of Philhellenism, and under the influence of the Romantic

---

[1] Thr. Georgiadis, *Der neugriechische Rhythmus*, Hamburg, 1949, pp. 98–121.

[2] See S. Baud-Bovy, 'Sur la strophe de la chanson cleftique', *Mélanges H. Grégoire*, vol. 2, Brussels, 1950, pp. 53–78.

[3] τὴν τῶν συρτῶν πάτριον ὄρχησιν θεοσεβῶς ἐπετέλεσεν, *I.G.* vii. 2712, lines 66 f.

movement, Fauriel became interested in the demotic songs, and published them in two volumes (1824–5); at the same time the German scholar Werner von Haxthausen was making a collection, but he gave it up when he learned of Fauriel's intention; his collection was published only a few years ago.[1] The collections of A. Manousos (1850) and S. Zambelios (1852) come from the Heptanesian circle of Solomòs. The versatile and rich collection of the German scholar A. Passow (1860) used the basic methods of textual criticism. There are also many collections of songs of particular regions.

How much confidence are we to place in the accuracy of these collections? The early and the partial collections perhaps give us the most genuine texts; the comprehensive collections often alter the text because of entirely subjective criteria and arbitrary taste. A typical example is the collection of Zambelios. The *Selections from the Songs of the Greek People* of N. G. Politis (1st edn., 1914) were edited with absolute philological conscientiousness. The editor compared the variant versions of each song, and thus established his text, 'putting in' as he said 'nothing of his own, not a word nor a letter'. But this conscientious philological method is not the one most recommended for a form so peculiar as the demotic song, as the criticism of Apostolakis has shown us.[2] The verses of the various versions may, in isolation, be genuine, but when thus arbitrarily put together by the editor they do not constitute an organic whole, but an inorganic compilation. The motifs of equal value, used by the variants to express the same or a similar meaning, lose their independence and are jumbled together by Politis. Though the sense proper is retained by this method, the aesthetic connection of the song is lost.

The problem of editing the songs has not yet found a solution. Among later collections only those of D. Petropoulos and of the Academy of Athens have taken account of the criticism of Apostolakis and have tried to deal with the difficulty.

[1] Werner von Haxthausen, *Neugriechische Volkslieder, Urtext und Übersetzung*, herausgegeben von Karl Schulte Kemminghausen und Gustav Soyter, Münster i. W., 1935.

[2] J. Apostolakis, *Τὸ δημοτικὸ τραγούδι*, I : *Οἱ συλλογές*, Athens, 1929, pp. 134–273.

# Part Two

## THE NINETEENTH AND TWENTIETH CENTURIES

154125

# VI

## THE DECADES PRECEDING THE
## WAR OF INDEPENDENCE
### RIGAS—CHRISTOPOULOS—VILARÀS

THE LAST DECADE of the eighteenth century and the first
two of the nineteenth were most critical and important
years for modern Hellenism. Everything shows that the enslaved and scattered nation was slowly but surely approaching
a new unity and was nearing the final liberation. Political and
social conditions were radically changed for the better, particularly after the Russo-Turkish war of 1787–92 (although the
failure of the Orloff rising brought about terrible destruction,
especially in the Peloponnese). An enlightened Greek aristocracy
had sprung up in the Danubian principalities around the Phanariot princes; education was becoming ever more widespread, new
schools were founded (for example, at Kydoniai and elsewhere),
and old schools were reformed in accordance with new principles.
Commercial companies were organizing an export trade, founding branches abroad, and amassing considerable wealth; as early
as 1771 Koraïs went to Amsterdam as representative of his
father's business firm. Islands such as Chios, Hydra, and Spetsai
created a whole merchant navy; other commercial companies
and partnerships in Thessaly and northern Greece were in direct
contact with Vienna, and extended their activities throughout
the whole Austro-Hungarian empire. In small towns in western
Macedonia (such as Siatista and Kastoria), in Ambelakia in
Thessaly, and in Hydra and Spetsai great mansions were built
that looked from the outside like towers, but inside had a refined
decoration where European rococo blended happily with motifs
taken from local folk art. The period is marked by economic
prosperity, the rise of the middle class, the widening of interests,

and the thirst for education, and at the same time by a deeper national consciousness and a desire for liberation.

In the fiery personality of Rigas all the tendencies of contemporary Hellenism seemed to meet, and his activities coincided with the last decade of the eighteenth century. He was born (probably in 1757) in the small Thessalian village of Velestino (he always called himself 'Velestinlìs'; 'Pheraios' is an archaism invented in later times). He received the basic education offered by the schools of his home country; at about the age of twenty he went to Constantinople as clerk to the noble family of Ypsilantis, and thence to Wallachia, as clerk to the prince Mavrogenis (1786–90) and as sub-prefect (*kaimakam*) of a small area. In 1790–1 he went to Vienna where his first books were printed; he returned to Wallachia (where he seems to have held some landed property) and went back again to Vienna in 1796. Here he launched out upon a vigorous political and national line of activity. He printed his famous maps (especially his great map of Greece) and a picture of Alexander the Great; he translated Metastasio and the Abbé Barthélemy and published revolutionary pamphlets and songs (the *Constitution of Greece* and the *War Song*). This caused him to be eyed with suspicion by the Austrian authorities, who arrested him at Trieste when he was about to leave for Greece, and after close examination handed him over to the Turkish provincial governor of Belgrade, where Rigas and seven of his companions were secretly strangled on 24 June 1798 and their bodies thrown into the Danube. Thus Rigas consummated his patriotic activities by the sacrifice of his life. Koraìs, his senior by ten years, made prompt mention of the fact in his hortatory pamphlet *Brotherly Teaching*. Two months earlier, in April 1798, Dionysios Solomòs was born at Zakynthos.

Rigas is the forerunner and the first martyr of Greek liberty. Later history and the national conscience have rightly given him that place.

$$\Sigma\pi\acute{\epsilon}\rho\mu\alpha\tau' \ \acute{\epsilon}\lambda\epsilon\upsilon\theta\epsilon\rho\acute{\iota}\eta\varsigma \ \acute{o} \ \Phi\epsilon\rho\alpha\tilde{\iota}o\varsigma \ \sigma\pi\epsilon\tilde{\iota}\rho\epsilon\nu \ \acute{\alpha}o\iota\delta\acute{o}\varsigma.[1]$$

So runs the inscription in classical Greek on the pedestal of his statue in front of the University of Athens. His importance in the history of the nation is infinitely greater than in its literature.

---

[1] The Pheraean singer sowed the seeds of Liberty.

Nevertheless, Rigas was a vigorous and versatile personality; the descriptions of his contemporaries and such portraits as have come down to us show him to have been full of vitality and the joy of life, highly imaginative, and easily moved. He was agreeable in manner, spoke many languages, sang his own songs, and accompanied himself. As we have said, all the tendencies in the Hellenism of his time meet in this vital character, and his intellectual and literary work must be counted as part of his patriotic activity.

His first work, *The School for Delicate Lovers* (Vienna, 1790), is a collection of six short love-stories, the first in modern Greek literature, which research has lately shown to be translated from Restif de la Bretonne, a voluminous and second-rate French author;[1] in the preface, the translator expresses the wish 'to please and be of use'. And indeed these tales, with the fascination of the smart Parisian world, now rendered in a language without literary cultivation, yet simple and easy to understand, had a considerable success. In 1792, two years later, and again in Vienna, an unknown writer published a similar work, *The Results of Love*, 'for the pleasure and delight of noble youths'. These are three original tales, in which the Greek *tselebìs* and *kokones* of Constantinople and Wallachia replace the *messieurs* and *dames* of the *School*. The unknown writer, far more than Rigas, inserts in his stories little popular poems which circulated either with their music or in manuscript anthologies. They represent the taste of a wider public, and it is strange how they combine eastern voluptuousness and melancholy with a premature and confused romanticism.

Simultaneously with the *School*, in 1790, Rigas published (also in Vienna) a handbook of physics derived from French and German books. He also announced for future publication a translation of the *Esprit des Lois* of Montesquieu. The spirit of the French Enlightenment together with popular science was to be offered to the service of the nation. This parallel publication of learned and literary works also took place during Rigas's second stay in Vienna; but at that time he also published his maps and revolutionary pamphlets. Out of all this abundant work we should

---

[1] J. Thomopoulos, *L'Original de l' 'École des amants délicats' de Rhigas Velestinlis*, Athens, 1949. See now the introduction in the new edition by P. Pistas (*Νέα Ἑλληνικὴ Βιβλιοθήκη*, 1971).

give particular attention to an original poem, the *War Song*, his verse declaration of independence.

> How long shall we dwell in the dales, lads,
> Like lions alone on the hills?
>
> .    .    .    .    .
>
> Better a single hour of life in liberty
> Rather than forty years' prison and slavery!

The *War Song* is not to be judged by the ordinary standards which we apply to poetry; it does not easily stand such criticism. It would, however, be a mistake to judge it that way. The *War Song* is a revolutionary voice, finding utterance in verse, a voice that shows a fiery enthusiasm and a soul really aflame. It is not a poem as such, nor it is a mere manifesto; its warmth gives it a character superior to mere rhetoric and at times brings it near to the confines of poetry. The way it circulated is a moving tale: Rigas invited friends to his room, played the tune on the flute, and taught them to sing it, or he sought out Greeks in the cafés of Vienna and secretly gave them the text. Most of them were merchants from Vienna, Semlin, and Trieste, and they passed it on to the Ionian Islands and the rest of Greece. The poet's death as a martyr gave a special consummation to his work.

In his second volume of *Chants populaires de la Grèce moderne*[1] Fauriel published the *War Song* and related the following story: a friend of his was travelling with other companions in Macedonia in 1817, and in one village they met at the baker's shop (which was also the khan) a tall and handsome youth from Epirus who worked there. He looked at them earnestly and asked the traveller: 'Can you read?' When the answer was in the affirmative, he took him aside, and pulled out something that hung round his neck like an amulet; it was a little book of Rigas's songs. He begged the stranger to read it, which he willingly did, but almost at once he saw the boy had undergone a complete change; his whole countenance was aflame, his lips trembled, and tears poured from his eyes. 'Is it the first time you've heard the book read?', asked the traveller. 'No; I always ask travellers to read me some of it; I've heard it many times.' 'And are you always moved like this?' 'Always', answered the boy.

Among the papers which the Austrian police found in the hands of Rigas was a letter in his own hand to Bonaparte, then

---

[1] Vol. 2, pp. 18–19.

fighting in Italy, inviting him to liberate the Greek nation. The young general, representing the ideals of the French Revolution, had an extraordinary effect then upon the imagination of the Greeks as he approached their shores. In June 1797 the thousand-year-old aristocratic republic of Venice was abolished, and in the following month French forces reached Corfu, planted the tree of liberty, and promised freedom to the Ionian Islands. These islands, the only part of Greek soil which (as we have seen) had remained under western suzerainty for centuries, were thus immediately involved in the whirl of events that succeeded the French Revolution. By the treaty of Campoformio (October 1797) they were officially annexed to France, but a year later, in the autumn of 1798, the Turks and Russians occupied them and restored the old order and the privileges of the nobility. In 1800 a half-independent 'Ionian State' was constituted, to fall under the first French empire in 1807, and in 1809 under British domination. This unstable order of things was not ended until the Council of Vienna in 1815, when the 'United State of the Ionian Islands' was formed, and placed under British protection, with a High Commissioner and a Greek parliament and senate. This constitution (which Solomòs called 'fictitious liberty') lasted till 1864 when Great Britain offered the Ionian Islands to the new king, George I, and they were incorporated into Greece proper.

This dramatic history of nearly twenty years (1797–1815) had its effect on intellectual life, just as the long subjection to Venice had influenced it, and as the fact that the islands did not yet belong to Greece was to influence it in the following years. This was a sensitive time in the history of Greek culture and literature. Verse was written about the French occupation of the islands, especially in Zakynthos, which reflects the social and political situation. Many of the writers are known by name. We shall make mention of the outstanding personality of Antonios Martelaos (1754–1818). He was of aristocratic origins, but a fanatical adherent of democratic ideals. In 1797 he wrote a *Hymn to France, to Bonaparte, and General Gentilly* (who had occupied the Ionian Islands). Later, with an equal enthusiasm he was to hail the foundation of the Ionian State, the French imperialists, and the British; he had an inextinguishable desire for freedom rather than a political or social conscience. Of course Martelaos is not a poet—even less so than Rigas—and he is somewhat pedantic

An unsupported statement makes him the teacher of Solomòs; he was certainly the teacher of Ugo Foscolo. At the beginning of his democratic hymn we find a reference to the 'bones of the Greeks', as in that of Solomòs.

Nikolaos Koutouzis (1746–1813), a few years older than Martelaos, was an entirely different personality. He too was of noble stock, had studied in Venice, and was one of the most representative painters of the new Italianate school. He took no part in the revolutionary upheaval. He is chiefly remarkable for satire and mockery, a pitiless satire and an unbridled tongue. Besides his merciless satire we find in him an incredible obscenity of language: a critic calls him 'prince of scandalous satirists'.[1] The odd thing is that Koutouzis was a priest, in charge of the Faneromeni, one of the most famous and beautiful churches of Zakynthos. Ten years after his death, when Solomòs wished to attack a usurer, he put his biting satire into the mouth of Koutouzis.

This disposition towards satire and humour brought about a new development of comedy in Zakynthos at about the same time. The memory of the Cretan theatre was indeed still alive there, and the Cretan dramas and comedies were certainly played. On the other hand, we know that at carnival and on other occasions outdoor theatrical performances were given, known as 'speeches'. Most frequently they were theatrical sketches or isolated scenes from the Cretan dramas. Some, however, were of greater interest. Savogias Roúsmelis (or Soumerlìs) wrote, perhaps in about the year 1745, a comedy in mockery of the quack doctors of Janina, a comedy of manners, with contemporary characters. The same features are found in another comedy of his, *The Moreans*, this time with a social theme. We know that this work was played by a troupe of amateurs in 1798, but it gave rise to violent reactions and to police intervention and an inquiry (from which we derive our information about the work).

Undoubtedly the most remarkable comedy was the *Chasis* of Dimitrios Gouzelis. The writer (1773–1842) was of a younger generation, and a nephew of Martelaos. As was natural, he too was inspired by the democratic fever of 1797–8 and lived a life

---

[1] Gr. Xenopoulos, ʽΗ ζακυνθινὴ ποίησις, in J. Tsakasianos, Ἅπαντα, vol. 1, Athens, 1926, p. 22.

full of adventure. He fought for Napoleon, then for the Greek revolution, was captured, and imprisoned. He translated Tasso and wrote heroic epics and patriotic dramas. None of this was of much account; his only significant work was his youthful comedy. *Chasis* was written in 1795 when Venice was still dominant. The eponymous hero of the work is a sort of braggart, brave in words but cowardly at bottom. This, of course, is a type well known to comic tradition, though here he seems to have had a living prototype. There are other stock characters, also taken from life: Chasis's son, an idler; the cunning woman who plays with both father and son; the soldiers of the Venetian garrison of the island who speak in their own dialect and create comic misunderstandings, etc. The language is entirely dialectal—the language of Zakynthos exactly as it was spoken—and the verse is the Cretan decapentesyllabic couplet, which proves, if not the immediate influence of Cretan models, at least a submission to the same tradition.

It is proper, I think, to lay emphasis on the fact that during those twenty years of political upheaval there was a group of verse writers in Zakynthos, since this was happening during the youth of Solomòs, and in his own birthplace. We may call them his local precursors, and we have remarked on his relationship with Martelaos and Koutouzis. None of them, however, achieved a genuine poetical personality. We must seek his real ancestors elsewhere, in a place which at this critical period had more importance than provincial Zakynthos, that is the Phanar. There in Constantinople, and in the Danubian principalities, we hear the first voice of true poetry.

This begins in 1811 with the publication of Christopoulos's *Lyrics*. For the first time since the fall of Crete, and after nearly a century and a half of silence, a lyric voice is heard: it is still feeble, but is undoubtedly genuine. The *Lyrics* are decidedly on a higher level than the insignificant verse-writing of his contemporaries. Christopoulos (and later Vilaràs) are, from a national and not from a local point of view, the real precursors of Solomòs, and indeed of all modern Greek poetry. The *Erotokritos* closes the first period, the *Lyrics* inaugurate a new period. 1811 is a key date in the history of modern Greek poetry.

Athanasios Christopoulos was born in 1772 at Kastoria in western Macedonia. He went at an early age to Bucharest, and later studied medicine and law at Buda and Padua. In 1797 he returned to Bucharest and became tutor in the household of the prince Mourouzis; he followed him to Constantinople when Mourouzis retired into private life (1806–12) and there, it would seem, he found the leisure and the right environment for writing poetry. Later (1812–20) he held a high position with the prince Joannis Karatzàs and reached the rank of Grand *Logothetis*, and at the prince's orders drew up a legal code on liberal principles. He naturally lost his place in 1821, with the War of Independence and the extinction of the Greek principalities. He attempted to settle in Greece but he could not acclimatize himself, and he returned to Bucharest, where he could live in comparative ease; he died there aged 75 in 1847.

We have already spoken of his participation in the dispute over the language question, and of his *Grammar* (1805). His *Achilles: a heroic drama*, which was published with the *Grammar*, need not occupy us. His other works, *Political Parallels* (Paris, 1833), his curious and only recently published *Political Sophisms*,[1] and his *Studies in Greek Antiquity* (Athens, 1853), posthumously published, fall outside the field of literature.

We shall confine ourselves to the *Lyrics*, which brought no small honour to the poet. Previously there had indeed been signed and anonymous Phanariot poems (like those in the *School* of Rigas, and in the *Results of Love*). These were his precedents; but he also knew the French and Italian literature of his time, and was unquestionably influenced by it. On a first glance we can see that his 'Erotic' and 'Bacchic' songs (for so he distinguished them) belong to the realm of contemporary European classicism. We are in the same world of classical mythology and allegorical personification, with Love the child of Aphrodite, with Tithonus and the Dawn, etc. The 'Bacchic' songs, for which his contemporaries called him the 'new Anacreon', were imitations of the post-classical anacreontics in which the age abounded. Written in short, pliant lines and in demotic language (but used in a literary way), the songs of Christopoulos have a grace and lightness, though at the same time they are discreet and restrained. He sings of love and wine, and represents himself as continuously lovesick; but this love is never a *grande passion*, but

---

[1] The entire work was published only recently in A. Christopoulos, Ἅπαντα, ed. G. Valetas, Athens, 1969.

rather a sport or an amusement. The tone is always mild; the
passion is lacking that would have dissolved all the cold mythology. Critics have already observed this. Christopoulos might
write:

> May I never live in bliss
> If one day I fail to kiss!
> And when I must come to death,
> Be a kiss my latest breath!

or

> Books away! And make a pyre.
> Throw the rubbish on the fire—
> Let the library so fine
> Be filled up with tubs of wine.

All this is the fashion of his time, a mere literary convention; he
himself led an entirely sober life, quite the reverse of that suggested by his 'Erotic' and 'Bacchic' songs. Nevertheless, in that
generally cold and conventional world, it is surprising to find in
him (and not infrequently) a true lyric sensibility and a genuine
feeling for nature. The language then becomes warmer, and
nearer to popular speech.

> Spring is grown old
> And summer grown cold
>    And wintry winds blow.
> Where blossom was glad
> The trees are now sad
>    And covered with snow.
>
> No leaf is now green,
> No flower is seen,
>    And bare is the earth.
> Its beauty is dead,
> To chaos is fled,
>    First source of its birth.

Christopoulos's poems are mostly light and charming, and,
however we may judge them today, they brought a new freshness, a new message into their own age. The age completely
understood it and honoured the poet, and his *Lyrics* went into
many editions. We may add that Solomòs began to write his
first Greek poems with the *Lyrics* in his hands. Modern Greek
poetry had began its history.

A decisive step forward was made by Jannis Vilaràs. Born in 1771, Vilaràs was a year older than Christopoulos; he was from Janina, where he lived nearly all his life. He too studied medicine at Padua and, on his return, became a doctor at the court of Ali Pasha, and the personal physician to his son, Veli, whom he followed on his various military expeditions in Greece (to Macedonia, Thessaly, and the Peloponnese). When the Sultan's army besieged Janina in 1820, Vilaràs fled, like most of the Greek population of the city, and took refuge in a village in the canton of Zagori, where he died in solitude and poverty in December 1823. Vilaràs, therefore, lived far from the courts of the Danubian princes in a comparatively small city, and he had the opportunity (particularly on his journeys) to come into contact with country people and learn their language and its means of expression. We see this in his poetry. If we leave Christopoulos and turn to Vilaràs, we feel that a warmer and more truly poetical personality is speaking to us. But his work cannot be conceived of apart from the Phanariot poetry, with which it is closely connected. We may also mention that Janina was a considerable intellectual centre, and that well-known teachers had taught in its school.

In 1814 (three years after the *Lyrics* of Christopoulos) Vilaràs published a curious little book at Corfu: it was called *The Romaic Language* and was printed in revolutionary spelling, which approached the phonetic, without, of course, accents or breathings. He explained his system in a brief 'Explanatory Note', and then, as examples of the 'Romaic Language', in verse and prose, he published four original poems, and translations from Anacreon, Plato, and Thucydides. His complete poems were posthumously published in Corfu in 1827. We are in the same world as that of Christopoulos: there is the same classical allegory and the same light playful tone. Vilaràs is a more genuine 'Arcadian', and Chloë, Phyllis, Thyrsis, and Daphne often recur in his lines. One of his better poems, 'Spring' (published in *The Romaic Language*), may well be an imitation of an Italian model, but it has also an unquestionable originality of his own.

> Spring the sweetest season
> With every flower bespread,
> With roses round her head,
> This earth of ours beguiles.

With grass the earth is clad,
Their shade the forests throw,
And melted is the snow,
And all the heaven smiles.

There is a direct breath of spring, coming from nature herself,
without the interposition of frigid allegories and symbols; and
the verse with its graceful flexibility seems to follow Italian models,
and not the somewhat rigid forms of Phanariot poetry.

At the same time as the influence of Phanariot and Italian
prosody, we are occasionally pleased and surprised by echoes of
the long-forgotten decapentesyllabic couplets of the *Erotokritos*
or of *Erofili*.

As a moth turns about the flame, so about you I turn;
Nor have I any wit to shun the fire in which I burn.

It was in that metre that Vilarás wrote what is rightly regarded
as his masterpiece, the translation of the pseudo-Homeric
*Batrachomyomachia*. Here his richness of expression, his fertility in
invention of words, and his handling of the language are truly
marvellous.

Vilarás was a vital and dynamic personality; with regard to
the language question (including that of spelling) he shunned
compromise and sought extreme and revolutionary solutions.
Satire, good-natured but sharp, forms a great part of his work,
either in original satirical poems of his own or in his versifications
of 'Myths', when Aesop and La Fontaine are his models. He was
a man of great culture, wisdom, and wit; he expressed his ideas
on the then burning questions of the language and of education
both in prose tales and dialogues (for instance, *The Most Learned
Traveller* or *The Learned Pumpkin*) and in epistolary diatribes
addressed to his friend Athanasios Psalidas, the headmaster of the
high school at Janina. He also prepared in 1822, shortly before
his death, a 'Vocabulary of the Romaic Language' and a 'Short
Geography', both designed for children.[1] It is a great pity that
so vital and forceful a personality should not have made his
due impression on his age. After the liberation the scholars of
Greece were to follow very different lines.

[1] Both works have been edited from the autograph manuscripts: (*a*) the
'Vocabulary' by Sp. Lambros, Ἡμερολόγιον Δωδώνη, 1 (1895), 35 ff.; (*b*) small
fragments from the 'Short Geography' by M. Triantafyllidis, Δελτίο Ἐκπαι-
δευτικοῦ Ὁμίλου, 3 (1913), 264–8 (= Ἅπαντα, 6, pp. 154–8).

# VII

## SOLOMÒS

WHEN the *Lyrics* of Christopoulos were being published in 1811, and *The Romaic Language* of Vilaràs in 1814, Dionysios Solomòs was still a schoolboy, studying at Cremona. In 1815 he was to go to the University of Pavia, to return three years later, at the age of twenty, to Zakynthos. He had been born there in April 1798 during the brief period of French Republican rule. His father was a rich nobleman to whom Venice had granted the tobacco monopoly. His mother, Angelikì Nikli, was a woman of the people, a servant in his father's house. The elderly tobacco merchant had two sons by her: he was over sixty when Dionysios was born, while Angelikì was not yet sixteen. In spite of their illegitimacy (not unusual in the upper class of Zante), the boys were brought up in their father's house as young noblemen—that is to say their education was Italian—and their father was to declare in his will that 'he loved them as if they were legitimate', and was to endeavour to secure for them a due share of his property. He even legalized his relations with Angelikì by a deathbed marriage. Solomòs had therefore none of the bastard's feeling of inferiority during his youth, while his mother's plebeian origin connected him with the world of popular tradition and mythology—a thing which stamped his personality with a mark of its own. On the other hand his Italian tutor, the priest Don Santo Rossi (an exile from his country on account of his liberal ideas), exercised a decisive influence upon the young Dionysios.

In 1808 at the age of ten, a year after his father's death, Solomòs went to Italy, accompanied by Rossi; first he studied with his tutor at the lyceum at Cremona, and later (1815–18) at the University of Pavia. He acquired a solid culture and a wide knowledge of classical and modern literature. These were critical

years in the political and literary history of Italy—the years of
the triumphant beginning of the romantic movement. Solomòs
knew the young poets and was friendly with Vincenzo Monti,
then the doyen of the Italian classicists. A dispute between them
over the interpretation of a line of Dante has been recorded:
'One must not think so much, one must feel, one must feel!',
said Monti angrily. 'First the mind must comprehend vigorously',
said the young Solomòs mildly; 'then the heart must feel warmly
what the mind has comprehended.'[1]

His first essays in poetry (naturally in Italian) have come down
to us from that period in his life. There is the first canto of a
long poem in *terza rima*: *La Distruzione di Gerusalemme* (perhaps no
more than a scholastic exercise); there is also the more considerable *Ode per prima messa* (for which he later showed some
regard), and a few sonnets on religious subjects. They display
technical perfection, but no sign of anything more remarkable:
it is the sort of Italian poetry that was then being written in
literary circles at Milan or Cremona, with perhaps some added
symptoms of a precocious romanticism.

When he returned to his native island in 1818 at the age of
twenty, after ten years of study in Italy, he found the political
system changed and the upheavals now over. The social background of Zakynthos was not then very different from that of
a small town in north Italy. Solomòs found several men who had,
like himself, studied abroad; some were his seniors and others his
contemporaries. Naturally they welcomed him into their company with enthusiasm. We may mention, for example, the doctor
Tagiapiera (who had studied in France, practised in Janina, and
was connected with the tradition of Vilaràs), the Italian Gaetano
Grassetti, Antonios Matesis, and George Tertsetis. This amusing
and lively group composed impromptu sonnets in Italian (on
set rhymes) or made the doctor Dionysios Roidis (who also
wrote Italian verse, but full of the comic bombast of the old
school) the butt of their biting satire. Some of Solomòs's impromptu sonnets were printed in Corfu in 1822 under the title
of *Rime Improvvisate*; we know some eighty of the same period.
A number of them are religious, of the sort then written in Italy;

---

[1] The incident is referred to by Polylàs in his Προλεγόμενα (in Solomòs, Ἅπαντα,
ed. L. Politis, vol. 1, p. 12); also, slightly differently, by G. Regaldi, *L'Oriente,
Memorie, Isole Ionie, Corfu, Il Conte Dionisio Solomos*, Genova, 1853, p. 398.

others are distinguished by a more idyllic content, pictures of
the landscape of Zakynthos. They were all written before 1822;
the later sonnets, composed on particular occasions up to 1827,
are not impromptu, and are marked by seriousness of theme
and careful craftsmanship: one is addressed to Lord Guilford,
another is on the death of Pius VII, another on that of Ugo
Foscolo. On the occasion of the death of this great Italian poet,
also a native of Zakynthos, he delivered a funeral oration in
the Catholic church on the island. This is a very succinct text,
remarkable for its flights of rhetoric, and for the depth of its
ideas. These were his last writings in Italian; he was not to use
that language again until the last decade of his life.

It is of the greatest interest (since Solomòs is a Greek poet) to
see when he first wrote in Greek, when he forsook a language that
had been formed for centuries in order to write in one which had
almost no poetical tradition and which, though it was his mother
tongue, he had never studied properly. From this point of view
his meeting with Spyridon Trikoupis at the end of 1822 was
decisive: Trikoupis, a relative of Alexandros Mavrokordatos,
a politician who was later to write a history of the Greek War of
Independence, had studied in England with a bursary provided
by Lord Guilford, and had come to Zakynthos to wait for Lord
Byron. He asked to see Solomòs, who read him his Italian *Ode
per prima messa.* Trikoupis was silent for a while and then told
him that what their country now wanted was a Greek poetry:
'Greece is waiting for her Dante.'[1] Solomòs, however, had
already taken the vital decision a little time before: his friend
Lodovico Strani, in a dedicatory letter to Foscolo prefixed to the
*Rime Improvvisate* (January 1822), wrote that Solomòs was no
longer writing in Italian, apart from impromptus, and that
all his thought was now directed towards the formation of the
modern Greek language; he makes specific mention of his poem
the 'Mad Mother'.

We shall not go far wrong if we suppose that Solomòs began
his first poetical exercises in Greek immediately after his return
from Italy in 1818. Nothing could be more natural, uneasy spirit
that he was, than that immediately he found himself at home

---

[1] Trikoupis himself records the meeting in a letter to Polylàs from London,
6 June 1859. See Ἔκθεσις Πεπραγμένων Ἐπιτροπῆς Ἑκατονταετηρίδος Σολωμοῦ,
Zakynthos, 1903, pp. 221–4; cf. Παναθήναια, 4 (1902), 221–2.

again he should be seized by the idea of putting his thoughts into his mother tongue, the language that he had imbibed with his mother's milk, as Trikoupis was later to tell him. His literary education, orientated towards the Romantics and their teachings on traditional culture, was a contributory influence. We are told that he collected popular words and expressions, and listened with rapture to the lines of a blind singer of folk-songs, which preserved many elements of the Cretan tradition.

His early poems (1818–23) are mostly written in short flexible lines, trochaic or iambic, which remind one of Italian prosody, but also frequently of that of the Phanar (Trikoupis tells us explicitly that they studied Christopoulos together). Sometimes, in his least successful verses, he attempts an approximation to the popular decapentesyllabic couplet, an approximation which is only superficial. It is odd that while his Italian sonnets are mature and terse, the Greek poems in content and even more in form are simple and almost naïve. It is as if Solomòs, when writing Greek, was adapting himself to the primitive stage at which Greek poetry then found itself. Among his poems are many that are 'Arcadian' or pastoral such as 'The Death of the Shepherd', 'The Death of the Orphan Girl', and 'Eurykome'. We can also see the influence of the Romantic movement, particularly in those poems which are variations on the favourite theme of the child and death. Of these the most typical is the 'Mad Mother' with the essential romantic setting: its sub-title is 'The Cemetery'. The gentle figure of the woman, a basic theme in all Solomòs's poetry, is first seen in the two most successful and certainly the most mature poems of these five years, 'The Unknown Woman' and 'Xanthoula'.

> The Fair-haired Girl, I saw her,
> Saw her late yesterday,
> Boarding the boat that bore her
> To lands far, far away.

Just a record of fact, no emotional description. The emotion is stirred by the lack of anything superfluous in the expression, and by the very simplicity of the rhythmic movement.

However, the Greek poet was profoundly stirred by the revolution of 1821. In his *Dialogue* of 1824 he wrote: 'Have I anything else in my mind but liberty and the language?' In May

1823, in one month full of continual lyrical excitement, he wrote
the 158 stanzas of the *Hymn to Liberty*. This is a youthful, vigorous
work, far above the level of his earlier poems; it meant success
and the immediate recognition of its twenty-five-year-old author
as a poet.

Liberty, a poetical figure, neither fictitious nor allegorical but
identified with Greece, from the first moment flashes before the
poet's eye as familiar to him:

> Well I know thee, by the rending
> Of the terrible sharp sword,
> Well I know thee, . . .

In the prelude he speaks of the past miseries of slavery and the
present strength of Liberty. Then he describes, one by one, her
achievements, that is, the principal events in the war up to the
time of writing: the sack of Tripolitsà, the capital of the Morea,
the first important Greek victory, takes on an epic and dramatic
form; the annihilation of Dramali's great force near Corinth is
like a slow movement in a symphony, and has an idyllic strain;
he returns to the vigorous descriptive style of the beginning for
the first siege of Missolonghi (Christmas 1822) and for the defeat
of the Turks at the Acheloos which followed. Later the tone
drops, particularly when the poet gives advice to the warriors
(even if he makes Liberty his spokesman), or when he appeals
to the foreign sovereigns on behalf of Greek freedom.

The *Hymn* had great renown; it was translated into most
foreign languages, and its lyric voice gave fresh inspiration to
Philhellenism. For Solomòs the *Hymn* was a beginning; it is in
*The Cretan* that ten years later we shall find him at the next stage
of a continuous progress. In the intermediate decade, a fruitful
and creative period, he advances steadily towards a fuller possession of his language, and of a finer lyrical expression. An ode
*On the death of Lord Byron* is a failure; it is a feeble copy of the
*Hymn* in the same metre and with much the same subject-matter.
The manuscripts survive, with many corrections and with phrases
of sharp self-criticism by the author. Nevertheless the severely
laconic epigram on the destruction of Psarà (1825) and still more
the elegy on the *Farmakomeni* (1826) exhibit a remarkable progress. The latter begins with a moving lament for the poisoned
girl, and imperceptibly, while keeping its purely musical

character, turns into a defence of the young girl against the slander of the world, with an invincible persuasiveness that we may call lyric rhetoric. In these years there also takes place, gradually, a profound change in Solomòs's poetry: in his youthful works he was the inspired singer and the amazingly facile writer of impromptus; now he tries to control his natural facility and submit it to a sterner discipline and to a higher conception of the art of poetry, to what he himself called 'the meaning of art'. 'The difficulty that a writer experiences is not in the exhibition of imagination and emotion, but in the subjection of those two, with time and labour, to the meaning of art.' This is a note by Solomòs on his poem on Byron. Earlier, in a note on the *Hymn*, he had said: 'The harmony of the verse is not merely a mechanical thing, but an overflowing of the soul.'[1] The progress from the 'overflowing of the soul' to 'the meaning of art' was achieved in this creative decade.

He had by now a clear consciousness of his vocation and was exclusively devoted to his art. At the end of 1828 he left the narrow provincial setting of Zakynthos and the cheerful company of his friends, and settled in Corfu, seeking solitude and contemplation. The capital of the small Heptanesian Republic could offer him what he sought: it had the warm-heartedness of a small town, without the disadvantages of provinciality. The local aristocracy frequented Government House; Sir Frederic Adam and his Corfiot wife were Philhellenic in policy, and things after Navarino were very different from what they had been when Maitland was High Commissioner. There was also the small University of Corfu, The Ionian Academy, founded by that noble visionary, Frederick North, fifth Earl of Guilford; and there were men of considerable culture, among whom an outstanding personality was the composer Nikolaos Mantzaros, who was to be united with the poet by a sincere and lasting friendship. The first years at Corfu were the happiest in his life. Letters to his friends and his brother show the cheerfulness of that isolation into which he had now withdrawn: 'It is delightful, in the quiet of your small room, to express what your heart says.'[2] The same feeling

---

[1] Note to the *Ode on Byron*: Ἅπαντα, ed. L. Politis, vol. 1, p. 133, no. 2; Note to the *Hymn of Liberty*: ibid., p. 99.

[2] Letter to George Markoràs, September 1830, see L. Politis, 'Ο Σολωμὸς στὰ γράμματά του, Athens, 1956, p. 29.

is expressed in his song 'To a Nun', about a girl who took the
veil in April 1829:

> Sweet it is to ponder on
> The joys of Paradise.
> Bitter and fearful are the storms
> That in the world arise—
> Hither the echo only comes
> There comes not here the swell . . .

At the same time he tried to give final form to a poem entitled
*Lambros*, begun at the same time as the *Hymn*. In 1834 a large
part of it was published in the *Ionian Anthology*, a periodical
founded by the cultured and liberal governor Lord Nugent.
The story is sombre and Byronic: Lambros is a minor Don Juan,
'bad in conduct but great in soul'; Maria, the girl whom he
seduces, is fifteen. There is a basic contradiction in the work: it
was conceived at a period when he was tormented with romantic
visions (the time of the 'overflowing of the soul') and was now
worked over much later, when he had already created figures
like the Nun and was now serving 'the meaning of art'. The
finely wrought stanzas with their limpidity of expression are in
direct contrast with the sombreness of the conception. For this
reason, apart from three or four complete episodes, we have
only fragments of this work. Solomòs himself said, 'Lambros
will remain fragmentary'.

Solomòs's only two Greek prose works belong to the same
decade. The first is *The Dialogue* (1824), Solomòs's credo about
the demotic language, a kind of sequel to the *Dream* and *The
Learned Traveller* of Vilaràs. The weapons used on his enemies
(the archaists and Koraìs) come from the same arsenal of the
French Enlightenment. The second part, which contains his
personal contribution, that of the poet as a creator of language,
is the most important: no one has the right to change the
language of the people, and we cannot improve or ennoble it
by external changes in its forms; only the poet, basing himself
entirely on the popular language, can enrich and ennoble it
from within, and deepen and widen the meaning of every word,
until the language is able to express the most delicate movements and feelings of the soul.

The second prose work, *The Woman of Zakynthos*, which has

remained unpublished until fairly recently,[1] is strange and enigmatic. Perhaps it began as a satire against a particular woman, but it has taken on a more universal meaning, and has become a lament, a prophecy, or a nightmare. In notes for the further development of this work, the Devil appears as the initiator of the entire action, twisting his horns in pleasure, like a moustache. The prose is excellent, in pure and vigorous demotic, the expression is succinct, the tone frequently apocalyptic. There are many similarities with *Lambros*. Perhaps the two works were written to free Solomòs once and for all of his debt to the Romantic age.

1833 was a critical year for Solomòs. A family lawsuit troubled his happy life in Corfu; at the same time, with *The Cretan*, he entered a new period of complete maturity, a period of the highest inspiration and achievement. The lawsuit was initiated by his half-brother Leontarakis, the first son of his mother's second marriage, who wished to prove that he had been born within the period that would entitle him to be considered a legitimate son of old Solomòs and one of his rightful heirs. This miserable case obliged Solomòs and his full brother, Dimitris, to fight for their interests. It dragged on for six years, and their rights were vindicated by all the courts, including finally the Supreme Court of Justice.[2] But Solomòs had received a psychological trauma. His mother, for whom the poet had had a very great love, supported the false claim for the sake of her new family. This family tragedy cast its shadow over the rest of his life; the happy solitude of his early Corfiot years turned to a tragic isolation.

But 1833 was also the year in which he wrote *The Cretan*, the first of his major works. It has come down to us as a fragment, but this is a matter more of appearance than of reality. Solomòs, following the custom of his time, intended to write an epic lyric, which he never finished. *The Cretan* was to be an episode in the poem; but the episode has become an independent and

[1] First edition, not satisfactory, by K. Kairofylas, Σολωμοῦ Ἀνέκδοτα "Ἔργα, Athens, 1927. New critical edition by L. Politis, Athens, 1944 (now in Ἅπαντα, vol. 2, pp. 31–75).

[2] Much has been written about the family lawsuit that cannot be relied on. An objective account of the facts is given by L. Politis, 'Ο Σολωμὸς στὰ γράμματά του, Athens, 1956, pp. 34–8. The decision of the Supreme Court was published in the official *Journal of the Ionian Islands*, no. 380, 7 April 1858, see L. Politis, Γύρω στὸ Σολωμό, Athens, 1958, pp. 98–9.

complete poem in itself. The shipwrecked Cretan tries to save his
beloved from the storm. The storm suddenly comes to an end,
and before him is a divine, 'moon-clad' female figure; when the
vision fades, a marvellous, other-worldly sound is heard, and
enraptures the soul of the shipwrecked man; when this stops,
he reaches the shore, on which he lays his beloved, now dead.
Many explanations have been given of the moon-clad figure,
which shows the enigmatic and deep lyricism of the poem. We
may say it is like a confession of the poetical mind, and that it
reveals to us a whole new feeling of lyricism, similar to that of
the major European poets of the time. More than any of his
former works this poem shows how he had gone down to the
very roots of the nation, to a far deeper consciousness of modern
Greek lyric speech. It is written in decapentesyllabic couplets
with the same internal movement as that established in the great
Cretan literature of the seventeenth century. Solomòs is taking up
the severed thread of tradition; we know that he was studying
the Cretan texts at this time. His poetical maturity is now complete. An entirely new lyricism is revealed to him, and at the
same time he penetrates ever more deeply into the mysteries
of his language and of the poetical style of the folk-tradition.
Almost all his later poetical work was on the same lines.

The Free Besieged is the poem that above all occupied his mind.
The besieged are those of Missolonghi in the second great siege,
from 1825 until the heroic sortie of the garrison on the eve of
Palm Sunday 1826, perhaps the noblest and most decisive episode in the War of Independence. Solomòs was living near—
the cannons fired in the besieged fortress were often heard in
Zakynthos—but the poem was not written with recent impressions in mind, but much later. We have a first draft, something
more like a trial essay, of c. 1830. We have a second draft (the
most important), in the metre of The Cretan, on which he worked
for more than ten years, from 1833 to 1844. Then, when he was
some way advanced in the composition, he began to put it into
a different verse form, again in decapentesyllables but without
the ornament of rhyme and without the elision, so usual in
Greek; a severe, almost ascetic prosody, with an internal
harmony that still puzzles us today.

Solomòs never completed the work. We have a series of 'fragments' (as we are accustomed to call them) of the second and

third drafts. The name is misleading; they are not fragments of a whole, broken off by chance like the remains of Sappho or Archilochus. Solomòs never achieved completion. He seems to have been indifferent to the setting of these lyric passages in a narrative or 'epic-lyric' whole. He aimed at pure lyric expression, with little interest in any non-lyrical binding material in the composition, and may be said to have been a forerunner of the modern poetical feeling. We saw something of the same sort in *The Cretan*, and the same is true of his other 'fragmentary' works. It would be better to speak of them as lyric entities or episodes. If we approach them in this way we shall find that each has its indubitable completeness, and one has an internal connection with another. The besieged overcome, one after another, the difficulties against which they have to contend; at first these are physical (such as hunger) and later spiritual, until they reach the highest moment of sacrifice. One of the most important episodes is that of the leader (ii. 6) who, in the moment of utmost despair, remembers that in the same spot he first learned from the lips of his beloved of his renown—a thing still unsuspected by his simple, humble nature. There is also the passage about the enchantment of spring, which recurs persistently in more elaborate forms both in the second and third drafts (ii. 2 and iii. 6). Nature, in spring, at her sweetest hour, is a force bringing cowardice and hesitation to the besieged (a theme particularly dear to Solomòs).

> Over the waters of the mere, where she comes flitting by,
> With her reflected image plays the sky-blue butterfly—
> She who has passed a scented sleep in the wild lily's flower.
> Even the humble little worm enjoys the blessed hour.
> All Nature is a magic world of beauty and of grace;
> The black rock is all turned to gold, so is the desert place;
> A thousand springs are gushing forth, a thousand voices cry.
> He who is doomed to die today a thousand deaths shall die.

At that time Solomòs seems to have worked exclusively on *The Free Besieged*, but during the last ten years of his life (1847–57) he produced a lot of work, some complete, and some fragmentary or merely in the form of a rough plan; at the same time he returned to Italian verse, which he had forsaken after his Zantiot period: a rare and late poetical flowering. The most remarkable of his Greek poems is *Pórfyras* (1849). 'Pórfyras' is the Corfiot word for shark. An English soldier from the garrison had been torn apart by a shark while swimming carefree off Corfu; Solomòs (taking this event as subject) wrote a poem of lofty ideas. Here his favourite theme of the enchantment of nature (the young man in the water, 'in nature's embrace') takes on a different dimension; in the moment of ecstasy appears the 'reasonless and monstrous strength' of the sea monster, but in that moment of trial the young man finds strength to resist, and get to know his true self:

> Before the noble breath was spent his soul was filled with joy.
> Suddenly in a lightning flash the young man knew himself.

It is odd that Solomòs should have returned in the last part of his life to Italian poems. They are, indeed, not many, and most were 'subjects' that he suggested to the well-known Italian improvisers Borioni and Regaldi at public gatherings. Some, however, were written for various occasions: the sonnet on the death of Stylianòs Markoràs, the epigram on Alice Ward, the High Commissioner's daughter, another addressed to his intimate friend John Fraser, the Commissioner's secretary, etc. Of particular interest are the Italian prose sketches that he meant to work up later into Greek poems: they are like a painter's rough notes for his pictures. And in the construction of the prose, which is not at all like that of Italian, we can see clearly how the Greek verses were to be arranged. Oral tradition has preserved for us a fine line from 'The Greek Mother':

> Great was the pit that opened up to close my giant in.

Other such sketches, which would surely have turned into poetic masterpieces, are 'La Donna Velata' (his one real love-poem), 'The Nightingale and the Hawk', 'Orpheus'.

There is something in common between the Greek and Italian poems and the sketches of the last decade. One characteristic is a return to the words 'mystery', 'occult', 'secret'. The poet seems to be tormented by some kind of doubt; he wants to learn the mystery of life and death, and is asking poet or prophet, Sappho or Orpheus, to unveil this mystery to him. The theme of the prophet is connected with another theme, basic in all Solomòs's poetry, that of the girl, the virgin, and the visionary power that connects the two beings, the poet and the girl. The fragmentary poem on the death of Emilia Rodostamo and the short epigram on Francesca Fraser are two excellent examples:

> A little prophet cast his eyes upon a maiden's face . . .

Solomòs died in February 1857; he was just fifty-nine years old. His contemporaries were ignorant of the great poetry of his prime—*The Cretan, The Free Besieged,* or the *Pórfyras*; at the time of his death he was still honoured as the national poet, the author of the *Hymn to Liberty*. It is to the self-denial and conscientiousness of his disciple Jakovos Polylàs that we owe the first edition of his *Remains,* arranged from the disorderly manuscripts of the poet two years after his death (1859). Since that date all commonly used editions of his works have essentially been based on this first publication. But at first it did not arouse the interest that might have been expected. The poet was much in advance of his time, and his message was incomprehensible; many years had to pass before modern Greek poetry could make use of his teaching.

# VIII

## KALVOS, THE HEPTANESIAN SCHOOL,
## AND VALAORITIS

DURING THE DECADE of the War of Independence all the forces of the nation were focused on this great event, and the poets wrote hymns and revolutionary odes. Solomòs's *Hymn*, written in 1823, was printed in 1825 both at Missolonghi and in Paris. In 1824 Andreas Kalvos printed his *Lyra* (ten patriotic odes) in Geneva, and in 1826 the *Lyrics*, a further ten. These are his only appearances in Greek poetry.

### A. KALVOS

Kalvos too was born in Zakynthos, in 1792, six years earlier than Solomòs. The social position of his parents was the reverse: his mother was of an aristocratic family, and his father a plebeian. The latter would appear to have been an adventurer; he soon abandoned his wife and went abroad with his two sons. Andreas's youth and childhood were unhappy, and he had no chance of acquiring a solid education. But in 1812 came the decisive meeting of his life: in Florence he made the acquaintance of Ugo Foscolo, became his secretary, and accompanied him into exile, first to Switzerland, then to London, till in 1820 they quarrelled and parted. As we have seen, he published his two poetical collections in 1824 and 1826; in the preface to the second, in a dedicatory letter to General Lafayette, he declares his intention of going to revolutionary Greece: 'Je quitte la France avec regret: mon devoir m'appelle dans ma patrie, pour exposer un cœur de plus au fer des Musulmans.'

Words are easier than deeds; he arrived at Nauplia, but remained there only a short time before leaving for Corfu, where he settled permanently, and was for a time professor at the Ionian

Academy. We know very little about the twenty-five years of his life at Corfu. His poetical silence was complete; only from time to time he published sharp philosophical or theological diatribes in the local newspapers. He seems to have been a strange and solitary man; he does not appear to have had even the slightest acquaintance with Solomòs, who lived so near him. In 1852 he suddenly left for England, where he made a second marriage, and became partner with his wife in the management of a girls' school at Louth in Lincolnshire; he also translated books for the Church of England. He died there in 1869 and was followed to the grave by his wife in 1888; the oldest inhabitants remembered them until recent years. Their bones rested there until 1960, when they were transferred with great honour to Zakynthos.

The twenty odes are Kalvos's sole contribution to modern Greek poetry—small in extent but in many ways remarkable. As was natural, he was already well trained in writing Italian verse. As early as 1813, under the influence of his first acquaintance with Foscolo, he wrote two classical tragedies, *Theramenes* and *The Danaids*, and in the following year *Ode agli Ionii*, a protest against the fate of the Ionian Islands. By his own account we know that at the age of nineteen he had written an ode to Napoleon; the work was lost, but a few years ago a fragment was discovered.[1] The astonishing thing is that it is not in Italian, as we should have expected, but in Greek, and in a language not very different from that of the Odes.

As we might expect, the subjects of these twenty odes have a connection with the War of Independence; there are, however, exceptions: the 'Philopatris' (the first ode) is a hymn to the island where he was born, Zakynthos; the third ode, 'To Death', is a moving recollection of his dead mother. All the others are about the great event: 'To the Sacred Legion', 'To Chios', 'To Parga', 'The British Muse' (on the death of Byron). His metre is original: four heptasyllabic lines (which may also have six or eight syllables, according to whether the last accent is oxytone, paroxytone, or proparoxytone) and a pentesyllabic catalectic (the 'adonic'). This classical form reminds one of the Alcaic or Sapphic stanza, though the basis is the demotic decapentesyllabic line cut in two. Sometimes one hears it in its entirety: Στὰ πλούσια περιβόλια σας |

---

[1] It was first published from Kalvos's autograph by M. Vitti, *A. Kalvos e i suoi scritti in italiano*, Naples, 1960, pp. 325–8.

βασιλικὸς καὶ κρίνοι: 'In the rich gardens that are yours | are basil plants and lilies.' The language is also entirely original, a mixture of demotic and archaistic, and it has presented students with many problems. Mr. Dimaras[1] has found the best explanation: in writing Greek, Kalvos applied to it the poetical and aesthetic theories of the Italian classicists, and in particular of his master Foscolo. The spoken language is taken as a basis and is enriched with archaic expressions and rare words (even taken from ancient lexicons), while at the same time demotic words are transformed by archaic endings. The case of Kalvos is entirely unique. He wished to celebrate the Greek revolution and the return of Liberty to the country where she was born, and naturally, Greek poet as he was, he wished to write in Greek, not in Italian, which until now had been his natural mode of expression. But he had lived for twenty years far from Greece ('the fifth part | of a century beheld me | mid foreign nations'). He was cut off both from the demotic and the Phanariot tradition; he certainly did not yet know Solomòs, and it is doubtful if he knew the poems of Christopoulos or Vilaràs. Thus, in adapting the lessons of his teacher to his mother tongue, he was more or less alone as he made up his poetical instrument, and half-forgotten memories were to give it their warmth.

It is not only in his language that he follows the example of Foscolo: the lofty tone of the odes is in keeping with their classical form. There are classical recollections: the Parnassian maidens, the zephyrs, and the Olympian gods occur as well as the archaistic vocabulary; and he exalts noble actions, a lofty spirit, and above all Virtue. But in the classicist poetry of Kalvos, as in his language, there is a deep contradiction, which stamps its originality and, ultimately, is the reason for its worth. For all this apparent classicism is nothing but an outer garment, which conceals the movement of the uneasy soul of a genuine Romantic. The cloak is that of Pindar or Foscolo; the voice is that of Ossian or of Edward Young. The ode 'To the Muses' begins with references to the 'Leto-born', to 'the Zephyr-footed Graces', to 'the garden of the Pierides', and to 'the feasts of the Olympians', but in the later stanzas this frigid setting is at once quickened by a warm breath and a feeling for Nature:

---

[1] K. Dimaràs, Οἱ πηγὲς τῆς ἐμπνεύσης τοῦ Κάλβου, Athens, 1946 (reprinted from Νέα Ἑστία).

Where there tremble infinite
The lights of the night time;
There on high is spread out
The Milky Way and pours down
    Sprinkling of dewdrops.

This drink in its pureness
Gives health to the foliage;
And where it leaves the verdure
The sun finds the roses
    And all their perfume.

Night, stars, winds, clouds, blood, death, the tomb, tears: it has
been proved[1] that Kalvos makes his poetical pictures out of this
romantic material far more than from classical types. Of his ode
'To Death', Seferis[2] has written that it is essentially an ode by
Young. At his genuinely romantic core, we find Kalvos a true
and really original poet. Perhaps his moments of poetic ease are
relatively few, and there is more of what critics have called 'poetic
vacuum'. But criticism must rejoice when it meets excellence, even
in a small degree; and excellence is undoubtedly to be found in
the poet of the Odes.

Kalvos followed no tradition, and himself left no following.
His work, so unlike anything else either in the Ionian Islands
or in the poetry of Athens, was destined to remain in oblivion
for many years. It was only in 1888 that Palamàs, with his critical
acuity and his sensitivity, rediscovered the poet of the Odes. The
younger poetical generation of 1930 was in its turn to find some
kinship with him, and to speak of 'his genuine personality and
his lyric daring'.[3]

### THE HEPTANESIAN SCHOOL

The lesson of Solomòs, on the other hand, was received in
Heptanesian circles and gave birth to a whole school. The poets
of this school were so closely involved with Solomòs that we may
divide them into two classes: on the one hand his friends and
contemporaries, and on the other his disciples or followers. We

---

[1] See Dimaràs, op. cit.

[2] In Δοκιμές, 2nd edn., Athens, 1962, p. 24.

[3] O. Elytis, " 'Η ἀληθινὴ φυσιογνωμία καὶ ἡ λυρικὴ τόλμη τοῦ Ἀνδρέα Κάλβου",
*Νέα Ἑστία*, 40 (Christmas 1946), special fascicule dedicated to Kalvos, pp. 84–
106; reprinted, vol. 68 (September 1960), special fascicule, pp. 240–69.

have already made mention of a close friend, a little his senior, Antonios Matesis (1794–1875), who wrote anacreontic imitations, like Christopoulos, or approached the simple lyricism of Solomòs's early poems, and even translated Ossian and Gray. His most significant contribution to literature was his drama *The Basil Plant* (1830) on the subject of the social contrasts in the islands at the beginning of the eighteenth century. A young man from 'the second-best families' loves a girl from 'the best'. It is written in prose, in lively demotic, and is enriched with many picturesque elements, particularly when personages 'from the lowest class of the people' are presented. There is a sort of Iago in the character of the agent of the Venetian Provveditore.

George Tertsetis (1800–74) was also among Solomòs's friends at Zakynthos. He studied law in Italy, and went to Greece under Kapodistrias. As a judge in 1833 he strongly opposed the proposal of the Regency that he should condemn Kolokotronis to death, and he was obliged to leave his country. He returned with the change of politics in 1843, and remained thenceforward in Athens until his death, as librarian to the House of Parliament. On every anniversary of the national holiday (25 March) and on other occasions he delivered an oration in demotic, thus keeping the tradition of Solomòs alive amid the archaism of Othonian Athens. In 1833 he greeted Otho's arrival with a poem, *The Kiss*. In 1847 he published anonymously a collection, *Simple Language*, an obvious recollection of the *Romaic Language* of Vilaràs, in which he includes prose and verse by himself and by others. In the following decade he also took part in the poetical competitions that were in fashion at the time, and protested when he got no more than praise, e.g. with *Corinna and Pindar*, *The Marriage of Alexander the Great*, and *The Dream*. The last is inspired by contemporary events: it is a dream of King Otho; the others have classical subject-matter. All are written in un-rhymed decapentesyllables, like the demotic songs or the poems of Solomòs's last period. Tertsetis, his close friend, is perhaps here influenced by him. But Tertsetis's verse has nothing of the enig-matic harmony of the third draft of *The Free Besieged* or of the *Pórfyras*. It is stiff, with no kind of flow. We get the impression that Tertsetis is not at home in verse, and that poetic expression troubles him. On the other hand he is perfectly at ease in prose; he is the prose writer *par excellence* of the Heptanesian school. Two

early prose works of his are particularly noteworthy: one is a
letter of advice to Dimitris, son of the warrior Markos Botsaris,
when he was going to Munich in 1826 as a bursar of King
Ludwig I of Bavaria; the other is a speech in commemoration
of the Philhellene Frank Abney Hastings (1828). Both are
written in pure but carefully handled demotic and with an extraordinary freshness, such as we find only in *The Woman of
Zakynthos* or in the *Memoirs* of Makrygiannis. In his later prose
works, the speeches on 25 March, this freshness has vanished;
but the prose deliberately retains the character of the spoken
word and has a peculiar charm. We are told that it enchanted
his audience, and we can understand why. As a personality he
himself always had a charm of his own, though his appearance
was anything but attractive. We are also indebted to Tertsetis for
his initiative in getting Kolokotronis in his old age to dictate his
memoirs to him; he apparently did the same with Nikitaràs and
other heroes of the War of Independence, but the documents
have not come down to us. It is not worth our while to pause over
two works of his last period, a comedy (1858) in which he makes
fun of a poetical competition, and his play in Italian, *The
Death of Socrates* (1866).

We come now to the disciples of Solomòs. The eldest of these,
and scarcely thirteen years younger than the master, was Andreas
Laskaratos. He was born at Lixouri in Cephalonia in 1811, and
died there in 1901 after a long and stormy life. He was personally
acquainted with Solomòs in Corfu, where he had studied at the
Ionian Academy as a pupil of Kalvos. From 1836 to 1839 he
studied law in Paris and at Pisa, and on his return practised for
a short time at Lixouri; but he soon gave it up and retired into
private life. In 1851–2, and also after 1856, he lived in London,
giving Greek and Italian lessons and studying in the British
Museum.

Laskaratos, as he himself confessed, did not have the nature of
a poet: 'I always wanted to climb Parnassus, but every time I
got tired half way up and turned back. I hadn't the wings of
my friend Valaoritis.' He wrote a great many satirical lines,
starting, as in his earlier 'satiric epyllia' of 1840–50, from local
events, and sometimes advancing to more general social criticism.
But his satires are laden with intolerably prosy elements and are
quite unreadable. More successful are his parodies; of the Old

Testament ('Why dollars are called dollars') or of the *Iliad* ('The quarrel between Agamemnon and Achilles'). Palamàs rightly said: 'Laskaratos is no painter of passions, but a persecutor of prejudices; he is not a creator, he is an observer.'[1] Living in a restricted society he was irritated by its smallness and the falsity of its conventions and he wished to become a social reformer. Therefore his most characteristic writing is his prose work, *The Mysteries of Cephalonia*, printed in 1856; its sub-title is 'Thoughts on family life, religion, and politics in Cephalonia'. The book is, in fact, divided into these three parts, and the writer states his views on these subjects; his intention is ethical and didactic, but his mood is often satirical. The section on the family is certainly the best. The religious part caused scandal. Laskaratos was attacking prejudice and superstition, ikons that shed tears, the ignorance and the avarice of the clergy; but it is not always easy to make clear what is essential, what is mere formality, and what is prejudice. Laskaratos, with his intellectualism and his puritan ethics, was not the man to make that distinction. It was impossible for him to understand, perhaps because he was so little an artist, the particular hue that religious faith and ritual take on among the Greek people. He saw everything as black or white, and had no eye for the rich colours of a popular festival; his approach is therefore that of a foreigner. Not unnaturally *The Mysteries of Cephalonia* provoked a stormy reaction, which went so far as the author's official excommunication by the Church. Laskaratos was obliged to go away, first to Zakynthos, and later to England; he wrote polemical pamphlets, edited a periodical, and when the storm had somewhat subsided he tried to start it up again by publishing his 'Answer to the Excommunication' in 1868. The excommunication was not lifted until 1900, just before his death. Meanwhile, from 1875 onwards, he collaborated with different Athenian periodicals, and in 1884 went to Athens where he gave a lecture at the literary society 'Parnassòs'. Things were much changed by then, after nearly thirty years, and the Athenian public was mature and advanced enough to understand his value, and this gave him much moral satisfaction.

In 1886 he published another prose work, *Behold the Man*, and a collection of *Characters*, in imitation of Theophrastus and

[1] K. Palamàs, *Τὰ πρῶτα κριτικά*, Athens, 1913, p. 69 (= *Ἅπαντα*, vol. 2, p. 82).

La Bruyère. First he draws his own portrait with irony, yet also with fighting spirit: 'The Quarrelsome Man'.

In 1866, at the request of a Danish friend, he started writing an extremely interesting autobiography in Italian, which he finished about twenty years later, adding to it constantly until the end of his life.[1] The last lines are highly impressive, as they reveal a deeply ethical and, at bottom, religious personality:

Now recapitulating my long existence, I shall say this: I was endowed with what is called a good nature, and all who knew me intimately loved me and wished me well. I have indeed known grief, misfortune, and insults in the course of this long existence. . . . Today, in the eighty-seventh year of my life, I thank God for what He gave me in this world, and I trust in His fatherly benevolence for what is to become of me after death.

Julius Typaldos (1814–83) was also of Cephalonian aristocratic origins. He studied law in Italy, and on his return followed the juristic branch. In 1857, posted in Zakynthos, he delivered a commemorative speech on Solomòs, a noteworthy token of his critical admiration. From 1867 he withdrew to Florence, but in 1881 he went back to Corfu, where he died. Of all the Heptanesians, Typaldos is perhaps the purest lyric poet, though his work is small in bulk. His one collection of poems, *Divers Poems* (1856), is dedicated to Solomòs: a few poems (and not his best) were added later. His poetry, formed in the school of Solomòs, has an undoubtedly lyrical quality, and a rare nobility, but is somewhat monotonous and feeble in sound. He moves in the same world of idealism as all the Heptanesians, and his few poems are marked by a sweetness and a delicate grace. Words such as 'hidden' and 'secret' frequently recur in his lines, and a dim moonlight seems to illuminate the gentle and aristocratic creations of his imagination. 'Poet of the moonlight', Palamàs called him.[2] However, this gentle world of idealism does not lead him astray into the abstract; his genuine lyric feeling is always in touch with the world of reason, while his musical

---

[1] This fuller text has been published in a French translation by H. Pernot, *Études de littérature grecque moderne*, vol. 2, Paris, 1918, pp. 146–276. Greek translation from the French text by Ch. Antonatos, Athens, [1927], reprinted in *Ἅπαντα*, vol. 1, pp. 2 ff. A different version of the text (in Italian) is published by Al. Papageorgiou, *Ἀνδρέου Λασκαράτου Βιογραφικά του ἐνθυμήματα*, Athens, 1966.

[2] K. Palamàs, *'Ἰούλιος Τυπάλδος*, In *Ἅπαντα*, vol. 8, pp. 285–310.

sensibility converts his idealistic visions into pliant musical verse
in melodious stanzas of six or eight lines:

> Thou like a dream appearing
> The very first thou art
> To kindle sleepless passions
> Within my guileless heart.
> Ah, say, where art thou love?
> Where art thou my sweet hope?
> Say, is this earth thy home,
> Or are the stars above?

The atmosphere of Typaldos's poetry is that of Solomòs's first
Corfiot period, a likeness which extends to the versification;
perhaps of all his disciples Typaldos is the one who went furthest
into his world.

Typaldos devoted his later years in Florence to the translation
of the *Gerusalemme Liberata*, which is his most perfect work. The
*ottava rima* hendecasyllabic stanzas of the original are rendered
in the Cretan decapentesyllabic couplet, and it is clear that
Typaldos studied Kornaros in order to learn how to render the
epic force of Tasso. Moreover in a letter to De Viazis in 1880 he
speaks without hesitation of the poetic excellence of the *Erotokritos*, which he places next to Solomòs. His admiration for
Kornaros is realized by this poetical translation, and though it
is not an original work it is nevertheless a work of the highest
importance both for the poetry of Typaldos and, more generally,
for that of modern Greece.

If Laskaratos is the satirist and Typaldos the lyric poet,
Jakovos Polylàs inherited Solomòs's critical spirit. He was born
in Corfu of a good local family in 1826. He did not study abroad
as a young man, but in 1852–4 he accompanied his sick wife to
Naples, where he had the opportunity of studying German
idealistic philosophy, and in particular Hegel and Schiller, by
whom he was profoundly influenced. After the death of Solomòs
he undertook, almost unaided, the heavy task of editing the
poet's works from his incomplete manuscripts. His edition of the
*Remains* in 1859 is a wonderful critical monument, valuable not
only for the edition of the text itself, but also for the 'Prolegomena', which is one of the most precious pieces of evidence for
the poetry and personality of Solomòs. Before this, when still at

Naples, he was working on a prose translation of *The Tempest* which he published, with a critical introduction, in 1855. Years later he published another Shakespearian translation, *Hamlet* (1889), this time in verse, in a melodious thirteen-syllable line which is his own invention. His translations are the creative expression of his critical spirit; they are the fruit of his inclination towards idealism and of his need to know, and to make known to others, the greatest works of the great masters. From 1875 he had been engaged on the translation of Homer, first of the *Odyssey* and then of the *Iliad*. His translation, especially of the *Odyssey*, is outstanding for its elegance and rhythm.

His original work is small; Polylàs was not a creative artist but, as he said himself in the best of his sonnets, an 'amateur'. But he was an amateur in the highest sense of the word. His own small body of original writing, his criticism, and his translations complement each other and combine to make up a most distinguished personality of the utmost sensibility. In the last years of his life he came into closer touch with the literary circles of Athens, on whom he exercised a great influence, for his former friendship with Solomòs gave him especial authority. Thus in 1892, taking as his occasion the results of the third 'Philadelphian' competition, he took part in the discussion and published his study, *Our Literary Language*. At the same time he also came under the influence of the Athenians and wrote three 'genre' stories,[1] but with the firm imprint of his own personality. In 'A Little Mistake' he introduces an admirable female character; in 'The Three Gold Coins', a longer tale, there is an atmosphere of spiritual nobility that makes credible the supernatural. Polylàs died in Corfu in 1896. In the previous year Palamàs had paid tribute to him and to Markoràs in one of the sonnets in *Countries*,[2] as heirs of Solomòs and his own poetical forerunners.

Gerasimos Markoràs, another Corfiot, was born in the same year as Polylàs, 1826. His father, a justice, was a close friend of Solomòs and in general had close relations with the poet's family. Between 1849 and 1852 he studied law in Italy and on his return led a quiet and solitary life, especially after the death

[1] On the 'genre' story and its significance for the prose of the generation of 1880, see below, Chapter XI, p. 164.
[2] "Πατρίδες", 4th sonnet, in *Life Immovable* (= Ἅπαντα, vol. 3, p. 16).

of his parents, looking after his country estate. In 1857, like all the poets of the Ionian Islands, he wrote a lament for the death of Solomòs. In 1863 he printed a satire against the British protectorate. The subjects of his poetry are not particularly original; they deal with such commonplaces as love, death, and the fatherland, but they are distinguished for their gentleness, by a language refreshed by the Heptanesian tradition, and by an uncommon perfection in form. When his *Poetical Works*, the first collected edition, was published in 1890, his poetry made a great impression in Athens because of both its form and its content, and decisively influenced the younger poets. Like Polylàs, he brought to Athens the tradition of Solomòs, at a time when it was ready to receive it. But like other artists who lack the power of self-renewal, Markoràs, after influencing his juniors, was influenced in his turn by them. His second collection, *Short Journeys* (1898), clearly shows the influence of Athenian Parnassians, and in addition the weakening—and also the attendant graces— of old age. This is the end of the Heptanesian school. In 1911, when Markoràs died at the age of eighty-five, we are a long way from its beginnings.

Markoràs is the poet of the minor key *par excellence*. An exception is his big epic–lyric work, *The Oath*, first published in 1875, and based on the Cretan insurrection of 1866 and the blowing up of the monastery of Arkadi by its abbot Gabriel—an action comparable with the most heroic events of 1821 and one which has always evoked admiration. Markoràs constructs his work round two personages, Eudokia and Manthos, who are betrothed. Eudokia returns to Crete three years later, after Manthos has been killed at Arkadi; as she follows his tracks, his ghost appears to her and relates all the events, the resistance, and the blowing up of the monastery. Markoràs uses the rhymed decapentesyllabic couplet, a technique which he learned from *The Cretan* and from *The Free Besieged*. The verse is very precise, and has a carefully constructed harmony, sometimes with a masculine roughness and at other times with a feminine tenderness, corresponding to its two chief characters. It is both gentle and vigorous, and ranks with the *Fotinòs* of Valaoritis as one of the most remarkable achievements in poetry after Solomòs, particularly of the decade 1870–80.

## A. VALAORITIS

Aristotle Valaoritis occupies a place of his own in the Heptanesian school. He was almost an exact contemporary of the two last-mentioned poets. Born in 1824 in Leucas, the Ionian island nearest to mainland Greece, he studied in Italy and France, and returned to the Ionian Islands in 1848, playing an energetic role in politics both before and after the union with Greece. He was a man of strong constitution and athletic appearance, violent in his reactions and bitter in dispute. For the last ten years of his life he retired to the islet of Madourì off the coast of Leucas, and gave himself up to writing and study. He died there, prematurely, in 1879.

His first volume, *Verses* (1847), is insignificant. He made his first important appearance with *Elegies* in 1857, the year in which Solomòs died. The collection includes his most significant and best-known lyric poems: 'Funeral Ode', 'Thanasis Vagias', 'Samuel', 'The Flight', 'Efthymios Vlachavas'. Valaoritis is a strange phenomenon; he was a genuine Heptanesian, but his orientations brought him nearer to the demotic song and to French Romanticism than to Solomòs and the ideals of his school. His subjects are mostly taken from the War of Independence and the pre-revolutionary period, the struggles of the klephts, of the *armatolì*, and of the Suliots. His heroes move in an impossibly exalted atmosphere where the supernatural element blends with Romantic exaggeration. Meanwhile, unlike the Romantics of Athens, Valaoritis, like a true Heptanesian, used the demotic. He did not modify it creatively, as Solomòs taught, but followed superficially the style of folk-poetry, transforming it with much romantic bombast. In his more mature works such as *Astrapogiannos* and above all in *Athanasis Diakos* (1867) many of these faults are less prominent. However, in the second, perhaps the more significant work, symbolism and allegory prevail, rendering the essentially human figure of the hero–martyr indistinct. The last ten years of his life he lived on his estate at Madourì, and in 1879, the year of his death, he worked on *Fotinòs*, his last and most remarkable poem, which unfortunately he was unable to finish. The subject is taken from the earlier history of Leucas, a rising of the Greek inhabitants against the Frankish dynast in the fourteenth century. Fotinòs, the hero, an old countryman, retires to the mountains of his homeland after a quarrel with the Frankish ruler. There we find him with his daughter in his poor cottage, planning revolution. This aged champion of freedom is distinguished by his gentle humanity and his quiet determination and a certain aristocratic pride. All the poem centres round this warm human character. Valaoritis no longer wishes to impress us with the supernatural, his verse is free from bombast or rhetoric, everything is simpler and at the same time warmer and more human. It seems that Valaoritis had to wait until the end of his life to free himself from the faults that spoil his other work—faults that were, to a large degree, those of his age. Or perhaps he had sought solitude and contemplation in order to discover his real self. Unlike the other works of Valaoritis, the *Fotinòs* has a place of its own in modern Greek poetry.

The Heptanesian school has also a rich crop of less significant names. Spyridon Zambelios (1815–81) wrote some early poems under the influence of Solomòs, but then turned rather to the study of history; in 1852 he published a collection of demotic songs (with many arbitrary emendations), and in 1857 his *Byzantine Studies*, one of the earliest proofs of interest in this subject. *The Cretan Wedding* (1860) is a historical novel, set in the time of Venetian rule in Crete, and has no literary merit. Spyridon Melissinòs (1823–88) dedicated his youthful *Tombs* to the memory of Solomòs, but his later work departs from his school. Of Gerasimos Mavrogiannis (1823–1906) we shall mention only one poem, *The Ionian Sailor*, written in demotic, in imitation of the demotic songs. Antonios Manousos (1828–1903) wrote some light stanzas that are not without freshness, and some technically superior sonnets, in which he tried to imitate the style of Petrarch. His long poem, *The Blind Woman's Death*, Romantic both in style and conception, is written in very competent Dantesque *terza rima*. Stylianòs Chrysomallis (1836–1918), a friend of Polylàs, wrote satirical poems and also a few lyrics and translations. Andreas Martzokis of Zakynthos (1849–1923) was much more in the Heptanesian tradition; he was much influenced by the Romanticism of Valaoritis in his larger compositions, and in his purely lyric work he shows an affinity with the poetry of Typaldos. Others, such as P. Panàs, M. Avlichos, and D. Iliakopoulos, gradually lost their Heptanesian character, merging in the great melting-pot of Athens.

# IX

## THE NEW GREEK STATE
## THE PHANARIOTS AND THE
## ATHENIAN SCHOOL
## GREEK ROMANTICISM

ISTORICAL CONDITIONS favoured the independent
development of the Heptanesian school: the small 'independent state' of the Ionian Islands continued to exist
until 1863, when, with the accession of the new dynasty, Great
Britain consented to the union of the islands with Greece. Meanwhile, as a result of ten years of revolution, the new Greek state
had been founded upon a democratic basis, and was officially
recognized by the western powers and by the Porte. Since 1828
its leader had been the Corfiot Joannis Kapodistrias, whose political sagacity had been trained by his having been a minister
of the Tsar's. In Nauplia, the first capital, and in Athens, the
capital after 1834, intense intellectual and literary activity was
developing side by side with political life.

Nevertheless the newly founded state was shaken by political
and social conflicts. Kapodistrias's attempts to organize a well-
governed state, following western models, were sure to meet with
every sort of opposition; the first tragic consequence was his own
murder in 1831. Moreover the arrival of the young king Otho
in 1833, and above all the exercise of power by the Bavarian
regents, caused the situation to deteriorate further. Some im-
provements were brought about by the political change of 1843
and the granting of the first constitution.

The new state only extended as far as Mt. Othrys, and
excluded vital areas of Hellenism such as Thessaly, northern
Greece, and the islands. In this stiflingly restricted area, mani-
fold and (in many respects) opposing elements, free and unbridled

during the Turkish regime, were now crowded together and were creating an explosive atmosphere. The Phanariots, who came down from the Danubian principalities, with their political and administrative experience, obtained the highest positions; Heptanesians who had received an education in western universities also played an important part; while the Peloponnesians and Roumeliots, who were also at rivalry among themselves, whether simple men of the people or leaders in the War of Independence, saw or thought themselves to be cold-shouldered. The vision of their country's freedom, which had warmed their hearts throughout the revolution, like all attractive visions seemed to have little correspondence with reality. At the same time the language of the people, that of the demotic songs or of the simple decrees of the village elders, was unable to satisfy the increased demands of a more complicated state organism, and was set aside. In state documents, in the press, even in literature we observe a continual tendency to further archaism: katharevousa, a creation of the learned, was gradually established as the official language.

There is no work that better reflects this situation than the *Memoirs* of General Makrygiannis, even though he is a quite individual case. Makrygiannis was born in 1797 in a village in Epirus, and was a prominent figure in the War of Independence; he was courageous and determined, he distinguished himself in several battles, and attained the rank of general. Like nearly all the leaders in that war, he was illiterate; but when, at the end of the conflict, he was made a 'chiliarch' by Kapodistrias, he felt the need to record his own deeds and what he had seen, and at the age of thirty-two he sat down and learned to read and write; he began to write his *Memoirs* in his own hand, with no knowledge of punctuation or spelling, and continued them up to the eve of his death. His language is entirely that of the people, without a touch of learned influence; it has the liveliness of actual speech and the warmth of a man who was not only an observer but also a part of the events which he described. This lively, personal style is entirely fitting as the expression of his vehement and peculiar character, which made him the violent opponent of any high-handed action or of any opportunist compromise. The *Memoirs* are the most genuine expression of the spirit of the generation that took part in the War of Independence;

at the same time there is perhaps no other text that gives us the language of the people so unadulterated and in a work of such length. It remained unpublished, and when Vlachogiannis first brought it out in 1907 it aroused no interest in literary circles. Only during the years just before the Second World War, the younger generation became fascinated by the general's purity of language, and tried to learn from him, the 'illiterate master' as Seferis calls him.[1]

### GREEK ROMANTICISM

The literary tendencies in the decade 1830 to 1840 were entirely different from those reflected in the *Memoirs* of Makrygiannis. Romanticism, the new, lively movement of the time, imposed itself upon literature at about the same time as it was making itself predominant in France. At present neither Romanticism nor the katharevousa receives much sympathy; and when the demotic first predominated, Romantic poems in katharevousa became the butt of an easy satire. However, in an objective historical account there is no place for prejudice of that kind; besides, during the fifty years of Greek Romanticism there were not only bad or mediocre poets, but also a few with a genuine lyric voice, who succeeded in making a virtue out of katharevousa and Romanticism.

*The Traveller* by Panagiotis Soutsos (1806–68) was the work with which romanticism first came into Greece. It is a 'dramatic poem' as the sub-title of the first edition announces. The poet, the youngest of three brothers, was a Phanariot of a princely family; he was born in Constantinople, and educated at the Chios School and later in Paris. His eldest brother fought beside Alexandros Ypsilantis and was killed at Dragatsani; his second brother was Alexandros, of whom we shall be speaking later. *The Traveller*, as the author tells us, had been inspired when he was eighteen years old 'in the cloudy horizons of northern Europe', was written in Greece in 1827, and published in Nauplia in 1831. The two principal characters, the Traveller and Raloù, meet again, fail to recognize each other, swoon, lose their senses, see

---

[1] G. Seferis, *Ἕνας Ἕλληνας, Ὁ Μακρυγιάννης*, in *Δοκιμές*, 2nd edn., Athens, 1962, p. 174. See also: *Makriyannis*, edited and translated by H. A. Lidderdale, p. vii (letter of Seferis to C. M. Woodhouse).

visions, run mad, and finally commit suicide, exchanging with their last breath the most heart-rending words of love.

*The Traveller* is the genuine first-born offspring of Romanticism, and therefore had an immediate success and great influence, as if that age were hungry for such improbabilities and for such an escape from reality. Besides, the work has positive virtues: the Romantic passion here finds most genuine expression, combined with an indubitable lyric nobility, and in the better parts the language has warmth and expressive power. This, at least, is true of the first edition; for Soutsos was led astray by the archaistic tendency of his time, and in every further edition made the language of *The Traveller* colder and less poetical. In 1853 he wrote the most curious of all documents on the archaistic tendencies in poetry, the *New School of the Written Word*, making his theoretical ideal a complete return to the ancient language. This was answered with remarkable cool-headedness and acuteness in the *Soutsiad* by K. Asopios, professor of classical literature at the Ionian Academy first and later at the University of Athens; he was the first to attack without reserve Romantic and linguistic extravagances, and to refer to Solomòs and to the *Erotokritos* as examples of real poetry.

Before *The Traveller*, Soutsos had written short lyric poems, mostly love-poems, in the manner of the 'Arcadian' poets and of Christopoulos, who was acknowledged as their master by all the young Phanariots. During the decade 1830 to 1840 he published an epistolary novel, *Leander* (1834), the prose counterpart of *The Traveller* and obviously inspired by Foscolo's *Letters of Ortis*. He also published a collection of poems, *Guitar* (1835). In the last volume, as well as love-songs and drinking-songs, there are patriotic and politico-satirical poems, of the type that his brother Alexander cultivated still more; pure lyricism appears to be fading here, and his poetic power was clearly failing. His subsequent work, tragedies, lyric dramas and novels, is not worth our attention. Panagiotis Soutsos could not recover the moments of genuine poetic inspiration that the young author of *The Traveller* had achieved; moreover his language, progressively more archaic, cast its chill and spoiled his poetic creation.

Alexandros Soutsos was three years older than his brother. He arrived in Greece a little before him and was at Nauplia under Kapodistrias. He published *Satires* in 1827. His poetry was never lyrical; it was always political and satirical in tone. He wrote violent polemics against Kapodistrias, and even went so far as to praise his murderers as 'tyrannicides'. Nevertheless, later, he attacked the Regency and King Otho with equal vehemence. He was a poet–journalist, of the type (always Romantic) of Béranger. He took a vigorous part in politics, and for that reason his life was a stormy one; he was frequently attacked for political reasons, was imprisoned, and was obliged to leave his country, and finally died in a hospital at Smyrna in 1863.

His most interesting poems are collected in *Panorama of Greece* (1833). The language is still near to demotic, and his ironic and playful disposition often shows the beneficial influence of the school of Christopoulos. *The Wanderer* is a long and miserable poem, a poor imitation of *Childe Harold*, with a number of political gibes in it; *Greece against the Turk* (1850), a poem hailed in its own time as the highest example of lofty poetry, is an unsuccessful attempt to describe the struggle of 1821, in which the author cannot escape from prosiness. We should make mention of his early comedy, *The Prodigal* (1830), which is in ordinary living speech, but we can ignore his other dramatic works and his prose book *The Exile* (1835), 'a mass of bombast', as one critic called it.[1]

Alexandros Rizos Rangavìs (1809–92) was of a noble Phanariot family, and a cousin of the Soutsos brothers. In the course of his long life he was to take part in many activities and to write many books, of both a literary and a non-literary nature. He too was born in Constantinople; he attended a military academy in Munich with a scholarship from Ludwig I of Bavaria, and later occupied various positions in Greece; he was a professor of archaeology at the university, a senior administrative official, ambassador to Washington and to Berlin, and a government minister. He was also a man of letters. His complete literary works, published by himself, amount to nineteen volumes. We shall later speak of his short stories and his novels. For the moment we are exclusively concerned with his poetry, which made its earliest appearance at the same time as that of Panagiotis Soutsos. *Dimos and Eleni* (1831) has a purely Romantic structure, but at the same time an artificial overlay of Greek popular colour, which can also be seen in the demotic names of

[1] Angelos Vlachos, *Ἀνάλεκτα*, vol. 2, Athens, 1901, p. 46.

the principal personages; the language is a demotic that has been tidied up, with an admixture of learned frigidity. Rangavìs on the whole, unlike Panagiotis Soutsos, is moderate both in his Romanticism and in his use of language; and this is his defect. In his comparatively early collection, *Various Poems* (1837), there are poems in the newly established katharevousa of the Phanariots, side by side with a greater number of poems in which demotic is felicitously used either in brief, light songs (most of them to well-known western airs) or on the familiar Romantic themes. The Romanticism of Rangavìs seems to be influenced by the German poets, and this gives it a special character. *The Woman Traveller*, for example, is another variation on the theme of the wanderer.

During the first decade of Romanticism, the poetry of the new state accepted the coexistence of the two languages. But as time went on—and we have already seen it happen in the case of P. Soutsos—the poor sister was ousted by the rich one. In 1864 Rangavìs published a poetical 'tale', *The Voyage of Dionysos*; the theme is taken from Greek mythology, the episode of the god Dionysos and the Tyrrhenian pirates that is carved on the frieze on the monument of Lysicrates in Athens (fourth century B.C.). The language is very skilful and elegant, but extremely archaistic, and the five-line stanzas are highly wrought and polished:

> The richest brooches gatherèd
> The mantle of the maiden,
> With precious stones enamellèd,
> But richer yet her golden head
> With wealth of curls was laden.

We are far from the demotic and the Romanticism of *The Woman Traveller* and of *Dimos and Eleni*; this has been succeeded by a neo-Classicism, which was more and more to control the life of the country. This neo-Classicism did harm enough. Yet today we value the neo-Classical houses of Athens (those that remain standing), the skilled marble work on the public buildings of the time, and the rosettes and palmettes carved on tombs in the cemetery of Athens. Rangavìs worked with the same elegance (and frigidity) on the neo-Classical verses of his *Voyage of Dionysos*, and the other poems of his last period.

The linguistic question tormented the poets of Athens who did not have Solomòs's good fortune of immediately realizing the right road to tread. Panagiotis Soutsos and Rangavìs began with demotic, and as we have seen ended up in a severe archaistic manner. George Zalokostas (1805–58), from Epirus, impartially divided his poetic activity between katharevousa and demotic. It is not only in language that he had a double personality; his poetry fluctuates between two extremes, some being on great 'epico-lyrical' themes (he had lived through the revolution and wished to celebrate it) and other poems being in more familiar tones, more tender, whether erotic or (more frequently) elegiac (he had lost seven of his children). He does not use katharevousa for epic, and demotic for his more lyrical poems; in both types of poem he uses either language indifferently. He is typical of a generation and an epoch that was struggling to find itself, faced by two conflicting traditions.

His long epico-lyrical poems, *The Khan of Gravià, Missolonghi,* etc., frequently exhaust us with their grandiloquence. He is much more successful in his shorter lyric poems in which he uses a more melodious metrical scheme (a four-line stanza with one decapentesyllable and three shorter lines); in this he seemed to find the perfect means for his individual expression. By this metrical scheme, and by his use of demotic, he drew near to the Heptanesian school, with which moreover he had other ties both of origin and of education. In a letter to the Italian Regaldi he shows unreserved admiration for Solomòs.

While Zalokostas stood aloof from the Athenian school, Theodore Orfanidis from Smyrna (1817–86) was absolutely a part of it, and followed the politico-satirical line of Alexandros Soutsos rather than the lyrical line of his brother. At an early age he wrote satires, later he studied botany in Paris, and in 1849 was appointed professor at the university, and distinguished himself in his own branch of study. He continued, however, to write poems, most of which were epico-lyrical (attempts to imitate Alexandros Soutsos's *Greece against the Turk*), and he won one prize after another in literary competitions; such poems were *The Man without a Country, Enslaved Chios* about the medieval history of that island, and *St. Minàs* about the massacres of Chios in 1822. The only work which need detain us is the satirical *Tiri-Liri,* 'or the shooting season in the island of Syros, an heroico-comical poem'. The odd title (taken from a line of

Soutsos) means something like 'a joke', or 'senseless babble'. The 3,000 fifteen-syllable lines are careless and flabby; but there is a genuine satirical feeling and much comic invention (for example, the pun on the cuckoo eaten by sportsmen, and the name of Captain Cook), and felicitous gibes at the Erasmian pronunciation, the antihellenism of Edmond About, etc.

We return to the true line of Romanticism (and of Panagiotis Soutsos) with two younger poets who are worth our mention, Joannis Karasoutsas and Demosthenes Valavanis, both born in the third decade of the century. The former (1824–73) came from Smyrna where, while still very young, he published two volumes of collected verse; the second of these, dedicated with admiration to Rangavìs, was an early sign of his poetical direction. The decade 1840–50 was that of his prime; his best poems are to be found in two collections, *Melodies of Dawn* (1846), and even more in *Barbitos* (1860). Karasoutsas lived a wretched life, earning his living as a teacher of French; at fifty years of age in 1873 in 'a fatal hour of painful frenzy'[1] he put an end to his days.

He was a genuine lyric poet; his Romanticism is never exaggerated, and his pessimism is irradiated by a true feeling for nature, in which there is a breath of spring:

> March, you are here, are here,
> And fields again are green,
> And bright the spring's eyes shine,
> Shine on the whole earth's cheer.

His true poetical sensibility was nourished by memories of Ionia, his homeland, and by the warmth of his faith in Christianity. In Karasoutsas the flabby Phanariot language takes on a firmer expressiveness and becomes subtle enough to render fine shades of meaning, and his lines and his well-managed stanzas achieve a more composite harmony. These are not mean virtues, and in other circumstances they would have been more fully developed. As it is, beneath the ice-bound katharevousa of convention, we sometimes seem to hear echoes of something warmer. One has the impression that the poet first conceived his impressions in demotic and later in his study 'translated' them into the established archaistic katharevousa. Perhaps his is the most pleasing voice that finds utterance in that language.

---

[1] A. Vlachos, Ἀνάλεκτα, vol. 2, p. 57.

Demosthenes Valavanis was the first poet to be born in liberated Greece. He was born at Karytaina in the Peloponnese in 1824; he studied medicine, but died in 1854 at the age of thirty before he had time to bring out a collection of his poetry. In his few poems, scattered over the anthologies and periodicals of the time, we can nevertheless discern a most interesting poetic individuality.

He, also, was unable to escape from the general climate of his age. He paid particular attention to the language and used it with skill; it is remarkable that of his small body of work a large proportion is in demotic. In some of these poems he seems to draw directly on folk-literature, particularly songs of the Peloponnese. In the best and the most mature of his work demotic preserves all its life force, and is used as a vehicle for the purest poetical expression. Such lines completely distinguish Valavanis from the other poets of the Athenian school. It is a sad thing that he died so young, but it would be useless to ask ourselves whether he would have managed to continue on this course, or whether he would have ended by compromising with his times.

Valavanis died in 1854, Zalokostas in 1858, Karasoutsas did nothing after the *Barbitos* (1860). The years following 1860 seem to have been unpropitious to poetry. 1863, the year of political change and of the introduction of the new dynasty, may be taken as a milestone. Romanticism had now lost its better exponents and with them its justification; it had also lost its balance and was on the decline. Its last phase is marked by exaggeration and by carelessness of style.

The decade 1863–73 is occupied by two poets whose births and whose early deaths were almost exactly contemporaneous. Dimitrios Paparrigopoulos (1843–73) was a son of the great historian Konstantinos Paparrigopoulos. He studied law, and published essays and philosophical studies at an early age; from these works we can see that he was a restless and revolutionary spirit. He wrote a great deal, epico-lyrical poetry and prose. His poems (1867) are marked by a strong sense of pessimism, and despair like that of Leopardi (as Palamàs said),[1] turning into complaints, discontent, and hatred—a death wish, which in its strength and persistence became his chief merit as a poet. He lacked the lyric vein, the sensibility of Karasoutsas, and the

[1] K. Palamàs, Ἕνας λεοπαρδικὸς ποιητής (= Ἅπαντα, vol. 10, pp. 267–82).

freshness of immediate contact with things; as a poet he was greyly and grimly philosophical. He made verse out of his despairing death wish, without 'baptizing it with the double baptism of feeling and imagination'.[1] His prosody is unstudied and careless and near to prose.

Spyridon Vasiliadis was born at Patras a year later than Paparrigopoulos, and died of consumption in Paris a year after the latter—the third poet whom we have seen dying at thirty. Is this, like the suicide of Karasoutsas and of others of less significance, a biological consequence of Romanticism, as it has been said?[2] Vasiliadis also studied law, and was friends with Paparrigopoulos, though his character was very different. He was ardent and enthusiastic, exuberant and charming. His volumes of poems often won praise and honourable mention in poetical competitions. He was more spontaneous than Paparrigopoulos, but also more shallow, with a tendency to empty rhetoric and to exaggeration. He wrote a great deal in verse and prose, also tragedies and other plays, which were often performed. His best known work, *Galatea* (in prose), makes use of the myth of Pygmalion, and at the same time of the demotic ballad 'The devoted brothers and the evil wife'. In spite of its frigid archaism, his dialogue is not without dramatic tension. It is interesting that Vasiliadis should have turned to the demotic songs as a source of inspiration.

With Vasiliadis we already feel the gradual collapse of Greek Romanticism. The end of it is represented by Achilles Paraschos (1838–95). Though he was a little older than the two whom we have just named, their careers coincided, and after their deaths he remained almost alone in the field of poetry. From 1870 to 1880 he lived at the centre of Athenian intellectual life and was much honoured. In 1881 he collected his poems into three volumes, grouping them into three classes: epic, patriotic and elegiac, and love poems. In the third group, the 'Myrtles', Romanticism seems to collapse into a parody of itself:

> I want her weak, my loved one, and I want her swift to fade,
> I want her pallid, and dead-white as is a dead man's shroud,
> With twenty autumns on her brow, and not a single spring . . .

---

[1] Solomòs, cited by Polylàs, Προλεγόμενα (= Ἅπαντα, vol. 1, p. 28).
[2] See e.g. K. Dimaràs, 'Ιστορία, 4th edn., Athens, 1968, p. 300. Id., Ποιηταὶ τοῦ ΙΘ′ αἰῶνα, Athens, 1954, Introduction, p. κζ′.

Obviously an empty shell is all that remains now of Romanticism. Poverty of ideas and of images and a disproportionate grandiloquence characterize this representative of its decline. He wrote with fantastic facility; his matter was unoriginal, his verse clumsy, and his language unstudied. His katharevousa is pompous and rhetorical, his demotic is commonplace and flabby. His intolerable repetitions were noticed and satirized even by the critics of his own time.

Achilles Paraschos is the end of Greek Romanticism, and of the Athenian school. As we have seen, it was a world without the warmth of genuine art, though there were some flashes of brilliance, and some real achievement, but it ended in a blind alley. At this time other forces, which derived from a more living source, and which were to bring about something new, now made their first appearance. The decade of Paraschos's prime (1870–80) was precisely when this change was preparing.

## PROSE AND THE THEATRE

Greek Romanticism mainly confined itself to poetry; perhaps it was afraid of the sobriety of prose. It is true that both Panagiotis and Alexandros Soutsos wrote in prose, but these are not their most characteristic works. Alexandros Rangavìs was much more successful in prose: he wrote interesting tales, and a long historical novel inspired by the medieval *Chronicle of the Morea*; this book, *The Lord of the Morea* (1850), very clearly shows the influence of Walter Scott. Rangavìs makes no concession to demotic, and this certainly gives a frigidity to his work and limits the effect of his ingenious plot and his lively dialogue.

The historical novel, with its return to a past age, and with the feuds, adventures, and intrigues, and the violent emotions that it describes, is particularly suited to the Romantic atmosphere, and therefore is the genre that flourished to some extent round the middle of the century. Stefanos Xenos, in *A Heroine of the Greek Revolution* (1852), draws on the recent past, and so does K. Ramfos in *Katsantonis* (1860) and *The Last Days of Ali Pasha* (1862), novels which aim at giving pleasure to a wider and less exclusive reading public. A particular place in any account of the historical novel should be given to *Pope Joan* (1866), a youthful work by Emmanuel Roidis, which provoked violent hostility, and was censured by the Church. His rationalism, his irony, and even his elegance of style place Roidis in contrast with the Romantic school, although his novel is undoubtedly its fruit. We shall have more to say of this interesting personality later.

*Thanos Vlekas* by Pavlos Kalligàs stands out from the rest of the prose work of the time as a genuine novel. The writer (1814–96) was one of the outstanding men of his time, a distinguished lawyer, a historical writer, a professor at the university, a member of Parliament, and a minister. *Thanos Vlekas*, published in 1855, represents a side-line of his, but an important side-line. The subject is not taken from the idealized historical past, but from contemporary actuality: the misery of the new Greek kingdom, tormented by misgovernment and banditry. There is no Romantic whitewash of the gloomy picture, which is drawn with a realism and irony that amount to sarcasm. The book has true literary qualities, imagination, a well-developed plot, skilfully drawn characters, and picturesque and lively descriptions rendered with realistic accuracy. Above all, we find the outstanding characters of Thanos and Euphrosyne presented, with no Romantic distortion, as a ray of light in this world of evil and misfortune. Naturally Kalligàs also uses the archaistic language of his time, which is frigid even in dialogue, though he employs it with some artistry.

Romanticism and the katharevousa were no more beneficial to the theatre than to non-dramatic prose. It is true that the poets of the Athenian school wrote dramatic works (even the *Traveller* had the sub-title 'a dramatic poem'), but without any theatrical plot, and in an unnatural and undramatic katharevousa. But although they were acted frequently by the (as yet impermanent) companies in Athens, in the provinces, and in the still unliberated Greek cities, and sometimes with success (as, for example, was the *Galatea* of Vasiliadis), we can hardly speak of the existence of a modern Greek drama during the fifty years that we are examining. The one successful theatrical play was the comedy *Babel* (1836) by the amateur playwright Dimitrios Vyzantios. The scene is laid at Nauplia in 1827; the writer brings forward people from different parts of the Greek world, each speaking in his own dialect, and thus creating comic misunderstandings. The motif was well known (from the older Venetian dialect comedies, and the *Korakistika* of Neroulòs), and was very popular. Vyzantios, however, as well as his skill in 'snap-shots', is able to distinguish and to represent the different 'ethos' for example of the man from Asia Minor, the Chiot, the Corfiot, etc. For this reason his *Babel* had a great success, and is still acted today. Together with the *Chasis* of Gouzelis and *The Basil Plant* of Matesis it ranks with the few genuine theatrical works of that earlier period.

Dimitrios Vernardakis, who wrote almost exclusively for the theatre, is another who wrote in katharevousa. He was born in Mytilene in 1833, and was not a professional writer, but (together with his much younger brother Gregorios) was one of the best Greek classical scholars and a professor at the university from 1861. As an innovator with a quarrelsome disposition (since 1855 he had been attacking the exaggerations of Romanticism) he came into conflict with the established professors, and particularly with Kontos; he therefore retired in his later years and lived in Mytilene (d. 1907). In another chapter we shall speak of his important influence upon the development of the language question. Here we are only concerned with him as a man of letters and a dramatic writer.

His first work, *Maria Doxapatrì* (1857), on a story taken from the period of Frankish rule in Greece, is genuinely Romantic and shows the strong influence of Shakespeare. However, on his return from his studies in Germany, he 'recovered', as he himself said, 'from the mist of Romanticism' and turned towards the ancients. His conversion to neo-Classicism was like that of Rangavìs. Henceforward his themes were to be taken from the ancient world. The *Cypselids* (1860), with choruses—a work of his transitional period—was never acted on the stage. But his other works, for all their anti-theatrical archaistic language and their iambic verse, were frequently performed with great success, especially the two best, *Merope* (1866) and *Fausta* (1893); the first performance of the latter was given twice on successive days by the companies of two rival leading actresses. The work is not without dramatic qualities, but in spite of the great success it won it is obviously a relic of an earlier age. In the last decade of the century very different forces were at work, which were to influence intellectual life in another direction and to lead to very different achievements.

# X

## THE GENERATION OF 1880
## THE NEW ATHENIAN SCHOOL
## KOSTÌS PALAMÀS

### THE DECADE 1870–1880

THE YEARS in which Romanticism had fallen into decline (1870–80) were, as we said, also years during which much fermentation was going on, and in which change and a creative resurrection were on their way. The young, those born after the middle of the century, were looking for something new in poetry, in science, and in intellectual life, and were dissatisfied with the forms sanctioned by convention. In 1877, the literary society Parnassòs (which was founded in 1865 and mainly composed of young men) organized a drama competition of its own, and invited Emmanuel Roidis, the author of *Pope Joan*, to be the judge. His criticism, in which he turned down all the works that had been submitted, was at the same time an important essay: *On the present state of poetry in Greece*. In his report he said there neither was nor could be poetry in Greece; for she lacked the 'milieu' that Taine thought essential, and what Roidis called the 'circumambient atmosphere'. Greece found herself in a transitional period; she had abandoned her traditional mode of life, but was not yet taking part in the intellectual life of the younger nations; this transitional state was not at all propitious for poetry. Among living poets Roidis made an exception only for Valaoritis and (oddly) for Paraschos.

Angelos Vlachos replied to Roidis's critical essay. They were both distinguished for their learning, culture, and acumen. Vlachos (1838–1920), however, had more respect for the established, and was less far-sighted as a critic. He lacked Roidis's ability to scent the new life that still only hovered unformed in the air. He expressed, rather, the spirit of the older generation; he felt that he belonged to a world that had, in the past fifty years, given a degree of order to its language, its poetry, and its *Weltanschauung*, and he had no desire to destroy the world to which he belonged. He had brought out his own first volume of collected verse very young, in 1857; others followed in 1860 and 1875. But he was no poet, and literature was his weak point. He was rather a man of learning. He had a fine feeling for the language, which he used with elegance, and was continually studying. His translations are always accurate, and his Greek–French Lexicon is of great value. Vlachos showed a special interest in the theatre, was a central figure in intellectual life, and became an important member of the state organization during the government of Charilaos Trikoupis.

Emmanuel Roidis (1836–1904) was a very different personality. He was born in Syros and spent his early life at Genoa, being brought up and educated abroad until his final return to Athens in 1863. The foreign models on which he was nourished formed his taste and his cosmopolitanism has left its stamp on his work. Literature is certainly not his strong point; it is also to be noted that he never wrote poetry. As we have seen, his first youthful work, *Pope Joan*, was less remarkable for its creative power than for its spirit of sarcasm, and for a rationalism that went so far as disbelief; the style is sparkling, but it becomes wearisome as an exhibition of wit. This quality, and the scandalous theme, assured it a great success; it was translated into many foreign languages, but provoked, as in the case of Laskaratos, the violent opposition of conservative circles and of the Church, an opposition which the writer left by no means unanswered.

Of more literary consequence are the short stories which he wrote in the later part of his life (after 1890) when deafness and financial difficulties isolated him and rather crushed his arrogance. These are not 'genre' stories like most of that time, though inspired by recollections of his childhood in Syros. His particular talent was for criticism, and it is as a critic that he exercised an undoubted influence on all the younger generation, who recognized him as an intellectual leader. After his sharp controversy with Vlachos in 1877, he was to be the first to recognize the *Journey* of Psycharis in 1888; and in 1893, in order to support demotic, he wrote (in katharevousa!) a linguistic study, *The*

*Idols.* It has been justly said of Roidis that, with all his cultivated taste and his acumen, his criticism is unconstructive and lacks that basic quality of a good critic, sympathy. He could destroy but not build. Nevertheless a pitiless criticism was perhaps what the times needed.

### THE GENERATION OF 1880: PARNASSIANISM

In the controversy between Vlachos and Roidis, it was natural that the younger generation should side with the latter; his censure satisfied some of its anxiety, and was in harmony with the desire for change that was floating in the air. In 1878 two journalists expelled from Constantinople, Kleanthis Triantafyllos and Vlasis Gavriilidis, published a satirical and political paper *Rabagàs*. Here such young men as Drosinis, Palamàs, Souris, and Polemis, who were later to make their names, made their first appearance. Their verse was satirical, and they took subjects out of everyday life, deliberately avoiding the conventional 'poetical subject', and they made an assault on Romanticism and the katharevousa of their elders, clamouring for the end of 'wordy, lachrymose idealism'.[1]

It was destruction that preceded construction. We can date the new construction from 1880, a year that is a watershed in Greek literary history. Two collections of poems then came out, the *Verses* of Nikos Kambàs, and the *Spider's Webs* of George Drosinis; this was the official début of the new poetical generation, that of 1880. It had matured among the inquietude and hesitations of the past decade, and now had something new and positive to introduce. First and foremost, its attitude was definitely anti-Romantic; it condemned the pomposity, the rhetoric, and the false heroism of the last period of Romanticism, and sought simplicity of expression, the familiar, even the everyday theme, and thus brought about a new order and a new measure in place of the uncontrolled passion of the Romantics. The new movement looked for guidance to western Europe, above all to the French *Parnassiens* (and chiefly the lesser of these, such as Sully Prudhomme or François Coppée). The same teachers taught them to take care to polish the form and the lines, a thing neglected by the Romantics. There now returned to

[1] K. Palamàs, Τὸ θαμποχάραμα μιᾶς ψυχῆς (1900) (= Ἅπαντα, vol. 4, p. 440).

common poetical practice, rhythmical and melodic combinations, and skilfully worked stanzas, and even the sonnet. Last, but most importantly, the new poets repudiated not only Romanticism, but also katharevousa. Together with the familiar subject, the demotic language came into poetry; katharevousa was no longer tolerated.

The poets who published these two collections in 1880 both belonged to the group of young men connected with the *Rabagàs*. They had studied in Athens where Kambàs shared a room with Palamàs; they were full of literary inquietude, and dissatisfaction with Greece as it was made them turn to foreign models for inspiration. Today we notice the faults in their poems much more than their virtues; they are full of commonplace and shallow ideas, the verse is flabby, the rhymes too facile, and above all there is too much of the anti-poetical and down-to-earth atmosphere of the *salon* of 1880. Nevertheless, in their own day they were a turning-point; the familiar and everyday subject was a deliverance from Romantic exaggeration and affectation; and the warmth of common (even if it were everyday) speech was a relief after the learned chill of the artificial katharevousa.

But how long a life is there for a poetry that is deliberately prosaic? The more gifted naturally passed beyond this stage, but there were some who were to remain rooted in it. Such were Joannis Polemis (1862–1924), who was prolific and shallow, or George Souris (1852–1919), both of whom came from the circle of the *Rabagàs*. The last mentioned, who had immense facility, went on writing verses in his paper, the *Romiòs* (which was much appreciated by the petty bourgeois); his superficial, journalistic satire was more in the nature of self-complacent mockery than severe censure.

There were also writers, a little senior in age, who continued to hover between the old and new, ceasing to belong ideologically to the former, and yet unable to embrace the latter. Such were Vikelas and Vizyinòs: we shall become better acquainted with them in the following chapter, particularly with the latter, as prose writers. In the *Breezes of Atthis* of Vizyinòs, printed in London in 1883, we find poems still written in the polished katharevousa of Rangavìs, and others in a demotic that is emotionally warm but rather flabby. Most are narratives, a kind of ballad, in which the poet already betrays the hypersensitiveness of his mind. In his last four years of life he was mentally disturbed, and then it was that he wrote his most moving lines, a dramatic testimony:

> Within me, deranged,
> The world's rhythm is changed.

Another poet of the transition is Aristomenes Provelengios (1851–1936). His early poems are still in the manner of the Athenian school, and near to Romanticism or to the neo-Classicism of Rangavìs. He was touched but not deeply affected by the change of 1880; in the first 'Philadelphian' competition of 1889, when Palamàs won the prize, he was *proxime accessit*. In 1890 he was himself judge, and awarded the prize to Palamàs. In 1896 he collected all he had hitherto written into *Poems Old and New*; the title was almost symbolic. Provelengios lived his long life between the old and the new, writing nostalgic poems about his Cycladean island and the Aegean; they were not without grace and musical charm, the very type of a minor poet.

Very different was the case of Joannis Papadiamantopoulos (1856–1910), five years younger than Provelengios and only one year older than Kambàs. He came of an outstanding family, was well educated, and made an early appearance in literary circles. In 1878 he published a pamphlet on the Vlachos–Roidis controversy, and in the same year his collected poems, *Doves and Serpents*. This collection was characteristic of the transition in its hesitation between new and old; Palamàs said of it that it 'bade farewell to something that was disappearing'.[1] This was his one appearance in Greek poetry; not long afterwards he finally settled in Paris, where he won an important place as a French writer under the name of Jean Moréas.

The change of 1880 was an intellectual occurrence of wide significance. After the romantic period, Greek society began to set itself more realistic aims; the progressive party and a new and more enlightened bourgeoisie began to demand better state organization and to place its faith in Parliamentarianism and in democratic principles. On the political front these tendencies were incarnate in the outstanding personality of Charilaos Trikoupis who, as prime minister precisely during this decade,

---

[1] K. Palamàs, *Τὰ τραγούδια τῆς πατρίδος μου*, 2nd edn., Athens, 1933, Introduction, p. ιβ΄ (= Ἅπαντα, vol. 1, p. 16); see also below, p. 156 n. 1.

organized the state and its policy along realistic lines. There was much progress in the language question, and Psycharis, more or less the contemporary of Drosinis and Palamàs, discovered entirely new paths and proposed revolutionary solutions. At the same time literary research abandoned the habit of exclusive devotion to the ancients and looked for national origins in the Middle Ages and in popular tradition. K. Sathas and Spyridon Lambros studied medieval texts and manuscripts; G. Chatzidakis laid the basis of modern Greek linguistic study and cleared the ground of former prejudice; Nikolaos Politis founded the science of folklore, in an attempt to systematize research into popular tradition and culture.

In a competition of 1869, when he was still a student, Nikolaos Politis (1852–1921) won a prize for his work *Modern Greek Mythology*. The set subject was the contemporary manners and customs of the people, and the comparison of them with those of the ancients. Modern Greek scholarship, which had received a shock from Fallmerayer's well-known theory of the Slav origins of modern Hellenism, refuted this theory responsibly by researching into the roots of the nation. During his whole life Politis devoted himself to the systematic collection of Greek folklore material, and (*c.* 1900) he produced his monumental edition of *Proverbs* and *Traditions*[1] (which unfortunately he never managed to complete); in 1915 he added his *Selection from the Songs of the Greek People*, while at the same time he was editing a periodical, *Laographia*, and at the end of his life he founded the Folklore Archives (which later belonged to the Academy of Athens). Our present interest in this matter is due to the fact that these researches of Politis revealed to writers at that time the rich world of popular tradition, in which they found not only a source of inspiration, but a deeper awareness of themselves. Drosinis acknowledged this in his autobiography, and so also did Palamàs.

Of the two poets of 1880 of whom we have made mention, Kambàs (1857–1932) produced nothing but that youthful volume; in the same year he went to Egypt, where he pursued a legal career. On the other hand George Drosinis (1859–1951) was to devote all his life to poetry. His second collection,

---

[1] *Μελέται περὶ τοῦ βίου καὶ τῆς γλώσσης τοῦ ἑλληνικοῦ λαοῦ, Παροιμίαι*, 4 vols., Athens, 1899–1902; *Παραδόσεις*, 2 vols., Athens, 1904. Photomechanical reproduction, Athens, 1965.

*Stalactites* (1881), does not differ essentially from his first; but the *Idylls* (1884) mark a definite advance. 'The *Verses* of Kambàs seemed to greet a new dawn', wrote Palamàs; 'the *Idylls* assured us of its arrival.'[1] The new generation was now mature, had passed through the phase of inquiry, and was ready to set in order what it had won. This collection of Drosinis also, for the first time, showed the beneficial influence of folklore.

Drosinis's collected volumes came out in quick succession. The two most characteristic of his prime are *Radiant Darkness* (1915) and *Closed Eyelids* (1918); the poet was then between fifty-five and sixty, and by this time Palamàs had already completed his poetical journey. But Drosinis was not influenced by his fellow traveller's course; in fact he followed no course, but remained always in the same limited field. His poetry is distinguished by human dignity, but is always too detailed and superficial. He lacks power of construction and his poems are rather poetical sketches; one single idea is made into a poem, with a natural and pleasing facility, and also with fineness and delicacy. In the collections of his later years another note is sounded, the touching fertility of his robust old age; the titles are characteristic: *Halcyon Days, Evening Draws On, Sparks in the Ashes*. Beside the sonorous voice of Palamàs, the quieter tone of Drosinis preserves its own elegant individuality. In 1925, in his poem addressed to Drosinis, Palamàs said:

> How else
> Can I name you? The fellow traveller . . .

Drosinis replied with modesty, though not without some complacency:

> Yes, fellow travellers, we made together
> Our first steps, in the dawn of Art's new day—
> Yet as the years went by, there was appointed
> To each of us his very different way.
>
> .    .    .    .    .
>
> For you stretched up to reach the laurel branches,
> I stooped to any plant that I could see;
> And you have won and wear your wreath of laurel—
> A little mountain thyme will do for me.[2]

---

[1] K. Palamàs, op. cit. (The continuation of the sentence cited above, p. 154 n. 1.)

[2] Palamàs, on sending him his volume *The Five-Syllables*, in Δειλοὶ καὶ Σκληροὶ Στίχοι (1928) (= Ἅπαντα, vol. 9, p. 215); Drosinis, in Φευγάτα Χελιδόνια (1936).

## KOSTÌS PALAMÀS

Kostìs Palamàs (1859–1943) was undoubtedly, of all the 'young' poets of 1880, the most representative of his generation, and is certainly one of the great poets of modern Greece. Though he was slow in declaring himself (his first collection of poems was published in 1886), he quickly rose above the average of the age and for fifty to sixty years was the central figure in the intellectual life of the country. These fifty to sixty years were particularly critical in the development of modern Greek culture. The small state of the first dynasty was spreading in area, was taking in more of the places that were historically Greek, and was internally strengthened by the government of Charilaos Trikoupis. The defeat of 1897 was, however, a serious setback, though it was also a stimulus to the progressive element. At the same time there was a great deal of intellectual progress. The literary world was enlarging its interests, and was extending them beyond the still narrow land of Greece. Palamàs stands in the forefront of this progress, not only because of his poetry but by reason of his criticism and his continued presence on the scene. If in this creative period the genius of Eleftherios Venizelos places him first in the field of politics, there is no doubt that a similar leading place in literature belongs to Kostìs Palamàs.

But was his poetical, his purely lyrical production on the same high level? Critics have often called this into question, and there is still doubt on the subject today. Much has been said of his grandiloquence, his lack of depth, of the absence of pure lyricism, and of his 'anti-poetical' character. Nevertheless, as time passes, the more established is the opinion that his lyrical contribution really was great, and in him Greek poetry attains a calibre unknown since the time of Solomòs. Naturally in the case of so extensive an output there are failings and unfortunate moments. These, however, should not incline the balance against him.

Critics have observed that a dualism exists in his poetical thought, and that he hovers between two poles, accepting or rejecting both at once: on the one hand energetic action, affirmation, faith, and on the other retirement, denial, disbelief. But all these contradictions revolve round one central point, which we may call 'the meaning of art': the outlook and the volition of the poet. His work moves between two extremes, in a major or in a minor key. There are poems that are more lyrical, where he writes of home, of retirement, of the 'immovable' life (what he called 'lyricism of the Me'), and others ('lyricism of the Us') in which he extends his range into large epic compositions and 'great visions'. In his own day his poetry in the major key was over-estimated; it appears that it is his poetry in the minor key that has better stood the test of time.

Kostìs Palamàs was born at Patras in 1859, where his father was a magistrate. At the age of seven he lost his parents and from then on was brought up in the house of an uncle at Missolonghi, the place from which the family came; in 1875, aged sixteen, he went to Athens to study, and began publishing poems in the journals of the time and in the *Rabagàs*, and in 1886, comparatively late, he brought out his first collected volume of verse, *The Songs of My Country*. In 1889 his long poem, *Hymn to Athena*, received the prize in the first 'Philadelphian' competition (N. G. Politis was the judge); this was like an official sanctioning of the new school of poetry. In 1890 Palamàs also received the prize in the second 'Philadelphian' competition; the collection, *Eyes of My Soul*, with a quotation from Solomòs as its title, shows how much he desired a fusion between the Athenian school, in which he had his roots, and the tradition of Solomòs, which he was now gradually discovering. Nevertheless his early volumes, whether they received prizes or no, do not yet express his personality; the poet is still struggling to free himself from the conventions and commonplaces of the time, and to set out on his own path.

This, we may say, was first achieved in *Countries*, a series of twelve fine Parnassian sonnets, first published in 1895 and later included in *Life Immovable*. Then one important stage in his work follows another: *Iambs and Anapaests* (1897), and *The Tomb* (1898). The former is a small collection of forty poems in similar metres: three quatrains in which iambic and anapaestic verse alternates —a breaking up of the traditional fifteen-syllable line, and at the same time a reminiscence of Kalvos, whose musical verse particularly fascinated Palamàs at this time. We also discern something else in this collection, the first appearance of 'symbolism' in Greek poetry; the vague and the undefined, the extension of the meaning of words that the French *Symbolistes* sought, are here in *Iambs and Anapaests*. Jean Moréas, the author of *Stances*, while in Athens on a visit, took notice of these short poems, and held them in high esteem.

*The Tomb* (1898) is also a small collection, and the poems are all on one subject, an elegy on the death of his little son. But the next collection, *Life Immovable* (1904), is one of his most important and one of the richest, including poems of the last decade, beginning with *Countries*, to which we made reference above. In compositions such as *The Return* or *Lines to a Well-Known Tune* the poet draws on reminiscences of his childhood and renders sounds 'that awake in him like sighs'. *The Palm-Tree*, a long poem in thirteen-syllable lines, is one of his most lyrical poems and, perhaps for this very reason, one of the most difficult to understand. It was written in 1900, and this year, the turning-point of one century into another, may be called a watershed in his poetry. In the years that followed, his inclination for large compositions, for 'great visions',[1] will be dominant. He will abandon the pure lyricism of *The Palm-Tree*. First among the 'great visions', *The Ascraean* (i.e. Hesiod), a long and inspired poem in the same collection, is an attempt at a synthetic approach to the world, and is influenced by mystic theories and by Orphism.

The most representative of these 'visions' is his great poem, *The Dodecalogue of the Gipsy* (1907), divided into twelve 'words' (parts), and in a variety of rhythms, among which an entirely original free trochaic verse is dominant. The gipsy, the central personage, follows the path of negation, of a complete nihilism with regard to everyone and everything, until finally a violin reconciles him with life. The symbolism could easily become too obvious, but the poet escapes this danger by the wide range of his poem, which is sometimes near to pure epic, and at other moments has happy flashes of genuine lyric inspiration. More-over the poet situated his action in a historical setting, on the eve of the fall of Constantinople, and this gives a richness of colour to its development; an interesting complication of the action is produced by an account of the flight of the Greek scholars from Constantinople to the West, and the burning of the works of the neo-Platonist Gemistòs-Plethon. In this manner (and it is this that is of most consequence) the ideas and problems

---

[1] *From the Great Visions* is the title of the last section of *Life Immovable*, which includes the lengthy poems 'The Ascraean' and 'The Chains'.

of the poem are connected with the anxieties and struggles of the poet's own time. The date of publication was ten years after the defeat of 1897, and five years before the Balkan wars; it falls within the first decade of our century, a decade marked by progress and tension (see Chapter XIV), and is its most authoritative poetical expression. People understood the words of the prophet in the eighth 'word' as being a prophecy about the nation:

> For thy ascension back where thou art called
> Thou wilt feel grow again, o joy!
> The wings,
> The wings of thy past glory.

At this time the learned world was discovering Byzantium, and this meant a further familiarity with the roots of Greek life; Byzantine history, literature and art were being studied, and this not only in Greece but also abroad (it will suffice to mention, for example, Krumbacher and Schlumberger). It was under the influence of *The Byzantine Epic* of the latter that Palamàs wrote another long epic composition, *The King's Flute* (1910), this also in twelve 'words', and in fifteen-syllable lines. It is a poetical appraisal of Byzantium at the height of its glory under the Macedonian dynasty and an account of the journey of Basil II into Greece proper as far as Athens (the symbol of the unity of the ancient with the Byzantine world, and of the continuity of modern Greek tradition). Palamàs considered this his most important work, but it may be doubted if poets are the best judges of their own works; the mere breadth of range is often fatiguing, the numerous innovations in the fifteen-syllable line end by destroying its traditional harmony, the manner of the poem is far more bookish than epic. But Palamàs's art is here seen at its full maturity, and in his handling of the language and the verse he introduces in a masterly way reminiscences both of learned and popular Byzantine texts (for instance, *Digenìs* and the *Erotopaignia*).

After these two large compositions, Palamàs collected what we might call his left-over lyrical poems in two volumes in 1912. These were *The Sorrows of the Lagoon*, and *The City and the Solitude*. The lagoon is that of Missolonghi, and the poems are lyrical reveries about his life there. This is where we find two of his most musical poems.

> I lived my early years, the unforgettable,
> By the seaside,
> There where the sea is shallow and calm,
> There where the sea is great and wide. ('A Bitterness')

> O songs of Smyrna, Janina, the City,
> Or you, long-drawn-out Anatolian ditty
> So full of woes,
> Ah, how my soul by you is torn apart!
> Out of your music moulded is my heart,
> And on your wings it goes. ('Orient')

*The City and the Solitude*—the title is characteristic of what we called Palamàs's dualism—contains poems either on national subjects (the whole last book refers to the 1912 war, which had just broken out), or expressing the 'secret speech' of the soul (the 'Scent of the Rose' is a minor masterpiece). The collection of 1915, *The Altars*, is more confined to the major key, and contains many long compositions. The poet himself wrote[1] that they 'complete *Life Immovable* in a more pathetic and more controlled tone; they are more dramatic in thought, and the verse is more polished'. It is a collection of his prime.

After *The City and the Solitude*, *Untimely Poems* (1918) suggest by their title that the poet thought their minor key ill adapted to a world that had just emerged from the First World War. The following volumes already show decline—the poet was over sixty. Often he republished old poems in a new recension or, following his passion for formal perfection, he devoted himself to the cultivation of one or another verse form: *The Fourteen Lines* (sonnets with a great deal of freedom in construction), *The Five-Syllables and the Pathetic Whispers* (1925). The *Timid and Cruel Verses* (asked for by friends in America, and published in Chicago in 1928) are, as he wrote in the prologue, 'taken out of the bottom of drawers and out of envelopes belonging to every period of my life'—they make no addition to our general picture of him; we might say the same of *Passings and Greetings* (1931), his

---

[1] In a draft for a preface to *The Altars*, published in his Ποιητική (1933) (= Άπαντα, vol. 10, p. 542).

penultimate collected volume. On the other hand *The Cycle of Quatrains* (1929) and even more *The Nights of Phemius* (1935), his last collection, are distinguished by a different point of view. The poet of the great epic compositions, who had so often been blamed for grandiloquence, was now trying his voice in the limited range of the quatrain. His voice, indeed, no longer had its former vigour: it was low and elderly; but its sadness and its nostalgic reverie make it particularly appealing, his voluntary self-limitation to the simple metrical form often increases its expressiveness, and by his elliptical character of expression they acquire an almost dramatic tension:

> The Lord's day: for a child, life by the shore,
> The joys of home, the teacher's holiday.
> Now I am waiting for the great Lord's day
> That is to give me rest for evermore.

*The Nights of Phemius* are dated 1931–2. Palamàs was silent for the last ten years of his life; a few intervals of brilliance were not enough to break the darkness and silence which oppressed him. He died in February 1943, during the enemy occupation. A crowd of people of every class and age gathered spontaneously at his funeral. His long and continuous service to poetry had made him a symbol, and those who did honour to the dead poet felt at the same time that they were making a mute but decisive act of resistance.

We may say that Palamàs was, first and foremost, a poet; his personality is fully expressed in his eighteen volumes of poetry. His prose work is not remarkable; of the few short stories that he published between 1884 and 1900 the most important is *A Man's Death*, where he exposes a typically Greek view of life and misfortune. His single theatrical work, *Trisevgeni* (1903), is particularly significant: a poetic drama in an age of realism in the theatre. The heroine is clearly drawn: an exceptional, uncompromising character whom other people do not understand, not even those who love her or are loved by her.

Finally, Palamàs wrote a number of articles in newspapers and periodicals; at one time, indeed, when he was pressed by financial need he wrote articles almost every day (in katharevousa, and signed 'W') in the paper *Embròs*. The admirable *Bibliography of Kostìs Palamàs* by George Katsimbalis enumerates

2,500 'essays, articles, or notes'. Some of these are of exceptional importance and merit preservation in the *Complete Works* now being issued by the Palamàs Foundation (sixteen volumes to date in 1971). Particular mention should be made of his polemical articles (he was always an advocate of the demotic language, and never wavered, even in difficult times), and also of his articles and essays on modern Greek literature. In a sense he is the first scholar of modern Greek letters; he wrote about all the personalities of modern Greek literature, and he spoke authoritatively and with the sharpness of a critic, the accuracy of a scholar, and the sensibility of a poet. He was the first to discover Kalvos, he wrote felicitous articles about Vilaràs and Typaldos, Markoràs and Krystallis, and (even in a time of hostility over the language question) he recognized the virtues of poets writing in katharevousa, such as Paparrigopoulos and Valavanis. These essays complete the picture, which we have already drawn, of Palamàs as an authoritative, responsible man of letters.

# XI

## PROSE AFTER 1880
## THE 'GENRE' STORY, THE LANGUAGE
## QUESTION, AND PSYCHARIS

### THE 'GENRE' STORY

THE CHANGE OF 1880 became a general intellectual movement. The flight from Romanticism and the attachment to
the familiar and concrete was especially favourable to prose,
which now abandoned the historical novel of the Athenian
school, and turned to the short story, particularly to what we
may call the 'genre' story, that is, one that describes the Greek
countryside, the villages, and their simple inhabitants. We may
say that this was the first appearance of a literary prose in
modern Greek literature; in the constricted framework of the
short story concentration upon one central character or one
episode permits a high state of literary finish. On the other hand,
the folklore movement opened the way towards the exploitation
of village life and the wealth of popular tradition.

In the borderland between historical novels and the genre
story we find the *Loukìs Laras* of D. Vikelas (1833–1909). We
have already met this writer among others slightly his senior,
wavering between the old and the new (see p. 153). He made his
fortune as a merchant in London (1852–72). From 1872 he lived
in Paris, was in contact with the Hellenists there, and influenced
scholarly research into earlier Greek literature. After 1896, when
he settled finally in Athens, he was intensely active socially and
intellectually, principally with the 'Society for the Distribution of
Useful Books', of which he was himself the founder. In his youth
he had translated many of the tragedies of Shakespeare, though
with no poetical feeling and in a flabby prosaic language; but

it was by these translations that the English poet was introduced to the Greek public.

In *Loukìs Laras* (first published in 1879) the plot develops during the revolution of 1821, but the hero does not play an active role in the events. It is the unromantic, realistic setting that is the most interesting in this book; moreover the characters, the style, and the language, a moderate katharevousa without the mannerism of Rangavìs or Pavlos Kalligàs, are consistent with the unromantic approach.

*Loukìs Laras* had a great success, it was translated into many languages and had a decisive influence upon future generations. Vikelas also, influenced by younger writers in his turn, wrote a series of genuine 'genre' stories in the decade 1880–90, where we discern the same lack of excess. The most successful, perhaps, is 'Papa-Narkissos', where with clarity and sympathy he depicts the character of a newly married priest who by means of his simplicity and natural goodness (the characteristics of most of Vikelas's heroes) manages to overcome the revulsion which he feels on seeing a dying man, and himself emerges a new man from the trial.

It was George Vizyinòs (1849–96) who really introduced the 'genre' story into modern Greek literature; we saw him as a poet wavering between the old and the new (p. 153). He was born in Vizyi, a small village in eastern Thrace. After a penurious youth in Constantinople and Cyprus, the help of a rich Greek living abroad enabled him to study in comfort in Athens and later in Germany (1874–82); he studied philosophy and psychology and took a doctorate at Leipzig in 1881. A visit to Paris and acquaintance with Vikelas turned him towards the short story, and in only two years, 1883 and 1884, he had already published most of his tales. He became assistant professor at the University of Athens in 1884 with his thesis on *The Philosophy of Beauty according to Plotinus* (Athens, 1884); he also wrote psychological essays and educational handbooks until 1892, when mental illness put an end to his career.

'My Mother's Sin' is Vizyinòs's first story—and the first modern Greek short story. The central figure of the mother (his own mother) who in her sleep unwittingly smothered her small daughter, and who was tortured by this 'sin' all her life, is drawn with all its tragedy and its human tenderness. Other stories also

draw upon the writer's recollections and render the background
of Thracian village life, which derives a colour of its own from
the coexistence of Greek and Turkish elements and the warm
human relations that often unite people from the two races.
They are few in number, and often exceed the limits of the short
story. In most of them the psychological description of the
people is excellent, there is firmness of composition and graceful
narration. The language is the katharevousa then still usual in
prose, but the demotic dialogue, enriched with many northern
Greek dialectal elements, gives a special liveliness.

In 'The One Journey of His Life' he draws the tender picture
of a grandfather, seen through the admiring eyes of the grandson–
narrator—the grandfather who knew so many tales about strange
and distant lands, but had never actually travelled further than
the nearest hill outside his village. But without doubt his masterpiece is the lengthy story of 'Moskov Selim'—the tale of a worthy
Turk to whom his own people (family and compatriots) had
given nothing but bitterness and disappointment, and who finds
humanity and love from the Russians, by whom he was taken
prisoner. The hero is an 'outsider', considered mad because of
his love for Russians, to which is owed his nickname, Moskov
Selim. His moving story is told by his own mouth, and is therefore in a simple and lively demotic.

The appearance of Vizyinòs's stories in 1883 seemed to give
a signal, and in the five following years most of the well-known
story writers published their first stories. They came at the
right time. In the same year, 1883, the established periodical
*Estia* (which supported the modernist movements) announced
a competition for a short story, on a Greek theme; the selection
committee consisted of E. Roidis, S. Lambros, and N. G. Politis.
Drosinis won the prize and M. Mitsakis (then a boy of fifteen)
was *proxime accessit*. The competition was repeated in the following year, with less satisfying results; nevertheless the *proxime
accessit* was won by Gregorios Xenopoulos, and this was his first
appearance in literature.

Drosinis wrote other short stories and also impressions and
memoirs; he attempted too a longer narrative work, *Amaryllis*
(1885), which met with a good deal of success. But the best of
Drosinis is his lyric poetry. (An odd but not altogether successful
return to prose in his later years was his *Ersi* (1922).) As we have

seen, Palamàs also wrote stories during those years, and so did Polylàs, who belonged to another age and school (see pp. 132–3). Among the earliest we may mention E. Lykoudis (1849–1925), Dimitrios Kambouroglou (1852–1942) who was chiefly engaged upon the history of Athens and whose tales are mainly historical, and J. Damvergis (1862–1938) who gave typical pictures of Cretan life (collected in *My Cretans,* 1898). Merely to give the names of the many other short-story writers would serve no purpose.

Out of the many writers of short stories two are distinguished for their particular devotion to the 'genre' story: they are Alexandros Papadiamantis and Andreas Karkavitsas. The first and elder (1851–1911) made his appearance with historical and adventure novels (1879), but then went over to the 'genre' story, to which he devoted himself almost exclusively for a quarter of a century. His tales, which exceed 200 in number, are not on the same level; many are only hasty sketches or 'snapshots', others are more like essays than stories. But the successful stories are many and remarkable. Almost all of them describe events and human characters to be found on his island, Skiathos; and the writer's homesickness gives them life and movement. Nostalgia is the permanent basic element in Papadiamantis; it is his strength and his weakness. Since his own time his work has been the object of criticism, which sometimes went so far as excessive praise and admiration, and at others erred as far in the opposite direction by underestimating him. Hostile criticism picked on the loose construction of his stories, the absence of plan, the lack of artistic intention. In a large degree these objections are sound; but the lack of construction is usually owing to the nature of his nostalgia and reverie; the ideas, not bound by any pre-determined plan, follow the course of reverie—and this very lack of connection is a virtue and has charm. As with many painters, Papadiamantis's main strength lay in the free sketch. On the other hand, beyond an underlying tendency for the 'genre' style, he had caught many aspects of the modern Greek character that are not easily caught, and had captured something of what might be called 'modern Greek popular mythology'. His child-hood years on the island, his bond through his father, a priest, and through other members of his family, with the world of Orthodoxy (he himself was a cantor, and he loved to take part in

all-night services), his retiring life in Athens, and his companion-
ship with humble people, all give an authority to his accounts.
They go deeper than mere 'genre' tales, or folkloristic studies,
and it is this that his supporters admired.

In language, unlike many others of his generation, Papadiamantis made no decisive step from katharevousa to demotic. His
katharevousa, however, is entirely personal, individual, and in-
consistent. What has been said about the influence of the language
of the Church upon Papadiamantis is irresponsible and without
proof. I should say there were three levels in his language: in
dialogue he uses the popular spoken language, almost photo-
graphically recorded, and often with idioms from Skiathos. In
the narration there is another language, based indeed on katharevousa, but with an admixture of many demotic elements (and
this is his most individual style); finally there is a pure katharevousa, the traditional prose language of the earlier generation,
which Papadiamantis reserves for his descriptions and his lyrical
digressions.

From his abundant output we may set aside stories that are
hardly more than mediocre. Before 1900, 'The Homesick
Woman' and 'Round the Lake' stand out, the latter for its strikingly poetical tone; so does the long story 'Guardian of the In-
fected Ships', which is like a picture with many figures in it, with
the mother and her love in the centre, and 'Love in the Snow'
with its lyrical melancholy. After 1900 the lyric tone dominates,
and to this period belong the much-read 'Dream on the Wave',
'Reverie on 15 August', and the longest of them, which is like a
lyric confession, 'Rosy Shores'. But the work of his last decade, if
not the most personal, is the most powerful: *The Murderess* (1903).
The central figure in this long story is Frangogiannoù (the murderess); she is now sixty years old and, as she thinks over the past,
she realizes that woman is always a slave, first to her parents, then
to her husband, then to her children, and then to their children.
Thus she conceives the idea of killing little girls, to spare them all
this trouble. With this fixed idea in her mind she accomplishes a
series of murders; the police are after her, she seeks sanctuary in
a church near the sea, and drowns 'on an isthmus that joined the
rock of the hermitage with the mainland, half way between divine
and human justice'. *The Murderess* is a powerful work; this woman
with her perverted mind, who puts herself outside human society,

is an enigmatic figure and altogether unlike the islanders who people the other stories; they may be crafty, but are always good-hearted. The psychological description is given with a quite different fullness; the construction is compact and more care is taken over the artistic execution.

Andreas Karkavitsas (1866–1922), his junior by fifteen years, is in many ways different from Papadiamantis; he is the second most important exponent of the 'genre' story. He was born in Lechaenà in Elis, a small Peloponnesian town; by profession he was an army doctor and had the opportunity to know Greek village life (especially in Roumeli) at first hand, and also to know Greek sailors; he drew on both these subjects in his stories.

In 1885, before he was twenty, he began publishing 'genre' stories in periodicals, and he collected them into a volume: *Stories* (1892). They were written, naturally, in the katharevousa usual at the time. But the emergence of Psycharis in 1888 influenced him decisively, and already in the introduction to the *Stories* he condemns the language in which they are written. Thenceforward he was to write only in demotic, a demotic that he cultivated with all the zeal of a convert. His extravagantly coloured epithets, his recherché compounds, and his persistent exploitation of the language of demotic poetry may seem faults to us today, but they were absolutely natural in an age that had done little to cultivate the artistic elements of prose writing. His linguistic study led to the creation of a particularly polished style —unlike that of Papadiamantis—where his artistic intention is obvious. Perhaps his style is Karkavitsas's chief contribution to prose.

He himself collected his later stories into two volumes: *Words from the Prow* (1899, his sea stories) and *Old Loves* (1900); they certainly belong to the 'genre' type. They are not characterized by a nostalgia and reverie like those of Papadiamantis so much as by accurate observation and a psychological strength; there is in general a realistic tone, which sometimes goes so far as roughness. His energy sometimes exceeds the limits of the short tale and leads him into more complicated stories and novels. In the still early *Lygerì* (first published in 1890), set in the plain of Elis, we already have firm characterization and a happy end with a bitter tang to it. His best work is undoubtedly *The Beggar* (1896); the central character is a professional beggar from

Kravara near Naupactus, who gets rich by exploiting the misery and ignorance of the villagers of Thessaly that had just come under Greek rule. The novel is a dark picture of human baseness on the one hand, and of misery on the other, and at the same time an inexorable criticism of the society of his time (we must remember it was in 1896, just before the disaster of 1897). The literary merits of the work are of a like kind, the style and language are highly polished, the construction is firm, and the descriptions effective (for example, that of the fire which destroyed the bey's residence).

*The Beggar* is Karkavitsas's finest achievement; his next novel, *The Archaeologist* (1904), was a failure. The burning satire of *The Beggar* here turns to a cold and obvious allegory, which neither moves nor convinces. Had he exhausted his creative talent, and given all he had to give in the tales and *The Beggar*? Karkavitsas wrote no more for the rest of his life.

### THE LANGUAGE QUESTION AND PSYCHARIS

An event which was one of the most important in the decade now under consideration (1880–90) and which had a decisive influence not only on literature but on intellectual life in general, was the appearance of *My Journey* by Psycharis in 1888, with his revolutionary declaration in favour of the demotic language. After 1880 demotic had already become completely dominant in poetry; prose, however, was still written in katharevousa, which moreover was now, after fifty years of cultivation, predominant in all forms of intellectual life. But in those years of renaissance and new maturity it was natural that the spirit of change should enter this sphere which was never altogether peaceful. Thus, during the decade 1880–90, the language question again became acute, and demanded an immediate solution.

In 1882 the *Observations on the Language* of K. Kontos (1834–1909) were published in Athens, summing up what he had elsewhere published separately. He was a philologist, a pupil of the Dutchman Cobet, and professor at the university since 1868; he was a strange reincarnation in the nineteenth century of the 'Atticists' of late classical times; his linguistic teaching is the highest summit reached by the archaism which we have seen at work in the years 1830–80. The book was attacked by another classical philologist and university professor, who was also a creative writer, D. Vernardakis (see p. 149). His *Critique of Pseudo-Atticism* attacked the 'Atticism' of Kontos and asked for a gradual return to the popular language. A younger scholar took part in the argument, G. N. Chatzidakis (1848–1941), who was to be the founder of modern Greek linguistics. His position was at first ambiguous: he was against Vernardakis and supported Kontos, but recognized the rights of demotic. (Later Chatzidakis was to turn definitely against the demotic movement.) The dispute was becoming more bitter on either side until Psycharis appeared, at first with minor publications and then with *My Journey* (1888). Then the situation was radically changed.

Jannis Psycharis (1854–1929)—he preferred to call himself just 'Psycharis'—was of Chiot origins, born at Odessa, and educated in Constantinople. At the age of fifteen he went to Paris, and after sound philological studies there and in Germany, he taught modern Greek from 1885 at the École des Hautes Études (and from 1904 at the École des Langues Orientales Vivantes as the successor of É. Legrand). In the growth of his ideas his acquaintanceship with Taine and Renan played an important role (his wife was Renan's daughter); he remained in Paris all his life and occupied a central place in French intellectual circles. His was a many-sided and rich nature. A French citizen and a Greek patriot, a writer and a scholar, he was never an amateur in anything; on the contrary he always showed in all his activities a complete devotion, an insistence upon his own ideas, and a refusal to compromise that often went so far as obstinacy and fanaticism. Thus his position in the language question is decisive, daring, and uncompromising; he declared from the first that there was no need to wait, that demotic must be written everywhere, in prose and verse, and according to all its rules, in grammar and form, without any yielding to the established usage. Although the experience of the subsequent eighty years has obliged writers of the demotic language to make certain concessions that Psycharis rejected, it must be acknowledged, to his credit, that by his firm and bold position he promoted a decisive advance in the language question, which has had a continuous effect on all Greek intellectual life. Psycharis was undoubtedly the leader of 'demoticism', and his direct and indirect influence on his contemporaries and those who came after was immeasurable. With Palamàs, he is the most significant figure of the time.

Endowed as he was with a rich nature, Psycharis wrote many literary works; his creative ability is not insignificant, though it is not there that his real importance and value are to be found. His literary gift is at once clear in the *Journey*, which is pleasant to read. Of his purely literary work the most successful is *The Dream of Gianniris* (1897), a sort of beautified autobiography, which contains (especially in the second part) pages full of lyricism. He was influenced by the literary movements in France and attempted the psychological novel (*Life and Love in Solitude* (1904), *The Two Brothers* (1911), *Agnì* (1913), etc.), but he was not successful. Living far from Greece he could not adapt himself to the contemporary phase of modern Greek letters, then successfully going through the stage of the 'genre' story. On the contrary, Psycharis managed to create an entirely personal style in some of his lyrical prose writing (a sort of song in prose), where the tenderness of his feelings finds complete expression in the melodious delicacy of the language.

In 1888 Alexandros Pallis and Argyris Eftaliotis were working together in Bombay at the commercial house of Ralli Brothers; they had already met in Manchester. They were having lively discussions about language and literature when Psycharis's *Journey* reached those parts. Pallis was enthusiastic and gave it to Eftaliotis as soon as he had read it; 'just what I told you; read it and see'.[1] From thenceforth until their death they had a close friendship with Psycharis; they were the most orthodox writers of the school of Psycharis. All three were much the same age, and they were the most militant champions of demoticism.

The work of Pallis (1851–1935) is not voluminous. He was of Epirot origins and studied philology in Athens (his first publication was a critical edition of the *Antigone*); he went abroad very young and devoted himself to a commercial career (1869 Manchester, 1875 Bombay, 1894 Liverpool). In 1889 he published *Little Songs for Children*; he published his few poems in 1907 with the title *Lute and Stick*—the odd title means lyric and satirical poems. For Pallis poetry was really a hobby, a skilled amateur activity, though we pause over his lyric poems with

---

[1] Quoted by Eftaliotis himself in an autobiographical note: ‘Η ζωή μου, in *Νουμᾶς*, 8 (1910), no. 374 (= Ἅπαντα, ed. G. Valetas, vol. 2, Athens, 1962, p. 29).

their delicacy and grace and their demotic rhythm, and his satirical poems (especially the bitter poems called 'Tombstones') have verve and force. Pallis above all used his literary talent in translation: he has given us Euripides, Shakespeare, and Thucydides in translation, and also Kant—to show the possibility of using demotic for so difficult a text. He himself collected his minor works, poems, articles, and translations in a volume which he jestingly entitled *Bad Nuts* (1915). His two greatest achievements were the translation of the Gospels (which caused riots in opposition to it in Athens in 1901) and above all that of the *Iliad*. This was Pallis's life work. In its time it was praised and admired but also much condemned. Pallis proceeded from the assumption (then entertained by many scholars) that the Homeric poems were a popular creation, and he proceeded boldly to turn the epic into a contemporary demotic song, using the language and other features of the Greek traditional song. A version of this sort would not be tolerable today, and his popularized forms for names ('Leniò' for Helen, and 'Vrymedos') now annoy us in a different way from that in which they annoyed the reactionary circles of his time. But we must admit that, with his translation, Pallis succeeded in his aims, and that the 'faultless decapentesyllables' (as Palamàs called them)[1] are a creatively renewed form of the demotic song, while their robust style is highly suitable to the masculine art of the original. The translation of the *Iliad* is perhaps the most significant achievement of the generation of the first demoticists. One might call it the symbol of faith of that generation.

If the Epirot Pallis is distinguished by a Doric robustness, the islander Kleanthis Michaïlidis, known to literature by his pseudonym Argyris Eftaliotis (1849–1923), is marked by the sweetness of his nature. He was born in Mytilene, and he also went abroad young, to Manchester, Liverpool, and finally Bombay, where we saw him with Pallis. In his later years he sought a milder climate at Antibes, and died there aged seventy-four.

He first made his appearance with a collection of poems, *Songs of Exile* (exile was always his chief grief and the principal subject of his work), with which he was *proxime accessit* in the first 'Philadelphian' competition of 1889. (On that occasion the *Hymn*

---

[1] See the dedication of *The King's Flute* to Pallis.

*to Athena* of Palamàs won the prize; it was a year after the *Journey*
of Psycharis.) The songs are in the usual Parnassian mood, but
they are noteworthy for an individual sense of rhythm which
gives them an unusual charm and lightness. But in his next
collection Eftaliotis goes beyond this stage of 'descriptive music'.
The *Words of Love*, a series of sonnets addressed to his wife, and
clearly influenced in form and matter by Shakespeare's sonnets,
are distinguished by a rich and genuine lyricism (which does not
express the passion of love, but the contentment of married life),
and by the highly-wrought poetical language which goes beyond
the simple demotic of his first songs and becomes a more subtle
implement, able to render the high tone of his feeling and its
lightest nuances. The sonnets received no prize. The committee,
with Angelos Vlachos as president, could not properly appreciate
these particular virtues; but criticism took notice of them,
Palamàs devoted a series of articles to them, and the revered
Polylàs also wrote a series of articles about them entitled *Our
Literary Language* (see p. 133).

After the sonnets, Eftaliotis rarely occupied himself with
poetry, and devoted himself mainly to prose. As early as 1889 he
published stories which were collected in a volume in 1894 with
the title *Island Tales*. They are short 'genre' stories of varying
length, describing the peaceful life of the people on his island
with an exile's nostalgia. They may lack psychological force,
but Eftaliotis has the compensating merit of a narrative charm
and ease ('he is a king of narrators', Psycharis said),[1] and his
characters are rendered with infinite sympathy (e.g. the title-roles
in 'Marinos Kontaras' and 'Stravokostaina'), and the language
is genuine, warm demotic (he was the first prose writer after
Psycharis to write exclusively in demotic). His second work, *The
Pamphlets of Gerodimos* (1897), has many of the virtues of his first,
but also a tiresomely didactic tendency. Later, particularly after
1897, he turned to historical studies, which led to his *History of the
Romaic People* (1901), which was a failure; trying to be historical
and literary at the same time, he succeeded in neither. Eftaliotis
had a narrative talent and the capacity to rise above his personal
recollections and nostalgia for the island. With *The Olive Gatherer*
(1900) he gave us a well-constructed story, perfect in language

[1] In the dedication to Eftaliotis of his volume of short stories *In the Shade of a
Plane-Tree*, Athens, 1911.

and literary expression. In a Cretan village, with Greek and Turkish inhabitants, he sets a crowd of varied characters in motion and weaves a drama out of their contrast. The central character, the beautiful Asimo, an olive gatherer, has been dishonoured and becomes, as it were, the pawn of a diabolical destiny, a creature of antisocial habits and an instrument of the powers of evil, like the *Beggar* or the *Murderess*.

Eftaliotis's one dramatic work, *The Ghost*, makes not unsuccessful use of the moving demotic song *The Dead Brother*, but it has never been performed. In 1914 he began to translate the *Odyssey*, with Pallis's translation of the *Iliad* as his model; but the *Odyssey* of Eftaliotis has all the faults and none of the virtues of Pallis's work; it was a failure.

### YOUNGER PROSE WRITERS: GR. XENOPOULOS

The three writers, Psycharis and his two followers, lived permanently out of Greece. But the intellectuals in Greece had to adapt themselves to the realities of their time—and this was no misfortune. One of the most productive of these was Gregorios Xenopoulos (1867–1951) from Zakynthos. He gave much attention to the 'genre' story, but he soon began to write his first novels, which form the greater part of his work. Above all a professional writer, he wrote a great number of works, as well as articles, criticism, essays, etc. This immense productivity naturally affected the quality of his work, in which signs of carelessness are frequent, and also a pandering to the taste of the average reader (and sometimes of a reader below the average). But as well as these faults criticism has recognized (and it is clearly seen in his better work) a narrative facility, a sharpness of observation, and a faultless technique. His novels are influenced by realism and naturalism; he himself recognized Balzac and Zola as his masters, as well as Dickens and Daudet. He must also be credited with the great advance that modern Greek literature made, through him, from the limitations of the 'genre' story to the complicated novel of town life. Nor is it without significance that Xenopoulos was read by a very wide public, and thus increased the general interest in literature.

The setting of Xenopoulos's novels is sometimes in Athens and sometimes in Zakynthos; the writer wished to describe Greek society of his time both in the capital and in the province. In his first two novels (1888, 1890) he described the Athenian world, while in those that followed (*Margarita Stefa*, 1893, and *The Red Rock*, 1905) he gave a successful picture of life in Zakynthos. The first of these was the last book he wrote in katharevousa; the rest of his work is in demotic, but an easy demotic near the everyday speech. Three of his best works have a Zantiot subject (*Laura*, 1915, *Anadyomeni*, 1923, *Teresa Varma Dakosta*, 1925). The works which the critics have acknowledged as undoubtedly the best out of his many novels (twenty were issued as books and others came out in newspapers and periodicals) are *Rich and Poor* (1919) and *Honest and Dishonest* (1921). They belong to a 'social trilogy' (the third, *Fortunate and Unfortunate*, 1924, is not on the same level), in which the writer endeavours to examine social problems, and does so with success.

His dramatic works are also of importance (see Chapter XIV). Under the influence of Ibsen he issued his first plays in about 1900. From all his work, and he wrote a lot, we shall pick out *The Secret of Countess Valeraina* (1904), *Stella Violanti* (1909), which has a subject like that of *The Basil Plant* of Matesis, and the one-act play *All Souls' Day* (1911) whose dramatic tone is heightened by the power of the dead over the living.

Joannis Kondylakis from Crete (1861–1920) was more or less contemporary with Xenopoulos. He also was a professional writer, did much work as a journalist, and cultivated an individual style in essays (under the *nom de plume* 'Wayfarer'). As a man of letters he first appeared with the 'genre' story at the time when that form was flourishing (1884). But like Xenopoulos (and under his influence) he went on to the more tightly knit naturalistic novel: *Les Misérables of Athens* (1894) is a broad picture of the underworld of Athens, drawn with an indubitable narrative skill and abundant technique, but with much exaggeration and many improbabilities, to which he resorted to gain a popular reading public. His best work is *Patouchas* (1892), where the life of a Cretan village is portrayed with much charm, and there is a successful depiction of unsophisticated love, and of the delightful gaucherie of the eighteen-year-old hero. At the end of his life, using demotic for the first time, he wrote a lyrical novel *First Love* (1920) drawing on his early memories of Crete.

Unlike Xenopoulos and Kondylakis, who began with the

'genre' story and went on to the urban novel, others who were more or less contemporary with them were more faithful to the 'genre' story. Jannis Vlachogiannis (1867–1945), from Naupactus, published three tales in 1893 under the pseudonym of Jannos Epachtitis, and they attracted the notice of Palamàs. Vlachogiannis also interested himself in historical research; he saved many of the archives of the revolution of 1821, and (among other things) gave us an exemplary edition of the *Memoirs* of Makrygiannis. Many of his tales (particularly the shorter ones, written for children) revive the times of 1821 and the struggles of the Suliots. They are all written in uncompromising demotic, and the earlier tales have many Roumeliot dialect words, while in others the prose is rhythmical. The better of the later stories have delicate psychological nuances, such as the youthful love in *The Cock* (1914), or the devotion of a popular karagiozis player to his art, in one of his most mature tales, *The Bitterness of Art* (1935).

The Epirot Christos Christovasilis (1855–1937) remained more exclusively attached to the 'genre' story and to folklore; he settled in Janina in his later years. A. Travlantonis (1867–1943), an educationalist, also had a gift for narrative; he wrote in pure demotic, but lacked the power to create an individual style. His characters are simple people and the circumstances of their life lack interest. His one novel, *Pillage of a Life* (1936), is in the same sort of setting.

The prose of M. Mitsakis (1868–1916) is in a class of its own; in his tales (if we can call them tales) the story plays little part; what interests the writer, a true pupil of the naturalist school, is the description and faithful rendering of actuality, and at the same time the creation of a style distinguished for its sophistication. His language is unstable and mixed, and he made the experiment of translating a tale of his own from katharevousa into demotic. He did not write much and after 1896 he had a mental disorder, but notice was taken of his work by both his contemporaries and juniors.

## THE THEATRE

The modernist, realist tendency of the generation of 1880 had a beneficial effect on the theatre, that is, on theatrical performances. Contemporary plays were seldom performed, apart from

the tragedies of Vernardakis which were always successful. But
for about ten years from 1888 a new kind of play, the 'Comidyll',
was popular, a sort of comedy with songs introduced. This form
undoubtedly was due to the same wish to get away from
Romanticism and to get nearer to everyday life. The heroes are
men of the people, their language is demotic prose, the 'genre'
and folklore elements play a large role, but at the same time the
influence of naturalism is very obvious. The first real musical of
this type is *The Fortune of Maroula* by D. Koromilàs (1850–98),
which at once had an astonishing success. Previously, between
1874 and 1888, Koromilàs had published twenty-three theatrical
works of a quite different and more 'learned' kind; later he wrote
a 'dramatic' idyll, *The Lover of the Shepherdess* (1891), in bombastic
decapentesyllables, with a prettified (and rather falsified) picture
of pastoral life in the mountains. (The motif was continued in
*Golfo* by S. Peresiadis (1894) which became a popular entertain-
ment.) The real 'Comidyll' was charmingly continued by
D. Kokkos (1836–91) with the *Lyre of Old Nicolas* and *Captain
Giakoumìs*.

This lively and popular form did not last long: theatrical
historians date its eclipse from 1896 onwards. The theatre, moreover, was being revived by other forces, of which the influence of
Ibsen was the most important; the theatrical works of G. Kambysis and the theatre of ideas of the early Xenopoulos are the
first signs of this influence (see Chapter XIV).

# XII

## POETRY OF PALAMÀS'S TIME
## AND AFTER

FOR FIFTY TO SIXTY YEARS after 1880 Palamàs was the dominant figure in poetry. We may speak of three stages in poetry: poetry before, contemporary with, and after Palamàs. Of those poets who started out with him, Kambàs, as we said, was almost immediately silent, while Drosinis followed his own way. Of the others (see p. 153) Sourìs lapsed into metrical journalism and J. Polemis (1862–1924) cultivated a facile poetry, feeble both in language and prosody and poor in ideas, a poetry that leaves nothing unsaid and is directly addressed to the reader of average or less than average intelligence. It is not fortuitous that he was one of the first to condemn Palamàs for obscurity; Palamàs, however, in what appeared on the face of it to be a favourable criticism of one of his collections (1888),[1] struck a mortal blow at his weaknesses: 'fanciful, unstudied poetry, in easy, intelligible verse with pretty rhymes . . .'

Those who were a little younger walked level with Palamàs, 'under his heavy shadow' (to quote a happy phrase of K. Dimaràs);[2] nevertheless, each has his distinguishing characteristics. One of the most individual was Kostas Krystallis (1868–94). He started life in an Epirot village from which the Turkish authorities obliged him to flee, and when about twenty years of age he published two small and rather insignificant 'epyllia', in which the influence of Valaoritis was obvious. His chief poetical work is to be found in two collections, *Poems of the Fields*, which won a prize in the second 'Philadelphian' competition of 1890, and *The Singer of the Village and the Pasture*, which won

---

[1] Palamàs, Ἅπαντα, vol. 2, p. 460.
[2] 'Under the heavy shadow of Palamàs' is the title of the last part of his *History* concerning the years 1890–1922.

the prize in 1892. Two years later, aged 26, the poet died of tuberculosis.

The chief characteristic of his two collections is the strong and exclusive influence of the demotic songs, whose fresh sap this young villager has introduced pure and unadulterated into his own poems. In his first collection many of the poems are hardly distinguishable from demotic songs, and Krystallis never hesitated to incorporate lines of these into his own poems. This was what astonished the Athens of 1890 and won him the praise of the critics. But his poetry was condemned for the same reason: he did not transform the demotic song creatively, but imitated it rather slavishly. Moreover, they objected, the world of the genuine demotic song is infinitely deeper and richer than that expressed by his poetry (this was the criticism of J. Apostolakis).[1]

This severe judgement, in which many of the younger critics concurred, needs perhaps some revision. We shall form a juster idea of Krystallis's contribution if we do not try to compare it with the original. Naturally the world of Krystallis is different from that of the demotic songs—how could it not be? On the other hand, his poetry is not so slavish an imitation as appears at first sight. It is strong and robust, with much personal art, exploiting the strength and vigour of the demotic song. Moreover, the carefully controlled use of dialect words is an added charm, and the sign of no ordinary poet. If we consider the poems of Krystallis in their own time, when Palamàs, hardly ten years older, was still at the early stage represented by *The Eyes of My Soul*, and the exploitation of the demotic songs had so far yielded nothing but the polished sweetness of Drosinis's *Idylls*, we shall form a truer picture of the contribution made by this poet, who died so young, to modern Greek poetry. Lines as full of meaning as the following (from the posthumously published *Psomopatis*) were not a common thing in the poetry of 1890:

> When bent beneath the chilly dew and almost frozen dead
> The April flower in the fields remains there all the night,
> And when the sun beams kiss it in the early hour of dawn
> At once it feels its warmth again, and gently thaws and melts,
> So Chryso melted . . .

---

[1] J. Apostolakis, *'Ο Κρυστάλλης καὶ τὸ δημοτικὸ τραγούδι*, Thessaloniki, 1937.

Krystallis died in 1894. In 1895, as we have seen, the period of Palamàs's prime began, chiefly with his sonnets *Countries*. It was a particularly favourable time for the cultivation of this form of verse so dear to Parnassianism. A distinguished, delicate sonneteer was the Corfiot Lorentsos Mavilis (1860–1912). He was fortunate in the breadth of his culture, being first educated in Corfu, then for fifteen whole years in German universities, where, besides studying literature, he was initiated into the philosophy of Kant, Fichte, and Schopenhauer (the last of whom particularly influenced him). He also studied Sanskrit and Indian philosophy and translated passages from the *Mahabharata*. He wrote his early poems during his student years, but he turned more to poetry after his return from Germany in 1893, when he settled in Corfu ; his most popular sonnets were written from 1895 to 1900 : 'Forgetfulness', 'Kallipateira', 'Twilight', 'Olive Tree'.

In these few sonnets all Mavilis's poetical contribution is summed up. It is one of the rare examples of a small poetical output having great importance. For the sonnets of Mavilis, faultlessly wrought, have really a central position in modern Greek poetry. The language is full, the verse carefully polished, 'rich' (in the technical meaning of the word) in its rhymes. The poetical thought is as clear and crystalline as the verse. The pessimist tone of Indian philosophy and the influence of Schopenhauer have not tainted the freshness of the poet's immediate contact with reality. An 'amateur', like his master Polylàs, he pours into his verse an exalted moral and human nobility that characterized him all his life. It was therefore entirely consistent that he should take part in the struggles of Crete in 1896 and of Epirus in 1897, and that at the age of fifty-two he should wear the uniform of the Garibaldi Officer Corps, and die on the battlefield outside Janina in 1912.

In 1895, the year that Palamàs published his *Countries*, Joannis Gryparis also made a triumphant appearance in modern Greek poetry with a series of sonnets. Gryparis (1870–1942) was a Cycladean from Siphnos; he grew up and was educated in Constantinople, where in 1895 he was a master in a secondary school and at the same time edited a literary periodical. Next year he settled permanently in Greece and had a career as a teacher; later he became a higher Civil Servant and finally director of the National Theatre. His sonnets, under the general title *Scarabs*, made a great impression, as soon as they were published, because of their artistic polish and their resonant language with many rare words and newly-coined compounds:

> Come forward incense-breathing morn who puts the dreams to flight,
> And drive away from near me all the shadows of a shade;
> Come forward morn, and put to sleep the visions sleep has made,
> Which while I sleep are wakened by the nighthag's sleepless might.

Gryparis had a poet's feeling for language, he knew the language of the people well and also how to make use of popular medieval literature, while on the other hand he creatively absorbed the teachings of the pure Parnassianism of Hérédia or Théophile Gautier. Their influence is clearly seen on all his decapentesyllabic *Scarabs*, and also in the hendecasyllabic *Terracottas* (their influence is even seen in the recherché titles). But in *Intermedia* (1899–1901) he was turning towards the technique of the Symbolistes; his verse became freer and more musical, his images more strikingly suggestive. In *Tryphon and Chrysofrydi* he made an individual use of legends drawn from medieval books and popular tradition, and his language became warmer and more concrete. His most mature poems are certainly the three *Elegies* (1902–9), filled with an undefined grief and disappointment, with deeper and purer tones, which become in the 'Vestals' (the most important of the three) dramatic and self-revelatory:

> But once the sacred fire is out it is not lit again
> By human tinder or match . . .

The 'Vestals' closes the poet's creative period, and forms a close to his one collection *Scarabs and Terracottas*, put together ten years later (1919). 'Once the sacred fire was out' the poet stopped writing. He turned his unusual linguistic power and his sensibility to the translation of ancient tragedies, particularly to his admirable translations of Aeschylus.

In the last years of the century there was a greater tendency towards 'Symbolism'. We have already seen it in Gryparis and Palamàs. The short-lived periodical *Techni* (1898–9) expressed the new tendencies, under the editorship of K. Chatzopoulos, as did later *Dionysos* (1901–2) which continued in the same line under the editorship of Chatzopoulos's brother Dimitrios and J. Kambysis. The two periodicals wished to transcend the narrow national framework and wanted to direct themselves towards foreign literatures, particularly English and German, but also Scandinavian and Russian. The most thorough representative of Symbolism, K. Chatzopoulos (1868–1920), had published two early collections of verse in 1898; he was to issue two more (*Simple Ways* and *Evening Legends*) in 1920, the year of his death. Meanwhile, from 1900 till the First World War he had lived in Germany, and therefore the influence of German and of northern literature in general is clear in his work. In Germany he attached himself to the socialist movement, and wished to propagate it in Greece, connecting social ideology with the renovating tendencies of demoticism. His prose work was important; he brought out a series of tales and novels between 1910 and 1917 (see p. 211). His literary translations are of particular quality, especially those from the German (*Faust*, etc.).

In his poetry, following the teaching of the Symbolists, he pursued his effects through indefinite images and the musical charm of the verse. The dominant tone is that of vague, elegiac reverie, and there is an absence of the concrete. The same atmosphere prevails both in his early and his mature collections. Despite the greater artistry of the verse in the latter, there is no change in their dominant tone, upon which the poet skilfully weaves a large number of musical variations; but the monotony becomes tiring in the end:

> Of pain I am born;
> And I spread and I spread
> And beyond I am spread
> And around I am spread
> On the shores, in the deeps,
> My fragments to sow.

The poem goes on the same way for many verses more. Its title is typical, 'The Legend of the Fog', and so is the title of the collection, *Evening Legends*.

Lambros Porfyras (1879–1932) also came from the *Techni* circle, and his few poems are Symbolist; there is in them a delicacy of feeling and a tender sympathetic melancholy, but his powers of expression and language were much inferior to those of Chatzopoulos: a feeble voice, and a limited intellectual world. His one collection, *Shadows* (1920), influenced the muted tones of poetry in the years 1920–30. (After his death his other poems were issued under the title *Musical Voices* in 1934.)

On the contrary the short-lived Spilios Pasagiannis (1874–1909) was always seeking new means of expression, apart from the Parnassian technique of Gryparis and the Symbolism of Chatzopoulos. He came from a village near Sparta and tried to give new life to his diction by means of the robust popular language, and to a great extent he succeeded. His neologisms or purely dialectal words are used with quite a different intention from that of Gryparis or Krystallis, and subserve his lyric Symbolism. His one collection, *Echoes* (published by *Techni* in 1899), is really a single poem in decapentesyllables, in which the traditional firm rhythm turns into something entirely personal. A. Melachrinòs was influenced by Pasagiannis, and so, to some extent, was Sikelianòs.

In the same year, 1899, and also published by *Techni*, *Fragments* appeared, the first collection of M. Malakasis (1869–1943). But the two poets had nothing in common. Malakasis was free from schools and theories of art, though he was clearly influenced by Jean Moréas, with whom he had been closely linked in Paris for many years. His verse rolls on impulsively, without problems, without his seeking a lyric depth—and without our missing it. He is above all a 'singer'; his virtue lies in the shallow, pure babble of the stream of verse, which never grew troubled in all the forty years during which he wrote. Combined with a touch of Roumeliot gallantry and a greater robustness of expression, this music has its happiest moments in the poems inspired by his home, Missolonghi: the famous 'Batariàs', 'Takis Ploumas', and 'What the Nightingales Say'.

A symptom of the increased interest in poetry, and in literature generally, was the appearance of a large number of writers, mostly poets, who continued along the lines established by their forerunners and maintained a reasonable standard. The lesson of Palamàs, the art of Mavilis and Gryparis, the feeling of Chatzopoulos and Malakasis found parallels in their verse and enriched the picture of Greek poetry during the first two or three decades of our century. Alekos Fotiadis from Smyrna (1870–1943) wrote short poems of four or eight lines, like neo-Classical epigrams; Markos Tsirimokos (1872–1939) cultivated complicated metrical compositions with Parnassian care (terzine, triolets, decastichs, villanelles); N. Petimezàs (1875–1952), under the pseudonym Lavras, gave a certain genuine popular colour to his verse, as well as variety in rhythm. Zacharias Papantoniou (1877–1940), a learned man, an art critic, and a journalist, was above all a stylist. He wrote a great deal, essays, biographies, travel, and criticism. His poetical work is very small, but he also cultivated the hybrid genre of prose poem in his *Prose Rhythms* (1923). Sotiris Skipis (1879–1952) was prolific in his poetical production, but his facility and unimaginable carelessness in thought and expression were fatal to his work.

All these writers were more or less contemporary, born in the decade 1870 to 1880. With the poets born after 1880 (particularly A. Sikelianòs, N. Kazantzakis and K. Varnalis) poetry reached a new flowering. We shall examine them in the next chapter. Meanwhile we must mention two poets, who though they were younger, belong rather to the older generation and are a last echo of the poetry of Palamàs's circle. These are A. G. Kyriazìs (1888–1950) and the still younger G. Athanas (G. Athanasiadis-Novas, b. 1893). Both were Roumeliots and followed with devotion the orthodox Palamist tradition of verse and rhyme. The sheltered life of the province gives to both of them, particularly to the latter in his first two and most successful collections, a freshness and an idyllic tone to their writing. This survival of Palamism, already an anachronism in the pre-war years, is still more incompatible with the present time.

# XIII

## KAVAFIS SIKELIANÒS
## POETRY UP TO 1930

### KAVAFIS

IT IS STRANGE that while in Athens, the unique cultural centre of the Greek world after 1880, Palamàs was at his zenith and exercised a dynastic influence on poetry and intellectual life, in an isolated area of Hellenism in Alexandria a poet was working who was, in after years, to take the central place in modern Greek poetry, and to have a decisive influence upon its later development down to our own times. This poet was Kavafis. Alexandria, where he lived permanently during his maturity and the years of his creative activity, a city with memories of a rich Hellenistic past, had been, since about the middle of the nineteenth century, the seat of an important and flourishing Greek commercial colony. Rich national benefactors such as G. Averoff, and later Emmanuel Benakis, were members of it, but it had not yet given any sign of intellectual life. This isolation within the Greek world explains in part—but only in part—some of the peculiarities of Kavafis's poetry.

Konstantinos Kavafis was born in Alexandria in 1863, the last of nine children. His father was a prosperous merchant, his mother came from a good family from Constantinople. After the father's early death the family went to England where they stayed (in Liverpool and in London) for seven years from 1872 to 1878. Kavafis must have studied at an English school, and it was then that he acquired that perfect knowledge of the English language which he used for his notes. On his return to Alexandria he completed his education at a Greek secondary school.

His family was again forced to leave their city, this time owing to the political disturbances of 1882, which resulted in the British occupation of Egypt. His mother went with her children to Constantinople, where her father was living, and they remained there till October 1885. After his return the poet only left Alexandria for occasional journeys: to Paris and London in 1897, and to Athens in 1901 and 1903. His life passed tranquilly; he had a permanent position in the Civil Service; he lived first with a brother and then alone, surrounded in his latter years by the affection and admiration of his Alexandrian friends. He died on his birthday in 1933 of cancer of the throat.

His first publications begin in 1886, the year of Palamàs's first collection. They are in katharevousa, Romantic in their conception, and appear quite uninfluenced by the change of 1880; in their pessimism and their obvious cerebralism they seem to follow the line of D. Paparrigopoulos, with clear signs of influence by Hugo and Musset. But already in 1891 he published in a pamphlet of its own a poem, 'Builders', which foreshadows his subsequent development, and in 1896 he wrote 'Walls', a completely Kavafian poem. Kavafis disowned almost all this writing of a decade, and did not incorporate it in the publication of his work. He was to make many other 'purges' of the same kind; even at the height of his maturity he would write poems which, for one reason or another, he refrained from publishing. The corpus of his acknowledged poems amounts to 154; the first in chronological order is 'Walls' of 1896, and the last is 'In the Suburbs of Antioch' of 1933, the year of his death. The poems are all short; they rarely reach a second page, and only one reaches a third.

Kavafis's eccentricity is shown also in the manner in which his poems circulated, in small pamphlets. In 1904 he selected fourteen and printed them in a small brochure which he republished in 1910, adding another seven; these brochures, printed in editions of 100 to 200 copies at the most, were issued privately. After 1912 he issued separate broadsheets which he himself fastened together with metal clips into collections, some arranged simply chronologically, others according to subject. He often corrected a line by hand, or had the corrected poem reprinted and substituted it for the former version. The author thus remained in continual touch with his work.

The important years for his formation were certainly those round 1900—between 'Walls' of 1896, and 1904 when he published his brochure of fourteen poems (the year of Palamàs's *Life Immovable*). He had abandoned his role as a successor of the Romantics, and by continuous trial and effort was discovering his altogether individual personality. 'Walls', though its technique is still somewhat irresolute, astonishes us by its maturity; with extraordinary succinctness it gives us the tragic profundity of the feeling of isolation, the permanent tragic element in the life of our time. And in the other poems up to 1900—those which the poet himself approved and published—we recognize the basic elements, the stones that are to build 'the city of Kavafis' (to quote the critics) :[1] a post-Romantic melancholy in 'Candles', a high sense of art in 'The First Stair', the historico-mythological element and the opposition between the world of men and the gods in 'The Horses of Achilles', 'The Funeral of Sarpedon', and 'Prayer'. His personality becomes yet clearer and takes on its familiar form in the poems of the next five years (1900–4) : the human dignity in 'Chè fece . . . il gran rifiuto' and the admirable 'Thermopylae', a further development of the theme of 'Walls' in 'The City', and finally, in 1904, one of his most mature and characteristic poems (both historical and dramatic), 'Waiting for the Barbarians'. At the same time we find shorter, more lyrical poems, like epigrams, warmer and more personal (and more demotic in language), e.g. 'Voices' and 'Desires' :

> Ideal voices and beloved
> Of those who died . . .

(unfulfilled desires, which are)

> Like beautiful bodies of the dead who never grew old
> And were laid, with tears, in a splendid mausoleum,
> With roses at the head, and at the feet jasmine.

After these critical years round 1900, Kavafis, now forty years old and mature, had created his own poetic style, something personal and uniquely expressive. In the following thirty years, until his death, he deepened it from within and continually enriched the personality we know, sparingly producing new poems always of the same type, but with a richness of theme,

---

[1] T. Malanos, 'Η μυθολογία της Καβαφικής πολιτείας, Alexandria, 1943 (= id., 'Ο ποιητής Κ. Π. Καβάφης, 2nd revised edn., Athens, 1957, pp. 289–396).

meticulously worked in his workship. Some were written before 1910, more after 1911 (and there was something of an outburst in 1917–18); there is a marked falling off in his last years.

It seems that Kavafis himself saw his poems as belonging to three categories (or 'areas'): philosophical, historical, and erotic (sensual). This distinction corresponds to the facts, if we take it as referring to the form of expression rather than to the content. For on the other hand there is no doubt, as he himself said, that Kavafis's world is a single entity, and the fact that a poem is 'historical' in subject does not mean that it is not 'philosophical' or 'erotic', and vice versa.

Much has been said about Kavafis's eroticism, and the homosexuality which is the origin of poems of this kind, and (more generally) of all his poems; criticism has here gone too far, interpreting all his poems in terms of his sexual abnormality and the psychological complex of isolation and secretiveness which it created (T. Malanos). Later criticism, without denying that this particular eroticism was a basic element in his poetry, has avoided excessive insistence upon this element, and has called attention to others, for example, his love of drama, his didacticism (E. P. Papanoutsos), the relationship between his poems and the historical background of Egypt and the Greek colony there (S. Tsirkas)—though it has not always escaped exaggeration and one-sidedness. The world of Kavafis is many-sided and his work 'a prism with many facets', and therefore any attempt to seize its meaning from one point of view only is doomed to failure.

The purely erotic poems are few; the frankest ones begin to appear at a fairly late date (perhaps after 1915). But in the historical poems and elsewhere in Kavafis's poetry we see the figure of beautiful youth, an erotic fancy, and above all the remembrance of it, and the enjoyment of this in a lonely room. Human nobility and dignity, perhaps the leading characteristics of his poetry, are not absent even from his frankest poems; fundamentally what interests him is the transubstantiation of sentiment into poetry. Often the motifs of love and art are woven together in his poems:

> Sometimes the talk is of fine sophistry
> And sometimes of the delights of their love.
> ('Herodes Atticus')

> The theatre where there took place the union of art
> With the erotic tendencies of the flesh.
>
> ('Julian and the people of Antioch')

The poems we call historical are certainly the most characteristic. No other poet has so authoritatively expressed a continual return to the past in his poems. Already in his early (and
disowned) poems there are examples of this tendency. In those
before 1900 we already noticed some with mythological subjects
drawn from the *Iliad*, and already in 1904 we have 'Waiting for
the Barbarians'. There follow (all before 1910) 'King Demetrius',
'The Steps' (about Nero), and 'That One' (which is not about
a known historical personage, but a poet 'Unknown, stranger
to Antioch, from Edessa'). In 1911–12 come the masterpieces:
'The God leaves Antony', 'Philhellene', and 'The Alexandrian
Kings'.

There is no doubt that the historical poems express the same
world as the others. His didacticism (if we must call it so), his
philosophy, and his eroticism find the same mode of expression
in the historical poems. The historical past helps him to achieve,
in the obliqueness that is characteristic of his poetry, the exact
expression; behind the masks of history and its personages his
voice becomes—at least for the initiated—even more clear.
Critics have in many ways tried to explain the basic significance
of the secretiveness, the hints, and the indirect expression in
Kavafis's poetry; he himself speaks of 'half-seen faces or lines',
and of visions 'half-hidden in his phrases'. It is not because his
form of love is unorthodox, and still less because he is afraid of his
references to well-known current events being understood; it is
because the things he hides or reveals, deep in his esoteric world,
are not things that can be simply or directly said. Apart from
this fundamental explanation, the fascination of the historical
past, magically brought to life by the poet, adds to the
captivating charm of the poetry. The historical personages in
Kavafis, whether authentic, like Antony, Caesarion, or Antiochus
Epiphanes, or imaginary like Aimilianos Monaë and Temethos
of Antioch, have an existence of their own, in their own right,
independent of the poet's aim; they are as much alive as nature
in other poets (nature, be it said, plays little or no role in his
work). A few years before his death Kavafis said: 'I had two

talents, for writing poetry or for writing history. I haven't written history and it's too late now.'[1]

Most of the historical poems have to do with the Hellenistic period, and the world created by the conquests of Alexander the Great at its height ('a great new Greek world') and in its decline, in various distant colonies; the Greco-Roman world also takes up some space, and the struggle between Paganism and Christianity (Julian and Apollonius of Tyana), and then the Dark Ages until the Moslem capture of Egypt; finally, some are concerned with the Byzantine period ('our glorious Byzantinism'). Alexandria occupies a central place in most of them, his beloved city; its name gradually turns into a symbol, a magic clue, that the initiated will understand:

> Where the rhythm and every phrase shows
> That an Alexandrian is writing about an Alexandrian.
> ('For Ammon')

The third category (or 'area') in his poetry is the philosophical poems, which others have called 'didactic'. E. P. Papanoutsos[2] called Kavafis a didactic poet, and placed in a category of their own poems with advice to his fellow craftsmen (about poetry and aesthetics generally, and how a poet faces his work and is bound up with it); he sees the other 'didactic' poems as variations on certain themes: the theme of 'Walls' with the dominant feeling of the ineluctable and irrevocable, and others of a kindred nature where the heavy atmosphere of destiny is dominant, and the implacable course of events. In the motif of 'Thermopylae' the feeling of duty is united with that of the virtue of human dignity. This fundamental characteristic of Kavafis's poetry is heard even in the poems that present the vanity of human greatness ('The God leaves Antony'), or that of *hybris* in its ancient sense ('Nero's Time Limit', 'Ides of March'). The reader will have observed that many of these 'philosophical' or 'didactic' poems are 'historical' in form.

Kavafis is serious and melancholy: we shall find no merriment, no humour in his poems. There is much irony, but an irony accompanied by a tragic grimace. It is unimportant if the

---

[1] G. Lechonitis, *Καβαφικὰ αὐτοσχόλια*, Alexandria, 1942, p. 22.

[2] E. P. Papanoutsos, *'Ο διδακτικὸς Καβάφης*, in: *Παλαμᾶς, Καβάφης, Σικελιανός*, new edn., [Athens, 1955], pp. 121–222.

point of view is erotic, philosophical, or historical; the important thing is the consciousness of the dramatic essence of life, the sense of decadence and vanity. But this tragic feeling does not lead to nihilism or lack of faith; the sentiment of dignity and pride, the deeper consciousness of man are the counterbalance, and keep his faith steady. If the generation of the 'decadents' of 1920 turned to Kavafis, it saw his poetry only from the negative side.

Poetry of this sort, so different from what was then known and established, naturally employed altogether new modes of expression. The language of Kavafis is altogether individual, and bears no relation to the established Athenian 'poetic' demotic (e.g. that of Palamàs), but at the same time, for all its frequent use of katharevousa, it is far from the formal katharevousa, whether old or new. Extreme demoticists never forgave him for his non-conformity, and yet advocates of katharevousa could hardly admit him to their ranks. Basically his language is living and demotic, and his deviations into katharevousa are perhaps a deliberately prosaic and realistic element; the demotic basis, however, gives warmth and authenticity to his language, while his Constantinopolitan idioms, to which he clung with obstinacy and complaisance, add a valuable human touch.

His metre, like his language, cultivates prosaic instead of poetic elements aiming at the weight and authority of realism. The metre is always iambic (the nearest to prose), loose, in free verse, with an unequal number of syllables; often, most often in the earlier period, rhyme appears, and its sound is also playful and ironical; often the verse is cut or rather dissolved into two (e.g. 'Temethos of Antioch') as if it lacked the strength to complete itself. But this also is a poetical device. In Kavafis's poetry nothing happens by chance; he carefully works his poems to the last detail. The stress, the stops, the pauses are all calculated, and all serve 'the art of poetry'; so does the typographical appearance. Everything is always elegant and in good taste.

Kavafis's poetry did not immediately win a reputation. Gregorios Xenopoulos, with remarkable sensibility, was the first to appreciate its importance in an article as early as 1903.[1] Athens in general, however, overlooked and rejected him. An important moment was the publication of an article in the

---

[1] Gr. Xenopoulos, *"Ενας ποιητής*, in *Παναθήναια*, 7 (1903), 97–102. Reprinted in *Νέα 'Εστία*, 14 (1933), 749–55, and ibid. 74 (1963), 1443–9.

*Athenaeum* of 1919 by E. M. Forster,[1] who served in Alexandria in the First World War and knew the poet personally and had some of his poems translated into English. After 1920 Kavafis was discovered by the young of that generation; Tellos Agras gave a lecture on him in 1921, as did Alkis Thrylos[2] in 1924. During the last years of his life his poetry was read and studied and criticized (not without some hostility). After 1930 his influence on the younger generation was very strong, and critical essays and books on his work abounded, by Greeks and by foreign writers; we may mention G. Seferis, W. H. Auden, C. M. Bowra, and Marguerite Yourcenar. The centenary of 1963 gave an opportunity for a new critical appraisal of his work.

### A. SIKELIANÒS

Quite unlike the poetry of Kavafis is that of Angelos Sikelianòs (1884–1951), the greatest poet of Greece proper since Palamàs. It is not without significance that he came from the Ionian Islands, or that his fatherland, Leucas, is very close to the rugged mainland opposite. The tradition of the Heptanesian school was still alive in him, and this no doubt accounts for the deep feeling for and knowledge of the popular language in all its purity that Sikelianòs possessed, and also his familiarity with other literature, particularly with that of Italy.

At the beginning of this century, when still very young, he started to publish poems in literary periodicals, with clear signs of the influence of late Parnassianism and Symbolism. These youthful efforts gave no promise of his later development—he himself omitted them from the three-volume *Lyric Life* (1946), the corpus of his work. His first real poetical appearance is his great composition *The Light-Shadowed* (the title is taken from the well-known line in Solomòs's *Free Besieged*), written in the spring of 1907 and issued (in a handsome uncommercial edition in large format) two years later.

*The Light-Shadowed* is like a lyrical autobiography of the young poet, a poem full of youthful sentiment and happiness, a wonderful outpouring of lyricism flowing unsullied from the

---

[1] Reprinted in *Pharos and Pharillon* (see Selected Bibliography).

[2] Tellos Agras, 'Ο ποιητὴς Κ. Π. Καβάφης, Δελτίο 'Εκπαιδευτικοῦ 'Ομίλου, 10 (1922); reprinted in Νέα 'Εστία, 74 (1963), 1397–1402. Alkis Thrylos, Κριτικὲς μελέτες, vol. 3, Athens, 1925, pp. 155–97.

purest and most secret sources. The poet has gathered up within himself a hoard of immediate experience, while he wandered in complete freedom in total accord with nature, by the olive groves and shores of his island home.

This youthful and happy identification of the poet with nature is what most attracts us in this early but already mature poem. The separate parts are loosely linked, the poetic process is not everywhere clear, but the lyric tone is always intense, and the language, a robust demotic, has a fullness and richness of expression hitherto unknown in modern Greek poetry. Nature, we feel, is not an objective phenomenon which the poet contemplates with admiration and worship, but there is a 'direct communication' between them, which, to use a phrase dear to Sikelianòs himself, has the character of a 'profound devotional exercise':

> . . . And I worshipped,
> And in my joy I cried:
> 'Go put your ear close to the ground.'
> And then I fancied the profound
> Heart of the earth replied.

Features which later become the distinguishing marks of his poetry, and what he and his critics consider most characteristic in it, are already found in this youthful poem; the ideas are still undeveloped, but receive perhaps a more genuine and more immediate expression.

That which appears unconsciously in *The Light-Shadowed*, the 'cosmic (or Orphic) expansion into the soul of life' or his 'exercise',[1] was what he tried later to render more consciously. Immediately after the publication of the poem he began work on a vast composition, *Prologue to Life*, and in 1915–17 he brought out (in small volumes, again exquisitely printed) four parts, each entitled 'Consciousness'—the first of the earth, the second of the race, the third of woman, the fourth of faith (the fifth, the consciousness of the personal creativity, was first published much later). As he passed from youth to maturity he felt the need to 'take consciousness' of certain basic problems, which define his place in life—problems, which 'had been wrenched away from the primal core of his youthful entity'. He does not express

---

[1] All the quotations cited here and in the following pages are taken from Sikelianòs's 'Prologue' to *Lyric Life*, now edited in Ἅπαντα, ed. G. P. Savvidis, vol. 1, pp. 11–81.

himself clearly in his poetical compositions, and far less in his comments (especially the Prologue to *Lyric Life* of 1938). But his fundamental line is faith in the unity and roundness of the whole (the 'universal soul of the World') and in the coincidence of the 'feeling soul' (that of the poet) with the centre of the world. In the fragmented world of today, in its 'arbitrary, mechanical, mnemonic, distinguishing, and logocratic interpretation and ordering of life', he desires wholeness of the kind the ancients knew in myth (before the rationalism of the sophists), which secret cults and mysteries still preserved for them at a later date. Hence the poet's familiarity with the mystery religions, and above all with Orphism; hence too the deeper meaning that he sought in centres of ancient Greek religion, such as Eleusis, Olympia, and Delphi. He envisaged a universal religious myth, which should unite the primitive matriarchal religions with the ancient Greek spirit, and this with the teaching of Orphism and the symbols of Christianity. This is the reason for the frequent appearance of death in his poetry, in its ontological, existentialist aspect, and for the central place and the mission that the poet has as 'instructor of the whole of human life'. In all these there is sometimes an exaggerated and often tiresome egocentricity; perhaps, however, this living presence of the ego prevents these visions from evaporating into 'philosophy', and preserves the biological urge, and the initiation and participation which is the inalienable contribution of the poetry of Sikelianòs.

In the *Prologue to Life*, the fragmentation of his youthful unity and the weakness of the composition are felt more. However, at the same time, Sikelianòs was writing perfect smaller poems, such as the series inspired by the Balkan wars (*Songs of Victory I*), a series of sonnets and some poems in the series *Aphrodite Urania*: the marvellous 'Pan' (where we seem to be living with immediacy at the moment of the birth of the myth) and the charming and much loved 'Thalerò', 'By the Cold Waters, by Pentavlì', 'John Keats', 'The Mother of Dante', and so on.

But the diffuse power of *The Light-Shadowed* finds maturity and completion in the relatively long poem, *Mother of God*, written in 1917, 'the most musical poem written in Greek since the death of Solomòs'.[1] It is not musical only because of the

---

[1] R. Liddell, 'Η ποίηση τοῦ Ἄγγελου Σικελιανοῦ, Ἀγγλοελληνικὴ 'Επιθεώρηση, 4 (1949–50), 424.

charm of the rhythm, and the fifteen-syllable couplets that remind us of *The Cretan*—which the poet prints separately, as if they were complete stanzas—but because in the free flow of the images one follows another like motifs in music. Three years previously Sikelianòs had lost his sister Penelope (wife of Raymond Duncan, brother of Isadora) and a new consciousness, that of death, led him deeper into 'experience of that Mystery working with uninterrupted energy around and below him'. For the Orthodox, the *Panagia* is more the sorrowful mother of Christ than the Virgin. The maternal or matriarchal divinity—as in the mother goddesses or mothers of the gods of the past—is the source of life, but also of death, in a mystical connection, as in March the cult makes an almost mystical connection between the Annunciation, the 'salutations' of Our Lady, and 'All Souls' Saturday' (the commemoration of the dead in the Greek Church). The poem moves musically, imperceptibly from the warmth of the first lines to the central idea of death; the pain of the dead sister and the sweet presence of the Mother of Christ are mystically united, welded (one might almost say) into an organic whole, one of the finest things in poetry. The language, perfectly wrought, exploits all that is best in Greek poetical tradition; it is rich, robust, and musical and gives birth to the loveliest fifteen-syllable lines ever written in Greek (see Appendix, p. 281).

In the following years, 1918–19, the poet attempted a wider synthesis, a longer poem, divided into smaller parts (cantos), *The Easter of the Greeks*. It is an attempt to unite the symbols of ancient and modern religion, and to make poetic contact with the religious 'subconscious' expressed 'not in dogma or organization, but in the genuine myth of Christianity'. His purpose was high; it may be doubted if the poet managed to fulfil it. He printed a part of it in 1918, but did not put it into circulation, and from time to time he issued fragments of it. A whole note-book of his, he tells us, full of unpublished cantos was lost on a journey. Yet though the whole poem was not completed, this does not prevent parts of it from being among the most characteristic and the most perfect poems of Sikelianòs.

In 1927, twenty years after *The Light-Shadowed* and ten after *Mother of God*, Sikelianòs devoted himself to what he called the 'Delphic attempt', that is, an attempt to put his world theory into practice, that theory which he had expressed in his poetry. In the sanctuary of Delphi, which the ancients considered 'the navel of the earth', where the Greek spirit attempted the first synthesis of the Apollonian and Dionysiac elements, he dreamed of founding a new, world-wide, intellectual amphictyony, a 'Delphic union', and a 'Delphic university', whence might spring an intellectual independence and spiritual redemption of all peoples, and a unity beyond the fragmented individual of today, and above the ephemeral political creeds of our times. In May 1927 the first Delphic Festival was organized, with a performance of *Prometheus Bound* as its central feature, an exhibition of folk art, naked contests in the stadium, folk dances, and fairs. The Festival was repeated in 1930 with a performance of *The Suppliants* of Aeschylus. The soul of the whole enterprise was Sikelianòs's wife, Eva Palmer, an American by birth. She gave a more definite form to the poet's vaguer visions, and, initiated into the spirit of the dance by Isadora Duncan, she understood the inner connection between ancient tragedy, Byzantine music, and the folk culture of today, and she tried to make a synthesis of all these in her *mise en scène*. The music of the chorus was based on the modes of Byzantine melody, the costumes were woven by herself on popular models, and the movements of the chorus were inspired by the study of ancient monuments. It was the first serious attempt (and it was a revelation) to present tragedy in its home, the ancient theatre, with ancient equipment and a chorus that was really dancing.

The performances of Eva Sikelianòs were the one positive element in the Delphic Festivals. The other aims of the poet's 'Delphic attempt' were ultimately, and not surprisingly, unsuccessful. The Festivals were a complete financial failure. Eva went almost in voluntary exile to America, and only returned to Greece in 1952, when she died and was buried at Delphi.

Granted Sikelianòs's immediate way of feeling everything, it was natural that the erotic element should have a prime place in his work. He wanted this element to take its place in the universal vision of the world which his poetry expressed and to fulfil his need for 'a cosmic and integral participation of the whole of my being with the full erotic breath of the "god of the living" '. Already in his youthful 'Hymn of the Great Return' he shows his nostalgia for a cosmic erotic integrity, where 'deeper than the dense starlight' his 'first self' awaits him. In his more mature poems (1936–9) he makes a more marked advance towards or search for the primal essence of the feminine and for an identification of body and soul, which should finally lead to a redemption and freedom that could conquer time and death ('Study of Death'). But, as usual in the work of Sikelianòs, he never passes the dangerous frontier where poetry slips into metaphysics. The impulse of life in his erotic poetry is so genuine and deep that it never loses its uninterpreted biological origins but vibrates with the purest poetical pulsation.

The poet gave the title *Orphic* to some of his second series of lyric poems written between 1927 and 1942, and this title is a clear commentary on them. Here is the famous 'Sacred Way' (1935) with its rich symbolism, and the less well-known but equally fine poem 'Attic' (1942). It is no coincidence that they are both set on the sacred road that leads to the most venerable ancient shrine of the mother goddess, Eleusis.

The *Songs of Victory II* are poems inspired by the Greco-Italian war of 1940–1 and the occupation. Most of them circulated secretly at that time, and were a form of resistance. They are not all on the same level. We may single out the enthusiastic 'Apology of Solon' and 'The Unwritten' (sc. Gospel), with its deep reflectiveness, issued at the beginning of the most terrible winter of the war in October 1941.

In the last decade of his life Sikelianòs turned towards the composition of tragedies. It was the natural reaction of a man who had lived intensely in the spirit of ancient tragedy, and had made the productions of Aeschylus' plays the centre of his Delphic attempt. In fact his first attempts towards tragedy began at the time of the Delphic Festivals, or soon after. But the composition of most of his tragedies dates from the war years and after, and they follow the same line as the *Songs of Victory*. In these years, moreover, Sikelianòs showed a strong interest in political and social engagement, and wished to popularize his message and bring it to the masses (though it remained aristocratic in essence).

The beginning, as we said, went further back. *The Last Orphic Dithyramb* or *The Dithyramb of the Rose* was printed in 1932, and was acted in the open air on the hill of Philopappos in April 1933. Like the ancient dithyramb it is not actually a tragedy; it is a dialogue between Orpheus and the two leaders of the chorus, which often turns into a monologue.

Even earlier Sikelianòs had begun a tragedy about Byron, and an *Asclepios* of which he published fragments in 1919. The work was perhaps never completed; an unfinished extract was published after his death. But the idea of tragedy was continually gestating in his mind, though his first completed tragedy, *The Sibyl*, was written shortly before 1940, and was publicly read by the poet a few days after the declaration of the Greco-Italian war. In this tragedy the Greek spirit clashes with that of Roman despotism, and the central episode is Nero's excursion to Delphi, and his conversation there with the Sibyl, who is in ecstasy. The work is genuinely inspired, but it is hard to call it a tragedy and still less is it a theatrical work (some of the stage directions are in fact interpretative glosses by the poet). Moreover, the language of Sikelianòs, always difficult to understand, and the symbols (such as the 'promanteia', the 'upright tune', the 'paean'), incomprehensible to most people, cannot easily reach the large public at which the theatre is directed. For this reason the one attempt to perform this work was not a success.

The subsequent tragedies are altogether lacking in tension. The basic theme is always the same, the clash of spirit and matter, in different circumstances: Daedalus and Minos in *Daedalus in Crete*, Nero and Christ in *Christ in Rome*. The theme gradually loses the high (if difficult) symbolism of *The Sibyl* and becomes an easier symbolism of social and political clashes (people and rulers). In *The Death of Digenìs* (his last and feeblest tragedy, which has also the unwarranted title of *Christ Unbound*) Digenìs, leader of the Manichaean heretics, is a revolutionary against the emperor Basil, and the defender of the weak and poor against the rich and the rulers.

The tragedies (even *The Sibyl*, which is the best of them) do not show Sikelianòs at his best. The real Sikelianòs is the lyric poet, with his magnificent beginning with *The Light-Shadowed*, his full maturity in *Mother of God*, and in the erotic and Orphic poems of before the war. In 1938, when he meant to issue the collection of *Lyric Life*, he wrote a fine poem, which is a confession, and a worthy epilogue to his 'lyric life'. These are the first and the last lines:

> Because I deeply glorified and trusted in the earth
> Because I never opened out my mystic wings in flight
> But ever rooted deep in silence all my mind and spirit . . .
>
> .    .    .    .    .    .    .    .    .    .
>
> All that has been ephemeral has melted like a cloud,
> And here is the great Death, who has become to me a brother.

## POETRY UP TO 1930

Contemporary with Sikelianòs (his elder by only one year) was another poet like him in many ways, but in more ways different, Nikos Kazantzakis. His work is voluminous, and always bears the mark of his reflective and restless spirit. His chief poetical work is his epic *Odyssey*, but he used every literary genre. His work as a whole will be considered in the following chapter.

Kostas Varnalis (b. 1884) was the contemporary of these two poets. His beginning was like that of Sikelianòs, with finely wrought poetry influenced by the Parnassians and the Symbolists (*Honeycombs*, 1905). His later poems are marked by a strong Dionysiac flavour and a deep sense of music; he has a strong tendency towards satire, when his playful and agile verse emphasizes his sharp humour.

Varnalis studied literature in Athens, and after 1908 worked in secondary schools; in 1919 he went with a state scholarship to Paris and there, in the post-war atmosphere, he came to accept dialectical materialism and the Marxist ideology. Two long poetical compositions written in Paris, *The Light that Burns* (1922, under the pseudonym of Dimos Tanalias) and *The Enslaved Besieged* (1927), show his new orientations; at the same time they are his most genuinely lyrical work. In the first of these, after an introduction in prose (a dialogue between Prometheus, Christ, and Momus) there is a lyrical part, where 'The Mother of Christ' and 'Magdalene' must be singled out as rare lyrical achievements; the third part is satirical. The poet made many changes in subsequent editions. *The Enslaved Besieged* (an obvious contrast to *The Free Besieged* of Solomòs) is also, as the poet says, 'in its essence an anti-war and anti-idealistic work'. But his 'engagement' has not weakened his rich imagination and lyric intensity, particularly in 'The Sorrows of the Virgin', and the polished fifteen-syllable couplets of the 'Dialogue between Man and Woman'. His satire and sarcasm reach their height in short, forceful lines, which seem to resound with the tunes of a popular festival (see Appendix, p. 281).

In these compositions we clearly see his destructive attitude to established values and ideas. This is continued in his prose works, particularly in the two longest, *The True Apology of Socrates* (1933) and *The Journal of Penelope* (1946). Here lyrical gift and poetical imagination are absent and there is only (perhaps less in the first, but much more in the second) a bare and repellent impulse to destruction, and the denigration of 'heroes'. His prose is unquestionably well written, but it has not the power to win the sympathy of the reader—at least of a reader who is not already prejudiced in its favour. Varnalis's work in criticism is of considerable merit. *Solomòs without Metaphysics* (1923)—though the Marxist point of view is obvious—is full of detailed observation that shows a rare critical penetration. The same may be said of most of his later essays on older writers (*Living Men*, 1939).

We must here make mention of another almost contemporary poet, who had not however the importance of the last, Apostolos Melachrinòs (1880–1952). He was born in Rumania and lived till 1922 in Constantinople, where he edited the periodical *Life* after 1902, and thereafter in Athens. He was influenced by Gryparis (a contributor to his periodical), persistently cultivated the Symbolist technique, and sought the musical charm of verse. He seems later to have turned to the *poésie pure* of Mallarmé, but his language and expression have a recherché quality, and his exercises in verse rarely seem to have got beyond the stage of the work-room.

The spirit of destruction, which in Varnalis sprang from his ideology (and which appears late in his work), was to be a part of the personality, and an essential element in the poetry of later poets, born in the last decade of the nineteenth century (or a little before), who were to begin to make an appearance during the First World War. Romos Filyras (1889–1942), the pseudonym of J. Ikonomopoulos, brought out his first works in 1911, and in 1911–23 published poems marked by a new attitude and technique, very different from the exalted tone of Palamàs, and of poetry after him. In spite of this poet's eroticism and idealism, there is a flavour of bitterness and disillusionment, a grief for lost ideals, a subjectivity expressed in muted tones and everyday language; a poetry of the *salon*, apart from the established poetical language. His anti-heroism reaches the point of irony and self-mockery; the poet takes pleasure in assuming roles such as those of 'Dolls' or 'Pierrot' (1922), and he wrote a kind of satirical autobiography in prose under the title of *The Player of Life* (1916). Filyras spent the last years of his life (1927–42) in a lunatic asylum; we have some scattered publications of his dating from those years, which are of value; they show an attempt to escape from destructiveness and disbelief, and an advance towards a more solid manner of expression. We shall see the same thing occurring in other poets of the same generation.

We find the same intellectual atmosphere in Kostas Ouranis (1890–1953), who had considerable influence on his contemporaries and juniors (that is, the generation of 1920) by reason of *Nostalgias*, which is essentially his only collection of poems. He had previously published two collections, and a third entitled *Journeys* was not published until after his death. The titles are characteristic: Ouranis sought in travel and flight the refuge from everyday boredom and lack of faith: 'spleen' is a word that frequently recurs in his work. It was natural that poetry of this sort should remain faithful to the same tone, and should not know change. Ouranis travelled a great deal, and the cosmopolitan spirit that he brought into literature was perhaps his most marked characteristic. His impressions of travel are certainly among his best works (*Sol y Sombra* about Spain, *Azure Ways* about the Mediterranean, etc.), describing places that he had visited with lyric feeling.

Napoleon Lapathiotis (1888–1943) has a place of his own among these low-keyed poets; his first poems were influenced by the leaders of the aestheticism of the age (Walter Pater and Wilde), and he later developed a despairing and melancholy tone, dominated by the feeling of lost ideals and nostalgia. However, he was faithful to his aestheticism and, in contrast to Ouranis, he gave great attention to form in his most successful poems.

A poet of greater calibre, and the most representative of this generation, was Kostas Karyotakis (1896–1928). At the age of twenty-three he published his first collection, *The Pain of Man and Things*, and two years later his second, *Nepenthe*. Just before

his death in 1928 he published *Elegies and Satires*. In the July
of that year, when a Civil Servant in a small provincial town,
he committed suicide.

Karyotakis's poetry is serious; any trace of belletrism, aestheticism, or playfulness that one may have found in his predecessors
has vanished from his work. There is an overflowing desire for
life and a full awareness of reality, and—in strange contradiction
—a feeling of futility and of loss, which became more and more
stark till he reached the tragic impasse which resulted in his
suicide. He wrote poems about the 'Don Quixotes', about the
'inglorious poets of the age'; his position was always anti-heroic
and anti-idealist; he celebrated the inglorious, the insignificant,
even the absurd, as a protest that went so far as to become sar-
castic. Sarcasm pervades all his poetry with a peculiar bitterness
and becomes the one outlet (if outlet there were) for his permanent disillusionment. But in Karyotakis this feeling of emptiness,
which provides his work with rare firmness, is not facilely conveyed in conventional poetical forms, but creates out of its own
dissolution, one might say, a new form of expression. The verse
and the poetical language lose their sharp outlines without losing
their firmness; and this is their originality.

> Let us imagine that we have not found,
> After the hundred roads we have travelled by,
> The confines of silence; let us sing, and let the sound
> Be a trumpet of victory, the outburst of a cry
> To amuse the fire demons far beneath the ground
> In the bowels of the earth, and the men that live on high.

There is a complete nihilism, but the voice is clear. This is the
last stanza of one of his poems, published after his death. It has
the ironical title 'Optimism'.

The generation of 1920 cultivated in various ways this feeling
of the inadequacy of the poet, and of decadence. The poets—
'decadents' or *intimistes*—were many; they formed Bohemian
groups in cafés and published their verses in short-lived literary
periodicals. After the tragic suicide of Karyotakis, 'Karyotakism'
as a literary fashion flooded Greek poetry, as the verse-making
of the last Romantics had previously flooded it. There is no
point in simply recording names. We may single out Maria
Polydouri (1902–30) for a certain feminine sensibility, which did

not, however, compensate for the carelessness and commonplace quality of her verses, and Mitsos Papanikolaou (1900–43), who had much affinity with Lapathiotis and Ouranis.

Tellos Agras (the pseudonym of Evangelos Ioannou, 1899–1944) belonged to the same world. He made an early appearance in various periodicals, and published his first collection of poems in 1934, with poems 1917–24, and a second (*Everyday*) in 1940, with poems dating from 1923–30. In the first volume an idyllic tone is dominant, even a 'bucolicism', which is like an escape from the ennui of the town; but in the second collection the monotony and everyday boredom provide the dominant tone, a grey atmosphere of depressing afternoons, rain, the dreariness of the poor quarters of Athens, schoolgirls with tight uniforms (there is an undertone of repressed eroticism here). But this mournful monotony is not conveyed in a destructive manner in his verse, as it is in that of Karyotakis. Faithful to the last period of Symbolism in which he was educated (at first under the strong influence of Moréas, and later that of Laforgue), he showed a particular preoccupation with technique, and worked over his poems till he had given them final shape. This care for form offsets the dominant minor tone of his poetry. His *New Poems* (1930–40), announced in 1940 but only recently published in a volume,[1] reveal a new technique, new conjunctions of words, and a more solid versification: an attempt to escape from the stifling cycle of monotonous subjects dear to his generation. Agras however, was left, almost completely untouched by the revival of poetical language brought in by the generation of 1930. He was too heavily burdened with the past to throw it off easily. Yet his attempt is not without significance.

Takis Papatsonis (b. 1895) on the other hand, though of the same generation, is quite outside that monotonous atmosphere of decadence and disbelief. His work is firmly grounded in faith, above all religious faith (which in his early poems is linked with Catholicism), and generally with faith in values and meaning. His first poems were published early in his life, in 1914–15, and though they reveal many influences, they show from the first a completely individual personality and forms of expression that were revolutionary for his time; in contrast with the decadence

---

[1] Tellos Agras, *Τριαντάφυλλα μιανῆς ἡμέρας*, ed. by K. Stergiopoulos, Athens, 1965.

of his contemporaries they seem to foretell a revival, and to be leading towards a new synthesis. He followed on the same path and published a considerable body of work, first issued sporadically and recently collected into two volumes (*Selected Poems* I and II, 1962). His thoughtful nature may sometimes lead him into an abstraction that is hardly lyrical, but his poetry always preserves a solid architecture and the seriousness of its intentions.

# XIV

## THE FIRST DECADES OF
## THIS CENTURY

## PROSE AFTER PSYCHARIS
## N. KAZANTZAKIS

AROUND 1900 the young creative writers and other men of letters of 'the 1880 generation' were now mature men, and had a responsible position in intellectual life. Demotic had prevailed in poetry and was beginning to take possession of prose also; poetry was trying to enter into more obscure regions. For the men of that generation, who had accomplished one change and whose minds were open to progress and novelty, the unfortunate war and the defeat of 1897 was a bitter blow which left scars on all intellectual as well as on political life. By a somewhat facile generalization the old ideas, the fruitless worship of the ancient (and also katharevousa) were made responsible for the national decline: desire for novelty gained strength, and at the same time there appeared a feeling of greater responsibility, connected with a serious facing of the problems.

In the political field, after the death of Ch. Trikoupis in 1896, the old parties were in power, but they were meeting with more and more opposition. There was much nationalistic feeling, chiefly shown in the claim for two regions at the opposite ends of Greece—Crete and Macedonia. In Macedonia from 1904 secret missions were organized, which by a guerrilla warfare (the 'Macedonian Struggle') full of exaltation and sacrifice neutralized the underground activities of the guerrillas of the Bulgarian Committee whose purpose was ostensibly to promote the formation of an autonomous Macedonia. Pavlos Melàs, a young officer of a rich aristocratic family, was killed in a village near Kastoria, and became the symbol of this nationalist movement. In 1909 some officers who had founded the 'Military League' became the representatives of the common indignation against 'the old party system', and summoned to power from Crete Eleftherios Venizelos, whose political personality had been shown in the revolutionary struggles of that island, and in his opposition to Prince George (son of King George I, appointed Commissioner in 1898). The new political situation led swiftly to the Balkan wars of 1912–13.

The Balkan Wars added to the Greek nation the new provinces of Macedonia and Epirus, the Aegean Islands, and Crete, and radically changed the character of the small state. But the following decade was to be one of trials. The First World War led to a split: the opposition between the pro-Ally premier and the pro-German king, Constantine I. With the coup at Thessaloniki in 1916 Greece placed herself finally on the side of the Allies, and was able to claim the fruits of her struggle on the side of the victors. But the defeat of Venizelos in the election of 1920, and above all the crushing disaster to the Greek Army in Asia Minor in September 1922, put an end to this period of expansion and progress. The exchange of population that followed—the uprooting from Asia Minor of 1,500,000 Greeks, established there for thousands of years, and their incorporation in the narrow bounds of Greece proper—brought a radical, irrevocable ethnological change, causing new social adjustments involving new and complex problems. The disaster of Asia Minor was to remain deeply marked on the minds of responsible intellectuals in all the years that followed, and was to determine not only their psychology, but also their *Weltanschauung*.

Students of Greek intellectual history often speak of the first decade of this century as a time of *Sturm und Drang*. Nowhere are the vigour and elation more keenly felt than in the linguistic movement, which at this period was connected with the desire for reform in education. The first years of the decade were marked by two reactionary movements, the *Evangelika* (1901), riots about the translation of the Gospels into the new language, and the *Oresteiaka* (1903), other riots about the performance of Aeschylus' tragedy in a moderate demotic translation, in the newly founded Royal Theatre. These riots (which were not bloodless) were started by university students, urged on by conservative professors. But this reaction was not strong enough to stop the current of progress, and demotic continued to gain ground. In 1903 the periodical *Noumàs* began to appear (directed by D. P. Tangopoulos), and this was the tribune for demoticism. The other side won a victory in the sanction by the Council of Revision of 1911 of the article in the Constitution whereby katharevousa is the 'official language' of the state. But this provision could not prevent the progress of demotic.

As we have said, there was a parallel desire for progress in the sensitive area of education, where the dominance of katharevousa was particularly harmful, especially in the elementary school. In 1902 an enlighted doctor in Constantinople, Fotis Fotiadis (1849–1936), wrote a book *The Language Question and Our Educational Renaissance*, which first opened the way. At the same time there were three men studying in Germany who were to work for the establishment of 'educational demotic': D. Glinòs, A. Delmouzos, and M. Triantafyllidis. On returning to Greece they founded the 'Educational Society' in 1910, which had a decisive influence in preparing the educational reform.

Glinòs, with his deep philosophical thought and his clear head, was later (1926) to differ from the other two, and to seek to solve the problem by a Marxist political ideology. Delmouzos was the most purely interested in education; with enlightened intelligence and enthusiasm he sought to base his educational efforts not only on demotic, but on a deeper neo-Hellenic consciousness. He first carried out his ideas in the Higher Municipal Girls' School at Volos (1908–11), and later at the Marasleion Paedagogical School in Athens (1923–5) and in the University of Thessaloniki. Unfortunately the forces of reaction interrupted his efforts on each occasion. Triantaphyllidis was a scholarly linguist, pupil of E. Kuhn and K. Krumbacher, but he put his scientific training to the service of educational demotic; he was the man who put order and system into written demotic, and into its teaching in schools (*Modern Greek Grammar* [Demotic], 1941).

The revolutionary government of Venizelos in 1917 made the decisive step of establishing the 'educational reform'. Demotic (the mother tongue) was introduced and taught in the three first classes of the elementary school, and new lively reading-books were substituted for the old, which were in every way wretched. The programme envisaged the gradual introduction of the mother tongue into the higher classes of the elementary school, but the political change of 1920 delayed this reform, which is not yet complete.

## PROSE, 1900–1920

In the drive of the first decade, with its longing for self-knowledge we must include the work of Pericles Giannopoulos (1872–1910), though he represents another curious trend. He lived as a young man in Paris, close to Moréas with whom he had ties of friendship, and led a Bohemian life; on his return to Greece he discovered the Greek light and spirit, and tried to express a message focused on Greek feeling and tradition. He was not a creative writer, and his attempts at a new poetic synthesis were without fruit, but his two manifestos (*New Spirit*, 1906, and *Appeal to the Panhellenic Public*, 1907), combined with his attractive appearance and even, perhaps, the strange method by which he committed suicide, exercised an influence on the younger generation, and in particular on Angelos Sikelianòs.

Ion Dragoumis (1878–1920) was also undoubtedly influenced by Giannopoulos. He was of a distinguished political family (his father had been prime minister), and he himself began with a diplomatic career and later entered politics. He had many progressive ideas for the regeneration of political and national life, but ranged himself with the opponents of Venizelos and was murdered after the news of the attempted murder of the latter in Paris in 1920. Dragoumis was one of the founders of the 'Educational Society' and, though anti-Venizelist, he thoroughly expressed the new and progressive tendencies of the age. As a writer (with the pseudonym Idas) he published some good stories such as *Blood of Heroes and Martyrs* (1907), inspired by the Macedonian Struggle, *Samothrace* (1909), and *Those Living* (1911), perhaps the first examples of psychological writing in modern Greek letters. Critics remarked on the influence of Nietzsche and of Barrès upon him, and in his turn he decisively influenced the younger generation.

The work of Penelope S. Delta (1874–1941) follows a line parallel to this Hellenocentric movement, but is much nearer to educational demoticism. It began from the need to give children suitable books, freed from conventional prettified falseness; above all she wrote books for children, but her higher purpose and her undoubted literary talent together with her feminine sensibility, raised them above the ordinary level of juvenile literature and they may be considered historical novels (at a time when this genre was not much cultivated), in which Byzantium and Macedonia play a central role. *In the Time of the Bulgar-Slayer* (1911) is a tale set principally in Macedonia in the time of Basil II, and is still popular today; the subsequent *In the Secret Places of the Lagoon* (1937) is set in the time of the Macedonian Struggle.

It was not, however, only the ideals of progress and regeneration and Hellenocentric thought that nourished literature during the first decades of the century. Creative writers and other men of letters more closely in touch with literary developments in western Europe were influenced by them and went beyond Symbolism and post-Symbolism, not only in poetry but also in prose. Such was the case of K. Christomanos (1867–1911), who brought to Greece the climate of the European *fin de siècle* and the Aestheticism of Oscar Wilde. He studied in Vienna (where for a time he taught Greek at the university), and was tutor to the unfortunate Empress Elizabeth, whom he accompanied on her journeys; this resulted in *The Book of the Empress Elizabeth*, first published in German and then translated into many languages, a biography written with rare sensibility and some lyricism. It was published in Greek in 1907. Christomanos had been permanently established in Athens since 1899, and took an energetic part in intellectual life. In 1901 he took the lead in the foundation of the 'New Stage' and thus in the regeneration of the theatre (see p. 215), and in 1911 brought out a novel *The Wax Doll*, basically different in character from his first. Here there is a daring realism, though his form of expression is still that of extreme Aestheticism, with a great variety of nuances.

Platon Rodokanakis (1883–1919) was influenced by Christomanos, and tried to create a mannered style, without the realistic base and the other virtues of Christomanos. The style of Spilios Pasagiannis, deriving from entirely different principles, is also artificial. We have seen him as a poet (p. 183) continually seeking new forms of expression. Similarly, his prose has a deliberate harshness, achieved by the use of many rare and downright popular words, and the strong rhythm of his phrases which goes far to abolish the frontiers between verse and prose.

Two writers undoubtedly stand at the centre of prose writing in the first two decades of the century: K. Chatzopoulos and K. Theotokis. They continue the tradition of 'genre writing' and develop and advance it by introducing new forms and methods of expression. We have met Konstantinos Chatzopoulos (1870–1920) as a poet (pp. 182–3). For many years he lived in Germany, where he embraced the doctrines of socialism. His work, particularly that in prose, wavers between two poles, his socialist theories and his lyrical sensibility. His first stories, written before 1910, still retain traces of 'genre writing', which gradually disappear while psychological penetration and a lyrical colouring become more prominent. A longer story, *Love in the Village* (1910), moves within the framework of the 'genre picture', though nevertheless it is a work with a social content. This is even clearer in the case of *The Tower of the Akropotamos* (first published 1909), although the writer himself calls it a 'genre picture'.

But Chatzopoulos was not to follow this line of development. His last novel, *Autumn* (1917), is entirely different in its construction. There is again the provincial town, but what interests the writer is to describe not the decline of society or of a class, but the feeling and shifts of feeling of his characters by suggestion, and to suggest an atmosphere. To a great extent he succeeds in this. With *Autumn* Chatzopoulos brings Symbolism also into prose. The influence of northern literature, especially Scandinavian, is obvious. In its turn, this work influenced the young, particularly in the decade 1920–30.

The prose work of Konstantinos Theotokis (1872–1923) had obvious social interests and implications. He was a scion of an aristocratic family of Corfu and was brought up in the ideological background of that island (he was linked with L. Mavilis by a close friendship); he acquired a solid education and was able to increase his experience by reading and travel. Around 1900, like many of his contemporaries, he was dominated by the influence of Nietzsche (especially in his story 'Passion'), but later in Germany (where he met Chatzopoulos) he also was to follow socialist theories, and to give a strong social colour to his work.

In the stories that he wrote around 1900 there is, as with Chatzopoulos, a framework of the 'genre picture', but realism is their strongest quality. One or two of the best ('Prone', and

'Not Yet') are so short that they are like 'dramatic snapshots with action breathless and condensed'.[1] Before the Balkan wars he wrote a more lengthy story, *Honour and Money* (published 1914), with a clear social focus. Shortly afterwards he began to compose a big novel, on which he worked until the end of his life, *Slaves in their Chains* (1922). The action is set in Corfu, in the town, at a time of readjustment in social life. The old aristocracy was trying to keep up a form of life that had had its day; the bourgeoisie was also on the decline, while parvenus from the lower class were trying to force their way with their money and to 'arrive' socially—all 'slaves in the chains' of their fate, which was of necessity controlled by money. Among these, feeble and finally defeated, is Alkis Sozomenos, a young idealist with humanist and socialist theories.

More perfect from a literary point of view are Theotokis's two long stories: *The Convict* (1919) and *The Life and Death of Karavelas* (1920). Here, in contrast to the novel, there is a central character whom the author has conceived in all his realistic clarity and his human presence. In *The Convict* it is Tourkogiannos who is made by the author an ideal type of devotion and Christian love (the critics drew comparisons between him and heroes of Tolstoy, or Prince Myshkin in Dostoevsky), but this exalted idealism endangers the realistic depiction of the central character. He has, on the contrary, welded plot and character much more firmly together in his second story, *The Life and Death of Karavelas*, perhaps the most perfect work of Theotokis. 'Karavelas' is the disparaging nickname of the central character, who is most realistically presented as ill-natured and unpleasant (the scene where he waits unmoved for the death of his wife is one of the most powerful); nevertheless he has not reached this state through his own fault alone, and is still capable even of passionate feeling, while the cold bargaining about everything by his rivals (who have 'arrived' socially) is more repellent and inhuman. 'Money and passion are rivals', writes A. Terzakis characteristically,[2] 'and in the reader's conscience it is the second that is acquitted.'

Theotokis had a genuine literary vein, and his intellectual conception of some of his characters never degenerates into

---

[1] A. Terzakis, Κωνσταντῖνος Θεοτόκης, Athens, 1955, p. 15.
[2] A. Terzakis, ibid., p. 23.

empty outlines. His language represents a late stage on the path opened by the first demotic prose writers (Eftaliotis, Karkavitsas); it is an authentic, carefully wrought demotic, to which some Corfiot idioms give a pleasant flavour. Theotokis was always faithful to his initial realism, and never followed the Symbolist path in prose like Chatzopoulos, so his style remains always clear and pure.

The case of Demosthenes Voutyràs (1871–1958) is altogether different. He began writing short stories in the usual 'genre' line about 1900, and collected them in a small volume in 1902. His 'genre' pictures transfer the focus from the circle of the village (with nostalgic and prettified reminiscences) to the poor quarters and outer suburbs of the modern city, and the wretched and unsuccessful life of its inhabitants. The stories from 1920 onwards aroused a more lively interest, particularly among the young, and were brought out at short intervals from 1920. It is not a matter of chance; the readjustments in political and social life, and the feeling of decline which we saw expressed in poetry after the First World War, created an atmosphere of sympathy for the reception of Voutyràs's picture of failure and the feeling of fatalism. In the decade 1920–30 Voutyràs was at the centre of literary interest and influenced (one may say harmfully) a number of young writers. His work was prolific, but careless; writing was almost a necessity of life to him, and he did not take much pains over it; he went on producing until his death, continuing in the same vein throughout his long literary career.

N. Nikolaïdis (1884–1956), a Cypriot settled in Alexandria, was most individual in his writing. He has left a series of stories and some novels, much influenced by the Aestheticism of the period. There is something unadjustable in the human characters that he describes, some deviation from the norm, which neither makes them sympathetic to the reader, nor justifies them from a literary point of view; moreover he has made most of his characters vague. Perhaps this is why his work caused little interest (favourable critics found it unjustly neglected). On the contrary his junior, Petros Pikròs, followed clearly in the footsteps of Voutyràs. Pikròs belonged, ideologically, to the left, but did not sacrifice literature to his ideology. His naturalism is more violent than that of Voutyràs, and his characters are the dregs of society; they are really the *Lost Bodies* (the title of a collection of his stories published in 1922), who wander between brothels and prisons.

Pikròs did not write after 1930. The atmosphere of pessimism and decline (which he shared with Voutyràs) was anyway that which dominated the decade 1920–30. But in the same decade there were to appear the first attempts to get away from the habitually miserable climate and the decline of style and expression. Fotis Kontoglou in 1923 published his first work, which was particularly well received (especially by the critics who were hostile to the existing state of things). The same welcome was extended to the first appearance of Thr. Kastanakis (1924), as a change from the old and an omen of things to come. It seemed that something new was burgeoning comparable with what had happened in the decade preceding 1880. This was to take new form with the 'generation of 1930', in poetry as well as prose. The first work of Kontoglou, Kastanakis, and others will therefore be examined in the chapter on prose after 1930 (see pp. 248–9).

## THEATRE AND CRITICISM

We saw in a preceding chapter (p. 178) that the theatrical revival which introduced the 'comidyll' (a parallel development with the 'genre' picture in the short story) came somewhat abruptly to an end in 1896. But at the same time there were new currents that revived the theatre (both in print and in performance). *The Ghost* of Argyris Eftaliotis (1894) (see p. 175), though never performed, was distinguished for its exploitation of popular tradition happily combined with the spirit of naturalism. Naturalism, the influence of Ibsen, and the conscious cultivation of literary demotic for the stage were the factors that determined the attempts at revival of the theatre at the end of the nineteenth and beginning of the twentieth centuries. It was in those years that Symbolism in poetry made its appearance, and it was no chance that the theatrical activity was connected with the periodical *Techni*.

We find the new tendencies more consciously expressed in the prematurely lost Jannis Kambysis (1872–1902), a mediocre writer, strongly influenced by Germany and by the north in general (Strindberg and Hauptmann). His best work is *The Mother's Ring* (1898) where all these confused influences mingle successfully in a Greek theme, and are expressed in a lyrical manner. The young of that time placed great hope in this poetical theatre of ideas, and the composer Manolis Kalomiris, influenced by Wagner but also a follower of the national music movement, chose this play for the theme of one of his first operas.

But it was K. Christomanos, whom we have already encountered as a prose writer (p. 210), who gave the greatest impulse to the modern Greek theatre. He wrote theatrical works, such as *Three Kisses* (1908), a 'tragic sonata' (as he called it) in three parts, with many cross-influences from naturalism, D'Annunzio, and so on, and a social satire *Kontorevithoulis*; but his importance to the theatre is more in practical matters. One day in 1901 he assembled the intellectuals in Athens in the Theatre of Dionysus and read them a proclamation in which he called for a revival of dramatic poetry and of the art of the theatre in Greece. The result was the foundation of a new theatre, the 'New Stage', of which Christomanos was the life and soul. Performances began in 1901 with a demotic translation of the *Alcestis* of Euripides, and ended in 1905. Christomanos was often obliged to make a compromise with the taste of the Athenian public, which was still immature, but by his firm personality he made a new and distinguished contribution, particularly in the realm of *mise en scène* and setting—this was one of the most successful achievements in the history of the modern Greek theatre. At the same time (1901–8) the 'Royal Theatre', a new foundation, was functioning; it was more conservative both in its choice of plays and in their production, but here also a remarkable producer, Thomas Ikonomou, was at work. The two theatres gave a noticeable impulse to the stage in Greece, and were favourable to the discovery of gifted actors, for example, the two 'leading ladies' round whom the theatre revolved for the following decades, Marika Kotopouli and Kyveli. But dramatic writing also benefited from this movement. Palamàs wrote *Trisevgeni* for production on the 'New Stage' (though it was withdrawn, because Christomanos wanted something 'more theatrical', that is, more in harmony with the naturalism of the time). And both Spilios Pasagiannis and Angelos Sikelianòs were 'initiates' (as Christomanos called his actors) in the first years of 'New Stage'.

These same years saw the first theatrical successes of G. Xenopoulos. We have already encountered him (p. 176) as a prolific novelist and prose writer; nor was his theatrical output small. He began in 1895 with plays influenced by Ibsen, and in 1904 produced what was perhaps from a theatrical point of view his most complete work, *The Secret of Countess Valeraina*; its centre (as in Palamas's *Trisevgeni*) is a noble character, ill-adapted to the low level of the surrounding society. This ideological–poetical spirit in his first works did not win immediate appreciation, and Xenopoulos early abandoned it, and sought, as in his novels, to compromise with his public. He was a highly skilled writer who knew how to put a work together, and how, without shocking the spectator, to do more than to satisfy him with the clichés of a boulevardier. 'A smart, modern theatrical work, on a worthy level, without extremes, moderate and decent; lacking both irrationality and genius.'[1]

Pantelìs Chorn (1880–1941) was an exclusively theatrical writer. His first works appeared in that creative decade, 1900–10, and have some of the idealism and other marks of the age. His dramatic writing was prolific, for he produced a new work almost every year. One that stands out is *The Green Shoot* (1921), a truly theatrical piece with developed characters, set in the yard of a house in a poor quarter of Athens; but the setting goes beyond that of a 'genre' picture, and takes on social proportions. 'After the *Basil Plant* of Matesis, our theatre has had no other work in which events and feelings and the development of character are so smoothly and boldly interwoven.'[2]

Spyros Melàs (1883–1966) gave much of his energy to the theatre, among other literary work. He was a novelist distinguished by his fictionalized biographies (*The Old Man of the Morea* (Th. Kolokotronis) and *Miaoulis*), a journalist, and critic, but also a regular author for the theatre, with a rich and varied body of work. He began in the 1900–10 decade with a curious, uneven, but inspired work, *The Son of the Shadow* (1907), a mixture of idealism and realism, obviously influenced by Ibsen and Nietzsche. His dramatic works in the same decade (*The Red Shirt, The Ruined House*) are more solidly constructed as plays. About 1925 Melàs, following the example of Christomanos, demanded a revival of the theatre and created the 'Arts Theatre' (where Pirandello was first produced), while in the following

---

[1] F. M. Pontani, *Teatro neoellenico*, Milan, 1962, p. 42.
[2] J. Sideris, Νεοελληνικὸ θέατρο, Athens, 1953, p. 30.

decade he was to return to writing for the stage with historical plays (*Judas, Papaflessas*) or with satirical comedies in somewhat doubtful taste (*The Father goes to School*). He continued in this line after the war.

The need for appreciation by the public, which is felt above all by the professional theatre, led those writers who wished to be professional playwrights to make compromises and concessions. Theodoros Synadinòs (1880–1959) chiefly cultivated comedy, with overt satire on Athenian life. D. Bogris (1890–1964) with loftier intentions achieved a dramatic competence in his best works, which are *The Engagement* (1925) and *The Squall* (1934).

Meanwhile, when the 'New Stage' and the Royal Theatre ceased to exist, there were sporadic attempts at change and improvement: the 'Company of the Greek Theatre' (1919), the amateur company of the Athens Conservatoire (1918–24), the 'Professional Dramatic School' (1924), the 'Arts Theatre' (Sp. Melàs, 1925), the 'Free Stage' (Sp. Melàs and Marika Kotopouli, 1929). Finally with the foundation of the 'National Theatre' (1932) an entirely new period began. The first producer of the National Theatre, and its principal support at the beginning, was Fotos Politis, whom we shall meet later as a critic.

In this period criticism was practised with a greater spirit of responsibility (we should distinguish the circle of the periodical *Panathinaia* and above all the critical work of G. Xenopoulos), and chiefly in progressive circles, especially among those concerned with demoticism. Already the *Techni* group had chosen for the target of its criticism the values established by the progressives, such as Papadiamantis and Psycharis and even Palamàs. The demoticists, who had their own organ, *Noumàs*, were also concerned with criticism—particularly of established values and of katharevousa. But in the columns of *Noumàs* pure literary criticism also developed. Those who took part in it were themselves creative writers, such as D. Tangopoulos, the editor of the periodical, or Rigas Golfis (pseudonym of D. Dimitriadis, 1886–1957), to whom we are also indebted for poems of great sensitivity and technical mastery. Aristos Kambanis and Elias Voutieridis further cultivated criticism, and gave us the first attempts at a history of modern Greek literature.

Jannis Apostolakis (1886–1947), with an essentially critical mind and a solid philological and philosophical education, at once distinguished himself from the creative writers of the time, and was violently critical of them, especially of Palamàs. Apostolakis studied philosophy in Germany, and immediately after his return published in a periodical of his circle (*Criticism and Poetry*, 1915) a study on the life of Thomas Carlyle. His orientations are obvious. In this idealistic atmosphere (his adversaries were to call it 'metaphysical') he wrote *Poetry in our Life* (1923), which, apart from some unevenness and looseness of construction, is the best interpretation of Solomòs after the 'Prolegomena' of Polylàs. He was to devote himself significantly to the demotic songs; he was the first who abandoned a folklore approach and considered them from a purely critical point of view (see pp. 92–7). His observations on the demotic songs and his analysis of the works of Solomòs are his best pieces of criticism; his negative criticism, which is just from his point of view, is nevertheless often unjustified in its historical aspect. 'The critic sees correctly, but judges unjustly.'[1] Apostolakis, as was natural, aroused the anger of his contemporaries; but today, in spite of his negative and often unjust attitude, we can see how much more weighty was his own pregnant critical thought. From the foundation of the University of Thessaloniki in 1926, until 1940, Apostolakis held the chair of modern Greek literature there.

Fotos Politis (1890–1934), son of N. G. Politis, also exercised a negative criticism, first following a line parallel to that of Apostolakis, and influenced by him. He also had studied in Germany, and had a keen interest in literature and the theatre; he began publishing criticism in the daily press in 1915, and continued for twenty years until his early death. He was not, however, the usual type of literary critic. Like that of Apostolakis, his criticism began from general principles, and from a basic attitude; he demanded a higher ethical approach from the intellectuals, and attacked falsity, *cabotinage*, and shallow literature without any real grip of life. He also aroused the anger of his contemporaries, but the young acknowledged his just austerity and unflinchingness, and accepted him as their teacher— especially in his last years when his articles extended beyond the narrow borders of literature, and touched ethical and social subjects that were very burning questions in the years 1930–4.

[1] K. Dimaràs, 'Ἱστορία, 4th edn., Athens, 1968, p. 444.

But Politis was not only a critic; his passionate interest in the theatre was expressed by the plays (*Tsimiskìs*, 1915, *Karagiozis the Great*, 1924), but above all by his activity as a stage manager and a producer. Already in 1919 he produced the *Oedipus Rex* in an entirely original fashion, and ten years later he gave model performances with the students of the Professional Dramatic School of, among other works, *The Basil Plant* of Matesis and the *Korakistika* of Neroulòs. With the foundation of the National Theatre in 1932 he became its first producer, but death too soon cut short his career.

Others who have practised criticism as a sideline, and not as their chief work, have been Sp. Melàs, G. Spatalàs, M. Avgeris (b. 1884). The last of these was later influenced in his criticism by his leftish position in politics, but being himself a poet is sensitive in his criticism of Sikelianòs and Kazantzakis. Fanis Michalopoulos (1895–1960), uneven in his achievements, was less a critic than a historian; however, the lack of scholarly method and accuracy deprives his books of a solid basis.

A group of critics appeared round 1920; most of them were poets or prose writers, and the literary work of many of them is not to be lightly dismissed. But their literary achievement is outclassed by that of the better-known of their contemporaries or those a little younger. Perhaps an exception is Tellos Agras who, as well as producing remarkable criticism, not so much in the field of critical journalism, which he did not much cultivate, as in fine appreciations of the complete work of many writers, had a place of his own as a poet (see p. 204). Of the rest, we may first mention Kleon Paraschos (1894–1964), a critic of rare sensibility who has given us full-scale studies of Ion Dragoumis and E. Roidis and shorter essays on modern Greek poets (*Ten Greek Lyric Poets*, 1937). Leon Koukoulas (1894–1967), one of the most lyrical poets of the 1920 generation (he first appeared in 1912 in *Noumàs* and later in *Mousa*), wrote theatrical criticism only in his later years. Alkis Thrylos (pseudonym of Eleni Ourani, 1896–1971) wrote mainly theatrical, but also more general literary criticism, in periodicals and newspapers. Her criticism was more systematic, and she attempted more synthetic studies of Greek prose writers, of Palamàs, the folk song, etc. Her thought was distinguished by its rationalism, which was sometimes a hindrance to deeper understanding of the work under discussion. Timos Malanos (b. 1897) lived in Alexandria and was the first to write a book on Kavafis, immediately after his death, and to make use of psycho-analysis in his critical method. He gave his attention to other poets (Karyotakis and Seferis), but his criticism, which was not always cool and un-biased, frequently aroused opposition.

Three critics born after 1900 still hold a central position in modern Greek criticism. J. M. Panagiotopoulos (b. 1901) studied literature and first appeared as one of the editors of the periodical *Mousa* (1920). He wrote poems, stories, novels, lyrical prose, and impressions of travel. His criticism appeared in the form of many articles and reviews in the daily and periodical press (especially in *Nea Estia*), and in independent volumes of essays and critical studies (*People and Texts*, 6 vols., 1943–55). We owe to Panagio-topoulos a short history of modern Greek literature, first pub-lished as an article in the *Great Greek Encyclopaedia*.

Petros Charis (pseudonym of Jannis Marmariadis, b. 1902) made his first appearance in *Noumàs* with a series of short stories. In later years his work has chiefly consisted of short stories and impressions of travel. But the greater part of his writing is critical; for forty years he regularly reviewed literary work in the columns of periodicals and newspapers, and in 1933 he undertook the direction of the periodical *Nea Estia*. He also published essays and some longer studies on problems connected with our literature (*Greek Prose Writers*, 3 vols. 1954–68).

A prolific writer, like the two just mentioned, is Emilios Chourmouzios (b. 1904), a professional journalist (editor of the *Kathimerinì*) and also a very conscientious critic. He often wrote topical literary and theatrical reviews (for many years he was also Director General of the National Theatre), and he also published many books of criticism: *Palamàs and His Age* (3 vols.), *Konstantinos Theotokis, Eugene O'Neil*, etc.

### N. KAZANTZAKIS

Within the narrow limits of a history of literature it is not easy to describe or evaluate the work of Nikos Kazantzakis (1883–1957), so varied and of such bulk. He was a contemporary of Sikelianòs (sometimes they were great friends, and sometimes they could not get on together) and of Varnalis, but entirely idiosyncratic. In the flux of modern Greek literature it is hard to classify his work, whether poetry or prose. He was an unquiet spirit, athirst for every sort of knowledge, and he not only travelled a great deal, but also lived for long periods abroad (in France, Germany, and Russia), and almost deliberately cut himself adrift from the actualities of modern Greek life.

Kazantzakis was born at Heracleion in Crete, and there in that small Turkish-dominated town, where the fever of revolution was secretly burning, he received his elementary education. The revolution of 1897 obliged him to leave home and spend two years at a school run by Franciscans in Naxos. In 1902–6 he studied law in Athens, and in 1907–9 in Paris, where he was influenced by the teaching of Bergson. He returned to Athens and occupied himself with the translation of philosophical books, and in 1914 he became acquainted with Angelos Sikelianòs, with whom he travelled to Mount Athos and other places. In 1918 and 1919 he travelled in Switzerland and in Russia, and in 1922 he stayed in Vienna, and later for a longer time in Berlin; there he lived close to the misery and social disturbance of the post-war world and with Jewish friends, with whom he drew near to the communist ideology. He returned to Greece in 1924 (passing through Assisi on the way), and in Crete he planned an illegal political movement, without success. In the years 1925–9 he made three journeys to Russia (invited on the second occasion by the Soviet Government for the tenth anniversary of the revolution), and there became acquainted (though they were finally to separate) with the Rumanian-Greek writer Panait Istrati; together with him, or alone, he crossed Russia from Tiflis to Siberia. His knowledge of Russia was to inspire his impressions of travel, a French novel *Toda Raba*, etc. But Kazantzakis had already firmly in mind his work, the *Odyssey*.

At the same time he made short visits to France and a visit of some months to Spain (1932–3), another to Japan and China (1935), and he was press correspondent to an Athenian paper in the Spanish civil war (1936). In the summer of 1939 he went as the guest of the British Council to England, where he lived for the first months of the war. At the end of the year he returned to Aegina, where he lived throughout the war and the occupation. After the liberation he took some part in politics in Athens, where he founded a socialist group and was for a short time minister without portfolio. In June 1946 he left for England, stayed for a short time in Cambridge, and in September settled in Paris where, again for a short time, he was literary adviser to UNESCO. After 1948 he remained permanently at Antibes in the south of France, always at work, and supervising the continual translations and editions of his work. As a guest of the Chinese Government he started on a journey to China in 1957; he arrived sick in Copenhagen, and thence went to the university clinic of Freiburg in Germany, where he died on 26 October of the same year. He was honoured by his fellow Cretans by burial in a bastion of the Venetian walls of Heracleion.

Kazantzakis made his first real appearance in literature towards the end of the first decade of this century, after his studies in Paris. A tragedy, *The Master Builder*, was based on the demotic song, *The Bridge of Arta*, and contained obvious elements of Aestheticism; he also wrote a scholarly study of Nietzsche. The influence of Nietzsche was also clear in the tragedy, and was to be permanent in his work, both in the element of lack of faith, and in the conception of the superman. Bergson's philosophy of the irrational, and his theory of the life force, were also to set their mark on all his creative work. Kazantzakis in some things followed the intellectual attitude of the time (he was influenced by the pragmatist William James), but he was completely involved with the actuality of Greek life and the currents leading towards progress; he dedicated *The Master Builder* to Ion Dragoumis, and was one of the founding members of the 'Educational Society'.

But even in these early years the mind of Kazantzakis was unquiet, his spirit was tormented by anxieties and fundamental problems—his biographers were to call it a metaphysical (or existentialist) anguish. He sought to find relief in travel, in knowledge, in human relationships, and in every sort of experience. And though a Nietzschean unbeliever, he was troubled by religious problems; the person of Christ ('that so mysterious and so real union of man and God', as he wrote in a letter)[1] followed him as a permanent idea from his youth till his last years. In 1915, after his visit to Mount Athos with Sikelianòs, he wrote

---

[1] Letter to the writer Max Tau quoted by P. Prevelakis, '*O ποιητὴς καὶ τὸ ποίημα τῆς* '*Οδύσσειας*, Athens, 1958, p. 309. Id., *Τετρακόσια γράμματα*, Athens, 1965, p. λς'.

*Christ*, a tragedy, expressing his experiences. In 1922 two new tragedies, *Buddha* and *Odysseus*, shows his new orientations. P. Prevelakis, his most authoritative critic, makes a list of the 'prophets' who in turn possessed his mind: Nietzsche, Christ, Buddha, Lenin—Lenin, it is to be noted, not Marx, whose theories were totally opposed to those of Kazantzakis.[1] Finally, he was to repudiate this last also, and his hero and prototype (his 'parallel', as his critic calls him) was to be Odysseus.

The years that he passed in Germany (1922–3) were decisive for the formation of his *Weltanschauung*. He abandoned the 'aristocratic nationalism' in which he had hitherto believed (the nationalism of I. Dragoumis and of his own time), and was receptive to the communistic and revolutionary ideas that were then disturbing the political and intellectual life of Germany. In these years he wrote his *Asceticism*, one of his most important works, which was published for the first time in 1927 with the title *Salvatores Dei*.

This is a fairly short volume, very concise, expressing Kazantzakis's metaphysical beliefs. He considered it as 'the seed from which all his work grew, and that all he wrote was an illustration or comment on the *Asceticism*'; he himself described it as 'a *mystique* book describing the method by which the soul rises from circle to circle till it attains the highest contact. The circles are five: Ego, Humanity, Earth, Universe, God.'[2] The last part of the theory is 'Action', and the last step up to redemption is 'Silence'. The work has a strong, moulded style and—in spite of its metaphysical content—a charm that gives it a literary elegance. When it first came out, its ideological message was described as 'a cry from beyond communism'. After his visit to Russia Kazantzakis denied his former theories and turned towards complete nihilism; he then altered the text and added a final 'beatitude' for those who liberate God and say, 'You and I are one, and that one does not exist'.

As we have seen, Kazantzakis considered the *Asceticism* as the seed of all his later work. And what he thought of above all as his *work* (and all the rest as 'sidelines') was his *Odyssey*. He had formed the first core of it already in Crete in 1924, after his

---

[1] Ibid., pp. λθ′–ν′.

[2] N. Kazantzakis, Ἄνθρωποι καὶ ὑπεράνθρωποι, p. 100 (cited by P. Prevelakis, ʿΟ ποιητὴς καὶ τὸ ποίημα τῆς ᾿Οδύσσειας, Athens, 1958, p. 79).

return from Germany, and later he worked on it with intensity from time to time, and made seven different recensions before its publication in 1938. On his journey to Russia he was longing to get home and devote himself to writing, and later on his voyage to the Far East he wrote down experiences for use in the work. It is really a 'superhuman attempt to put to order and use all the vast intellectual experience of Kazantzakis'.[1]

The work is in twenty-four rhapsodies, and 33,333 seventeen-syllable iambic verses (the number was symbolic to Kazantzakis). It is naturally difficult to give a summary; there is a useful synopsis in P. Prevelakis's book,[2] and another, more analytical, in the translation by K. Friar. We shall confine ourselves to saying that the poem begins with the return to Ithaca, and is about further wandering by the insatiable hero. First he goes to Sparta, whence he steals Helen, then to Crete, where a con-spiracy dethrones the king, and to Egypt, where again there is a working-class revolution; after leaving there and living as an ascetic on a mountain, he founds a city (Utopia), which is destroyed, and reaches 'complete freedom'. He meets Managìs (a personification of the Buddha), Captain One (Don Quixote), and a virgin fisherman (Christ). Finally he sails to the South Pole, where death overtakes him and he is sublimated.

In fact the *Odyssey* embodies in its peculiar form all the *Weltanschauung* (if we may so call it) of the author, and all his metaphysical anguish, as well as all sides of his character: his heroic pessimism, his irrationality, his solitude, and finally his nihilism. It is hard to say that his ideas enter into a synthesis, for often they conflict; the central line of Kazantzakis, however, is negation, a struggle not for an end in view, but for the sake of the struggle itself, liberty that is like a denial of the idea of liberty, the apotheosis of the void.

Kazantzakis wished to write an epic, that of contemporary man (not only of the Greek or the European), and therefore he saw the *Odyssey* as his *work*, above all his other works; but his most sincere admirers will find difficulty in accepting the *Odyssey* as an epic with this significance (the significance that Virgil had for the Roman of Imperial times, or Tasso for the man of the Renaissance). But whether the poet succeeded in his aims or no, one indispensable element was lacking: the contact between the

---

[1] Prevelakis, op. cit., p. 49.     [2] Ibid., pp. 111–23.

public and the work. The *Odyssey* did not speak to wider circles, nor yet to narrow circles so that it might indirectly be assimilated. It remained an isolated work, both when it was first published (in an expensive, heavy, and unmanageable first edition) and (it is to be feared) it still remains so, thirty years later, even though it has been translated and is available to an international public. It is not only the weight of more than thirty thousand lines that discourages the reader, but also the harsh language which is far-fetched and full of idioms and unknown words, and even the content. This new Odysseus, an immoralist and a desperado, is so isolated that he is no longer human, a creation that cannot awaken sympathy. The ice-berg on which he dies all alone is a clear enough symbol.

Nevertheless, the *Odyssey* is certainly an astonishing work, and a poetic achievement. The author could put into it all the vast knowledge and experience of life that he had gained by asceticism and meditation. And although its basis is an intellectual conception, it goes far beyond mere cerebration. Kazantzakis is a writer who could give shape and reality to his intellectual conceptions, and at his better moments could even infuse a poetical inspiration. The *Odyssey* is a *work*; on this point its author was absolutely right.

At the same time as his work on the *Odyssey* (from about 1933 to 1939) Kazantzakis was also writing a series of cantos, poems in the Dantesque *terza rima*, his only lyrical work (if lyrical it may be called). They are dedicated to people who played an important role in the formation of his personality, ranging from Dante and El Greco to his parents and closer friends. He meant to write twenty-four, as there were twenty-four rhapsodies in his *Odyssey*, and he called them, playfully, 'the twenty-four bodyguards of the *Odyssey*'. They were printed after his death under the title *Tertsines*.

The decade following the publication of the *Odyssey* (1938) was mainly occupied by the difficult years of the war and the occupation, which Kazantzakis lived through in Greece, mostly in Aegina. Before the war he had written two more tragedies, *Melissa* (1937) and *Julian* (1939). But also after the war, and at the time of his creative activity as a novelist, he wrote another series of plays, into which many critics feel he poured out all the anguish of his later years, even more than into the novels.

The themes are varied and many, and are drawn from Antiquity or modern history.

As we have said, drama was the form in which this writer found it most easy to express himself in his first years of work. But drama (or rather the dramatic form) was for Kazantzakis a mode of externalizing his inner world. A remarkable thing, which several theatrical critics have mentioned, is the likeness between one work and another. You have the impression that the same theme is taken up in many variations. In the centre is a single, solitary man who confronts the rest, the man who 'knows' the 'great secret', as Kazantzakis repeatedly calls it—who knows, for example, that the struggle is in vain, but that one must struggle until the end. It does not matter whether this man is called Julian or Constantine Palaeologus or Kapodistrias or Christopher Columbus.

His turn to the novel during his last years was decisive, though this was a form which he had hitherto never touched, at least not in his own language. The reason for this change was his desire to communicate with a wider public, which he had hitherto failed to do. His literary instinct showed him that the right form for this was the novel; he himself reveals somewhere that his novels were an amusement and relaxation to him after he had finished his *work*.[1]

The first novel was *The Life and Manners of Alexis Zorbàs* (1946). Kazantzakis is here making a legend out of a real person, a primitive man of the people from Macedonia with whom he collaborated in a curious enterprise connected with mines in the Mani in 1916–17. The author has transferred the action to Crete, but the central figure, who dominates the novel, is this unpolished character with his tremendous zest for life, a man outside society whom the meditative and cultivated Kazantzakis regards, as from the opposite bank of a stream, with some envy. He is certainly one of the most lifelike characters in Kazantzakis's novels, and this first novel is in every way his best. In the others Kazantzakis poses ethical and metaphysical problems which sometimes confuse the work's purely literary value, as he did not give much attention to literary revision. In a letter of his he says, with some exaggeration, that he has no connection with what is

---

[1] P. Prevelakis, op. cit., p. 278 (cf. p. 318, n. 218). See also id., Τετρακόσια γράμματα, p. 597 (no. 344).

called literature and that he employs the same medium, that is, words, for an entirely different purpose.[1]

Apart from *Zorbàs* Kazantzakis wrote, or gave final form to, other novels in the last decade of his life, when he had permanently settled abroad. He met with international success, a success that was astonishingly widespread. One after another his novels were translated into various European languages, were widely read and criticized, or adapted to the stage or the screen (we may mention Dassin's film *The Man Who Ought to Die*) ; often they were first published in a foreign language, and later in the original. This sudden and later international recognition of a writer perhaps needs some explanation, full treatment of which would divert us too far. Part of the success, however, is no doubt due to the 'picturesque' elements which abound in his novels (to the Cretan life of the beginning of this century, and the curious primitiveness of the people), elements certainly bound up organically with the works, and genuinely literary in their presentation, but which are not the central 'core', or the 'message' that the author wished to give the public in a popular form.

His novels are numerous; we need not refer to them all. The most polished, after *Zorbàs*, are, in our opinion, *Christ Recrucified* and *Kapetan Michalis*. *Christ Recrucified* (1948) presents a whole world of characters. The Passion of Christ is performed on the stage in a Greek village in Asia Minor. The various villagers enact the characters in the Gospels, but finally identify themselves with the roles which they enact. Manoliòs, who takes the part of Christ, is finally 'recrucified' for standing up for the poor and for justice. There is a dramatic clash between the permanent inhabitants of the village, who do not want their peace disturbed, and the hungry homeless refugees from another Greek village. The conflict takes on broad human proportions, the plot is purely that of a novel, and the crowd is distinguished by light and shade and countless details, while in front of it the central figures, and particularly the saintly character of Manoliòs, stand out in bold relief.

*Kapetan Michalis* (1950) is less well constructed as a novel and the action is not always suitably motivated. In the central figure the author depicts his own father in all his dynastic severity, and

---

[1] Letter from Antibes, 2 March 1955, to A. Sachinis, cited by the latter, Πεζογράφοι τοῦ καιροῦ μας, Athens, [1967], p. 34.

he also tries 'to resurrect the Heracleion of his childhood' and above all the struggles of the Cretans for their liberty. Perhaps the two subjects do not fit well together or balance each other. The central figure is less a combatant for liberty than a new incarnation of Kazantzakis's heroes (Odysseus, Julian, or Kapodistrias), that is, of the writer's own spirit. The final words of the hero: 'Not liberty *or* death; liberty *and* death', are completely 'Kazantzakian'. Nevertheless there are many characters in action, and the atmosphere of Turkish-dominated Heracleion is authentically given.

Of the other novels, *The Last Temptation* (1950–1) has Christ for its main subject (and gave rise to many objections); *The Little Poor Man of God* (1952–3) is a fictionalized biography of St. Francis of Assisi; and *The Fratricides* (1954) is set in the time of the guerrilla warfare just after the liberation of Greece (in 1944–9). The dates given are those of composition; most of them were published in Greek much later, the last one after his death. Finally we must mention his *Report to Greco*, also published posthumously (1961), though it is not a novel but a poetical autobiography, indispensable to the interpretation of his work.

In order to complete the account of the impressive and many-sided personality of Kazantzakis we must refer to his translations and travel books. We may say that Kazantzakis became conscious of his experiences by turning them into literature. His translations of the masterpieces of world literature (Dante, *Faust*, Homer) are more like a careful reading and a commentary. One might say they were written chiefly for himself and not for anyone else, and they might be of less help to any other person. From epistolary sources we know that they were finished in incredibly little time—which may give rise to astonishment, but also to some doubts.

Kazantzakis made creative use of his travel experiences by writing his impressions; often the first core was reportage for newspapers, but later his impressions lost their occasional character, and show us an unquiet, speculative, and meditative spirit. Under the general title *Travel* he first published his impressions of journeys in Spain, Italy, Egypt, and Sinai (1927), and later of the civil war in Spain (1937), of Japan and China (1938), and of England (1941). In posthumous editions impressions of

Russia, Jerusalem, Cyprus, and the Peloponnese were added. Of the many places that he visited there can have been few of which he did not write descriptive impressions, and these are among the best of Kazantzakis's work.

# XV

## THE GENERATION OF 1930
## POETRY

G. SEFERIS

IN 1931 a slim volume of poems came out in Athens, *Turning-Point* by G. Seferis. His name was unknown to the literary periodicals of that day, and appeared now for the first time. The Greek title (*Strophe*) is ambiguous; it might merely be a term in prosody (stanza), or it might mean a real turning-point and a more profound change. Now we know that the title certainly had the second meaning. With this slender collection of poems there came into modern Greek poetry an unexpected change, a real 'turning-point', which has since become familiar to us in its many variants.

Criticism has often spoken of the '1930 generation' in poetry and prose. The term is not haphazard. Just as fifty years earlier the 'generation of 1880' brought in something new and revolutionary and contrary to what was then established, so the post-1930 poets freed themselves from the false ornaments of traditional poetry and created—in immediate conjunction with the fresh currents and the uneasy developments of European lyricism—a new form of expression, and a modern poetry. (The term now has its meaning established in the history of literature.) Of this poetry Seferis was the initiator in *Turning-Point*.

G. Seferis (the *nom de plume* of George Seferiadis) was born on 29 February 1900 in Smyrna, that great city of Asia Minor that was so thoroughly Greek. His father, an authority on international law, was from 1919 professor in the University of Athens (he was also author of some poems and verse translations). The Seferiadis family left in 1914 for Athens, where the poet finished his secondary schooling, he continued his law studies in Paris

(1918–24), with a brief visit to London in 1924–5. He therefore lived the formative years of eighteen to twenty-five abroad, in close touch with the intellectual and poetical movements that changed the forms of literature immediately after the First World War. Here the news of the Asia Minor disaster and of the destruction of Smyrna reached him, and this memory was to remain deeply rooted.

Directly after the end of his studies Seferis entered the diplomatic service, in which he made his career, first in Athens and then in London. He was consul at Koritsa in Albania (1936–8). Subsequently he was Press attaché to the Ministry of Foreign Affairs, and in 1941 followed the Greek Government in exile to Egypt, South Africa, and Italy, returning after the liberation to Athens, where he remained till 1948. He was subsequently appointed Counsellor to the Embassies in Ankara and London, ambassador to Lebanon, Syria, Jordan, and Iraq (1953–6), and finally ambassador in London (1957–62); after this he retired from the diplomatic service and returned to Athens. He died in September 1971.

Seferis's poetry won its first distinction with the Palamàs Prize (1946); later came his honorary doctorate at Cambridge (1960), and finally the Nobel Prize for Literature (1963). Other distinctions followed, including honorary doctorates at Oxford, Thessaloniki, and Princeton, and an honorary fellowship of the American Academy of Arts and Sciences.

In an interview soon after he was awarded the Nobel Prize[1] Seferis said that at the time of the publication of *Turning-Point* (1931) he was aware of two things: that he wanted to write simple poetry and that people would not like it. The latter is a surprising confession, the former is the most personal and permanent characteristic not only of his first collection but of all his poetical work.

*Turning-Point* at once took us into an atmosphere entirely different from that of decadence and decay that characterized the generation of the decade 1920–30, and that continued monotonously and without originality, particularly after the suicide of Karyotakis. From the first poem (with the same title, 'Turning-Point') the difference was felt: it was a new spirit and

[1] Interview given to Bernard Pivot, *Le Figaro littéraire*, 2 November 1963, pp. 1–2.

above all a different 'language'. Perhaps at the time this new language was not at once comprehensible, but the most sensitive readers realized that the poet had something new and serious to say. The expression was new, frugal, and Doric, but there was a wealth of newly coined images and bold forms of expression:

> On the secret seashore
> white like a pigeon
> we thirsted at noon:
> but the water was brackish.
>                               ('Denial')

The narcissistic ego, which dominated the poetry of the time, was not heard in this collection, but persistently and fundamentally we hear, like a leitmotif, 'we'. Even in the poems that are clearly confessions the ego spreads out towards its neighbour, and the personal drama is raised to the general character of tragedy.

In the middle of the collection is the large poem, *Erotikòs Logos*, written in decapentesyllables, in four-line rhyming stanzas. The poet has stored up memories of the finest moments of the national metre (the *Erotokritos*, Solomòs, Sikelianòs), but his markedly personal expression gives a melodic line of his own to these decapentesyllables, which are among the most beautiful in modern Greek poetry, but also among the last to be written in a poem of any length.

Passing over *Cistern*, privately printed in 1932, the next significant phase is *Mythistorima* (1935). Here we meet the Seferis we will come to know. He has definitely abandoned strict metre and rhyme, to create his own personal style in free verse. This collection consists of twenty-four poems or, rather, a poem in twenty-four parts. These were critical years for Greece and for Europe, over which, unresisted, hung the heavy shadow of totalitarianism. The poet found refuge in new researches or new conflations in *myth* and *history* (in Greek myth and Greek history). No other collection is so weighted with classical recollections. The tragic element, as the Greeks first conceived it, returns with tormenting insistence; a permanent element, like a counterweight to the tragic decay of our time.

*Mythistorima* is a mature work; his later collections follow the same firm line. *Logbook* appeared in April 1940. The time was yet more critical; the Second World War had begun, and though

Greece was still outside it, it was obvious that it would not be for long. This apprehension seems to be present throughout the collection; there is an atmosphere of anxiety, but it is an anxiety without panic, full of courage and decision. 'The Last Day' (not published at the time because of censorship), and 'The Decision to Forget' are most significant poems from this point of view. The last poem in the volume is 'The King of Asine', one of Seferis's greatest and most disturbing poems, in which by the shore, under the ruins of the Mycenaean acropolis, he obstinately searches for the King of Asine, a void behind his gold funeral mask.

A month earlier, in March 1940, as a kind of first summing up (in May he was to publish all his previously printed poems), Seferis issued under the title of *Book of Exercises (1928–1937)*, poems that had not yet found a place in his published collections, fugitive fragments given to friends, and 'exercises more or less advanced, I mean as far as working on them goes', as he himself commented. Among the exercises we must pick out the 'Sixteen Haiku' (an exercise in this laconic and elliptic style), the poems about Stratis the Mariner (a fictitious character invented by the poet), and the later and more finished 'Plans for a Summer'.

As we saw, Seferis lived in the Middle East and in South Africa after 1941 with the Greek Government in exile; as he wrote on the frontispiece of his previous collection, in the dry phrase of a logbook: 'We remain in the same place, awaiting orders'. The next collection had the same title: *Logbook II* and is a poetical transubstantiation of his war experiences. The poems were written in the places of his exile (he noted places and dates: Transvaal, October 1941; Pretoria, 1942; Cairo, August 1943). They present the anxieties of the time from the point of view of the exile:

> Jerusalem, ungoverned city,
> Jerusalem, city of refugees . . .
>
> We continue our tour
> Many fathoms below the level of the Aegean.

The last and perhaps the most significant poem in the collection is entitled 'Last Stop' (Cava dei Tirreni, 5 October 1944).

The last stop before the return from exile to his liberated country. Two years later, having retired to the calm of the small Saronic island of Poros, Seferis wrote *The Thrush*, perhaps his most enigmatic poem, and that which most resists the critic's attempt to get inside it. *The Thrush* is the name of a ship sunk by the Germans in the harbour of the island; by that depth and clarity that Seferis knows how to impart to symbols, the shipwreck becomes the starting-point of the poetical thoughts that follow and that make this poem (as many critics think) the most personal of Seferis's works, and the key to his whole poetry. Able for the first time for years to surrender himself to solitude and meditation, he lets his thoughts wander over the mysteries of life and of death, over the double nature of life that becomes death, and of light whose other side is darkness:

> Light, angelic and black,
> Laughter of waves on the sea's highways,
> Tear-stained laughter, . . .
>
> Day, angelic and black;
> The brackish taste of woman that poisons the prisoner
> Emerges from the wave a cool branch adorned with drops.

All the last part, with the title 'Light', outstanding for its poetical richness, is one of the greatest achievements in Seferis's poetry. 'The double nature of light is sung with a sudden elevation of tone in the finale which is among the most exalted pages in modern poetry.'[1]

Ten years passed before Seferis published another collection. In these years he was again outside Greece, in London and Ankara and Beirut; then in 1953-5 he visited the monasteries of Cappadocia, and Cyprus. This last visit was more decisive. In December 1955 he published a small volume under the title of *Cyprus, where it was Decreed* . . . (words of Euripides). When it was reprinted he gave it the title *Logbook III*.

In fact the poems of this collection are not a continuation of *The Thrush* so much as of the two *Logbooks*. In this he conveys a new experience, in a way a continuation of his others: that of Cyprus' struggle for its liberty. 'The poems of this collection', he wrote, 'were given to me in the autumn of '53 when I travelled in Cyprus for the first time. It was the revelation of

---

[1] *Giorgio Seferis Poesie*, a cura di F. M. Pontani, 1963, p. 332.

a world and still more the experience of a human drama that, whatever may be the expediency of everyday give and take, must judge and measure our humanity.'[1] As well as the topicality (the 'experience of human drama'), the new world 'revealed' to him dominates this collection of poems, the natural and human background of the island, and a personal, warmer, almost sensual feeling; the two motifs blend in the poems with a particular charm—I use the word with its primal and not its decorative meaning.

> The nightingales won't let you sleep in Platres . . .

In this musical magic of a Mediterranean night begins one of the most important poems in the collection, 'Helen', which ends in one of the most piercing cries to be heard in modern poetry:

> And my brother?
> > Nightingale nightingale nightingale
> What is a god? What is not a god? And what is there in between them?

The words are given to Teucer, brother of Ajax, but in the symbolical language of Seferis in which there is continuous correspondence between myth and actuality, 'the brother' takes on another existence, especially when it is interwoven in the poem (in the same 'magical' manner) with a third motif, that of guile and deceit, which is heard more definitely in these questions with their existentialist agony, which continue, more tragically, the question-mark and the void of the 'King of Asine'.

Already in 1940, with the title of *Poems 1*, Seferis had made a first general collection of the volumes previously published; in 1950, with the title *Poems, 1924–46*, he made a second general collection in which in 1961 he incorporated the poems about Cyprus. We may call this the Corpus of his poetry, and it represents thirty years of intense artistic activity (from 'Fog'—the title is in English—in *Turning-Point*, dated London, Christmas 1924, till November 1953, the date of 'Salamis in Cyprus' in the last volume). It is certainly not everything that he wrote (recently a youthful 'ballade' in the manner of Villon and the language of the *Erotokritos* was published),[2] but Seferis is not only a laconic

---

[1] Seferis's own note to *Logbook III* (= Ποιήματα, 5th edn., Athens, 1964, p. 280). Not translated in *Collected Poems*.
[2] In the newspaper Μεσόγειος (Heracleion, Crete), 12 April 1967.

poet but also particularly sparing of his appearances before the public (like Kavafis, and most unlike Palamàs and Sikelianòs). After 1955 he was silent until 1966 when he published *Three Secret Poems*, which more or less continue the esoteric line of *The Thrush*; in these we hear his familiar voice, but it is now more austere and hermetic.

This body of work gives us a complete poetic personality—one of the most weighty not only in modern Greek, but in all contemporary poetry. In its fundamental character this personality is dominantly Greek, rooted in the soil of Greece which gave him birth. The Greece of Seferis has not the shining lucidity of an external view, but is a consciousness full of weight and responsibility; it is indivisible in time, place, and human elements —'with the ancient monuments and contemporary sorrow'.[1] Despite this 'classicism', Seferis's language is thorough demotic, and there seems to flow through it all the working of the Greek language throughout its long history. These reminiscences do not adulterate his voice, but make it all the more characteristic and personal, and on the other side it finds its natural parallel in the contemporary poetical language.

All this does not mean that Seferis is narrowly Greek and nothing else. In his earlier poems the influence of the *poésie pure* of his French contemporaries is evident (for example, Mallarmé and Valéry); from *Mythistorima* onwards we feel the influence of Eliot and Pound (though not to the degree that some critics have supposed). But 'influences' are the least important things about Seferis. The important thing is that this poet, so Greek in his outlook, is wholly rooted in the anxieties of our time and those of contemporary man. The poem may begin with the King of Asine or Helen, but its symbolism pierces through successive strata and reveals the 'soulmonger' War and the 'friends of the other war'; its centre is always directed towards man 'in offering insights that carry with them the weight of universal truths and that thus serve to reveal the deeper meaning of our times' (E. Keeley and P. Sherrard).[2]

Seferis is not an easy poet, and his reputation grew slowly and with difficulty. But he is not obscure. The language he speaks is difficult, but in this language his voice is clear and straight-

---

[1] μὲ τ' ἀρχαῖα μνημεῖα καὶ τὴ σύγχρονη θλίψη, 'The King of Asine'.
[2] *Collected Poems*, p. xiii.

forward; you feel he has hit upon the perfect expression, for what could not have been said otherwise. It is this perhaps that is most lovable about his poetry: the simplicity which attains the warmth of a confession, and the stability, so much opposed to the decadence of expression in the previous generation— a stability which we may call 'classical'. We must add another characteristic. Seferis's poetry is not at all cheerful; it is pessimistic and melancholy. It has the grief of a man often meditating on mankind, and also that of the Greek with the undercurrent of bitterness for national servitude and other sufferings (the 'grief of Greekdom', as it is called). However, his temperament never leads him to negation or destruction. On the other side of darkness is light, black but angelic, and 'on the sunny side' of the castle of Asine, there will rise 'the shield-bearer, the sun warring'. Behind denial there is a faith which protects him from despair, and a strong sense of reality that protects him from decadence or nihilism.

Seferis is a profound thinker and a student of persons and things concerned with history and literature. Thus he considered the problems of poetry and language: his dialogue with K. Tsatsos, 'Dialogue on Poetry', was followed by a 'Monologue', and by 'Language in Our Poetry'.[1] He has also written about Kalvos, Makrygiannis, Kavafis, and Eliot. He collected these studies in *Essays* (1944, 2nd edn. 1962). The few things he has written in interpretation of his own poetry are significant (especially 'A letter about *The Thrush*').[2] Other important prose writings are his impressions of a visit to the Byzantine rock churches of Cappadocia and an essay on Delphi.

Seferis has given much time and patience to translation, and in this he has indicated his preferences. His first publication in 1928 was a translation of Valéry, but his most considerable translations have been from Eliot (*The Waste Land, Murder in the Cathedral*, etc.). He has recently made a provisional collection of his other translations under the title of *Transcripts* (1965). It contains translations from Yeats, Pound, MacLeish, and Gide,

---

[1] 'Dialogue' and 'Monologue' now in Δοκιμές, 2nd edn., Athens, 1962, pp. 69–112. 'Language in Our Poetry', in: Aristotelian University of Thessaloniki, 'Ο Γ. Σεφέρης ἐπίτιμος διδάκτωρ τῆς Φιλοσοφικῆς Σχολῆς, Thessaloniki, 1965, pp. 17–33.

[2] Letter to G. Katsimbalis, in Ἀγγλοελληνικὴ 'Επιθεώρηση, 4 (1950), 501–6; the end reprinted in Δοκιμές, 2nd edn., pp. 365–8.

Jouve, Eluard, and Michaud. Lately he has attempted the translation of *The Song of Songs* and the *Revelations of St. John*; the rendering of these works from an older form of the Greek language into that of today (he calls it 'transcription' not 'translation') and all the problems that it raises were of the greatest interest to him.

### SURREALISM AND THE YOUNGER POETS

In 1935, the year of Seferis's *Mythistorima* (and, oddly, the year also of Palamàs's last volume of poems), a strange pamphlet was issued in Athens in an elegant edition; it was the *Furnace* of Andreas Embirikos. In content it was like no literary genre, and made no sense. Under paradoxical titles like 'The Vibrations of the Necktie' or 'The Appearance of Angels in a Steam-Engine', the reader found phrases to which he could attach no logical meaning. Public reaction ranged from astonishment to mockery and indignation, and few were the 'initiates' who could understand something. The only orientation provided by the writer was a citation on the front page from André Breton, where he spoke of the *voix surréaliste*. Thus eleven years after André Breton's first manifesto, and nearly five after his second, and almost at the time when the movement was at its height in Europe and America, the Surrealist school made its first appearance in Greece with the *Furnace*—just as Romanticism had made its first appearance with *The Traveller*, and Parnassianism with the *Verses* of Kambàs. The *Furnace* may have been incoherent and incomprehensible to the ordinary reader of 1935, but it was to have a direct or indirect influence on subsequent poetry, even when it was necessary for this to go beyond it.

Following the methods of the movement, the poet made use of 'automatic writing', and thus released from the subconscious a wealth of images without logical connection but with the charm of a surrealist sensation. The text is written in prose (this verbal release is hard to fit into metre and rhythm), with unsparing use of elements from katharevousa and clichés from newspapers or from scientific terminology. It is hard today to find poetical or literary virtue in these pieces; their value was that they were a landmark in history, and examples of a new genre.

Ten years after the *Furnace* Embirikos published a new volume,

*Hinterland* (1945), but containing poems written directly after the *Furnace*, between 1934 and 1937, that is, in a period very rich in new developments in modern Greek poetry. Here the poet goes beyond the limits of pure Surrealism and automatic writing, makes use of verse, and organizes a new poetical style full of gaiety out of the preceding chaos; here a principal place is given to the dream and to the all-powerful sexual instinct of Freudian theory. The result was the revelation of an original and fresh world, and a lyrical expression, unfettered by anything old, full of the joy of liberty. 'The transatlantic liner that sings and sails' (in the most mature and the best poem of the collection) takes on a peculiar symbolic value.

Embirikos, who was born at Brăila in Rumania in 1901 and lived many years in France and England, is a well-read man, and has particularly studied philosophy and psycho-analysis. As a writer he is prolific, though he has published little. He had written extensive prose works (*Argo or the Voyage of a Balloon, Zemphyra or the Secret of Pasiphaë*), of which the few friends who have heard them read speak favourably, though the eroticism is so unbridled in expression that they cannot be published. Lately he has published some poems (which seem to be more recent), *Words* and *The Road*, which have been recorded in an exciting reading by the poet himself.[1] In these poems, with succinctness and clarity, and an altogether new maturity, an idealistic faith is expressed, and a heavy feeling of death and doom.

N. Engonopoulos (born 1910) has followed the orthodox Surrealist line. He has followed the same line in painting, and is one of the most important painters of the new school. He is more revolutionary and, one might say, wilfully provocative— he kept to the left wing of the movement—and therefore his volumes (especially those of 1938 and 1939) annoyed the reading bourgeoisie and aroused scorn and indignation. Engonopoulos remained uncompromising in his Surrealist determination also in his post-war volumes. He is distinguished by an inward and bitter lyricism and pictorial clarity; he is also idiosyncratic in language, making use of many deliberately learned (Phanariot) elements.

During the enemy occupation this orthodox Surrealist gave us a long poem in which, temporarily going beyond Surrealism, he

[1] Record: " 'Ο 'Εμπειρίκος διαβάζει 'Εμπειρίκο", ed. Dionysos, XDL 0853.

reached the peak of his achievement. The poem, written in the winter of 1942–3, is entitled *Bolivar* (characteristically subtitled 'a Greek poem'). The poet took as his central theme the figure of the South American revolutionary and combatant for liberty, but, taking advantage of the freedom that modern poetry affords, he has extended his symbolism into a Greek setting and Greek history, both earlier and recent (Rigas Pheraios, Odysseus Androutsos, as well as the war of Albania), achieving a non-realistic and particularly charming synthesis, one of the most successful works of modernist poetry.

In 1935 began the publication of *Nea Grammata*, which in the last pre-war years was to play an important role in poetry and, generally, in all intellectual life. The director was A. Karantonis, whom we shall meet again as one of the most sensitive critics of the 1930 generation. G. Seferis, G. Katsimbalis, and others belonged to the circle of this periodical. *Nea Grammata* was intended as a reaction against the then low poetical level and the atmosphere of 'Karyotakism' that prevailed; on the one hand there was an exaltation of older values (Palamàs, Sikelianòs, and even P. Giannopoulos) and on the other hand new tendencies in poetry were given support. Thus it became a tribune for young poets, and many of them appeared for the first time in its pages.

In the penultimate issue of that year were published the first poems of Odysseus Elytis, who within a few years was recognized as one of the most gifted and representative poets of the new school. O. Elytis (the pseudonym of O. Alepoudelis) was born at Heracleion in 1911, but his place of origin was Mytilene. He had lived from childhood in Athens and studied there, passing his summers in different islands in the Aegean. In 1929—so he wrote in an autobiographical note[1]—a chance event, a volume of Paul Éluard, brought him into touch with Surrealism. Dreams, automatic writing, the liberation of the subconscious, the all-powerful imagination, freed from aesthetic or ethical examination, allowed him (as he wrote about the poets of Surrealism generally) 'to render the vision of the world with all the sacred joy of its material existence, but with all the "*frisson*" of the truly poetical moment'.[2]

---

[1] Not published as far as I know.

[2] In an article "Τὰ σύγχρονα ποιητικὰ καὶ καλλιτεχνικὰ ρεύματα", in the review *Καλλιτεχνικὰ Νέα*, i (1943–4), nos. 29–33.

From its first appearance the poetry of Elytis was hailed as a youthful, optimistic poetry, full of light, where the Aegean ('the cool and bright mystery of the Greek archipelago') has a central place. In these early poems are all the elements of the new school: the neologistic combinations of words, the images that immediately project themselves as free and unique, and are woven together in a 'super-realistic' unity. But there is something further, a desire to create form which subdues the torrent of images and gives them shape—not indeed that of traditional lines and stanzas, but something that calls them to mind: an order and spirit.

*Orientations* (1940) is a volume in which Elytis collected all he had published up to that date. Here we find some of his most characteristic early poems, such as 'Marina of the Rocks', 'The Age of Azure Remembrance', 'The Mad Pomegranate Tree'. *Sun the First* (together with 'Variants on a Sun-Ray'), a volume published in 1943, obviously followed the same line, being concerned with the Aegean, the sun, the joy of life. Meanwhile, beneath this positive attitude a bitter taste was sometimes felt in some poems, which foretold a different future development.

In 1940 Elytis, aged twenty-nine, was called up, and served on the Albanian front. This new trial was to mark his future development. There was no revolutionary change, but a note of mature seriousness was to enter his work and it was to have wider horizons. In 1945 he published a long poem, the fruit of a high inspiration and of great poetical eloquence, his *Heroic and Tragic Song for a Second Lieutenant Lost in Albania*. The *Song* illustrates all the poetical virtues of Elytis—the virginity of his speech, his daring and vibrant expression, the almost classical balance of his construction—all in a more mature form. The work was well received (a thing which would have been impossible five or ten years previously), and was appreciated by a large section of the public—though it is true that the subject was in its favour.

After the publication of the *Song* Elytis was silent for nearly fifteen years, at least as a poet. But in 1960 he published a smaller volume, *Six and One Regrets for Heaven*, where the compactness of the verse and the fullness of the poetical thought show the persistent work that had gone into it. Almost at the same time he published a long poem, *Dignum est*. The silent years were thus revealed as years of fertile work and reflection, 'one of the finest examples of an unwavering artistic conscience in the history of European poetry' (as G. P. Savvidis wrote,[1] one of the first scholars who unreservedly recognized the new work). Otherwise the critics (with few exceptions) were cautious about *Dignum est*.

The poem is really difficult both to understand and to evaluate. It is a severe architectural construction, consisting of three parts: 'Genesis', 'Passion', 'Gloria'. As in a Christian church, where the central nave is the widest, so the middle part of the poem is the most important: 'Genesis' is like an introduction, and 'Gloria' like a conclusion. In this work the poet's personal experience is blended with the historical experience of the nation, the 'Passion' of Hellenism, in a range, both synchronic and diachronic, interwoven with subjective feeling ('this world— small and great'), and leads up to the metaphysical dimension of the last section, which is a series of hymns of praise where the beauty of the infinite things of this world takes on an unearthly radiance, and where the Now and the Always (*Nunc et Semper*), earth and heaven, are joined in an other-worldly unity. The *Dignum est* is an epic in lyric form (not 'epico-lyric'), an epic where the poet is bound by the tradition of his country and race and goes in search of the secrets that compose it.

The epic composition of this poem has been well served by the language, which is a new poetical creation. The poet has made use of all the long tradition of the Greek language, from Homer to Solomòs, but chiefly (as the title hints) he has exploited a new vein hardly touched hitherto, the language of ecclesiastical hymnology, and from this source he has contrived to enrich his own poetical expression, and at the same time to give a strange new life to this traditional language by contact with his own fresh lyricism.

The renovation of poetical idiom in the decade 1930–40, with Seferis and Elytis as the forerunners and leaders, had a decisive and fertilizing influence on other poets who, though they began within the framework of tradition, at some later moment revived their means of expression and accepted the new language, with beneficial results to their own work. Such was the case particularly with N. Vrettakos and J. Ritsos, who both in quality and quantity of their work may be mentioned beside Seferis and

[1] In the weekly *'Ο Ταχυδρόμος*, 10 December 1960, pp. 14–15.

Elytis. They are more or less contemporaries of the latter; the devotion of both of them to a left-wing ideology has made critics speak of them together, although as poets there are major differences between them.

In the most important things their careers have been parallel. They both started under the strong influence of Karyotakis, which was the obvious influence of the time. Nikiforos Vrettakos (born 1911, near Sparta) published his first volume in 1929, and until 1937 remained faithful to 'Karyotakism', though he made vain efforts to shake it off. In two longer compositions, the *Epistle of a Swan* (1937) and the *Journey of the Archangel* (1938), an extensive, important, but uneven poem, we notice a change in the atmosphere and the means of expression. The later volumes, which closely follow each other, show the poet in his mature phase. The shorter poems are more numerous, and better express his lyric gift, a restricted lyricism with a happy disposition, an optimism that has been called 'neo-Christian', and above all a love of mankind. In later volumes (*Silence and Taygetus*, 1949, and *Time and the River*, 1957) a return to nature and his native province bring him further into touch with the demotic tradition.

With Jannis Ritsos (born in Monemvasia in 1909) we come to a poet with a clearer poetic voice, and a wider range. His first volumes (*Tractor*, 1934, and *Pyramids*, 1935) do not escape the 'Karyotakism' of the time, but are outstanding because of their accuracy of expression and their revolutionary content. *Epitaphios* (1936), the lament of a mother over her son, killed in a demonstration of out-of-work tobacco-workers, has deeper tones, but follows the same line. In his long *Song of the Sister* (1937) we notice, as in Vrettakos, a change of form and also of feeling, due to the influence of the new poetical technique. Thenceforward the volumes until 1945 were to establish his poetical personality. Ritsos was involved in political activity during the years of the occupation and the guerrilla war which followed. From 1948 to 1952 he was in exile on an island, and on his return he published a number of volumes, in which his harsh experience is naturally reflected. In 1961 he collected all his hitherto published work in two large volumes, but he continued to publish further collections. The *Poems* of 1961 were completed by a third volume in 1964. Since April 1967 the poet has again been in exile and now lives on Samos.

Ritsos is a prolific poet, and undoubtedly gifted with genuine inspiration and truly poetical qualities. His poems are on a large scale, with a continuous flow which springs spontaneously but uncontrolled. He draws his inspiration from the magic land of childish and youthful life, his images are rich and fresh, his language carries weight and significance, and is at the same time delicate and passionate. But this broad torrent of his lyric language, which is the most characteristic feature and the chief merit of his poetry, is also at the same time its weak point. This current is often disproportionately broad and confounds the necessary with the superfluous, insists too much, and sometimes does not avoid rhetoric. He also lacks power of composition; his long poems have no internal coherence, but loosely crowd together impressions and images, among which are some of the most fresh and fascinating in modern poetry.

Ritsos's poetry certainly touches the problems of contemporary man, both as an individual and in society. Sometimes he wishes to do so in a more immediate way (that is, less poetically) in order to serve his social ideology; these are not his better poems. Sometimes the social aim may exist as an intention (often only to be discovered by the hypercritical attitude of his interpreters), but is the least interesting thing about the poem. Aragon,[1] who spoke most flatteringly of Ritsos, when he was told that the 'Moonlight Sonata' (1956) 'expressed the tragic impasse into which individualism and all bourgeois civilization has fallen', waved aside this interpretation and confined himself to stressing the purely lyrical elements of the poem.

Here we should make mention of an estimable poet, G. Th. Vafopoulos (b. 1903), who comes from a different background, Thessaloniki, which as we shall see had a particular character, especially in prose writing. He had published as early as 1921; in 1931 he issued his first collection, *The Roses of Myrtale*, which was marked by an individual kind of neo-Classicism, and the strong influence of Karyotakis. A bereavement made him find a more laconic and personal form of expression (*Offering*, 1938), and he made a further advance in this direction in the post-war years, when he was to find his real personality. Vafopoulos has not written much and has a general tendency towards restriction and

---

[1] In *Lettres françaises*, 28 February 1957; translated in 'Ἐπιθεώρηση Τέχνης, 5 (1957), 209–12.

a severe and economical mode of expression. In his post-war collections of poems (and chiefly in the most typical of these, *The Floor*, 1951) we see his poetry dominated by a metaphysical death agony, and willingly casting off everything lyrical or suggestive in order to arrive, at times, at a deliberated coldness and bareness. It has been called a monotonous poetry; it is principally directed at the intellect and expresses itself in ideograms (perhaps it is relevant to mention that Vafopoulos studied mathematics). It is perhaps a result of these characteristics that he has preferred some formulas of katharevousa and the ecclesiastical tradition (with a particular partiality for the anapaestic rhythm), which give a certain stiffness to his expression, but also something particularly personal.

Around *Nea Grammata*, Seferis, and Elytis there gathered other poets who believed in the new poetry and expressed themselves with the new technique. A. Drivas, the oldest of these (1899–1942) had already made his appearance with the poets of the 1920 generation, but he soon began to express himself in the manner of *poésie pure*. A completely different personality was George Sarantaris (1908–41). Brought up in Italy, he came to Greece for the first time in 1932 and came in contact with the circle of *Nea Grammata* (he was the first to discover the poetical talent of Elytis). He was influenced by the new poetical achievements in the West and began even then to publish poems, which he collected in slender pamphlets up to 1940; at the same time, for he had a philosophical and inquiring mind, he published a series of critical studies. He had faith in life and beauty, and a bitterness because he was deprived of its enjoyment; he was profoundly idealistic (in his last years he was turning towards a Christian mysticism), and expressed himself with nostalgic reverie in short poems, succinct in their expression, which never reached completion and are like outline drawings. Though he made such an early appearance, Sarantaris always remained an isolated case, unable to reach completion or to exercise any influence; moreover he died young: he was mobilized in October 1940 and died in the following February from the hardships of the Albanian war.

D. Antoniou (b. 1906) is also individual and isolated, 'the marine friend' of whom Seferis has spoken so affectionately.[1] He spent

[1] In *Tὰ Νέα Γράμματα*, 2 (1936), 936–7, now in *Δοκιμές*, 2nd edn., pp. 13–15.

his early years in long sea voyages and poured into his poetry not
so much the seaman's usual nostalgia as the meditative concentration of a man alone on vast ocean journeys. Laconic and
sparing in his communication, he has nevertheless a genuine
poetic voice, severe and firm in its impact, without facile concessions. He collected his poems in 1939 and published some
others in 1944 (*Of Music*: music is, after the sea, the second
constant theme of his poetry). Since then he has appeared from
time to time in periodicals, and lately he has published a long
poem, *India* (1967), also based on experiences of his former
journeys and later worked over.

Of younger poets, A. Matsas (1911–69) kept himself outside
groups and schools. Delicate and aristocratic, with many
reminiscences of Kavafis, he clearly renders Hellenism both
as nature and as history. However, this apparent belletrism
approaches a more anxious questioning of a mysterious un-
explored world. Matsas also composed three tragedies on
classical subjects (see p. 265).

Surrealism, which seemed to have come to an end with the
later poems of Elytis, before the war, made a late and unexpected
appearance in the *Amorgos* of Nikos Gatsos (b. 1915), his only
poem. When it was first published in 1943 it caused astonishment
by its novelty and had an undoubted influence on younger poets.
It is said that the poet wrote this longish poem in a single night,
using the method of 'automatic writing'. The novelty introduced
by this experiment was the release of numerous memories of lines
and reminiscences of the demotic songs, here combined with
other experiences, a new freshness and purity, and a rhythm that
attracts one by its genuine force. It was as if streams, unsuspected
by the new poets, had been freed and were now irrigating poetry.
This had consequences for other poets, but not for Gatsos himself, who has remained more or less silent since then, and has
turned his sensibility to use in translating Lorca, and—rather
oddly—writing words for composers of popular songs.

# XVI

## THE GENERATION OF 1930
## PROSE

THE SO-CALLED 1930 GENERATION, that is, those writers who appeared about that time, gave new life not only to poetry but also to prose, which, as we have seen, was vegetating, and continuing a belated survival of genre writing and descriptions of life in the slums. The new writers turned their eyes to broader horizons, tried to trace more complicated psychological conditions, and to face more serious social and human problems, and also to cross the narrow limits of Hellenism and to make an advance parallel with that of European prose. Finally, they made a determined attempt to go beyond the limits of the short story or the *nouvelle* and to express themselves in the contemporary form *par excellence*, the novel. With a purely literary conscience, they also attempted a renovation of style and language, drawing on the tradition of the most esteemed demotic prose writers (e.g. Karkavitsas or Vlachogiannis), but at the same time enriching their picturesque vigour with a fuller, up-to-date feeling for language.

One event exercised a great influence on the writers of this generation, an event which was to cast its heavy shadow over all subsequent literary production and the whole intellectual and social background: the Asia Minor disaster and the exchange of population which followed (see also p. 207). The dreams and ideas of former generations of a revival of Hellenism within the previous limits of the Byzantine empire suddenly collapsed in September 1922, and a new tragic seriousness replaced the former, somewhat chimerical, romanticism. The 1930 generation gave literary expression to this new maturity.

This revival had its first beginnings (as we said above, p. 214) in the 1920–30 decade, though then it was but the appearance of a herald. In 1923 (a few months after the Asia Minor disaster), a hitherto unknown writer, Fotis Kontoglou (1895–1965), made his first appearance with a book oddly entitled *Pedro Cazas*. He was born at Ayvalik in Asia Minor (the ancient Cydonia), had travelled in France and Spain, and had studied art in Paris. The book was the story of a Spanish corsair, written with unusual force, in vibrant tense language, drawn from popular sources and popular writing of an earlier time. This book troubled the waters: Fotos Politis (then at the peak of his negative criticism) hailed it as a good omen.[1]

Throughout his subsequent development Kontoglou remained faithful to the uniqueness of his first appearance. Also a most estimable painter, he was in his two capacities inspired by Greek tradition and devoted himself almost fanatically to all that he thought truly Greek, drawn from Byzantine and Orthodox tradition. A new current both of tradition and experiment in Greek painting begins with Kontoglou, and many of the better younger painters (Vasiliou, Tsarouchis, and others) learned from him. In literature his tendency had less influence. He remained attached to the same style, and his many publications take up the same subject, while the language and style—at first so genuine and spontaneous—were later to become dry, sometimes tainted with a disagreeable revival of the archaisms of katharevousa.

Kontoglou came from Asia Minor, Kastanakis from Constantinople. Most of the writers of the 1930 generation came from this border region of Hellenism (forever lost to Greece after 1922), and their wider vision is not unconnected with their origins. Thrasos Kastanakis (1901–67) was born in Constantinople but educated in Paris, where he lived permanently all his life; he was lector in the Modern Greek Institute of the Sorbonne, and in his first years in close touch with Psycharis. In 1924 his novel *The Princes* received the prize in a competition instituted by a publishing house. It was something new, above all it was the first successful attempt by a member of the inter-war generation at producing an integrated novel. *The Princes* was above all an analytic novel, in which the writer examined the psychological states and changes of his characters.

[1] In a review of the book in the newspaper Πολιτεία, 8 April 1923; see Βιβλιογραφία κριτικῶν ἄρθρων Φώτου Πολίτη, Athens, 1940, no. 307.

For twenty years Kastanakis was extremely productive: he wrote five novels (three under the general title *Greek Soil*), and more collections of stories. After 1945 he appeared to have become silent, but later (1956–62) he issued two more novels, inspired by the setting of Constantinople and his early recollections there. Kastanakis was a worthy if uneven prose writer. He was distinguished by his power of composition, his psychological ability, and his humour and irony, which were sometimes caustic. His style was vigorous and idiosyncratic, at times to the point of paradox. In his early work sarcasm mixed with pessimism is dominant, and his eccentric or perverse human types do not seem to have been created with sympathy. But in his later work, particularly in the stories under the title *Raskagias* (1939), the sarcasm gives way to a tone of sympathy for mankind, and the characters are lifelike and unique in their human essence (such are the excellent Raskagias, Sapsalos, Madame Baraillac, and others). Lyrical feeling combined with a solid and perfected technique give a definite literary value to these stories of Kastanakis.

Certainly one of the most powerful of prose writers was Stratis Myrivilis (pseudonym of S. Stamatopoulos, 1892–1969) who, though older, belongs to the generation of 1930. He was born in Mytilene and took part in all the 1912–22 wars; as early as 1915 he published his *Red Stories*, and in 1924 in Mytilene appeared the first edition of *Life in the Tomb*. This novel, however, became better known with the 1930 edition, published in Athens; it established the author as the foremost prose writer of his generation.

*Life in the Tomb* is a war book, in the form of a journal kept by a sergeant in the trenches, inspired by the pacifist and humane spirit that gave birth to the contemporary work of Remarque or Dorgelès. In this, essentially his first book, Myrivilis shows himself a mature author, with great narrative skill, able to combine violent realism with more lyric feeling. His language is rich, sappy, and full of variety of shade, continuing and refreshing the demotic tradition (he may have been influenced by the recent example of Kontoglou).

*Life in the Tomb*, for all its epic content, is not in itself a novel; but, as we have said, the aim of the writers of that generation was the novel. In 1933 Myrivilis wrote a pure novel, *The Schoolmistress with the Golden Eyes*. The war had been a bitter experience from which he emerged with difficulty. His chief character returns to Mytilene after the war, and is tormented by the conflict between his devotion to a friend killed in the war, and love for his widow. The critics, who had greeted *Life in the Tomb* without reserve, showed much more caution about the new novel, but they recognized the literary qualities of the writer, particularly the lyrical, almost sensuous feeling for nature that is felt throughout the book (one of the most permanent characteristics of Myrivilis).

Myrivilis then produced a series of stories, later collected into volumes, each entitled with a different colour: *The Green Book* (1935), *The Blue Book* (1939), *The Red Book* (1952), and lastly *The Purple Book* (1959). His dynamic prose is shown at its full force in this narrow framework, the style is polished, and the phrases are colourful. He gave particular care to the revision of one story from *The Blue Book*, the admirable *Vasilis Arvanitis*, and brought it out in a separate edition (1943); it is the story of a hero of the people, full of life and boldness and love of freedom, an outstanding man who despises the compromises of convention and relies only on his force of character—but this goes beyond the bounds, and leads him to *hybris* and destruction: a lively, purely Greek, and wholly human character.

At the same time he was working on a novel which he published later in 1949, *The Mermaid Madonna*, the story of some refugees from Asia Minor who settle in a small seaside village in Mytilene. But war and exile are far from being the central theme of this novel. The writer's aim is to reproduce the social life of these simple island fishermen. The continuity of the novel is due to the warm tone, the vivacity of everyday life, and the earth and sea by which these simple folk are moulded; there is also the strange symbolism of the church with its extraordinary icon of the Mermaid Madonna: a Madonna represented as a mermaid, that figure of popular mythology, half-woman, half-fish.

Elias Venezis (pen-name of E. Mellos, born 1904) comes from the same 'Aeolic' region and, like Kontoglou, was born at Ayvalik opposite Mytilene. When still a boy, in 1922, he was conscripted by the Turks into the compulsory work corps in which they dispatched Greeks into the interior of Asia Minor, and thus, though he did not experience war, he had a similar experience of inhuman barbarity. His first book, *Number 31328*

(1931), is the chronicle of his captivity, produced with all the realism of immediate recollection. But Venezis is a more delicate and lyric spirit. In *Calm* (1939) he gives us, in the form of a novel, the drama of the refugees and their difficulty in adapting themselves to their new country. Through the whole story runs the nostalgia for the lost homeland, and thus the drama of isolated individuals gains a collective significance. Symbolism, a lyrical frame of mind, and a deep love of humanity characterize this novel—and indeed all Venezis's work.

This lyrical and nostalgic spirit brought him to recreate his childhood in his homeland Aeolia in *Aeolian Earth* (1943). Venezis is not a writer with abundant creative fancy, and his themes are all drawn from his personal experiences and recollections. In this book the recollections are given with the vagueness of memory, and the enchantment of dream and legend as they appear to the bemused eyes of a child. This air of youthfulness, with its firm roots in the soil, gives the novel particular charm. But these positive virtues are counteracted by the looseness of the structure, the lack of a centre, the absence of the concrete, an emotional exaggeration, and even a certain flaccidity of style and language.

*Aeolic Earth* is the last of Venezis's three major works. He has not ceased from creativity, nor have his literary qualities lost their strength, but in his later work the faults we mentioned become more obvious, and critics have observed 'a literary feebleness, and an exhaustion of the lyric impulse'.[1]

Like Stratis Myrivilis, Kosmàs Politis (pseudonym of Paris Taveloudis, born 1888) was older, but made his first appearance in 1930. The first representatives of the 1930 generation seem generally to have hesitated to appear under their own names. He was over forty when he published his first work *Lemon Grove* (1930), an uneven work, hardly that of a professional writer, but which at once revealed the ripe worldly personality of an idiosyncratic character who had a great deal to say. The charming background of the lemon grove of Poros gives a springlike enchantment to the book; this love of nature is bound up with the feeling of love and the psychological problems of the characters. In *Eroica* (1938), perhaps his most polished novel, he escapes

---

[1] A. Karantonis, Πεζογράφοι καὶ πεζογραφήματα τῆς γενιᾶς τοῦ '30, Athens, 1962, p. 138.

from the atmosphere and the orthodox prose expression of his first works, and in a musical and suggestive manner that is quite his own he presents a band of boys in a wonderful chronicle of youthful life, full of melancholy and yet also of happiness, in an atmosphere of dream and of poetry.

Politis's poetic feeling seems to change in the works published after the war, which are marked by greater maturity and thought-fulness, and a turning towards every-day triviality, to the people and their toil. In *Gyrì* (1946) he presents his recollections of the district of Patras of that name, while his last novel, *At Chatzifrangos'* (1963), is a more mature handling of the theme of *Gyrì*. It has the sub-title *Forty Years of a Lost City*, and it brings to life Smyrna, and one quarter of it in particular, forty years back, and a group of boys (the author's contemporaries); throughout the book a nostalgia is felt for this great Greek city where the author spent his childhood, which takes most definite form in the lyric (or dramatic) parenthesis, 'Parodos', where one of the boys of the neighbourhood, now old and a refugee in Athens, describes the great days of Smyrna, and the tragic catastrophe.

While Myrivilis and Venezis first appeared with work inspired by their personal experience, George Theotokàs (1905–66) made his first appearance with an essay, *Free Spirit* (1929), thus showing from the beginning the thoughtful direction of his mind. Of a well-to-do family of Constantinople, he studied in Athens, and later in Paris and London. He entered the literary world full of anxieties and questions, particularly about literature, anxieties and questions common to young men at that time. His essay revealed him as immature in many ways, but it was a work of youthful sincerity; it was a sort of manifesto, as was said, of the still unpublished 'generation of 1930'.

However, like others of his generation, Theotokàs felt the need to express himself in the novel, even though this need was more the result of a logical conclusion than a natural necessity. He published three novels before the war. Of the pre-requisites of the novelist he chiefly lacked the power of plot creation (which we shall find superabundant in Karagatsis); moreover his personal experience and reminiscences have neither the passion of Myrivilis nor the poetical nostalgia of Venezis, and never take flesh in fictional characters that are living in their own right, but only in symbols or classes of people. His fine sincerity, his civilized writing, and the clarity of his phrase never finally outweigh these basic limitations.

In *Argo* (1933–6) he rendered the anxieties and ideological conflicts of the young of the post-war generation; in *The Demon* (1938) the characters are too much commented on by the author, instead of convincing us by their fullness of life. In *Leonìs* (1940), perhaps his best achievement, the action is set in Constantinople, in the world of his childhood recollections; here the author tried to present the youthful anxieties and the development of his chief character against the historical background of a troubled time.

The short story was not the form most cultivated by Theotokàs, yet in *Euripides Pentozalis* (1937) the principal character is perhaps the most alive of all his creations. After the war, he devoted himself with enthusiasm to the theatre (see p. 265) and at the same time continued to write essays, with a strong political interest in the last years. He also published a fourth novel, *Sick Persons and Travellers* (1964), an account of the Greco-German war, the collapse of 1941, the Occupation, and the rising of 1944. 'I feel the time has come when we can look steadily at the theme of that terrible period . . . with the novelist's eye.'[1] Critics have not yet decided how far he succeeded in this attempt.

Among Theotokàs's last works, his travel books merit most distinction: *Essay on America* (1954) and *Travel in the Middle East and the Holy Mountain* (1961). The first is rather an examination of the many problems that an acquaintance with the great transatlantic state poses to a cultivated European (as Theotokàs always was). It is a book of rare sensibility, among the best on this theme. The second takes us into more familiar places which were once either part of or neighbour to the Greater Greece: Theotokàs, born in Constantinople, saw them with special emotion and expressed it with characteristic warmth. Particularly remarkable is the revelation that he, a convinced Cartesian, received from the enclosed world of Mount Athos, and in consequence from the world of Greek Orthodoxy. It was a plunge into the interior of the soul from a new direction and an opening of his eyes to aspects of the Greek tradition closed to most of our writers.

[1] In a short note he wrote on the work, published in Ἐποχές (cited by A. Sachinis, Πεζογράφοι τοῦ καιροῦ μας, Athens, [1967], p. 118).

A. Karantonis, one of his severest critics, wrote of him as 'a fine conscience'.[1] In fact the most important thing about Theotokàs, more important than his work, was his presence in our world of letters: the presence of a cultivated mind, conscious of the responsibilities of the intellectual, sincere in his aims, open to all ideas, and above all honourable in every aspect of his intellectual or personal life. An irreplaceable personality, and one of the most lovable men of letters, not only among his own generation.

M. Karagatsis (1908–60, pseudonym of D. Rodopoulos) was a very different character, impulsive and explosive. One of the youngest of his generation, he made an early appearance, and by 1940 had already published four novels and two volumes of stories. By the time of his early death his literary works amounted to twenty or more. He was one of the most prolific of modern Greek authors. His productiveness chiefly sprang from his inventiveness of plot, his main virtue. Although there are many autobiographical elements in his work, he did not limit himself to these, but created types and had the gift of giving them life in his fiction. A permanent characteristic of his work is his persistent return to sex, which becomes boring and even repulsive in his less successful works. At his better moments sex, always at the centre of his characters' action and psychology, takes on the nature of a biological force, a mysterious power which governs man and leads him into a tragic impasse. Karagatsis's eroticism is far from being light-hearted; it is tragic; his characters are brought to disaster by the unquenchable passion that masters them.

Realism is the atmosphere dominant in all his works, or rather a naturalism pushed to its extreme limits. For all his study of psycho-analysis, Karagatsis is not so much a depictor of psychological states and shades of mind as a keen observer of reality, which he knew how to represent to its last detail. This flavour of realism without sentimentality or poetical vision, and his tragic conception of man's destiny, often led him to a nihilistic pessimism or a humour full of irony, mockery, and sarcasm. Deeply realist and anti-idealist, he was dominated by a fundamental disbelief in every kind of ideal or heroism. His characters are profoundly, sometimes cynically anti-heroic. Often he

[1] A. Karantonis, op. cit., pp. 116–17.

deliberately chose well-known historical figures, in order to see them through his own prism as anti-heroic (in such a way he tried to write a *History of the Greeks*, an unsuccessful work).

With these positive and negative qualities, Karagatsis was a writer who occupied a doubtful position in his time, with many admirers and many hostile critics. No one, however, doubted his unique literary vein or his power to create a real novel. He was indeed uneven; his work is full of contradictions and sudden bathos, and his style (being natural) is unstudied, unliterary, and—particularly in his last work—almost descends to the level of journalism.

In his two first novels, *Colonel Liapkin* (1933) and *Junkermann* (1936), his principal characters are foreigners from the north (a Russian and a Finn) who come to Greece, acclimatize themselves, are successful, and lead a vigorous love life, but finally end in failure and disaster. In *Chimera* (1936, revised in 1953)—which some critics consider his best work—the main character is a woman, also a foreigner, and he gives the story of her love and her final collapse. After the war Karagatsis wished to write a *roman fleuve*, entitled *The World that is Dying*, in a number of volumes, a broad picture in which were to appear characters typical of Greece from before the War of Independence until today. He published only the first three books (1944–9), which revolve round the central figure of Michalis Rousis (the 'kotzambasis of Kastropyrgos'), a typically Karagatsian hero. Meanwhile he had issued one of his best works, *The Great Sleep* (1946), a psychological novel with many autobiographical elements; it stands apart from his other work by reason of its content and form. In his last fifteen years he wrote some of his strangest and most peculiar work, such as *Amri a mugu* (= In the hand of God, 1954), where his eternal erotic theme is set in the African jungle, *The Yellow File* (1956), a work remarkable for its technical and psychological experiments, and *Sergius and Bacchus*, a doubtful joke, 573 pages long.

While Karagatsis was above all a novelist, he also published a number of short stories; they do not add much to his personality, though some are distinguished by originality and force, such as 'Gust' from an earlier collection (1935) and 'The Man with the Cats' Meat', and others from the collection *Fever* (1945).

Th. Petsalis (b. 1904), of a well-known Athenian family, first appeared in 1925 with a volume of stories situated in a bourgeois setting; they were a welcome change from the lower-middle-class monotony in Voutyràs and P. Pikròs. He really began his career with a novel, *The Vocation of Maria Parni* (1933), the first part of a trilogy in which he wished to present the story and development of an upper-middle-class family. The three successive novels (1933–5) were later revised (1950) under the general title *Maria Parni*. Petsalis is not a vigorous writer, and his novel is not the broad epic of bourgeois society that undoubtedly he intended (e.g. like the novels of Galsworthy). But he is sensitive and delicate, and accurate in his recording, and he was able to render the warmth and spirit of a rich bourgeois household.

The experience of the war and of the occupation made Petsalis turn to other sources. Some stories in his volume *Our Own Children* (1946), sub-titled *Chronicle of Servitude*, are stories of the revolution of 1821, but leave a clear impression of the contemporary servitude. In 1942, 'at the time of the Italo-German occupation' as he himself noted, he wrote the brilliantly moulded *Bell of Holy Trinity* (published in 1949), a mixture of story and chronicle, in which he relates the vicissitudes of a small church from 1304 till 1885, and, in the adventures of a small place the history of the nation during six centuries is condensed. This interest in the roots of the nation led him to tackle the same theme within the broader framework of the novel. In the two volumes of *Mavrolyki* (1947–8) he follows a Greek family throughout the Turkish occupation through all the adventures of the nation, particularly from the mid seventeenth century till the time of Rigas (1799). However, the condensation which gave its force to *The Bell* is missing from this broader historical picture and, as critics complained, the historical outweighs the fictional character of the book. Petsalis also published a book, in the form of a chronicle, inspired by the struggles of Cyprus (1956)— a fictitious chronicle of the twelfth century with obvious parallels with modern times. More recently he published another work with a historical basis, the fruit of many years, and more perfect in its prose and fictional form, *The Greek Dawn* (three volumes, 1962). Here the work gains by the action being condensed into far fewer years, those just before and after the revolution of 1821; and instead of the fictional Mavrolykos family, the well-known

statesman Joannis Kolettis is at the centre and provides a link
between the people and happenings, and the atmosphere of the
time is more authentic.

Like Petsalis, Angelos Terzakis (born 1907) first appeared
before 1930 with two volumes of short stories, which, in the
manner of the time, followed the line of D. Voutyràs, but showed
also the influence of the Symbolist prose of Chatzopoulos. The
grey background of petty bourgeois life persists in his first two
novels (1933 and 1934); but the third, *Violet City* (1937), already
shows a significant change. Here the characters move in the same
surroundings, but are described with more clarity; their conflicts
are more dramatic, and the chief of them—especially the heroine
—have a real existence as human beings.

Immediately after the war Terzakis attempted something altogether different, a historical novel, *Princess Ysabeau* (1946), which
is thought to be his most perfect prose work. In this lengthy
work he brings a past age to life, the Frankish Peloponnese
of the thirteenth century, and his achievement is purely within
the frame of the novel. A number of characters of secondary
importance revolve round the principals and add a lively
colour to the broad picture. More significantly, in the Frankish
princess Ysabeau, and the young Greek Nikiforos Sgouròs, and
their dramatic love we see the opposition of two races and
civilizations, one worn out and approaching its end, and the
other still immature, but on the way of progress. In the enslaved
villeins' struggles for liberty we recognize memories of recent
painful experience.

Terzakis is perhaps the writer with the most problems in his
generation. At the centre of his investigations we always find
contemporary man with his distressing problems. Perhaps that
is why he has devoted so much time to the essay, and has sought
expression in the theatre (see p. 265) which allows the writer to
communicate his ideas and anxieties more immediately to the
public.

*Ysabeau* is itself in the midst of such a world of conflict and
anxiety, though the form of the historical novel presents these
ideas in a different aspect. In the three novels that followed
Terzakis returned to the low-toned bourgeois novel; but now
a more violent pessimism is discerned, and the writer's problems
and ideas are expressed with greater literary ease. *Without God*

(1951), a novel, has already a sufficiently emphatic title. His latest book, *Mystic Life* (1957), has a place of its own, on account of its barely hidden, dramatic, confessional tone, expressing the distress of a man tormented by doubts and difficulties, and unable to adapt himself to the commonness of life around him.

The youngest of the 1930 generation is Pantelis Prevelakis (born 1909), from Rethymno in Crete. After a youthful 'epyllion' (1928), he made his real debut with a 'romance', *Chronicle of a Town* (1938), in which he gives us his childhood reminiscences, and shows his native town in the process of silent decay. The sensibility and careful style of this young writer at once made an impression. Prevelakis, moreover, is one of the most cultivated men of his generation; he has written valuable studies on aesthetics and the visual arts, and has nourished his sensibility upon the models of the Renaissance (he has translated comedies of Macchiavelli and of Calderón). After a historical story, *The Death of the Medici* (1939), he brought out two books after the war, both drawn from the history of his island, which are certainly his most perfect and representative work. *Wretched Crete* (1945) is, as the sub-title tells us, a 'Chronicle of the Rising of 1866', the biggest of the risings in Crete. *The Cretan* (in three parts, 1948–50, and revised for the second edition of 1965) refers to events from the 1866 revolution until 1910. It was not the author's intention to analyse any one individual, but 'to express the whole soul of the Greek people at one period of its history'. Thus historical personages, particularly Venizelos, are introduced into the two later parts, and in consequence (as critics have observed) history outweighs fiction.

Prevelakis is meticulous about style, although, in his attempt to render the rough heroism of his theme, he never quite escapes from affectation. He is a pupil and imitator of Kazantzakis; but while Kazantzakis's indifference to literary style makes many of his faults acceptable, the same defects are disagreeable in the obviously polished language of Prevelakis.

Until now we have referred to the chief representatives of the 1930 generation. If we cast an eye back, we must agree that modern Greek prose made a great advance between 1922 and 1945, despite some isolated failures and some unsuccessful attempts.

Beside those authors whom we have examined there were other members of that generation who either did not reach the same standard, or else failed to stay the course, or for one reason or another have a lesser importance in literary history. Nevertheless some of their names should be recorded.

Near in style and subject to the first work of Myrivilis and Venezis is the *History of a Prisoner* (1929) by Stratìs Doukas (who also came from Aeolia). It is a short tale about a prisoner during the Asia Minor disaster and his adventures and escape. The author lets his character speak in the first person, in a popular style suitable to the subject, but condensed and without superfluity; without ornament, he goes straight to his point.

Many have tried to make literary material of the Second World War, and especially of the Albanian campaign of 1940–1, but the national exaltation of that time has seldom found a worthy transubstantiation into letters. Among the best of such novels is *Men in Arms* (1947) by the Cypriot Loukìs Akritas (1909–65), who was a journalist from 1931 onwards and sent remarkable articles to the newspapers from the front. In his later years Akritas took an active part in politics, and was undersecretary for education in the Papandreou Government (1964).

A second book on the Albanian war, *The Broad River* by Jannis Beratis (1904–68), is broader in composition, and more literary. It is a subjective story like a journal, in which the day-to-day events are related in every detail. The value of the book, however, is in the individual way in which the writer relates these everyday happenings, fascinating us by the immediacy of his description. In the same manner, though perhaps with less success, he composed the *Itinerary of '43* (1946), referring to the national resistance at the time of the occupation. His prose work is completed by *Whirl* (1961), a very interesting experimental novel.

A powerful novel, in spite of its imperfections and unevenness, is *Land and Water* (1936), the first work of G. Abbot (born in 1906 of a Hellenized English family), in which he describes the lives of lepers in the remote island of Spinalonga (off Crete). But it is neither document nor fiction; the writer has a rich inner world of ideas which he expresses with passion. There are scenes (like the revolt of the lepers), which are extremely tense, and others (such as the birth of a child to a leper) which are most tender and human. His last book, *Dimitrios Gabriel* (1960), develops the theme of the Greeks of the diaspora, and gives him the opportunity to explore a theme fundamental to modern Hellenism.

A great stir was caused by the publication of *The Lost* (1935) by Lilika Nakou (born 1903): it was a testimony and confession given with rare realistic power, with a deep tone of pessimism. But her woman's intuition and narrative skill are not accompanied by other literary attributes, or by sufficient strength, and the style is careless to a degree. This defect becomes more evident in her later work, while her talent has lost its first powers.

More and more genuine literary qualities are shown by another woman writer, Melpo Axioti (born 1906): her first book, *Difficult Nights* (1938), with its originality and boldness of technique, its lack not only of plot but of elementary sequence of narrative, produced various reactions, and even a certain amount of scandal. The most authoritative critics perceived the qualities of a new style and the vigorous originality behind the apparent collapse. Among those who praised it was a veteran writer with acute critical powers, Gregorios Xenopoulos; he described the book as having been written 'with the most modern and the most attractive inconsistency'. Next year Mme Axioti issued a poetical effusion (*Coincidence*, 1939), of unrestrained sensitivity and facility, not unlike that which we shall later see in Ritsos. Her second novel, *Let's Dance, Maria* (1940), with many digressions into poetry, is on the same lines as the first. In the first years after the war (1945–6), she issued what she called a series of 'chronicles'; they record recent events, but the definite political commitment has had a bad effect on the quality of the writing.

With the exception of Kavafis's Alexandria (a real exception), literary activity in Greece has been centred in the capital, at least since the death of the Heptanesian school with Mavilis and Theotokis. The generation of 1930 was no exception in this respect; though many of its representatives came (as we have seen) from Greater Greece (Mytilene, Smyrna, Constantinople), they almost all settled in Athens, and here printed and circulated their work.

But in the decade 1930–40 another great Greek city, Thessaloniki, began to make its individual character felt. It had been incorporated in the Greek state in 1912, and in 1926 the second Greek university was founded there (though at first only an

Arts Faculty). In 1932 a small circle of men of letters founded a periodical, *Macedonian Days*, which gradually became a paper of the vanguard with a line of its own, both in poetry and much more in prose. (We may mention that the first Greek translations of Kafka appeared in its pages.)

One of this circle, Stelios Xefloudas (b. 1901), published in 1930 *The Notebooks of Pavlos Fotinòs*, a prose work in the then new form of the 'interior monologue', in which the author (as he himself wrote) wished to express 'the inner world and its states that pass through us like a music dissolving in the infinite'. By 1940 he had written five prose works, and in 1944 issued a somewhat different novel, *Men of Fable*, his experiences on the Albanian front. In his last years (1957–62) he brought out three novels, with the same technique of self-analysis (sometimes coming near to the essay in form); he gives the drama of human loneliness in the contemporary world, and the pursuit of the unattainable dream.

A. Giannopoulos (b. 1896), also of the circle of *Macedonian Days*, never got away from the atmosphere of inner life and suggestion cultivated by the school of Thessaloniki. His culture and finesse led him towards the short story, which he sought to infuse with new life. Eleven stories make up his first collection, *Heads in Line* (1934), which are distinguished by originality of expression, youthful vivacity and grace, and (as was said) a sort of 'nervous sensibility'. Giannopoulos continued to write stories, and published three collections (1938, 1944, 1962) and a longer story (1950). His one novel, *The Salamander* (1959), has the same peculiar character as his stories, and his introvert and almost confessional personality finds expression in the epistolary form of the novel.

A low-toned writer of the inner world is G. Delios (b. 1897), to whom we owe four novels (1934–65) and many stories (clearly under the influence of Katherine Mansfield and Virginia Woolf). His work is less distinguished by tension and more by a tendency towards psychological analysis and a polished style that is sometimes 'fine writing' for its own sake. *Chamber Music* is the typical title he gave to one collection of stories, and *Shore of Cassandra*, the title of his last stories (1967), shows the kinship between his atmosphere and the landscape of northern Greece which is so rich in finer shades.

The youngest of this group of Thessaloniki, N. G. Pentzikis (b. 1908), though belonging to the same atmosphere, is more personal and individual, with a rich creative vein and a broader field of expression; he has written verse and prose, and is also a very original painter, always consistent in the steady continuity of his unadaptable originality. He first appeared in 1935 with a prose work under the pseudonym Stavrakios Kosmàs, and his last work, *The Novel of Madame Ersi*, was published in 1966.[1] Pentzikis pushed the interior monologue to its furthest limits, abandoning logic and sometimes even grammatical connection in his writing, which can be called neither stories nor novels, ('instalment' he labels one of his books), but are always interesting and attractive. The title of one of his books, *Knowledge of Facts* (1950), is typical, for this scorner of logic shows himself as a lover of fact and of concrete detail. Moreover this very modern writer and painter found an outlet from the decadence of our age in the stiff forms of Byzantium and eastern Orthodoxy, and his style is influenced by Byzantine chroniclers and the fathers of the Church. These roots, together with his 'knowledge of facts', give his style an uncommon solidity, and counteract his odd idiosyncracy.

Together with the school of Thessaloniki and close to Pentzikis, we may mention another eccentric prose writer and poet, Jannis Skarimbas (b. 1897), who lived his whole life far from the capital in the small provincial town of Chalcis. He made an appearance with a series of short stories in 1930, and two novels followed, and a collection of poems, *Ulalume* (1936). Paradox and improbability are his chief characteristics, a fancy pushed to the most arbitrary extremes, and a completely revolutionary form of expression which at its furthest limit leads to a perversion of syntax and the language.

The prose writers of the 1930 generation had all appeared before the war, and most of them had published their most characteristic work in the decade that preceded it. The years of enemy occupation, especially 1942–4 (after the famine of the winter of 1941–2 and before the rising in December 1944), were, in spite of difficulties, very productive. With few and insignificant exceptions the nation, after the exaltation of the Albanian war, lived through those years in proud endurance and a steady belief

[1] More publications have followed in recent years.

in ultimate victory. At the same time it felt the need for greater self-awareness, for knowledge of its historical foundations and of its literature, ancient and modern. Never at any other time have Greek books been so much read, and production was also plentiful. We saw established prose writers continuing their activity in those years, even with work immediately influenced by the situation (*Aeolian Earth, The Bell of Holy Trinity*). At the same time new prose writers appeared (as had Gatsos in poetry) who followed the line of the 1930 generation, and thus found their place among those already mentioned and in the rich production of the post-war years. One who continued until later times and achieved a considerable body of work is Tasos Athanasiadis.

He also originated in Asia Minor (b. 1913) and came as a refugee to settle in Athens. Then still very young, he made a short study of Fotos Politis (1936) and of why the younger generation turned to his criticism, and in 1943 published a volume of stories, *Pilgrims of the Sea*. It is concerned with inner moods, with lyrical colouring, and is exquisitely written. His second book, *Journey into Solitude*, a lyrical biography of Kapodistrias, is in the same manner. After the war he abandoned this type of lyrical prose and attempted the composition of a vast *roman fleuve*, *Panthei* (1948–61), his main work. He endeavours to present the adventures of a family, the Panthei, in three successive generations, from 1897 to 1940. Besides the biographical details of his particular heroes it was his object to give a broad and comprehensive picture of Greek bourgeois society during the first forty years of our century.

T. Athanasiadis turned his attention to another branch of prose, to biography. Not the lyrical biography (which he had created in the case of Kapodistrias), but a form owing much to fiction, yet more to fact, and more objective (what he called a 'fictional representation'). Thus he gave us a biography of Dostoevsky (1955)—in which he is particularly successful with the Russian atmosphere—and lately a more genuine biography, *Three Sons of Their Century* (1957) about Hugo, Dostoevsky, and Tolstoy, and *Albert Schweitzer* (1963).

## THEATRE AND CRITICISM

In a former chapter (p. 217) we saw that between 1920 and

1930 there were attempts at a theatrical revival; the prevailing situation, however, was that of more or less extemporized professional performances grouped round a protagonist, without direction and with very rough and ready scenery. Things changed definitely when (at the instigation of G. Papandreou, then minister of education) the 'National Theatre' was founded in 1932; this at once caused an improvement in the theatre, and influenced also the independent theatres.

Although the two great 'leading ladies', Marika Kotopouli and Kyveli, were not part of its company, the National Theatre gathered a complement of good actors, and in the first years enjoyed the direction and general artistic supervision of Fotos Politis; it gave performances of high quality, and was fully recognized by the public. There were older, trained actors such as E. Veakis, N. Rozàn, N. Papageorgiou, Eleni Papadaki, and Sappho Alkaiou, and younger ones such as Katina Paxinoù, Katerina, A. Minotìs, and M. Katrakis, and others at the very start of their careers. The works performed represented the most important stages of world drama from the ancient classics to Stefan Zweig, and also important works from the older Greek theatre (such as *The Sacrifice of Abraham* and *Babel*). After the premature death of Fotos Politis the theatre followed the same lines under the artistic direction of his pupil, D. Rontiris, though there was a gradual falling off and a lack of the creative spirit.

The independent theatre competed with the National Theatre in the quality of its performance. Kotopouli and Kyveli, rivals all their lives, collaborated under the direction of Spyros Melàs. At the same time new groups were being formed. Karolos Koun (b. 1908), who started his career with Aristophanes performed at Athens College, gave a remarkable performance of *Erofili* in 1934 (on the 'Popular Stage', with scenery by Tsarouchis and a strong folklore character); he founded later his own 'Arts Theatre', which was to become one of the most important theatrical centres after the war. We should also mention Socrates Karantinòs (b. 1906), who studied production in Vienna and founded the 'New Dramatic School' (1933), and with a body of devoted students gave performances distinguished by their seriousness. After the war he was for a time producer at the National Theatre and director of its Dramatic School, and from

1961 to 1967 the first director of the newly founded State Theatre of Northern Greece at Thessaloniki.

A number of the prose writers of this generation tried their hand at drama. Those most concerned with the theatre were Theotokàs and Terzakis; it is no accident that it was they who also were most concerned with the essay and criticism. For a time Theotokàs was director of the National Theatre and (after 1961) president of the administrative committee of the State Theatre of Northern Greece. His works are set in a historical background, and were not successful on the stage; the best is *The Game of Madness and Prudence*, a somewhat cerebral work, set in Comnenian times, in which there is an attempt to make use of popular Byzantine legend.

Angelos Terzakis has certainly a stronger theatrical personality. He also likes historical themes, especially those drawn from Byzantium, as in his first play, *The Emperor Michael*, and the tragedy *Theophano* (1953), which many think his best. His characters are convincingly drawn and his great success and especial interest is in presenting dialectical conflicts through dramatic conflicts; we note particularly *Two-Souled Thomas* (1962), which puts forward the subject of unbelief.

The subjects of Pantelìs Prevelakis's four plays are also historical: the Florence of the Medici, the blowing up of the monastery of Arkadi, etc. We may speak here of a poetical theatre. To the poetical theatre (and in the line of Sikelianòs) belong also the tragedies of A. Matsas on ancient themes (*Clytemnestra*, *Jocasta*), in which there is an attempt to revive ancient myth and to use the methods of ancient tragedy (especially the chorus) together with the sensibility of contemporary lyric speech.

It was natural that the 1930 writers, so marked by maturity and thoughtfulness, should give great weight to criticism; in particular they tried to cultivate that difficult and autonomous form, the essay. We have spoken of the *Essays* of Seferis, models of richness of thought and of a responsible confrontation of problems. Elytis at one time wrote literary articles and art criticism, while another poet, G. Themelis, pursued an active critical career in recent years (see p. 273).

As we saw, G. Theotokàs made his first appearance with an essay, and in later years he systematically cultivated this form;

it was well suited to his meditative and inquiring nature, and also to his clear and enlightened mind. The volumes *On the Threshold of New Times* (1945), *Problems of Our Time* (1956), and *Intellectual Progress* (1961) show his continual thoughtfulness, especially on general literary and critical subjects.

A. Terzakis (see p. 257) is a regular critic, chiefly in newspapers and periodicals. His articles go far beyond the limits of ordinary criticism; he enters upon fundamental themes and shows deep thinking and a solid philosophical training. For many years he has had a regular column in *To Vima*, and till 1967 he was director of *Epochès*, a fine magazine in which there was free exchange of ideas. Some of his essays are collected in *Adjustments to the Century* (1963).

An older man, but one who first appeared after 1930, was P. Spandonidis (1890–1964); he was of the circle of Thessaloniki. As a man of letters he published some uneven and unsystematic studies on philological subjects, but as a critic he was often just in his aim, particularly on subjects relating to contemporary poetry and prose. Jannis Chatzinis (b. 1900) has sensibility and a true critical eye. From 1941 he was the regular critic (especially for prose) in the *Nea Estia*, and had the opportunity of judging old and new prose writers in his column. His most important criticism is published in *Greek Texts* (1956), *Preferences* (1963), etc.

But the title of critic-in-chief of the 1930 generation must go without doubt to Andreas Karantonis (b. 1910), who was editor of the periodical of the generation, *Nea Grammata*. Karantonis has written a great deal, and this has perhaps damaged his writing, but his criticism is always sensitive and penetrating, sharp in its judgements and direct in its aim. His criticism springs from a centre, which may be identified with the *Weltanschauung* of his generation, and is based on a solid knowledge of European literature, especially poetry.

Side by side with Karantonis we should mention (from the group of *Nea Grammata*) George Katsimbalis (b. 1899), who turned his attention to systematizing the bibliography of modern Greek literature, and published many exhaustive annotated bibliographies of Palamàs, Kavafis, Sikelianòs, and others. He also translated Greek poetry into English and French, or assisted in the translation. Although he had contributed no critical or literary work, his lively appearance in our world of letters and his abundant vivacity and enthusiasm (he is the hero of *The Colossus of Maroussi* by Henry Miller) have markedly influenced the literature of our time.

V. Varikas (1913–71) was also a regular critic, and from 1953 occupied the columns of literary and theatrical criticism in two influential Athenian papers, *To Vima* and *Ta Nea*.

The case of the prematurely dead D. Kapetanakis (1912–44) is quite exceptional. He was born at Smyrna and studied law, philosophy, and social science in Athens under P. Kanellopoulos. He first published poems and a dramatic work in 1933, and a philosophical essay in 1934. His was an unquiet spirit, gifted with subtlety of feeling and open to every vibration, able to take to any new environment. From 1935 to 1937 he studied in Heidelberg where he was initiated into the philosophy of K. Jaspers and the school of Stefan George, taking a doctorate with a thesis on *Love and Time*. He returned to Athens and continued to write on philosophical and aesthetic subjects (*Mythology of the Beautiful, Rimbaud*) and in 1939 went to Cambridge with a British Council scholarship. He remained in England during the war, an experience which radically changed him, and repudiated (not without exaggeration and injustice) his German teachers. He published critical studies in *New Writing and Daylight*—and (though he knew little English on his arrival in England) wrote English poems that were well received by John Lehmann, Edith Sitwell, and others. Kapetanakis died in England of leukaemia in 1944.

Apart from pure literature, the 1930 generation encouraged the development of literary studies and the creation of an independent branch of research in modern Greek letters. K. Th. Dimaràs (b. 1904) was from 1926 occupied with the essay and literary criticism, and later with responsible literary research, particularly for the period of modern Greek Enlightenment, on which he is the leading authority. His *History of Modern Greek Literature* (1948) is a fine book, the most perfect and authoritative on the subject. E. Kriaràs (b. 1906), professor of medieval Greek literature in the University of Thessaloniki, has published many philological and literary studies, and is mainly concerned with Cretan literature. G. Th. Zoras (b. 1909) held the chair of modern Greek literature in the University of Athens, and has issued many publications, especially editions of older texts and studies in literature of the Heptanesian school.

Philosophical thought was also pursued by two university professors. V. Tatakis (b. 1896) has been mainly concerned with the history of philosophy, and in particular with Christian and Byzantine philosophy (*La Philosophie byzantine*, 1949). Joannis Theodorakopoulos (b. 1900), from the Neo-Kantian school of Heidelberg, has studied in particular Plato, Plotinus, and Kant. From the same ideological atmosphere and from the school of Heidelberg come P. Kanellopoulos and K. Tsatsos, who have both played an active part in politics. P. Kanellopoulos (b. 1902) was several times deputy Prime Minister, and twice Prime Minister (1945 and 1967); he has published several studies in social science, many other writings, and a compendium, *History of the European Spirit*. K. Tsatsos (b. 1899) taught philosophy of law in the University of Athens till 1946, and apart from his learned works he has published many essays and literary works, and a monograph on Palamàs.

Special mention should be made of E. P. Papanoutsos (b. 1900), who, after studying philosophy and education in Germany and Paris, for many years served as an educationalist, and from 1944 to 1952 held a high office at the ministry of education. As Secretary for Education under the Papandreou government (1964–5) Papanoutsos initiated a progressive policy for educational reform. Apart from many articles and essays (he was a regular contributor to *To Vima* and directed the periodical *Education* from 1945 to 1961), he also published *Aesthetics* (1948), *Ethics* (1949), *Theory of Knowledge* (1954), and other works distinguished by their clarity of thought and a gift for popularization on a high level, and by his faith in liberalism and progress.

# Excursus

## POST-WAR POETRY AND PROSE

ALTHOUGH TWENTY-FIVE YEARS have passed since the end of the war, it would perhaps still be premature to attempt an objective historical account of literature in those years. The great trials of the war left their trace above all on the generation that lived through it as young men, and also on the following generation, as did the problems that tormented the post-war world. These have been reflected in creative literature, but have not found genuine expression. Unlike the pre-war generation, so rich in young writers of prose and verse, the post-war generation—perhaps on account of its trials and its inward lack of coherence—has not given us (it would seem) its poet or its prose writer. Nor must we forget that after the end of the war Greece had to face the difficult years of civil war (1947–9), and that life did not return to normality before 1950.

For all these reasons, a responsible historical account is still difficult. However, for the sake of some completeness, we shall attempt to indicate the main lines of development in this excursus.

Never have so many volumes of verse been published in Greece as in the twenty-five years since the war. This is deceptive and on the whole discouraging. Verse seems to have been the easiest form of expression for commonplace sentiments and at times for deeper forms of disquiet. Few of the volumes are better than mediocre, and they follow worn-out methods of expression considered modern by their writers. Nevertheless, among this disturbing multitude of poets, some personal voices are heard, more serious and apparently of a more lasting value; only these concern us here. If this poetry has nothing of the impulse and brilliance of the poetry before the war, yet it compensates with a personal atmosphere befitting the age: its tragic seriousness, its impasse, its lack of dreams and false sentiment. It is an atmosphere of depression and pessimism, accompanied by an attachment to things not for their attractive surface but for their inner essence—a poetry of 'essence', as it has been called. Some critics, poets themselves, have emphasized the positive side of this poetry, while sharply criticizing the poets of the 1930 generation. But it is doubtful whether they could have reached this advanced level if they had not taken advantage of the achievements of their forebears.

Minàs Dimakis, Aris Diktaios, and G. Geralìs, who were born between 1917 and 1919, began with poems published before the war. Miltos Sachtouris and D. Papaditsas, more or less their contemporaries, appeared a little later and are among the most productive and representative poets of the first post-war generation. So is Eleni Vakalò (b. 1921) who is working on a kind of 'essential' poetry that is deliberately anti-lyrical.

In Thessaloniki a short-lived periodical, *The Snail* (1945–8), represented modern tendencies. In this group G. Themelis and Zoe Karelli stand out. Themelis (b. 1900) was a prolific writer, brought out twelve volumes of verse in the years 1945 to 1968, distinguished by undoubted sensibility and sureness of writing, yet not free from verbalism and loquacity. The poetry of Zoe Karelli (b. 1901) is more cerebral, concerned with the problems of time and death. Manolis Anagnostakis (b. 1925), who belongs to the war generation, expresses the ideological world of the disappointed hopes of the young of his time with a peculiar intensity and succinctness, combined with a low-toned confessional mode.

Among poets who first appeared after 1950 two are outstanding on account of their constant output and their higher quality. The language of T. Sinopoulos (b. 1917) is particularly polished and clear; and N. Karouzos (b. 1926) seeks relief from anxiety in religious faith and the presence of Christ. In Thessaloniki D. Christianopoulos (b. 1931), who writes exclusively love poems, expresses himself in a realistic and laconic style which leaves nothing dubious.

Post-war prose is perhaps of greater interest and diversity than the verse of the period; it is based more, either directly or indirectly, on the problems of our time, and tries to get away from the narrative and the genre-writing traditions. On the whole the newer trends in European prose writing seem not to have reached Greece.

Immediately after the war many writers wished to write about the recent events, particularly about the occupation and the resistance. This writing, with its strong political feeling (coming mostly from leftist writers), was rarely more than a simple chronicle. An exception is the trilogy of Stratis Tsirkas (b. 1911 in Alexandria): three novels with the general title *Cities Adrift*, about the war in the Middle East, and in particular about the mutinies in the Greek expeditionary force. The trilogy characteristically was not published until after 1960. A. Kotziàs and N. Kasdaglis have presented with hard realism the conflicts between Greeks of opposing ideologies during the years of the occupation; the latter in *The Shaven Heads* (1959) has given us the chronicle of the infantryman undergoing his military service. His realism stems from that of Karagatsis.

Rodis Roufos (b. 1924) wrote a trilogy, *Chronicle of a Crusade*, also concerned with conflicts of the war and the occupation. It contains many autobiographical elements, and the tone is emphatically anti-communist. His later work, *Bronze Age*, is a chronicle, in the form of a journal, of the struggle of Cyprus for independence. Angelos Vlachos (b. 1915), a career diplomat like Roufos, has particularly favoured the historical novel, placing his characters either in the classical period (*My Lord Alcibiades*) or in that of the Comnenian emperors (*Their Last Serene Majesties*). Both these writers use a fluent language and have an elegant and witty style reminiscent of Theotokàs. On the other hand Renos (Apostolidis, b. 1924) has a tense, aggressive, and very personal style, qualities that in general colour his life as a writer.

The sensibility, the lyricism, and the emotionalism of feminine writing we find in the work of Margarita Lymberaki and Galatea Saranti. But while the first in her novel *The Other Alexander* showed herself capable at last of dealing with deeper psychological problems, the latter is a lyrical writer in the vein of Venezis. Tatiana Milliex (b. 1920), who started her career as a member of the resistance group of writers, showed in her latest novel that she has been creatively influenced by the new tendencies in French prose.

A critic has suggested that perhaps the most essential contribution of post-war prose writing has been the revival of the short story. One of the most considerable short-story writers is D. Chatzìs (b. 1913 in Janina, he now lives in Budapest). He describes the world of a small town collapsing because of changed economic conditions; in a later volume (1966) he writes about events during the occupation and the Civil War. He is successful in rendering the inner world of his people and the warmth of relationships. He is among the best writers of post-war prose. Spyros Plaskovitis (a judge of the higher court, now in prison), as time went by, developed as a writer, dealing with more urgent contemporary problems, his style becoming more epigrammatic and tight. Richer in symbolism (derived from Kafka and Camus) is his only novel, *The Barrage*. M. Lazaridis sets his stories in Africa, where he is working; he depicts well the tropical atmosphere and the fiery and violent sensuality of his characters. G. Grigoris, who began in 1938, is exclusively a short-story writer. G. Kitsopoulos (b. 1919) has in his stories followed the Thessaloniki tradition of the inward narrative.

A younger generation of writers has done more interesting work, in trying both to protest more clearly and more vehemently and to find new ways of writing through experiment. A. Samarakis (b. 1919) has a strong and uneasy personality and expresses himself with originality and a sarcasm that sometimes touches the absurd. V. Vasilikòs (b. 1933 in Thessaloniki) gave us one of the finest works of post-war prose with his trilogy, *The Leaf*, *The Well*, and *The Message* (1961), where in modern, succinct, and vital language he expresses, in a purely literary manner, the collapse, confusion, and protest of our time. I do not think that in his later work, which is more directly 'engaged' (nor in $Z$, which had great success as a film), he has surpassed the remarkable achievement of the trilogy.

We shall mention a few names of writers who have appeared since 1959: A. Frangiàs, G. Kachtitsis (d. 1970), who settled in Canada, and G. Ioannou; the last has a frequently repulsive realism, shattering in its accuracy. *The Third Wedding* (1962) of Kostas Tachtsìs, with its astonishing narrative fluency, is perhaps one of the best novels of the last decade.

Playwrights around 1950 wrote under the influence of Lorca or with a social message (N. Pergialis, J. Kambanelis, G. Sevastikoglou). The novelist M. Lymberaki has, with some success, sought new means of expression in the theatre, while

Loula Anagnostaki has written one-act plays in a modern, tense style, in the manner of the Theatre of the Absurd.

Criticism has been written notably by G. Themelis, by Manolis and Nora Anagnostaki, by Renos (Apostolidis), and A. Argyriou; G. Dallas and the calm and reflective Zisimos Lorentzatos have been essay writers. In the field of literary research we have the important contribution of Professor G. Savvidis (editor of Kavafis, Karyotakis, and Sikelianòs), the work of A. Sachinis, who has specialized in the criticism of prose, and of K. Stergiopoulos. Responsible literary criticism has appeared in the columns of *Nea Estia*, of *Epochès* (under the direction of A. Terzakis), and the *Review of Art*.

# Appendix

## TEXTS OF THE POEMS QUOTED

p. 26:    Ἀνάθεμαν τὰ γράμματα, Χριστέ, καὶ ὁποὺ τὰ θέλει!

p. 31:    Καὶ ἀργὰ βραδύ, ὅταν ἔφεξε καὶ ἐξέβην τὸ φεγγίτσιν,
ἐβγαίνουν εἰς τὸν ἡλιακὸν τῆς κόρης οἱ καυχίτσες,
νὰ στέκουν καὶ νὰ λέγουσιν, φίλε μου, καταλόγιν·
Ἄγουρος ποθοαιχμάλωτος, ἀπὸ τὰ γονικά του
εἰς τὸ ἐμνοστοαναλίβαδον ἦλθε καὶ κατουνεύει·
αὐγὴ ποτὲ οὐ κοιμίζει τον, νύκτα οὐ καταπονεῖ τον ...

p. 36:    Εἰπέ μοι, κακομούσουρε κουρώνη, τί 'ν' τὰ λέγεις;
Πικρόφωνε, κακόθωρε, μυριοατυχισμένη,
Αἰγύπτισσα μὲ τὸ μανδίν, Γιλλοὺ μὲ τὸ καρκάλιν.
Πάντως οὐ λέγω ψέματα, ἠξεύρουν πόθεν εἶσαι,
γυναίκα καρβουνάρισσα ἀπὸ τὸ Μαῦρον Ὄρος.

p. 38:    πάλι μὲ χρόνια, μὲ καιρούς, πάλι δικά μας εἶναι.

p. 41:    ἂν εἶναι κῆποι καὶ δεντρά, πουλιὰ νὰ κιλαδοῦσι,
κι' ἀνὲ μυρίζουν τὰ βουνιὰ καὶ τὰ δεντρὰ ν' ἀθοῦσι,
ἂν εἶν' λιβάδια δροσερά, φυσᾶ γλυκὺς ἀέρας,
λάμπουσιν τ' ἄστρα τ' οὐρανοῦ καὶ αὐγερινὸς ἀστέρας;

p. 44:    Δίδει τὴν βράστην στὸ λαμπρὸν ἡ φύση,
στὸ χιόνιν δίδει κρυότην, δίδει ἀσπράδαν·
λαμπρὸν ἀχ τὸ λαμπρὸν νὰ βγῇ ἔναι χρήση,
τὸ χιόνιν πάλε βγάλλει μαργωμάδαν.
Μπορεῖ τὸ χιόνιν τὸ λαμπρὸν νὰ σβήσῃ,
καλὰ κι' ἂν διώχνῃ τὸ λαμπρὸν τὴν κρυάδαν·
κι' ἐμέναν τὸ λαμπρόν μου δὲ μπυρίζει·
βγαίννει 'πού μιὰν ἡ ποιὰ πάντα χιονίζει.

p. 63:    Ἐννιὰ μῆνες σ' ἐβάσταξα, τέκνο μου κανακάρη,
'ς τοῦτο τὸ κακορίζικο καὶ σκοτεινὸ κουφάρι ...

καὶ τώρα, πέ μου, ποιὰ χαρὰ βούλεσαι νὰ μοῦ δώσῃς;
σὰν ἀστραπὴ καὶ σὰ βροντή, θὲς νὰ χαθῇς, νὰ λιώσῃς.

p. 65: Ἄπ' ὅ, τι κάλλη ἔχει ἄθρωπος, τὰ λόγια 'χουν τὴ χάρη
νὰ κάνουσι κάθε καρδιὰ παρηγοριὰ νὰ πάρη,
κι' ὁποὺ κατέχει νὰ μιλῆ μὲ γνώση καὶ μὲ τρόπο,
κάνει καὶ κλαῖσι καὶ γελοῦν τὰ μάτια τῶν ἀθρώπω.

p. 66: Βιτσέντζος εἶν' ὁ ποιητής, καὶ στὴ γενιὰ Κορνάρος . . .

p. 76: Χιώτισσα εἶμαι, Χιώτισσα, τί μὲ ρωτᾶς, παπά μου,
γιὰ τοῦτο εἶμαι, ὡς θωρεῖς, εὔμορφη, δέσποτά μου.

p. 84: Ὁ Ὄλυμπος κι' ὁ Κίσσαβος, τὰ δυὸ βουνὰ μαλώνουν.

p. 85: Ὁ ἥλιος ἐβασίλεψε—Ἑλληνά μου, βασίλεψε—
καὶ τὸ φεγγάρι ἐχάθη,
κι' ὁ καθαρὸς αὐγερινὸς ποὺ πάει κοντὰ στὴν πούλια
τὰ τέσσερα κουβέντιαζαν . . .

p. 85: Ἦλθ' ἦλθε χελιδὼν     Ἦρθε, ἦρθε χελιδόνα
καλὰς ὥρας ἄγουσα     ἦρθε κι' ἄλλη μελιηδόνα,
καὶ καλοὺς ἐνιαυτούς.     κάθισε καὶ λάλησε
                        καὶ γλυκὰ κελάδησε.

p. 86: Κοιμήσου ἀστρί, κοιμήσου αὐγή, κοιμήσου νιὸ φεγγάρι,
κοιμήσου ποὺ νὰ σὲ χαρῆ ὁ νιὸς ποὺ θὰ σὲ πάρη.
Κοιμήσου ποὺ παράγγειλα στὴν Πόλη τὰ χρυσά σου,
στὴ Βενετιὰ τὰ ροῦχα σου καὶ τὰ διαμαντικά σου.

p. 86: Δὲ σὄπρεπε, δὲ σὄμοιαζε στὴ γῆ κρεβατοστρώση,
μόν' σὄπρεπε, μόν' σὄμοιαζε στοῦ Μάη τὸ περιβόλι,
ἀνάμεσα σὲ δυὸ μηλιές, σὲ τρεῖς νερατζοπούλες,
νὰ πέφτουν τ' ἄνθ' ἀπάνου σου, τὰ μῆλα στὴν ποδιά σου,
τὰ κρεμεζογαρούφαλα τριγύρω στὸ λαιμό σου.

p. 86: Γιά ἰδὲς καιρὸν ποὺ διάλεξε ὁ Χάρος νὰ σὲ πάρη,
τώρα π' ἀνθίζουν τὰ κλαριὰ καὶ βγάζει ἡ γῆς χορτάρι.

p. 87: Γιατί εἶναι μαῦρα τὰ βουνὰ καὶ στέκουν βουρκωμένα;
Μὴν ἄνεμος τὰ πολεμᾶ, μήνα βροχὴ τὰ δέρνει;
Κι' οὐδ' ἄνεμος τὰ πολεμᾶ, κι' οὐδὲ βροχὴ τὰ δέρνει,
μόνε διαβαίνει ὁ Χάροντας μὲ τοὺς ἀποθαμένους.
Σέρνει τοὺς νιοὺς ἀπὸ μπροστά, τοὺς γέροντες κατόπι,
τὰ τρυφερὰ παιδόπουλα στὴ σέλα ἀραδιασμένα.

p. 89: Στὰ ἔμπα του χίλιους ἔκοψε, στὰ ξέβγα δυὸ χιλιάδες,
καὶ στὸ καλὸ τὸ γύρισμα κανένα δὲν ἀφήνει.

pp. 92–3 :  Τί ἔχουν τῆς Ζίχνας τὰ βουνὰ καὶ στέκουν μαραμένα;
Μήνα χαλάζι τὰ βαρεῖ, μήνα βαρὺς χειμώνας;
Οὐδὲ χαλάζι τὰ βαρεῖ, οὐδὲ βαρὺς χειμώνας,
ὁ Νικοτσάρας πολεμάει μὲ τρία βιλαέτια.

p. 93 :  Τὸ λὲν οἱ κοῦκκοι στὰ κλαδιὰ κι' οἱ πέρδικες στὰ πλάγια,
τὸ λένε κι' οἱ Πλαγιώτισσες τὸ μαῦρο μοιρολόγι.

p. 93 :  Τρία πουλάκια κάθονταν στὴ ράχη, στὸ λημέρι,
τό 'να τηράει τόν Ἀλμυρό, τ' ἄλλο κατὰ τὸ Βάλτο,
τὸ τρίτο τὸ καλύτερο μοιριολογάει καὶ λέει . . .

pp. 93–4 :  Ἀπού 'ναι νιὸς καὶ δὲν πετᾶ μὲ τοῦ βορρᾶ τὰ νέφη,
ἴντα τὴ θέλει τὴ ζωὴ στὸν κόσμο νὰ τὴν ἔχη!

Νά 'σουν στὸν κάμπο λεϊμονιά, κι' ἐγὼ στὰ ὄρη χιόνι,
νὰ λιώνω νὰ ποτίζουνται οἱ δροσεροί σου κλῶνοι.

Ἐμίσεψες καὶ μ' ἄφησες σὰν παραπονεμένη,
σὰν ἐκκλησιὰ ἀλειτούργητη σὲ χώρα κουρσεμένη.

p. 94 :  Τῆς νύχτας οἱ ἀρματολοὶ καί τῆς αὐγῆς οἱ κλέφτες.

Θέλετε δέντρα ἀνθίσετε, θέλετε μαραθῆτε.

p. 94 :  Μάνα λωλή, μάνα τρελή, μάνα ξεμυαλισμένη.

Βαρεῖ δεξιά, βαρεῖ ζερβιά, βαρεῖ μπροστὰ καὶ πίσω.

p. 94 :  Φέρνει τ' ἀλάφια ζωντανά, τ' ἀγρίμια μερωμένα,
φέρνει κι' ἕνα λαφόπουλο στὴ σέλα του δεμένο.

Βάλε τὸν ἥλιο πρόσωπο καὶ τὸ φεγγάρι στῆθος,
καὶ τοῦ κοράκου τὸ φτερὸ βάλε γαϊτανοφρύδι.

p. 94 :  Ἐχάραξεν ἡ Ἀνατολὴ καὶ ρόδισεν ἡ Δύση.

p. 95 :  Καὶ μιὰ γιορτὴ, μιὰ Κυριακή, μιὰ πίσημην ἡμέρα.

p. 95 :  Τρία τουφέκια τοῦ 'ριξαν, τὰ τρία ἀράδα ἀράδα,
τό 'να τὸν παίρνει στὸ πλευρό, καί τ' ἄλλο στὸ κεφάλι,
τὸ τρίτο τὸ φαρμακερὸ ἀνάμεσα στὰ μάτια.

p. 95 :  Μοιρολογοῦσαν κι' ἔλεγαν, μοιρολογοῦν καί λέγουν.

p. 104 :  Ὡς πότε, παλληκάρια, νά ζοῦμεν στὰ στενά,
μονάχοι σὰν λιοντάρια στὲς ράχες, στὰ βουνά;

. . . . . . . . . .

Καλλιό 'ναι μιᾶς ὥρας ἐλεύθερη ζωὴ
παρὰ σαράντα χρόνοι σκλαβιὰ καὶ φυλακή!

p. 109:  Νὰ μὴ φθάσω, νὰ μὴ ζήσω
ἂν μιὰ μέρα δὲν φιλήσω,
κι' ἂν πεθάνω, ν' ἀπεθάνω
στὰ φιλάκια μου ἀπάνω.

"Εξω ἔξω τὰ βιβλία
στὴ φωτιὰ ἡ φλυαρία . . .
νὰ γενῇ βαρελοθήκη
ἡ χρυσὴ βιβλιοθήκη.

p. 109:  Ἡ ἄνοιξη ἐπέρασε,
τό καλοκαίρι γέρασε,
χειμώνιασε καί πάει.
Καὶ τώρ' ἀπελπισμένα
τὰ πρώην ἀνθισμένα
τὸ χιόνι τὰ χτυπάει.

Τὰ χόρτα ἐξεράθηκαν
καί τ' ἄνθη ἐμαράθηκαν,
γυμνώθηκεν ἡ γῆ.
Τό κάλλος της ἐσβήσθη,
στό χάος ἐβυθίσθη,
στὴν πρώτη του πηγή.

pp. 110–11:  Ἡ γλυκυτάτη ἄνοιξη
μέ τ' ἄνθη στολισμένη,
ροδοστεφανωμένη,
τὴ γῆ γλυκοτηράει.

Κι' ἡ γῆ τὴ χλόη ντύνεται,
τὰ δάση της ἰσκιώνουν,
τὰ κρύα χιόνια λιώνουν,
ὁ οὐρανός γελάει.

p. 111:  Σὰν πεταλούδα στὴ φωτιὰ σ' ἐσένα γύρες φέρω,
κι' ὄχ τὴ φωτιὰ ποὺ καίγομαι νὰ φύγω δὲν ἠξέρω.

p. 115:  Τὴν εἶδα τὴν ξανθούλα,
τὴν εἶδα ψὲς ἀργά,
ποὺ ἐμπῆκε στὴ βαρκούλα
νὰ πάη στὴν ξενιτιά.

p. 116:  Σὲ γνωρίζω ἀπὸ τὴν κόψη
τοῦ σπαθιοῦ τὴν τρομερή,
σὲ γνωρίζω ἀπὸ τὴν ὄψη,
ποὺ μὲ βία μετράει τὴ γῆ.

p. 118: —ˊΓλυκό 'ναι τῆς Παράδεισος
νὰ μελετᾶς τὰ κάλλη.
— Πικρή 'ναι ἡ φοβερώτατη
τοῦ κόσμου ἀνεμοζάλη·
μόν' ἐδῶ φθάνει ὁ ἀντίλαλος,
δὲ φθάνει ἡ τρικυμιά.

p. 121: Καὶ μὲς στῆς λίμνης τὰ νερά, ὅπ' ἔφθασε μ' ἀσπούδα,
ἔπαιξε μὲ τὸν ἴσκιο της γαλάζια πεταλούδα,
ποὺ εὐώδιασε τὸν ὕπνο της μέσα στὸν ἄγριο κρίνο·
τὸ σκουληκάκι βρίσκεται σ' ὥρα γλυκιὰ κι' ἐκεῖνο.
Μάγεμα ἡ φύσις κι' ὄνειρο στὴν ὀμορφιὰ καὶ χάρη,
ἡ μαύρη πέτρα ὁλόχρυση καὶ τὸ ξερὸ χορτάρι·
μὲ χίλιες βρύσες χύνεται, μὲ χίλιες γλῶσσες κραίνει·
ὅποιος πεθάνη σήμερα χίλιες φορές πεθαίνει.

p. 122: Πρὶν πάψ' ἡ μεγαλόψυχη πνοὴ χαρὰ γεμίζει.
Ἄστραψε φῶς κι' ἐγνώρισεν ὁ νιὸς τὸν ἑαυτό του.

p. 122: Μακρὺς ὁ λάκκος π' ἄνοιξε καὶ κλεῖ τὸ γίγαντά μου.

p. 123: Μικρὸς προφήτης ἔριξε σὲ κορασιὰ τὰ μάτια . . .

p. 127: Ὅπου τρέμουσιν ἄπειρα
τὰ φῶτα τῆς νυκτός,
ἐκεῖ ὑψηλὰ πλατύνεται
ὁ Γαλαξίας καὶ χύνει
δρόσου σταγόνας.

Τὸ ποτὸν καθαρὸν
θεραπεύει τὰ φύλλα,
κι' ὅπου ἀφῆκε τὸ χόρτον
εὐρίσκει ρόδα ὁ ἥλιος
καὶ μυρωδίαν.

p. 132: Ἐσὺ ποὺ πρώτη ἐπρόβαλες
σὰν ὄνειρο ἐμπροστά μου
κι' ἄναψες πάθη ἀκοίμητα
στήν ἄδολη καρδιά μου,
ἅ! ποῦ 'σαι, πές μου, ἀγάπη μου,
ποῦ 'σαι, γλυκιά μου ἐλπίδα;
Τὴ γῆν ἔχεις πατρίδα
ἢ τ' ἄστρα τ' οὐρανοῦ;

p. 142: Πλούσιαι πόρπαι πρὸς στολὴν
διάλιθοι συνεῖχον
τῆς κόρης τὴν ἀναβολήν,
κ' εἰς τὴν χρυσῆν της κεφαλὴν
τὸν πλοῦτον τῶν βοστρύχων.

p. 144: Ἦλθες, Μάρτιε, ἦλθες λοιπόν,
κ' ἐπρασίνισαν πάλιν οἱ κάμποι,
καὶ τὸ βλέμμα τοῦ ἔαρος λάμπει,
λάμπ' εἰς ὅλην τὴν γῆν χαρωπόν.

p. 146: Τὴν θέλω ἀσθενῆ ἐγώ τὴν φίλην μου, ταχεῖαν,
ὠχρὰν τὴν θέλω καὶ λευκὴν ὡς νεκρικὴν σινδόνην,
μὲ εἴκοσι φθινόπωρα, μὲ ἄνοιξιν καμμίαν . . .

p. 154: μετεβλήθη ἐντός μου
καὶ ὁ ρυθμὸς τοῦ κόσμου . . .

p. 156: . . . πῶς ἀλλιῶς
νὰ σὲ πῶ; ὁ συνοδοιπόρος . . .

p. 156: Συνοδοιπόροι ναί, μαζὶ κινήσαμε
στῆς Τέχνης τὸ γλυκοξημέρωμα — ὅμως,
μὲ τοῦ καιροῦ τὸ πέρασμα, χαράχτηκε
τοῦ καθενός μας χωριστὸς ὁ δρόμος·

.    .    .    .    .    .    .

Ἐσὺ στῆς δάφνης τ' ἀκροκλώναρα ἅπλωσες,
κι' ἐγὼ σὲ κάθε χόρτο καὶ βοτάνι·
στεφάνι ἔχεις φορέσει ἀπὸ δαφνόφυλλα —
λίγο θυμάρι τοῦ βουνοῦ μοῦ φτάνει.

p. 160: γιὰ τ' ἀνέβασμα ξανὰ ποὺ σὲ καλεῖ
θὰ αἰστανθῆς νὰ σοῦ φυτρώνουν, ὦ χαρά!
τὰ φτερά,
τὰ φτερὰ τὰ πρωτινά σου τὰ μεγάλα!

p. 161: Τὰ πρῶτα μου χρόνια τ' ἀξέχαστα τά 'ζησα
κοντὰ στ' ἀκρογιάλι,
στὴ θάλασσα ἐκεῖ τὴ ρηχὴ καὶ τὴν ἤμερη,
στὴ θάλασσα ἐκεῖ τὴν πλατιά, τὴ μεγάλη.
("Μιὰ πίκρα")

Γιαννιώτικα, σμυρνιώτικα, πολίτικα,
μακρόσυρτα τραγούδια ἀνατολίτικα,
λυπητερά,
πῶς ἡ ψυχή μου σέρνεται μαζί σας!
Εἶναι χυμένη ἀπὸ τὴ μουσική σας
καὶ πάει μὲ τὰ δικά σας τὰ φτερά.
(*"Ἀνατολή"*)

p. 162:   Κυριακή. Παιδάκι. Τοῦ δασκάλου πάψη.
Γλύκα τοῦ σπιτιοῦ. Ζωούλα στ᾽ ἀκρογιάλι.
Τώρα τὴν προσμένω τὴ μεγάλη
Κυριακή· γιὰ πάντα, λέω, θὰ μ᾽ ἀναπάψη.

p. 180:   Ὅταν ἀπὸ δροσόπαγο κλιτὸ καὶ μαργωμένο
μνήσκει στὸν κάμπο ὁλονυκτὶς τ᾽ Ἀπρίλη τὸ λουλούδι
καὶ τὴν αὐγούλα τὸ φιλοῦν μόλις τοῦ ἥλιου οἱ ἀχτίδες
κι᾽ ἐκεῖνο ἀναθερμαίνεται καὶ ξεπαγώνει ἀγάλια,
κι᾽ ἡ Χρύσω ἔτσι ξεπάγωσε . . .

p. 182:   Μπρόβαλε μέρα λιβανὴ κι᾽ ὀνειροξεδιαλύτρα
νὰ διώξῃς τὰ ἰσκιώματα τοῦ ὕπνου ἀπὸ κοντά μου·
μπρόβαλε μέρα, κοίμισε τὴν ὑπνοφαντασιά μου,
ποὺ ἐνῶ κοιμοῦμαι ξαγρυπνᾷ ἡ νυχτοπαρωρίτρα.

p. 182:   μὰ ἡ ἄγια ἡ φωτιά, μιὰ πόσβησε, δὲν τὴν ἀνάβει πλιὰ
ἀνθρώπινο προσάναμμα ἢ πυροδότης.

p. 183:   Γεννιοῦμαι ἀπ᾽ τὸν πόνο·
κι᾽ ἁπλώνω κι᾽ ἁπλώνω
κι᾽ ἁπλώνομαι πέρα
κι᾽ ἁπλώνομαι γύρω
σὲ ὀχτιὲς καὶ σὲ βύθη
συντρίμμια νὰ σπείρω.

p. 188:   Ἰδανικὲς φωνὲς κι᾽ ἀγαπημένες
ἐκείνων ποὺ πεθάναν . . .

. . . σὰν σώματα ὡραῖα νεκρῶν ποὺ δὲν ἐγέρασαν
καὶ τά 'κλεισαν, μὲ δάκρυα, σὲ μαυσωλεῖο λαμπρό,
μὲ ρόδα στὸ κεφάλι καὶ στὰ πόδια γιασεμιά.

p. 189:   ποὺ πότε ἡ ὁμιλία εἶναι γιὰ τὰ ὡραῖα σοφιστικά,
καὶ πότε γιὰ τὰ ἐρωτικά των τὰ ἐξαίσια.
(*"Ἡρώδης Ἀττικός"*)

p. 190:  (τὸ) θέατρον ὅπου μιὰ ἔνωσις ἐγένονταν τῆς Τέχνης
μὲ τὲς ἐρωτικὲς τῆς σάρκας τάσεις!
("Ὁ Ἰουλιανὸς καὶ οἱ Ἀντιοχεῖς")

p. 191:  ποὺ κι' ὁ ρυθμός κι' ἡ κάθε φράσις νὰ δηλοῦν
ποὺ γι' Ἀλεξανδρινὸ γράφει Ἀλεξανδρινός.
("Γιὰ τὸν Ἀμμόνη")

p. 194:  ... καὶ λάτρεψα,
καὶ στὴ λαχτάρα μου εἶπα:
"Βάλε τὸ αὐτὶ στὰ χώματα."
Καὶ φάνη μου πὼς ἡ καρδιὰ
τῆς γῆς βαριὰ ἀντιχτύπα.

p. 196:  Τοῦ ψυχοσάββατου φιλί — στὸν ὕπνο μου, ὡς νὰ φύγῃ
τ' ὄνειρο — ἀργά, τὰ μάτια μου στὴ νέαν αὐγή, π' ἀνοίγει!

Ἀπ' τὸ βαθὺν εὐτυχισμὸ τὸ πνέμα μου ὡς ξυπνάει
μὲς στὴν ἐγκόσμια χλαλοὴν ὁποὺ τὸ τυραννάει,

δὲ λέω ἡ ἄχραντη χαρὰ γιὰ μένα ἂν ἀναβρύζῃ
κι' ὁ γλυκασμὸς ποὺ ἀσίγητο τραγούδι μουρμουρίζει·

σιμά 'ναι ὁ ἴσκιος, ἄξαφνα, ποὺ ἀπάνω μου διαβαίνει
καὶ τὴν οὐρανομίλητη γλυκιὰν ἀχὼ βουβαίνει!

p. 200:  Γιατὶ βαθιά μου δόξασα καὶ πίστεψα στὴ γῆ
καὶ στὴ φυγὴ δὲν ἅπλωσα τὰ μυστικὰ φτερά μου,
μὰ ὁλάκερον ἐρίζωσα τὸ νοῦ μου στὴ σιγή,

.    .    .    .    .    .    .    .

νά πού, ὅ,τι στάθη ἐφήμερο, σὰ σύγνεφο ἀναλιώνει,
νά ποὺ κι' ὁ μέγας θάνατος μοῦ γίνηκε ἀδερφός! ...

p. 201:  Ἀϊ! μὲ τὸ γύφτικο ζουρνὰ
μὲ νταγερὲ ποὺ κουδουνᾷ
σύρε σκοπὸν ἀντάμικο.
Ἐστράβωσα τὴ φέσα μου,
ἔρωτας ποὺ 'ναι μέσα μου
γιὰ νὰ χορέψω τσάμικο.

p. 203:  Ἂς ὑποθέσουμε πὼς δὲν ἔχουμε φτάσει
ἀπὸ ἑκατὸ δρόμους τὰ ὅρια τῆς σιγῆς,
κι' ἂς τραγουδήσουμε — τὸ τραγούδι νὰ μοιάσῃ
νικητήριο σάλπισμα, ξέσπασμα κραυγῆς —
τοὺς πυρροὺς δαίμονες, στὰ ἔγκατα τῆς γῆς,
καὶ, ψηλά, τοὺς ἀνθρώπους νὰ διασκεδάσῃ.

p. 232:    Στὸ περιγιάλι τὸ κρυφὸ
                κι' ἄσπρο σὰν περιστέρι
                διψάσαμε τὸ μεσημέρι·
                μὰ τὸ νερὸ γλυφό.
                              (" Ἄρνηση ")

p. 233:    Ἱερουσαλήμ, ἀκυβέρνητη πολιτεία,
                Ἱερουσαλήμ, πολιτεία τῆς προσφυγιᾶς . . .

                            συνεχίζουμε τὴν περιοδεία μας
                πολλὲς ὀργιὲς κάτω ἀπ' τὴν ἐπιφάνεια τοῦ Αἰγαίου.

p. 234:    Ἀγγελικὸ καὶ μαῦρο, φῶς,
                γέλιο τῶν κυμάτων στὶς δημοσιὲς τοῦ πόντου,
                δακρυσμένο γέλιο, . . .

                Ἀγγελικὴ καὶ μαύρη, μέρα·
                ἡ γλυφὴ γέψη τῆς γυναίκας ποὺ φαρμακώνει τὸ φυλακισμένο
                βγαίνει ἀπ' τὸ κύμα δροσερὸ κλωνάρι στολισμένο στάλες.

p. 235:    Τ' ἀηδόνια δὲ σ' ἀφήνουνε νὰ κοιμηθῆς στὶς Πλάτρες . . .

p. 235:    Κι' ὁ ἀδερφός μου;
                      Ἀηδόνι ἀηδόνι ἀηδόνι,
                τ' εἶναι θεός; τί μὴ θεός; καὶ τί τ' ἀνάμεσό τους;

# Chronological Tables

*Modern Greek Literature*

IXth–Xth cent. Akritic Songs; Byzantine *Vulgärliteratur*
Early XIth cent. *Epic of Digenis Akritas*

XIIth cent. *Prodromika, Spaneas*
1159 Poem of Glykàs

c. 1300 *The Chronicle of Morea*

*History of Greece*

867–1025 Height of Macedonian dynasty
1042–54 Constantine IX Monomachus
1071 Disaster of Manzikert; the Byzantines lose eastern Asia Minor and S. Italy

1081–1180 Comnenian dynasty
1096–9 First Crusade
1192 Cyprus under the Lusignans
1204 Fourth Crusade; sack of Constantinople by the Franks
1204–61 Latin Empire of Constantinople; Greek Kingdom of Nicaea (1254–8 Theodore II Laskaris); Frankish Occupation
1261 Recapture of Constantinople by the Byzantines (Michael VIII Palaeologus)
1261–1453 Palaeologian dynasty

*History and Literature outside Greece*

c. 1100 *Chanson de Roland*
XIIth cent. Provençal Poetry in France

c. 1200 *Roman de Renart*

1213 Defeat of the Albigenses
c. 1235 Guillaume de Lorris: *Le Roman de la Rose*

1265–1321 Dante Alighieri

| Modern Greek Literature | History of Greece | History and Literature outside Greece |
|---|---|---|
| | 1261 Despotate of the Morea (Mystra) | 1304–74 Francesco Petrarca |
| XIVth cent. ROMANCES OF CHIVALRY; *Libistros and Rodamne*; *Assises* in Cyprus | 1309 The Knights of St. John at Rhodes | 1313–75 Giovanni Boccaccio |
| | 1354 The Turks land at Callipolis | 1338 Beginning of the Hundred Years War |
| 1310–40 *Kallimachos and Chrysorrhoe* | 1362 Sack of Adrianople | |
| 1364 *Tale about Quadrupeds* | 1396 Defeat of the Christians at Nicopolis by the Turks | 1359–89 Mourad I |
| 1388 *Life of Alexander* | | 1389–1403 Bajazet I |
| | | 1390–1400 Chaucer: *The Canterbury Tales* |
| 1400–50 Later Romances: *Belthandros, Florios*, etc.; *Belisarius, Achilleid*; Leontios Machairàs in Cyprus | 1430 Sack of Thessaloniki and of Janina by the Turks | c. 1400 Froissart: *Chroniques* |
| | 1439 Council of Florence. Vote for the unity of the Churches | |
| | 1444 Defeat of the Crusaders at Varna | |
| 1445 J. Laskaris b. | | |
| 1450–1500 Greek Scholars in Italy; *Erotopaignia* | 1453 Sack of Constantinople; Gennadius II, Patriarch | 1451–81 Mohammed II |
| 1452 G. Gemistòs Plethon d. | 1461 Sack of Trebizond | |
| | 1462 Occupation of Lesbos by the Turks | 1461 François Villon: *Le Testament* |
| | 1463–79 Turco-Venetian war | |
| 1472 Bessarion d. in Ravenna | | 1480 J. Sanazzaro: *Arcadia* (publ. 1504); Poliziano: *Orfeo* |
| | 1489 Cyprus passes from the Lusignans to the Venetians | 1492 Columbus discovers West Indies; Lorenzo de' Medici d. |
| 1490–1500 G. Choumnos (Crete); E. Georgillàs (Rhodes) | 1500 Capture of Methone and Korone by the Turks | |
| 1500–50 G. Sklavos, St. Sachlikis, M. Falieros (Crete); J. Trivolis, N. Sofianòs (Venice) | | 1512–20 Selim I |
| 1513–21 Greek Gymnasium in Rome | | 1513 Machiavelli: *The Prince* |
| | | 1516 Ariosto: *Orlando Furioso* |
| 1517 M. Mousouros d. (b. 1470) | | 1517 Luther's theses in Wittenberg |

| | | |
|---|---|---|
| 1519 | Apokopos of Bergadis | |
| 1524 | *Mourning for Death* | |
| c. 1530–1600 | Demotic prose, Venice | |
| 1535 | J. Laskaris d. (b. 1445) | |
| 1539 | *The Chap-book of the Donkey* | |
| 1544 | N. Sofianòs: *Pedagogue* | |
| 1560–70 | Cypriot love-poems | |
| 1571 | A. Achelis: *Siege of Malta* | |
| 1577 | Greek College of St. Athanasius | |
| | THE GREAT AGE OF CRETAN LITERATURE | |
| 1585–1600 | G. Chortatsis (*Gyparis, Erofili, Katzourbos*) | |
| 1593 | School of the Greek community, Venice | |
| 1602 | M. Margounios d. (b. 1530); M. Pigàs d. (b. 1532) | |

| | |
|---|---|
| 1522 | The Turks take Rhodes |
| 1537 | The institution of the *armatoli* becomes general |
| 1537–40 | Second Turko-Venetian war; Venice loses many of her possessions |
| 1540 | Surrender of Nauplia and Monemvasia to the Turks |
| 1566 | Occupation of Chios by the Turks; they control the Aegean |
| 1570–1 | Siege and occupation of Cyprus |
| 1571 | Battle of Naupactus (Lepanto) |
| 1572–95 | Jeremias II, Patriarch |
| 1573 | Peace between Venice and Turkey |
| 1590–1602 | M. Pigàs, Patriarch of Alexandria |
| 1595–1601 | Struggle against the Turks of Michael the Brave, Prince of Moldavia |
| c. 1600–25 | Movement of Charles, duc de Nevers |

| | |
|---|---|
| 1520–66 | Suleyman I, the Great |
| 1521 | Capture of Belgrade |
| 1522 | Luther's New Testament |
| 1530 | Charles V, Emperor |
| 1531 | Henry VIII; Reformation in England |
| 1532 | Rabelais: *Pantagruel* |
| 1541 | G. B. Giraldi: *Orbecche* |
| 1552 | Ronsard's first *Amours* |
| 1553 | Rabelais d. |
| 1558–1603 | Elizabeth Queen of England |
| 1564 | William Shakespeare b.; Galileo b. |
| 1564–70 | Siege and capture of Malta by the Turks |
| 1566–74 | Suleyman II, Sultan |
| 1570 | Camoëns: *Lusiads* |
| 1572 | Massacre of St. Bartholomew's Day |
| 1573 | Tasso: *Aminta* |
| 1580 | Montaigne: *Les Essais* |
| 1581 | Tasso: *Jerusalem Delivered* |
| 1583 | L. Groto: *La Calisto* |
| 1585 | Ronsard d. |
| 1586 | Tasso: *Il Re Torrismondo*; L. Groto: *Lo Isach* |
| 1590 | Guarini: *Pastor Fido*; Spenser: *Faerie Queene* (I–III) |
| 1594 | Shakespeare: *Richard II* |
| 1597 | Shakespeare: *Romeo and Juliet*; Bacon: *Essays*, 1st edn. |
| 1602 | Shakespeare: *Hamlet* |

| Modern Greek Literature | History of Greece | History and Literature outside Greece |
| --- | --- | --- |
| | | 1603 Queen Elizabeth d. |
| | | 1605 Cervantes: *Don Quixote* |
| | | 1611 Shakespeare: *The Tempest* |
| | 1611 Revolutionary movements in Thessaly and Epirus; execution of Dionysios the 'Skylosophist' | 1616 Shakespeare d.; Cervantes d. |
| | | 1619 Beginning of the Thirty Years War |
| | | 1623–40 Murad IV |
| | 1620–38 Kyrillos Loukaris, Patriarch | 1624 Richelieu becomes minister |
| 1627 *The Voskopoula*, 1st edn. | | 1625 Bacon: *Essays*, final form |
| 1631 Pseudo-Dorotheos: *Historical Book* | | 1633 Persecution of Galileo |
| 1635 *The Sacrifice of Abraham* | | 1636 Corneille: *Le Cid* |
| 1641 A. Landos: *Salvation of Sinners* | | 1637 Descartes: *Le Discours de la méthode* |
| before 1645 *Stathis*, comedy | | |
| 1645 Theophilos Korydaleus d. (b. 1560) | 1645 Beginning of the Cretan war; the Turks take Chania, Rethymno, and other towns and lay siege to Kastro | |
| 1647 *King Rodolinos*, tragedy | | 1648 Treaty of Westfalen |
| 1648 Foundation of Flanginis's School in Venice | | 1649 Execution of Charles I |
| *c.* 1640–60 Vitsentzos Kornaros: *Erotokritos* | 1656 Panagiotis Nikousios, Great Interpreter to the Porte | 1656 Kuprili, Grand Vizir |
| *c.* 1660 M. A. Foskolos: *Fortounatos* | | 1660 Pascal: *Les Pensées* |
| | | 1664 Defeat of the Turks by the Austrians; Molière: *Le Tartuffe* |
| | 1669 Surrender of Kastro; Turkish occupation of Crete | 1667 Milton: *Paradise Lost* |
| 1669 Elias Miniatis b. in Cephalonia | 1673 Alexandros Mavrokordatos, Great Interpreter | 1673 Molière d. |
| 1681 F. Skoufos: *Art of Rhetoric* | | 1677 Spinoza: *Ethics* (posthumous); Racine: *Phèdre* |

| | | |
|---|---|---|
| 1682–3 Zenon, tragedy | 1684–1715 New Turco-Venetian war | 1683 Siege of Vienna by the Turks failed |
| | 1687 Morozini in the Peloponnese; second Venetian occupation (until 1714); siege and sack of Athens; bombardment of Parthenon | 1687 Newton: *Philosophiae Naturalis Principia Mathematica* |
| | | 1689 Peter the Great, Tsar of Russia |
| 1703 *Chronicle of Galaxidi* | | 1690 J. Locke: *Essay concerning Human Understanding* |
| 1708 *Flowers of Piety* (Venice) | | 1693 J. Locke: *On Education* |
| 1713 *Erotokritos*, 1st edn. | 1709 Nikolaos Mavrokordatos, Prince of Moldavia | 1699 Treaty of Carlowicz; Fénelon: *Télémaque* |
| 1714 E. Miniatis d. | | |
| THE AGE OF THE PHANARIOTS; MODERN GREEK ENLIGHTENMENT | | 1714 Leibniz: *La Monadologie* |
| 1716 Eugenios Voulgaris b. | 1715 Sack of Nauplia; end of the Turco-Venetian war | |
| 1718 N. Mavrokordatos: *Parerga of Philotheos* | 1716 Siege of Corfu by the Turks | 1718 Peace of Pasarowicz |
| 1720–1 P. Katsaïtis's dramas | | 1719 Defoe: *Robinson Crusoe* |
| | | 1724 Metastasio's first drama for music |
| | | 1740 Frederick II, King of Prussia |
| | | 1742 E. Young: *Night Thoughts* |
| 1748 A. Koraïs b. in Smyrna | | 1748 Montesquieu: *L'Esprit des lois* |
| | | 1749–1803 Vittorio Alfieri |
| | | 1751 *L'Encyclopédie* (part 1) |
| | | 1753 Goldoni: *La Locandiera* |
| c. 1757 Rigas Velestinlis b. | | 1754–1828 Vincenzo Monti |
| 1760–79 Kosmàs the Aetolian | | 1760 J. Macpherson: *Ossian* |
| | | 1762–96 Catherine II, Empress of Russia |
| 1766–84 Works of K. Dapontes (d. 1784) | | 1762 Rousseau: *Du Contrat social* |
| | | 1767 Winckelmann, *Geschichte der Kunst des Altertums* |

| *Modern Greek Literature* | *History of Greece* | *History and Literature outside Greece* |
|---|---|---|
| 1771 J. Vilarás b. | 1768–74 Russo-Turkish war | 1768 Thomas Gray: *Poems* |
| 1772 A. Christopoulos b. | 1769–70 The Orloff movement; disaster in the Peloponnese | |
| | 1774 Treaty of Kutchuk Kainardji | 1774 Goethe: *Werther* |
| 1779 J. Moisiodax: *Education* | | 1776 Declaration of American Independence |
| | | 1781 Kant: *Critique of Pure Reason* |
| | | 1782 Rousseau: *Confessions*; Metastasio d. (b. 1698) |
| 1783–90 D. Katartzis's works | 1783 The Greeks acquire the right of navigation under the Russian flag | |
| | 1787–1803 Wars of the Suliots | |
| 1788 A. Koraïs settled in Paris | 1788 Ali, Pasha of Epirus | 1788 Barthélemy: *Le Voyage du jeune Anacharsis* |
| 1789 Correspondence between L. Fotiadis and D. Katartzis | | 1789 French Revolution |
| 1790–1 Rigas in Vienna; *The School for Delicate Lovers* | | 1790 Goethe: *Faust* (part 1) |
| 1792 A. Kalvos b. in Zakynthos | | |
| | | 1793 Decapitation of Louis XVI of France; V. Monti: *Basvilliana* |
| 1795 D. Gouzelis: *Chasis*, comedy | | |
| 1797 General Makrygiannis b. | 1797 Occupation of the Ionian Islands by the French republicans | 1797 Treaty of Campoformio; Destruction of the French fleet in Abukir |
| 1798 D. Solomós b. in Zakynthos | 1798 Execution of Rigas | |
| | 1799 The Ionian Islands occupied by the Russians and Turks | 1799 Napoleon, premier consul |

| | | |
|---|---|---|
| 1800 G. Tertsetis b. | 1800 The Ionian State | 1800 Novalis: *Hymns of the Night* |
| | | 1801 Ugo Foscolo: *Ultime lettere di Jacopo Ortis* |
| | | 1802 V. Hugo d.; V. Monti, Professor of Poetry at Pavia |
| 1803 A. Soutsos b. | 1803 Ali Pasha takes Suli | |
| | | 1804 Napoleon, Emperor |
| 1805 G. Zalokostas b.; A. Christopoulos: *Grammar of Aeolo-Doric*; A. Koraïs: *Prolegomena* | | 1805 Battle of Trafalgar; Mohammed Aly, Pasha of Egypt; F. Schiller d. |
| 1806 E. Voulgaris d. (b. 1716); P. Soutsos b. | 1806 Russo-Turkish war | |
| 1807 D. Katartzis d. (b. 1720-5) | | 1807 U. Foscolo: *I Sepolcri* |
| 1808-18 D. Solomòs in Italy | | |
| 1809 A. R. Rangavis b. | 1809 The English in Zakynthos | 1809 Metternich, Chancellor; Lord Byron's first visit to Greece |
| 1811 A. Laskaratos b.; A. Christopoulos: *Lyrics* | | |
| | | 1812 Byron: *Childe Harold* (I-II) |
| 1814 J. Typaldos b.; J. Vilaràs: *The Romaic Language* | 1814 Foundation of the 'Friendly Society' | |
| | 1815 The United State of the Ionian Islands (till 1864) | 1815 Battle of Waterloo; Manzoni: *Inni Sacri* |
| | | 1816 U. Foscolo in London |
| 1817 Th. Orfanidis b. in Smyrna | | |
| 1818-23 Solomòs's early poems | | 1818 J. Keats: *Endymion* |
| | | 1820 Lamartine: *Les Méditations poétiques* |
| 1821 | 1821 Outbreak of the Greek War of Independence; A. Ypsilantis at Jassy; rising in the Peloponnese (March); capture of Tripolitzà (October) | 1821 Congress of Laibach; Napoleon d. |

| *Modern Greek Literature* | *History of Greece* | *History and Literature outside Greece* |
|---|---|---|
| 1822 D. Solomòs: *Rime Improvvisate* | 1822 Destruction of Dramali in the Dervenakia (July); first siege of Missolonghi (Christmas) | 1822 Shelley: *Hellas*; Shelley d. (b. 1792) |
| 1823 J. Vilaràs d. (b. 1771); D. Solomòs: *Hymn to Liberty* | | |
| 1824 A. Valaoritis b.; J. Karasoutsas b.; D. Valavanis b.; D. Solomòs: *Dialogue*; A. Kalvos: *Lyra* | 1824 Destruction of Psara; Death of Lord Byron at Missolonghi; Thomas Maitland, Lord High Commissioner of the Ionian Islands | 1824 Leopardi: *Canzoni* |
| | 1825 Landing of Ibrahim in the Peloponnese | |
| 1826 J. Polylas b.; G. Markoràs b.; A. Kalvos: *Lyrics* | 1826 Sortie at Missolonghi | 1826 Hölderlin's poems |
| 1827 A. Soutsos: *Satires* | 1827 Election of J. Kapodistrias as Governor of Greece; Sir Frederick Adam, Lord High Commissioner; Naval battle of Navarino | 1827 Ugo Foscolo d. (b. 1778); V. Monti d. (b. 1754) |
| | | 1828–9 Russo-Turkish war; Treaty of Adrianople |
| 1829 Makrygiannis begins to write his *Memoirs* | | |
| 1830 A. Matesis: *The Basil Plant* | 1830 Protocol of London. Greece an independent state | 1830 Revolution of July; V. Hugo: *Hernani* |
| **GREEK ROMANTICISM** | | |
| 1831 P. Soutsos: *The Traveller* | 1831 Murder of Kapodistrias | 1831 Balzac: *Le Père Goriot* |
| 1833 A. Koraïs d. in Paris (b. 1748); Solomòs: *The Cretan, The Free Besieged* (2nd draft, 1833–44) | 1833 Arrival of King Otho in Nauplia | 1832 Goethe d. (b. 1749) |
| 1835 D. Vikelas b. in Syra | 1834 Athens the capital of the state | |
| 1836 D. Vyzantios: *Babel*, comedy; E. Roidis b. in Syra | | 1837 Accession of Queen Victoria |
| | | 1838 Dickens: *Oliver Twist* |
| 1843 D. Paparrigopoulos b. | 1843 Movement of 3 September; granting of a constitution | 1839 Stendhal: *La Chartreuse de Parme* |
| 1844 Sp. Vasiliadis b. | | |
| 1847 A. Christopoulos d. (b. 1772) | | |

| | | |
|---|---|---|
| 1849 | G. Vizyinós b.; A. Eftaliótis b.; D. Solomós: *Pórfyras* | |
| 1850 | A. Soútsos: *Greece against the Turks*; A. R. Rangavís: *The Lord of the Morea*, historical novel | |
| 1851 | A. Papadiamántis b.; A. Pallis b. | |
| 1854 | D. Valavánis d. (b. 1824); J. Psycháris b. | |
| 1855 | P. Kalligás: *Thanos Vlékas* | |
| 1856 | J. Papadiamantopoulos (Jean Moréas) b.; A. Laskarátos: *The Mysteries of Cephalonia*; J. Typáldos: *Divers Poems* | |
| 1857 | D. Solomós d. in Corfu (b. 1798); N. Kambás b.; A. Valaorítis: *Elegies* | |
| 1858 | G. Zalokóstas d. (b. 1805) | |
| 1859 | D. Solomós: *Remains* (edited by J. Polylàs); K. Palamàs b.; G. Drosínis b. | |
| 1860 | L. Mavílis b.; J. Karasoútsas: *Barbitos* | |
| 1863 | A. Soútsos d. (b. 1803); K. Kavafis b. | |
| 1864 | General Makrygiánnis d. (b. 1797); A. R. Rangavís: *The Voyage of Dionysos* | |

| | | |
|---|---|---|
| 1849 | Constitutional changes in the Ionian Islands | |
| 1850 | Blockade of Piraeus by Parker | |
| 1854 | Revolutionary movements in Epirus, Thessaly, and Macedonia | |
| 1862 | Abdication of Otho | |
| 1863 | George I, King | |
| 1864 | Cession of the Ionian Islands by Great Britain to Greece | |

| | | |
|---|---|---|
| 1848 | Revolution of February; Engels–Marx: *Kommunistisches Manifest*; Thackeray: *Vanity Fair* | |
| 1852 | Napoleon III, Emperor; Gautier: *Émaux et Camées* | |
| 1854–6 | Crimean war | |
| 1857 | Baudelaire: *Les Fleurs du mal*; Flaubert: *Madame Bovary* | |
| 1859 | Darwin: *The Origin of Species* | |
| 1862 | V. Hugo: *Les Misérables* | |
| 1865 | President Lincoln assassinated; *Le Parnasse contemporain* | |

U

*History and Literature outside Greece*

1866 Dostoevski: *Crime and Punishment*

1867 Ibsen: *Peer Gynt*; Marx: *Das Kapital*; Tolstoy: *War and Peace*

1870 Dante Gabriel Rossetti: *Poems*
1870–1 Franco-Prussian war
1871 Commune of Paris

1875 Third French Republic
1876 Mallarmé: *L'Après-midi d'un faune*

1880 Zola: *Nana*

*History of Greece*

1866–9 Cretan revolution. Burning of the monastery of Arkadi

1870 Independent Bulgarian Church (the Exarchate); Macedonian Question

1875 Ch. Trikoupis, Prime Minister

1877–8 Russo-Turkish war; revolutionary movements in Epirus and Thessaly
1878 Treaty of St. Stephen; Council of Berlin; Cyprus acquired by the British

*Modern Greek Literature*

1866 A. Karkavitsas b.; E. Roidis: *Pope Joan*
1867 Gr. Xenopoulos b.
1868 P. Soutsos d. (b. 1806); K. Krystallis b.; K. Chatzopoulos b.
1869 A. Kalvos d. (b. 1792); M. Malakasis b.; N. G. Politis: *Modern Greek Mythology*

1870 J. Gryparis b.

1872 K. Theotokis b.
1873 A. Karasoutsas d. (b. 1824); D. Paparrigopoulos d. (b. 1843)
1874 G. Tertsetis d. (b. 1800); Sp. Vasiliadis d. (b. 1844); Sp. Pasagiannis b.
1875 G. Markoràs: *The Oath*

1877–8 Controversy between Roidis and Vlachos
1879 A. Valaoritis d. (b. 1824); D. Vikelas: *Loukis Laras*; A. Papadiamantis's first novel

THE GENERATION OF 1880; GREEK PARNASSIANISM

1880 N. Kambàs: *Verses*; G. Drosinis: *Spider's Webs*

| | |
|---|---|
| 1881 | Annexation of Thessaly and the district of Arta |
| 1882–5 | Government of Ch. Trikoupis; organization of the State, strengthening of the finances |
| 1895 | Electoral defeat of Ch. Trikoupis (d. 1896) |
| 1897 | Revolution in Crete; Greco-Turkish war; defeat of Greece; Treaty of Constantinople; Bulgarian guerrillas (*komitadjis*) in Macedonia |
| 1898 | Autonomy in Crete; Prince George High Commissioner |

| | |
|---|---|
| 1883 | J. Typaldos d. (b. 1814); N. Kazantzakis b. |
| 1883–4 | Short stories of G. Vizyinòs |
| 1884 | A. Sikelianòs b.; K. Varnalis b.; G. Drosinis: *Idylls* |
| 1885 | A. Karkavitsas's first stories |
| 1886 | Th. Orfanidis d. (b. 1817); K. Palamàs: *The Songs of My Country* |
| 1888 | Psycharis: *My Journey*; Kosmàs Politis b. |
| 1889 | First 'Filadelfian' Competition |
| 1890 | K. Ouranis b.; Second 'Filadelfian' Competition; K. Palamàs: *The Eyes of My Soul*; G. Markoràs: *Poetical Works* |
| 1892 | A. R. Rangavis d. (b. 1809); Str. Myrivilis b. |
| 1893 | E. Roidis: *The Idols* |
| 1894 | K. Krystallis d. (b. 1868) |
| 1895 | A. Paraschos d. (b. 1838); F. Kontoglou b.; sonnets of Mavilis and Gryparis |
| 1896 | J. Polylàs d. (b. 1826); K. Karyotakis b.; K. Kavafis: *Wells*; A. Karkavitsas: *The Beggar* |
| 1897 | K. Palamàs: *Iambs and Anapaests*; Psycharis: *The Dream of Gianniris* |
| 1898 | K. Palamàs, *The Tomb*; K. Chatzopoulos's first collections |

| | |
|---|---|
| 1883 | Nietzsche: *Also sprach Zarathustra* |
| 1885 | Zola: *Germinal* |
| 1891 | T. Hardy: *Tess of the D'Urbervilles*; O. Wilde: *The Picture of Dorian Gray* |
| 1893 | J.-M. Hérédia: *Les Trophées* |
| 1897 | A. Gide: *Les Nourritures terrestres* |

| Modern Greek Literature | History of Greece | History and Literature outside Greece |
|---|---|---|
| 1898–9 *Techni*, periodical | | 1899–1902 Boer War |
| 1899 T. Agras b. | | 1899 J. Moréas: *Stances* |
| 1900 G. Seferis b. | | |
| 1901 A. Laskaratos d. (b. 1811); A. Embirikos b.; *Evangelika* (riots in Athens); 'New Stage'; 'Royal Theatre' | | 1901 Queen Victoria d. |
| 1903 *Oresteiaka* (riots); *Noumàs*, periodical; A. Papadiamantis: *The Murderess*; K. Palamàs: *Trisevgeni*, drama | 1903–8 Macedonian Struggle | 1902 D'Annunzio: *Francesca da Rimini* |
| 1904 E. Roidis d. (b. 1836); Elias Venezis b.; K. Palamàs: *Life Immovable*; K. Kavafis: *Poems* (first booklet) | 1904 Death of Pavlos Melàs | 1903 G. B. Shaw: *Man and Superman* |
| 1905 G. Theotokàs b. | | 1904 Anglo-French *Entente cordiale* |
| 1907 D. Vernardakis d. (b. 1833); A. Terzakis b.; K. Palamàs: *The Dodecalogue of the Gipsy* | | 1904–12 R. Rolland: *Jean-Christophe* |
| 1908 M. Karagatsis b. | 1908 Revolutionary government of Eleftherios Venizelos in Crete | 1905 Revolution in Russia |
| 1908–11 Delmouzos's girls' school in Volos | | 1907 Bergson: *L'Evolution créatrice*; Rilke: *New Poems* |
| 1909 Sp. Pasagiannis d. (b. 1874); J. Ritsos b.; P. Prevelakis b.; A. Sikelianòs: *The Light-Shadowed*; Gr. Xenopoulos: *Stella Violanti* | 1909 Military movement at Goudi | 1908 Movement of the 'Young Turks' |
| 1910 Suicide of P. Giannopoulos; N. Engonopoulos b.; K. Palamàs: *The King's Flute*; 'Educational Society' founded; Kavafis: *Poems* (second booklet) | 1910 Venizelos in Greece; general elections | 1910 Tolstoy d. (b. 1828) |

| Year | | Year | | Year | |
|------|--|------|--|------|--|
| 1911 | G. Markoràs d. (b. 1826); A. Papadiamantis d. (b. 1851); O. Elytis b.; N. Vrettakos b. | 1911 | Government of Eleftherios Venizelos; Revision of the Constitution of 1864 | 1913 | S. Freud: *Totem and Taboo*; D. H. Lawrence: *Sons and Lovers*; Proust: *À la recherche du temps perdu* |
| 1912 | L. Mavilis d. (b. 1860) | 1912 | The Italians take Rhodes | 1914–18 | First World War |
| | | 1912–13 | The Balkan wars | 1916 | Barbusse: *Le Feu* |
| | | 1913 | Murder of George I; Treaty of Bucharest: Greece obtains Epirus, Macedonia, Crete, and the Aegean Islands | 1917 | Russian Revolution; Valéry: *La Jeune Parque* |
| 1915 | K. Palamàs: *The Altars*; G. Drosinis: *Radiant Darkness* | 1914–18 | First World War | 1920 | League of Nations |
| 1915–17 | A. Sikelianòs: *Prologue to Life* | 1915 | Difference between King Constantine and Venizelos; resignation of the latter (October) | 1922 | Mussolini in Italy; T. S. Eliot: *The Waste Land*; J. Joyce: *Ulysses* |
| | | 1916 | Venizelos at Thessaloniki; Government of 'National Defence' | 1923 | Rilke: *Sonnets to Orpheus*; Pirandello: *Henry IV* |
| 1917 | A. Sikelianòs: *Mother of God*; K. Chatzopoulos: *Autumn*, novel; Educational Reform | 1917 | Abdication of King Constantine; King Alexander; government of Venizelos | | |
| 1918 | G. Drosinis: *Closed Eyelids* | 1919 | Treaty of Neuilly | | |
| 1919 | J. Gryparis: *Scarabs and Terracottas* | 1920 | Treaty of Sèvres; Greece obtains western Thrace and the mandate of administration of the region of Smyrna; electoral defeat of Venizelos (1 November); return of King Constantine | | |
| 1920 | A. Vlachos d. (b. 1838); K. Chatzopoulos d. (b. 1868); J. Dragoumis assassinated | | | | |
| 1920–30 | D. Voutyràs's short stories | 1921 | Movement of Mustapha Kemal | | |
| 1921 | K. Karyotakis: *Nepenthe* | 1922 | Asia Minor disaster; military revolution; abdication of King Constantine; King George II | | |
| 1922 | A. Karkavitsas d. (b. 1866); K. Varnalis: *The Light that Burns*; F. Kontoglou: *Pedro Cazas* | 1923 | Treaty of Lausanne; exchange of populations | | |
| 1923 | A. Eftaliotis d. (b. 1849); K. Theotokis d. (b. 1872); N. Kazantzakis: *Ascetism* | | | | |

| *Modern Greek Literature* | *History of Greece* | *History and Literature outside Greece* |
|---|---|---|
| 1924 S. Myrivilis: *The Life in Tomb* (1st edn.); Thr. Kastanakis: *The Princes* | 1924–35 Greek Republic (A. Papanastasiou) | 1924 G. B. Shaw: *St. Joan*; Lenin d.; Surrealist manifesto |
| 1927 First Delphic Festival | | 1926 F. Kafka: *The Castle* |
| 1928 Suicide of K. Karyotakis (b. 1896) | 1928–32 Government of Venizelos | 1927 V. Woolf: *To the Lighthouse* |
| 1929 J. Psycharis d. (b. 1854); G. Theotokas: *Free Spirit*, essay | | 1928 Lorca: *Romancero Gitano*; Yeats: *The Tower* |
| 1930 Second Delphic Festival | 1930 Greek–Turkish pact of friendship | 1929 E. Remarque: *All Quiet on the Western Front* |
| THE GENERATION OF 1930 | | 1930 D. H. Lawrence d. (b. 1885) |
| 1930 S. Myrivilis: *The Life in Tomb* (2nd edn.) | | |
| 1931 G. Seferis: *Turning-Point*; E. Venezis: *Number 31328*; K. Politis: *Lemon Grove* | | 1932 F. D. Roosevelt elected U.S. President |
| 1933 K. Kavafis d. (b. 1863); M. Karagatsis: *Colonel Liapkin* | | 1933 A. Hitler's government |
| 1934 F. Politis d. (b. 1890) | | |
| 1935 A. Pallis d. (b. 1851); K. Palamàs: *The Nights of Phemius*; G. Seferis: *Mythistorima*; A. Embirikos: *Furnace* | 1935 Restoration of the monarchy; return of King George II | 1935 Italy invades Abyssinia |
| 1936 G. Theotokàs: *Argo* | 1936 4 August, dictatorship of J. Metaxàs | 1936–9 Spanish Civil War |
| 1938 N. Kazantzakis: *Odyssey* | | 1938 The 'Munich Crisis'; Sartre: *La Nausée* |
| 1940 A. Sikelianòs: *Sibyl*, tragedy; O. Elytis: *Orientations* | 1940–1 Greco-Italian war | 1939 Italy invades Albania; S. Freud d. (b. 1883) |
| | 1941–4 German and Italian occupation; the Communist party (KKE) and the Communist army (ELAS) play | 1939–45 Second World War |
| | | 1940 Battle of France; Battle of Britain |

| | | |
|---|---|---|
| 1942 | J. Gryparis d. (b. 1870) | |
| 1943 | K. Palamàs d. (b. 1859); M. Malakasis d. (b. 1869) | |
| 1944 | T. Agras d. (b. 1899) | |
| 1945 | A. Terzakis: *Princess Ysabeau* | |
| 1946 | A. Sikelianòs: *Lyrical Life*; N. Kazantzakis: *Alexis Zorbàs* | |
| 1948–50 | N. Kazantzakis's novels | |
| 1951 | G. Drosinis d. (b. 1859); Gr. Xenopoulos d. (b. 1867); A. Sikelianòs d. (b. 1884) | |
| 1953 | K. Ouranis d. (b. 1890) | |
| 1957 | N. Kazantzakis d. (b. 1883) | |
| 1960 | M. Karagatsis d. (b. 1908); O. Elytis: *Dignum est* | |

the greatest part in the resistance; the Greek army in the Allied campaigns in Middle East, and later in Italy

| | |
|---|---|
| 1944 | October: Liberation of Greece; December: Communist Revolt; suppressed with British help |
| 1946 | March: Parliamentary elections; September: plebiscite; return of King George II |
| 1947 | 'Truman doctrine'; 1 April: death of George II; King Paul |
| 1947–9 | Civil war |
| 1948 | Union of the Dodecanese with Greece |
| 1951 | Government of General A. Papagos |
| 1954–5 | Cyprus question |
| 1955 | October: Death of A. Papagos; Government of K. Karamanlis (ERE) |
| 1959 | Agreements of Zurich and London: Cyprus an independent republic (August 1960) |

| | |
|---|---|
| 1942 | Battle of El Alamein; A. Camus: *L'Etranger* |
| 1943 | Mussolini falls |
| 1944 | Eliot: *Four Quartets* |
| 1945 | F. D. Roosevelt d. (b. 1882) |
| 1947 | Camus: *La Peste* |
| 1948 | Gandhi d. (b. 1869) |
| 1949 | Establishment of Communist Republic in China; G. Orwell: *Nineteen Eighty-Four* |
| 1950 | G. B. Shaw d. (b. 1856) |
| 1950–1 | Korean war |
| 1951 | A. Gide d. (b. 1869) |
| 1953 | J. Stalin d. (b. 1879) |
| 1955 | A. Einstein d. (b. 1879); Th. Mann d. (b. 1875) |
| 1958 | General De Gaulle President of France; B. Pasternak: *Dr. Zhivago* |
| 1960 | J. F. Kennedy elected U.S. President |

| *Modern Greek Literature* | *History of Greece* | *History and Literature outside Greece* |
|---|---|---|
| 1963 Nobel Prize to G. Seferis | 1963 May: murder of the EDA deputy, G. Lambrakis, at Thessaloniki; June: resignation of the Karamanlis government | 1963 President Kennedy assassinated (b. 1917) |
| | 1964 February: Centre Union (EK, under G. Papandreou) gains a clear majority in the elections; March: death of King Paul; Constantine II, King | |
| 1965 F. Kontoglou d. (b. 1895) | 1965 July: G. Papandreou obliged by the King to resign; beginning of political crisis | 1965 U.S. Offensive in Vietnam; W. Churchill d. (b. 1874); T. S. Eliot d. (b. 1888) |
| 1966 G. Theotokás d. (b. 1905) | 1966 December: Caretaker government of J. Paraskevopoulos (governor of the National Bank) | |
| 1967 Thr. Kastanakis d. (b. 1901) | 1967 April: Resignation of Paraskevopoulos government; government of P. Kanellopoulos (head of the ERE); dissolution of Parliament and proclamation of elections for 28 May; 21 April: military movement of the Colonels; establishment of a non-parliamentary government; 13 December: unsuccessful royalist movement; King Constantine and his family go to Rome | 1967 The Six-Day War |
| | 1968 G. Papandreou d. (b. 1888) | 1968 Student Troubles in Paris; Czechoslovakia occupied by U.S.S.R. troops |
| 1969 S. Myrivilis d. (b. 1892) | | |
| 1971 G. Seferis d. (b. 1900) | | |

# Selected Bibliography[1]

## A. GENERAL WORKS

### I. HISTORY OF MODERN HELLENISM

Aspreas, G., Πολιτικὴ ἱστορία τῆς νεωτέρας Ἑλλάδος, 1821–1921, 2 vols., Athens, 1922–3.

Heurtly, W. A., Darby, H. C., Crawley, C. M., Woodhouse, C. M., *A Short History of Greece, from Early Times to 1964*, Cambridge University Press, 1965 (modern Greek history by C. M. Crawley and C. M. Woodhouse.)

Markezinis, Sp., Πολιτικὴ ἱστορία τῆς νεωτέρας Ἑλλάδος, 1828–1964, 4 vols., Athens, Papyros, 1966–8.

Paparrigopoulos, K., Ἱστορία τοῦ ἑλληνικοῦ ἔθνους (from early times until 1830), 1st edn. 1872, many reprints (from the 4th edn. onwards, it contains a supplement by P. Karolidis for the years 1830–81).

Sophocles, S. M., *A History of Greece*, Thessaloniki, 1961 [Institute for Balkan Studies, 45].

Svoronos, N., *Histoire de la Grèce moderne*, Paris, P.U.F., 1953 ['Que sais-je?'].

Vakalopoulos, A. E., Ἱστορία τοῦ νέου Ἑλληνισμοῦ, 3 vols., Thessaloniki, 1961–8 (in progress).

—— Πηγὲς τῆς ἱστορίας τοῦ νέου Ἑλληνισμοῦ (1204–1669), Thessaloniki, 1965.

[1] This bibliography is not exhaustive. In Chapters I–V I have listed the (mostly rare) editions of the texts. In the remaining chapters the record of the editions of each writer would cause a disproportionate extension of the bibliography. (Such a record is to be found in my small *History of Modern Greek Literature; A Brief Outline*, listed below on p. 301.) Here I confine myself to mentioning trustworthy editions of complete works, where they exist, and translations into foreign languages, preferably into English. In the preparation of this bibliography I am much indebted to the publication of K. Dimarás, K. Koumarianoù, and L. Droulia, *Modern Greek Culture, A Selected Bibliography*, Thessaloniki, 1968, which records all publications in foreign languages; also to the extensive bibliography in the recent third edition (1969) of the *Letteratura neoellenica* of Bruno Lavagnini.

Woodhouse, C. M., *The Story of Modern Greece*, London, Faber & Faber, 1968.

Zakythinòs, D. A., Ἡ Τουρκοκρατία, Εἰσαγωγὴ εἰς τὴν νεωτέραν ἱστορίαν τοῦ Ἑλληνισμοῦ, Athens, 1957.

II. MODERN GREEK LANGUAGE

Browning, R., *Medieval and Modern Greek*, London, 1969.

Chatzidakis, G. N., Σύντομος ἱστορία τῆς ἑλληνικῆς γλώσσης, Athens, 1915.

Kapsomenos, S. G., *Die griechische Sprache zwischen Koine und Neugriechisch*, Munich, 1958 [Berichte zum XI. Internationalen Byzantinisten Kongress].

Megas, A. E., Ἱστορία τοῦ γλωσσικοῦ ζητήματος, 2 vols., Athens, 1925–7.

Mirambel, A., *La langue grecque moderne, description et analyse*, Paris, 1959.

Triantafyllidis, M., Νεοελληνικὴ Γραμματική, Πρῶτος τόμος : Ἱστορικὴ Εἰσαγωγή, Athens, 1938 (with extensive appendices of (*a*) Texts, (*b*) Testimonies, and (*c*) Supplements).

—— Ἅπαντα, 8 vols., Thessaloniki, 1963–5, and Γενικὸ Εὑρετήριο, 1969 (vols 1–2 : Ἐρευνητικά; vol. 3 : Νεοελληνικὴ Γραμματική, Ἱστορικὴ Εἰσαγωγή; vols. 4–7 : Γλωσσικὸ ζήτημα καὶ γλωσσοεκπαιδευτικά, vol. 8 : Διάφορα).

—— Νεοελληνικὴ Γραμματικὴ (τῆς δημοτικῆς), Athens, 1941 (edited by a committee under the presidency of M. Triantafyllidis).

III. HISTORY OF MODERN GREEK LITERATURE

Beck, H.-G., *Geschichte der byzantinischen Volksliteratur*, Munich, 1971 [Byzantinisches Handbuch, 2. Teil, 3. Band].

Dimaràs, K., Ἱστορία τῆς νεοελληνικῆς λογοτεχνίας (ἀπὸ τὶς πρῶτες ρίζες ὡς τὴν ἐποχή μας), 2 vols., Athens, 1948 (4th edn., 1968). There is also a translation in French : *Histoire de la littérature néohellénique; des origines à nos jours* (Athens, 1965).

Hesseling, D. C., *Histoire de la littérature grecque moderne*, translated from the Dutch by N. Pernot, Paris, Les Belles-Lettres, 1924.

Kambanis, A., Ἱστορία τῆς νεοελληνικῆς λογοτεχνίας, Athens, 1925 (5th edn., 1948).

Knös, B., *L'histoire de la littérature néo-grecque. La période jusqu'en 1821*, Uppsala, 1962.

Lavagnini, B., *La letteratura neoellenica*, revised edn., Florence–Milan (3rd edn., with detailed bibliography, 1969; 1st edn., 1965).

Mirambel, A., *La littérature grecque moderne*, Paris, P.U.F., 1953 ['Que sais-je?'].

Selected Bibliography 301

Politis, L., ʹΙστορία τῆς νέας ἑλληνικῆς λογοτεχνίας: Συνοπτικὸ διά
γραμμα, Βιβλιογραφία, 2nd revised edn., Thessaloniki, 1969 (pp.
79–143 a detailed bibliography of the editions of each author).
Voutieridis, E. P., Σύντομη ἱστορία τῆς νεοελληνικῆς λογοτεχνίας (1000–
1930), Athens, 1933 (2nd edn., with a supplement by D. Giakos
for the years 1931–65, Athens, 1966).

IV. ANTHOLOGIES

(a) POETRY

Apostolidis, H. N., Ἀνθολογία, 1708–1952, 2 vols., 9th edn., Athens,
1967 (1st edn., 1933) (from 1970 continued by Renos Apostolidis, under the title: Ἀνθολογία τῆς νεοελληνικῆς γραμματείας. Ἡ
ποίηση, λόγια καὶ δημοτική, ἀπὸ τὸν μεσαίωνα ὡς τὶς μέρες μας
(10th edn.)).
Politis, L., Ποιητικὴ Ἀνθολογία, 7 vols., Athens, Galaxias, 1964–7
(vol. 1: Before the Fall of Constantinople; vol. 2: After the Fall,
XVth and XVIth centuries; vol. 3: The Cretan Poetry of the
XVIIth century; vol. 4: The Phanariots and the Athenian
School; vol. 5: Solomòs and the Heptanesian School; vol. 6:
Palamàs and his contemporaries; vol. 7: Sikelianòs, Kavafis, and
the later poets).
Trypanis, C. A., Medieval and Modern Greek Poetry, An Anthology, Oxford,
Clarendon Press, 1951.

(b) PROSE

Apostolidis, H. N., Τὸ διήγημα ἀνθολογημένο, 3 vols., Athens, 1953–60.
Ikonomos, M., Διηγήματα μεγάλων Ἑλλήνων διηγηματογράφων,
Athens, 1951.
Mirambel, A., Anthologie de la prose néo-hellénique (1884–1961), 2nd edn.,
Paris, 1962 (1st edn., 1950).
Rosenthal-Kamarinea, I., Anthologie der neugriechischen Erzähler, Berlin,
1961 (2nd edn., 1965).
Valetas, G., Ἀνθολογία τῆς δημοτικῆς πεζογραφίας, 3 vols., Athens,
1947–9 (from the fifteenth century until today).
See also:
Βασικὴ Βιβλιοθήκη, 48 vols., Athens, Aetòs–Zacharovoulos, 1952–8
(a large anthology of texts, under various headings; each volume
with introduction, biographical notes of the authors, and bibliography).

(c) TRANSLATIONS

Axioti, M., and Hadzis, D., Antigone lebt; neugriechische Erzählungen,
Berlin, 1961.

Dalven, R., *Modern Greek Poetry*, New York, 1949.
Keeley, E., and Sherrard, P., *Six Poets of Modern Greece*, London, 1960 (poems by Kavafis, Sikelianòs, Seferis, Antoniou, Elytis, Gatsos, translated from the Greek).
—— —— *Four Greek Poets: C. P. Cavafy, G. Seferis, Od. Elytis, N. Gatsos*, London, 1966 (poems chosen and translated from the Greek).
Lavagnini, B., *Trittico neogreco, Porfiras, Kavafis, Sikelianòs*, Athens, 1954 (text and translation).
—— *Arodafnusa, Poeti neogreci (1880–1940)*, Athens, 1957 (text and translation).
Levesque, R., *Domaine grec, 1930–1946*, Geneva–Paris, 1947 (translations of twenty Greek writers).
Rosenthal-Kamarinea, I., *Neugriechische Erzähler: eine Anthologie*; übertragen, herausgegeben und mit einem Nachwort versehen, Freiburg i. Br., 1958.
—— *Griechenland erzählt*. 19 Erzählungen, ausgewählt, eingeleitet und aus dem Griechischen übertragen, Fischer Verlag, 1965.
Stomeo, P., *Antologia della lirica greca moderna*, vol. 1, [Lecce, 1955] (Solomòs and Kavafis; text and translation).
Trypanis, C. A., *The Penguin Book of Greek Verse*, Harmondsworth, 1971 (from Homer to Elytis, with plain prose translations of each poem. Parts 5–6, pp. 468–618, are devoted to modern Greek poetry).
Vitti, M., *Poesia greca del Novecento*, revised and augmented edn., 1966 [Collana Fenice, 10] (poets from the 1880 generation to post-war times; text, translation, and lengthy introduction; 1st edn., 1957).

V. MISCELLANEOUS STUDIES

(a) VARIOUS

Irmscher, J. (ed.), *Probleme der neugriechischen Literatur*, 4 vols., Berlin, 1959–60 [Berliner Byzantinistische Arbeiten, 14–17].
Karantonis, A., Φυσιογνωμίες, 2 vols., Athens, 1959–60.
Legrand, E., *Bibliographie hellénique, ou description raisonnée des ouvrages publiés par des Grecs*: (a) aux XVᵉ et XVIᵉ siècles, 4 vols., Paris 1885, 1903–5; (b) au XVIIᵉ siècle, 5 vols., Paris, 1894–6, 1903; (c) au XVIIIᵉ siècle, 2 vols., Paris, 1918, 1928 (the last is edited by H. Pernot).
Panagiotopoulos, J. M., Τὰ πρόσωπα καὶ τὰ κείμενα, 6 vols., Athens, 1943–55 (vol. 2: prose of the 1930 generation; vol. 3: Palamàs; vol. 4: Kavafis; vol. 5: Malakasis, Porfyras, Agras, Karyotakis).
Pernot, H., *Études de littérature grecque moderne*, 2 vols., Paris, 1916–18 (vol. 1: Digenìs, Prodromika, Erotopaignia, Cretan literature; vol. 2: Erotokritos, Kalvos, Laskaratos).

(b) POETRY

Baud-Bovy, S., *Poésie de la Grèce moderne*, Lausanne, 1946 (Kalvos, Solomòs, Palamàs, Kavafis, Sikelianòs).

Διαλέξεις περὶ Ἑλλήνων ποιητῶν τοῦ ΙΘ′ αἰῶνος, 2 vols., 2nd edn., Athens, 1925 (Kalvos, Soutsos, Laskaratos, Typaldos, and others).

Karantonis, A., Εἰσαγωγὴ στὴ νεώτερη ποίηση, Athens, 1950.

—— Γύρω ἀπὸ τὴ σύγχρονη ἑλληνικὴ ποίηση, Athens, 1961.

Politis, L., Θέματα τῆς λογοτεχνίας μας, Athens, 1947 (*Erotokritos*, Solomòs, Psycharis, Pallis, Palamàs, Sikelianòs, Seferis, Elytis).

Sherrard, Ph., *The Marble Threshing Floor: Studies in Modern Greek Poetry*, London, 1956 (Solomòs, Palamàs, Kavafis, Sikelianòs, Seferis).

Spyridaki, G., *La Grèce et la poésie moderne*, Paris, Les Belles-Lettres, 1954 (Palamàs, Kavafis, Sikelianòs, and others).

Thrylos, A., Κριτικὲς μελέτες, 3 vols., Athens, 1924–5 (vol. 1 : Solomòs; vol. 2 : Palamàs; vol. 3 : Gryparis, Chatzopoulos, Malakasis, Kavafis, Porfyras).

(c) PROSE

Charis, P., Ἕλληνες πεζογράφοι, 3 vols., Athens, 1954–68.

Chatzinis, J., Ἑλληνικὰ κείμενα, Athens, 1955.

Sachinis, A., Ἡ σύγχρονη πεζογραφία μας, Athens, 1951 (2nd edn., Galaxias, 1969).

—— Τὸ ἱστορικὸ μυθιστόρημα, Athens, 1957 (2nd edn., Thessaloniki, 1971).

—— Τὸ νεοελληνικὸ μυθιστόρημα, Ἱστορία καὶ κριτική, Athens, 1958 (2nd edn., Galaxias, 1970).

(d) THEATRE

Laskaris, N., Ἱστορία τοῦ νεοελληνικοῦ θεάτρου, 2 vols., Athens, 1938–9.

Pontani, F. M., *Teatro neoellenico*, Milano, Nuova Accademia, 1962 (introduction, and translation of: Matesis, *The Basil Plant*; Palamàs, *Trisevgeni*; Xenopoulos, *All Souls' Day*).

Sideris, J., Νεοελληνικὸ θέατρο (*1795–1929*), Athens, 1953 [Βασικὴ Βιβλιοθήκη, 40].

*The Modern Greek Theatre, A Concise History*, translated from the Greek by Lucille Vassardaki, Athens, 1957 (the concise history is due to J. Sideris. There are two introductory notes: (a) E. Chourmouzios, 'The Ancient Drama in our Time', and (b) L. Politis, 'The Theatre in Crete during the Time of the Renaissance').

Also in French: *Le théâtre néogrec. Histoire abrégée du théâtre néogrec, traduite du grec par Jean Gaitanos*, Athens, 1957.

Thrylos, A., Μορφὲς καὶ θέματα τοῦ θεάτρου, 2 vols., Athens, 1961–2.
Valsa, M., *Le théâtre grec moderne, de 1453 à 1900*, Berlin, 1960 [Berliner Byzantinistische Arbeiten, 18].

## B. WORKS RELEVANT TO INDIVIDUAL CHAPTERS

### CHAPTER I

#### (a) TEXTS

Collections:

Kriaràs, E., Βυζαντινὰ ἱπποτικὰ μυθιστορήματα, Athens, 1955 [Βασικὴ Βιβλιοθήκη, 2] (*Kallimachos, Belthandros, Imberios, Florios*).

Lambros, Sp., *Collection de romans grecs en langue vulgaire et en vers*, Paris, 1880 (*Kallimachos, Imberios*, and others).

Legrand, E., *Bibliothèque grecque vulgaire*, 9 vols., Paris, 1880–1902 (various texts, from the Byzantine period to the eighteenth century).

*Achilleid*: Hesseling, D. C., *L'Achilléide byzantine*, Amsterdam, 1919.
    Stomeo, A., *Achilleide, poema bizantino*, Lecce, 1958 (Italian translation with notes).

*Alexander, Life of*: Reichmann, S., *Das byzantinische Alexandergedicht*, Meisenheim am Glan, 1963 (edition from the cod. Marcianus 408).

*Apollonios of Tyre*: Janssen, A., *Narratio neograeca Apollonii Tyrii*, Amsterdam, 1954 (critical edition, not satisfactory, with Latin translation).

*Belisarius*: Follieri, E., 'Il poema bizantino di Belisario', in: Accademia Nazionale dei Lincei, *Atti del Convegno Internazionale sul tema: La poesia epica e la sua formazione*, Rome, 1970, pp. 583–651.

*Chronicle of Morea*: Schmitt, J., *The Chronicle of Morea*, London, 1904 (critical edition from the MSS. of Copenhagen and Paris).
    Kalonaros, P., Τὸ Χρονικὸν τοῦ Μορέως, Athens, Dimitrakos, 1940.
    Lurier, H. E., *Crusaders and Conquerors: The Chronicle of Morea*, New York and London, 1964 (translation with notes and introduction).

*Digenìs*: Kalonaros, P., Βασίλειος Διγενὴς Ἀκρίτας. Τὰ ἔμμετρα κείμενα, 2 vols., Athens, Dimitrakos, 1941 (the text of Andros–Trebizond, Grottaferrata, and Escorial; introduction and notes).

Selected Bibliography 305

Mavrogordato, J., *Digenes Akrites*, edited with an introduction, translation, and commentary, Oxford, Clarendon Press, 1956 (reprinted 1963) (the Grottaferrata text).

Trapp, E., *Digenes Akrites. Synoptische Ausgabe der älteren Versionen*, Vienna, 1971 [Wiener Byzantinistische Studien, 8] (critical parallel edition of the text of Escorial, Grottaferrata, and the combined Trebizond–Andros versions).

*Drunkard's Philosophy*: Lambros, Sp., *Νέος Ἑλληνομνήμων*, 1 (1904), 433–49.

*Florios and Platziaflore*: Hesseling, D. C., *Le roman de Phlorios et Platzia Phlore*, Amsterdam, 1919.

Glykàs, M., *Στίχοι οὓς ἔγραψε καθ᾿ ὃν κατεσχέθη καιρόν, Κριτικὴ ἔκδοση Εὔδ. Θ. Τσολάκη*, Thessaloniki, 1959.

*Kallimachos and Chrysorrhoe*: Pichard, M., *Le roman de Callimaque et de Chrysorrhoè*, Paris, Les Belles-Lettres, 1956.

*Libistros and Rodamne*: Lambert, J., *Le roman de Libistros et Rhodamnè*, Amsterdam, 1935.

Rotolo, V., *Libistro e Rodamne, romanzo cavalleresco bizantino*, Athens, 1965 (Italian translation with introduction).

*Porikologos*: Wagner, *Carmina* (see Chapter II).

*Poulologos*: Stamatia Krawczynski, *Ὁ Πουλολόγος*, Kritische Textausgabe mit Übersetzung sowie sprachlichen und sachlichen Erläuterungen, Berlin, 1960 [Berliner Byzantinistische Arbeiten, 22].

*Prodromika*: Hesseling, D. C., and Pernot, H., *Poèmes prodromiques en grec vulgaire*, Amsterdam, 1910 [Verhandelingen K. Akademie, 11. 1].

*Ptocholeon*: Wagner, *Carmina* (see Chapter II).

Schick, J., *Corpus Hamleticum*, vol. 5 (1930).

*Sinner's Prayer*: Legrand, E., *Bibliothèque grecque vulgaire*, vol. 1.

*Synaxarion of the Donkey*: Wagner, *Carmina* (see Chapter II).

*Tale of Consolation*: Lambros, *Collection de romans*.

*Tale about Quadrupeds*: Wagner, *Carmina* (see Chapter II).

(*b*) STUDIES

Gidel, A., *Études sur la littérature grecque moderne*, Paris, 1866.

—— *Nouvelles études sur la littérature grecque moderne*, Paris, 1878.

Grégoire, H., *Ὁ Διγενὴς Ἀκρίτας*, New York, 1942.

Implelizzeri, S., *Il Digenis Akritas, L'epopea di Bisanzio*, Florence, 1940 (in Appendix, pp. 121–89, Italian translation of the Grottaferrata text).

Kyriakidis, St. P., *Ὁ Διγενὴς Ἀκρίτας*, Athens, [1926].

—— *Forschungsbericht zum Akritas-Epos*, Munich, 1958 [Berichte zum XI. Internationalen Byzantinisten Kongress].

Manousakas, M., 'Les romans byzantins de chevalerie et l'état présent des études les concernant', *Revue Ét. Byz.* 10 (1952), 70–83.

—— 'Un poeta Cretese ambasciatore di Venezia a Tunis e presso i Turchi', in *Venezia e l'Oriente fra tardo Medio Evo e Rinascimento*, Florence, [1966], pp. 283–307.

Pertusi, A., 'La poesia epica bizantina e la sua formazione: Problemi sul fondo storico e la struttura letteraria del *Digenis Akritas*', in Accademia Nazionale dei Lincei, *Atti del Convegno Internazionale sul tema: La poesia epica e la sua formazione*, Rome, 1970, pp. 481–544.

Politis, L., 'L'épopée byzantine de Digenis Akritas; Problèmes de la tradition du texte et des rapports avec les chansons akritiques', ibid., pp. 551–81.

Veloudis, G., *Der neugriechische Alexander. Tradition in Bewahrung und Wandel*, Munich, 1968 [Miscellanea Byzantina Monacensia, 8].

—— *Alexander der Grosse. Ein alter Neugrieche*, Munich, 1969 [Tusculum].

CHAPTER II

(*a*) TEXTS

Collections:

Alexiou, St., *Κρητικὴ Ἀνθολογία*, Heracleion, 1954 (2nd revised edn., 1970) (anthology of Cretan poetry from the fifteenth to the seventeenth century, with introduction and notes).

—— (ed.), *Μπεργαδῆς, Ἀπόκοπος. Ἡ Βοσκοπούλα*, Athens, 1971 (*Ἑρμῆς, Νέα Ἑλληνικη Βιβλιοθήκη*, 15).

Bouboulidis, F., *Κρητικὴ λογοτεχνία*, Athens, 1955 [*Βασικὴ Βιβλιοθήκη*, 7].

Wagner, G., *Carmina Graeca Medii Aevi*, Leipzig, 1874 (various poems, especially of the fifteenth and sixteenth centuries).

A. Achelis: Pernot, H. (ed.), P. Gentil de Vendosme et Antoine Achelis, *Le siège de Malte par les Turcs en 1565*, Paris, 1910 (French and Greek text).

*Apokopos*: see Bergadìs.

Bergadìs: Alexiou, St. (ed.), *Ἀπόκοπος*, Heracleion, 1965 (reprinted from *Κρητικὰ Χρονικά*, 17); see also above, under Collections.

*Chap-book of the Donkey*: see Wagner, *Carmina*.

George Choumnos: Marshall, F. H. (ed.), *Old Testament Legends, from a Greek Poem on Genesis and Exodus by Georgios Choumnos*, Cambridge, 1925.

*Erotopaignia*: see *Katalogia*.

Falieros, M.: Zoras, G., "'Ο ποιητὴς Μαρίνος Φαλιέρος", Κρητικὰ
Χρονικά, 2 (1948) (edition of three poems).

Georgillàs, E.: see Wagner, *Carmina*.

*Katalogia*: Hesseling, D. C., and Pernot, H., *'Ερωτοπαίγνια (Chansons
d'amour*), publiées d'après un manuscrit du xvᵉ siècle, avec une
traduction, etc., Paris, 1913 [Bibliothèque grecque vulgaire, 10]
(from the London MS.).

Pernot, H., *Chansons populaires grecques des XVᵉ et XVIᵉ siècles*,
Paris, Les Belles-Lettres, 1931 (from the Vienna MS.).

Machairàs, L.: *Recital concerning the Sweet Land of Cyprus entitled
'Chronicle'*, ed. by R. M. Dawkins, 2 vols., Oxford, 1932.

*Mourning for Death*: Zoras, G., Πένθος θανάτου, ζωῆς μάταιον καὶ πρὸς
Θεὸν ἐπιστροφή, Athens, 1971.

Pikatoros, J.: Kriaràs, E. (ed.), "'Η ρίμα θρηνητικὴ τοῦ 'Ιωάννου
Πικατόρου", 'Επετηρὶς Μεσαιωνικοῦ Ἀρχείου, 2 (1942), 1–51.

*Rimada of the Girl*: Pernot, H., *Chansons populaires* (see under *Katalogia*).

Sachlikis, S.: see Wagner, *Carmina*.

Papadimitriou, S. (ed.), *Stefanos Sachlikis and his Poem 'Strange
Story'*, Odessa, 1896 (in Russian).

Siapkaras-Pitsillidès, Th. (ed.), *Le Pétrarquisme en Chypre, Poèmes d'amour
en dialecte chypriote d'après un manuscrit du XVIᵉ siècle*, Athens,
1952.

Sklavos, M.: see Wagner, *Carmina*.

Trivolis, J., Ποιήματα, herausgegeben, übersetzt und erklärt von
Johannes Irmscher, Berlin, 1956 [Berliner Byzantinistische
Arbeiten, 1].

(*b*) STUDIES

Cammelli, G., *I dotti bizantini e le origini dell'umanesimo*, I., Manuele
Crisolora, Florence, 1911.

Geanakoplos, D., *Greek Scholars in Venice*, Cambridge, Mass., 1962.

Hadjiantoniou, G. A., *Protestant Patriarch: The Life of Cyril Lucaris,
1572–1638, Patriarch of Constantinople*, London, 1961.

Kakoulidi, E. D., "'Ο 'Ιωάννης Μορεζῆνος καὶ τὸ ἔργο του", Κρητικὰ
Χρονικά, 22 (1970).

Knös, B., *Un Ambassadeur de l'Hellénisme. Janus Lascaris et la tradition
gréco-byzantine dans l'humanisme français*, Paris, 1945.

Manousakas, M., 'Η κρητικὴ λογοτεχνία κατὰ τὴν ἐποχὴ τῆς Βενετο-
κρατίας, Thessaloniki, 1965.

Meyer, P., *Die theologische Literatur der griechischen Kirche im sechzehnten
Jahrhundert*, Leipzig, 1899.

Morgan, G., 'Cretan Poetry: Sources and Inspiration', Κρητικὰ
Χρονικά, 14 (1960).

Papadopoulos, Chr., *Κύριλλος Λούκαρις*, 2nd edn., Athens, 1939.

Tsiter, Ch., *Λόγιοι Έλληνες μετὰ τὴν Ἅλωσιν*, Athens, 1935.

Tsourkas, C., *Les Débuts de l'enseignement philosophique et de la libre pensée dans les Balkans. La Vie et l'œuvre de Théophile Corydalée*, 2nd revised edn., Thessaloniki, 1967.

Xanthoudidis, St., *Ἡ Ἑνετοκρατία ἐν Κρήτῃ καὶ οἱ κατὰ τῶν Ἑνετῶν ἀγῶνες τῶν Κρητῶν*, Athens, 1939.

## CHAPTER III

### (a) TEXTS

Alexiou, St. (ed.), *Ἡ Βοσκοπούλα, κρητικὸ εἰδύλλιο τοῦ 1600, κριτικὴ ἔκδοση*, Heracleion, 1963, see also Chapter II, *under* Collections.

Chortatsis, G., *Ἐρωφίλη, τραγῳδία Γεωργίου Χορτάτση (1600), ἐκδιδομένη ἐκ τῶν ἀρίστων πηγῶν μετ᾽ εἰσαγωγῆς καὶ λεξιλογίου ὑπὸ Στ. Ξανθουδίδου*, Athens, 1928.

—— *Κατζοῦρμπος, κωμῳδία, κριτικὴ ἔκδοση, σημειώσεις, γλωσσάριο Λίνου Πολίτη*, Heracleion, 1964.

Foskolos, M. A., *Φορτουνᾶτος, κωμῳδία ἀνέκδοτος τὸ πρῶτον ἐκ τοῦ αὐτογράφου τοῦ ποιητοῦ ἐκδιδομένη ὑπὸ Στ. Ξανθουδίδου*, Athens, 1922.

Kornaros, V., *Ἐρωτόκριτος, ἔκδοσις κριτικὴ γενομένη ἐπὶ τῇ βάσει τῶν πρώτων πηγῶν ὑπὸ Στ. Ξανθουδίδου*, Heracleion, 1915 (with important introduction).

—— *Ἐρωτόκριτος, Ἀνατύπωση ἀπὸ τὴν ἔκδοση Στ. Ξανθουδίδου, Εἰσαγωγὴ Λίνου Πολίτη*, Athens, 1952 (2nd facsimile-edn., 1968).

—— *Ἐρωτόκριτος, Εἰσαγωγὴ Γιώργου Σεφέρη*, Athens, Galaxias (a paperback edition, with the essay of G. Seferis).

—— *Ἡ θυσία τοῦ Ἀβραάμ, Εἰσαγωγὴ Ἄγγελος Τερζάκης, Φιλολογικὴ ἐπιμέλεια Ἑ(λένη) Τ(σαντσάνογλου)*, Athens, 1971 (*Ἑρμῆς, Νέα Ἑλληνικὴ Βιβλιοθήκη*, 14).

—— *The Erotocritos*, translated by J. Mavrogordato, with an Introduction by Stephen Gaselee, London, 1929 (fragments).

Kriaràs, E. (ed.), *Γύπαρις, κρητικὸν δρᾶμα. Πηγαί–κείμενον*, Athens, 1940.

Marshall, F. H. (trans.), *Three Cretan Plays : The Sacrifice of Abraham, Erophile, and Gyparis; also the Cretan Pastoral Poem The Fair Shepherdess*, with an Introduction by John Mavrogordato, London, 1929.

Megas, G. (ed.), *Ἡ θυσία τοῦ Ἀβραάμ, κριτικὴ ἔκδοσις*, revised edn., Athens, 1954.

Sathas, K. N., *Κρητικὸν θέατρον ἢ συλλογὴ ἀνεκδότων καὶ ἀγνώστων δραμάτων*, Venice, 1879 (*Ζήνων, Stathis, Gyparis, Erofili*).

(b) STUDIES

Alexiou, St., ʿΟ χαρακτὴρ τοῦ ᾿Ερωτοκρίτου, Heracleion, 1952.

Cartojan, N., 'Le Modèle français de l'*Erotokritos*, poème crétois du xviie siècle', *Revue de litt. comparée*, 16 (1936), 265–93.

Embiricos, A., *La Renaissance crétoise, XVIe et XVIIe siècles*, vol. 1, *La littérature*, Paris, Les Belles-Lettres, 1960.

Kriaràs, E., Μελετήματα περὶ τὰς πηγὰς τοῦ ᾿Ερωτοκρίτου, Athens, 1938.

Manousakas, M., Κριτικὴ βιβλιογραφία τοῦ Κρητικοῦ θεάτρου, 2nd revised edn., Athens, 1964.

Mavrogordato, J., 'The Greek Drama in Crete in the Seventeenth Century', *Journ. Hell. Studies*, 48 (1928), 75–96 (and p. 243, 'A Postscript').

Politis, L., 'Il teatro a Creta nei suoi rapporti con il teatro italiano del Rinascimento, e in particolare con la commedia veneziana', in *Venezia e l'Oriente fra tardo Medioevo e Rinascimento*, Florence, 1966, pp. 225–40.

—— 'La Poésie pastorale en Crète à la fin du xvie siècle; rapports et différences avec la poésie pastorale italienne', in *Actes du IVe Congrès de l'Assoc. Intern. de littérature comparée*, The Hague–Paris, 1966, pp. 1000–7.

Seferis, G., ᾿Ερωτόκριτος, Athens, 1946 (now in Δοκιμές, Athens, 2nd edn., 1962, pp. 207–48).

Zoras, G., Περὶ τὰς πηγὰς τῆς "Θυσίας τοῦ Ἀβραάμ", Athens, 1945.

CHAPTER IV

(a) TEXTS

Ἄνθη εὐλαβείας εἰς τὴν μετάστασιν τῆς θεομήτορος Μαρίας, Athens, 1950 (reimpression of the 1708 edn., with notes by A. Papakostas).

Joannou, P. (ed.), ʿΟ πιστικὸς βοσκός, *Der treue Schäfer. Der Pastor Fido des G. B. Guarini von einem Anonymus im 17. Jahrhundert in kretischer Mundart übersetzt*, Berlin, 1962 [Berliner Byzantinistische Arbeiten, 27].

Katartzìs, D., Τὰ εὑρισκόμενα, ἐκδότης Κ. Θ. Δημαρᾶς, Athens, 1970.

Kriaràs, E. (ed.), Κατσαΐτης: ᾿Ιφιγένεια, Θυέστης, Κλαθμὸς Πελοποννήσου, ἀνέκδοτα ἔργα, Athens, 1950 (critical edition with introduction notes, and glossary).

Montselese, T., Εὐγένα, a cura di Mario Vitti, Napoli, 1965 [Istituto Universitario Orientale].

Sathas, K. N. (ed.), Χρονικὸν ἀνέκδοτον Γαλαξειδίου, Athens, 1865.

Valetas, G. (ed.), Χρονικὸ τοῦ Γαλαξιδιοῦ, δημοτικὸ ἱστόρημα τοῦ 1704, Athens, Ikaros, 1944.

(*b*) STUDIES

Angelou, A., *Πλάτωνος τύχαι* ('*Η λόγια παράδοση στὴν Τουρκοκρατία*), Athens, 1963.

Dimaràs, K., '*Ο Κοραῆς καὶ ἡ ἐποχή του*, Athens, 1953 [*Βασικὴ Βιβλιοθήκη*, 9].

—— *Φροντίσματα*, I., *Ἀπὸ τὴν Ἀναγέννηση στὸν διαφωτισμό*, Athens, 1962.

—— '*Ο νεοελληνικὸς διαφωτισμός*, Athens, 1964.

—— *La Grèce au temps des Lumières*, Geneva, 1969.

Iorga, N., *Byzance après Byzance*, Bucharest, 1935.

Michalopoulos, F., *Κοσμᾶς ὁ Αἰτωλός*, Athens, 1940.

Rotolo, V., *A. Korais e la questione della lingua in Grecia*, Palermo, 1965.

Tatakis, V., *Σκοῦφος, Μηνιάτης, Βούλγαρις, Θεοτόκης*, Athens, 1953 [*Βασικὴ Βιβλιοθήκη*, 8].

Therianòs, D., *Ἀδαμάντιος Κοραῆς*, Trieste, 1889–90.

CHAPTER V

(*a*) COLLECTIONS

Academy of Athens, *Ἑλληνικὰ δημοτικὰ τραγούδια* (*'Εκλογή*), vol. 1, Athens, 1963.

Fauriel, C., *Chants populaires de la Grèce moderne*, 2 vols., Paris, 1824–5.

Ioannou, G., *Τα δημοτικά μας τραγούδια*, [Athens, 1966], Tachydromos.

Lüdeke, H., *Neugriechische Volkslieder, Auswahl und Übertragung ins Deutsche*, 2 vols., Athens, 1947, 1964 (vol. 1: the texts; vol. 2: translations).

Passow, A., *Τραγούδια Ρωμαίικα. Popularia Carmina Graeciae recentioris*, Leipzig, 1860.

Petropoulos, D., *Ἑλληνικὰ δημοτικὰ τραγούδια*, 2 vols., Athens, 1958 [*Βασικὴ Βιβλιοθήκη*, 46–7].

Politis, N. G., *Ἐκλογαὶ ἀπὸ τὰ τραγούδια τοῦ ἑλληνικοῦ λαοῦ*, Athens, 1914 (6th edn., 1969).

(*b*) STUDIES

Apostolakis, J. M., *Τὸ δημοτικὸ τραγούδι, I.*, *Οἱ συλλογές*, Athens, 1929.

—— *Τὸ κλέφτικο τραγούδι: Τὸ πνεῦμα κ' ἡ τέχνη του*, Athens, 1950.

Baud-Bovy, S., *La Chanson populaire grecque du Dodécanèse, I.*, *Les textes*, Paris, Les Belles Lettres, 1936.

Deter-Grohmann, I., *Das neugriechische Volkslied*, Munich, 1968 [Tusculum].

Georgiades, Thr., *Der griechische Rhythmus. Musik, Reigen, Vers und Sprache*, Hamburg, 1949.

Joannidu, M., *Untersuchungen zur Form der neugriechischen Klagelieder*, Diss. Munich, 1938.

Kyriakidis, St. P., Ἡ γένεσις τοῦ διστίχου καὶ ἡ ἀρχὴ τῆς ἰσομετρίας, Thessaloniki, 1947.

—— Αἱ ἱστορικαὶ ἀρχαὶ τῆς δημώδους νεοελληνικῆς ποιήσεως, 2nd edn., with an appendix, Thessaloniki, 1954.

Petropoulos, D., *La Comparaison dans la chanson populaire grecque*, Athens, 1954.

CHAPTER VI

(*a*) TEXTS

Christopoulos, A., Ἅπαντα, ἀναστύλωσε Γ. Βαλέτας, Athens, 1969.

—— Λυρικά, Ἐπιμέλεια Ἑλένη Τσαντσάνογλου, Athens, 1970 [Ἑρμῆς, Νέα Ἑλληνικὴ Βιβλιοθήκη, 2].

Rigas Velestinlìs Pheraios, Ἅπαντα. Συναγωγὴ κειμένων, φιλολογικὴ ἐπεξεργασία καὶ παρουσίαση Λ. Ι. Βρανούση, 2 vols., Athens, 1968 [Ἅπαντα Νεοελλήνων Κλασσικῶν].

—— Σχολεῖον τῶν ντελικάτων ἐραστῶν, Ἐπιμέλεια Π. Σ. Πίστας, Athens, 1971 [Ἑρμῆς, Νέα Ἑλληνικὴ Βιβλιοθήκη, 13].

Vilaràs, J., Ἅπαντα, Ἐπιμέλεια Γ. Α. Βαβαρέτου, Athens, 1935.

Vranousis, L., Οἱ Πρόδρομοι, Athens, 1955 [Βασικὴ Βιβλιοθήκη, 11].

—— Ρήγας. Ἔρευνα, συναγωγὴ καὶ μελέτη, Athens, 1954 [Βασικὴ Βιβλιοθήκη, 10].

Zoras, G. and Bouboulidis, F., Ἑπτανήσιοι προσολωμικοὶ ποιηταί, Athens, 1953.

(*b*) STUDIES

Dascalakis, Ap., *Rhigas Velestinlis. La Révolution française et les préludes de l'Indépendance hellénique*, Paris, 1937.

—— *Les œuvres de Rhigas Velestinlis, Étude bibliographique*, Paris, 1937.

—— Μελέται περὶ τοῦ Ρήγα Βελεστινλῆ, Athens, 1964.

Lambros, Sp., Ρήγας, Βηλαρᾶς, Χριστόπουλος, in Διαλέξεις περὶ Ἑλλήνων ποιητῶν τοῦ ΙΘ′ αἰῶνος, vol. 1, Athens, 2nd edn., 1925.

Protopapà-Bouboulidou, Gl., Τὸ θέατρον ἐν Ζακύνθῳ ἀπὸ τοῦ ΙΖ′ μέχρι τοῦ ΙΘ′ αἰῶνος, Athens, 1958.

CHAPTER VII

(*a*) TEXTS

Solomòs, D., Ἅπαντα, Ἐπιμέλεια - σημειώσεις Λίνου Πολίτη, 2 vols. and Appendix, Athens, Ikaros, 1948–60.

—— Αὐτόγραφα Ἔργα, Ἐπιμέλεια Λίνου Πολίτη, 2 vols., Thessaloniki, 1964 (vol. 1 is a facsimile edition of the autograph MSS., vol. 2 a typographic transcription).

Solomòs, D., *The Hymn of Liberty*, translated by W. E. Blake, 1957.
—— *Neugriechisches Gespräch. Der Dialog des Dionysios Solomos*, über-tragen von R. Fahrner, Munich, 1943.
—— *Solomos, Introduction, Prose et Poèmes*, translated by R. Levesque, Athens, 1945 (*The Woman of Zante, The Cretan, Free Besieged, Pórfyras*).
—— *Éloge de Foscolo et autres textes*, traduits de l'italien par J. Peretti, présentés par O. Merlier, Athens, 1957.

(*b*) STUDIES

Apostolakis, J. M., *Ἡ ποίηση στὴ ζωή μας*, Athens, 1923 (2nd edn., Athens, Kollaros, n.d.).
—— *Τὰ τραγούδια μας*, Athens, 1934 (reprinted 1967).
Brandenburg, J., *Solomos et l'Italie*, Rotterdam, n.d.
Chatzigiakoumìs, E. K., *Νεοελληνικαὶ πηγαὶ τοῦ Σολωμοῦ*, Athens, 1968.
Jenkins, R., *Dionysius Solomos*, Cambridge, 1940.
Kriaràs, E., *Διονύσιος Σολωμός. Ὁ βίος, τὸ ἔργο*, Thessaloniki, 1957 (2nd edn., reprint, [1970]).
Palamàs, K., *Διονύσιος Σολωμός, Ἐπιμέλεια M. K. Χατζηγιακουμῆ*, Athens, 1970 [*Ἑρμῆς, Νέα Ἑλληνικὴ Βιβλιοθήκη*, 9] (a collection of all Palamàs's essays on Solomòs).
Politis, L., *Ὁ Σολωμὸς στὰ γράμματά του*, Athens, 1956.
—— *Γύρω στὸ Σολωμό. Μελέτες καὶ ἄρθρα (1938–1958)*, Athens, 1958.
Stochastìs (ed.), *Γύρω στὸ Σολωμό*, 2 vols., Athens, 1925–7 (Essays by J. Polylàs, Sp. Zambelios, G. Markoràs, J. Typaldos, K. Palamàs, and others).
Varnalis, K., *Σολωμικά*, Athens, 1957.

CHAPTER VIII

(*a*) TEXTS

Kalvos, A., *Κάλβου Ὠδαί, μετά τῆς πρώτης γαλλικῆς μεταφράσεως ὑπὸ St. Julien καὶ Pauthier de Censay*, ed. by G. Zoras, Athens, 1962.
—— *Ὠδαί, Κριτικὴ ἔκδοση* Filippo Maria Pontani, Athens, Ikaros, 1970 (with a word-index).
Laskaratos, A., *Ἅπαντα*, 3 vols., Athens, 1959 (ed. by Al. Papageorgiou and A. Moschovakis).
—— *Βιογραφικά μου ἐνθυμήματα, Ἀνέκδοτη αὐτοβιογραφία. Εἰσαγωγή, κείμενο, πίνακες Ἀλ. Γ. Παπαγεωργίου*, Athens, 1966.
—— *Ἰδοὺ ὁ ἄνθρωπος, Ἐπιμέλεια Γ. Γ. Ἀλισανδράτος*, Athens, 1970 [*Ἑρμῆς, Νέα Ἑλληνικὴ Βιβλιοθήκη*, 8].
Valaoritis, A., *Βίος καὶ Ἔργα*, 3 vols., Athens, 1907 [*Βιβλιοθήκη Μαρασλῆ*].

## Selected Bibliography 313

Valaoritis, A., *Φωτεινός*, *Ἐπιμέλεια Γ. Π. Σαββίδης*, Athens, 1970 [*Ἑρμῆς*, *Νέα Ἑλληνικὴ Βιβλιοθήκη*, 7].

Zoras, G., *Ποίησις καὶ πεζογραφία τῆς Ἑπτανήσου*, Athens, 1953 [*Βασικὴ Βιβλιοθήκη*, 14].

(b) STUDIES

Apostolakis, J. M., *Ἀριστοτέλης Βαλαωρίτης*, Athens, 1936.

Bouchard, J., *Γεώργιος Τερτσέτης*, *Βιογραφικὴ καὶ φιλολογικὴ μελέτη (1800–1843)*, Athens, 1970.

Dimaràs, K., *Οἱ πηγὲς τῆς ἔμπνευσης τοῦ Κάλβου (Ρωμαντικὰ σημειώματα, Γ')*, Athens, 1946 (reprint from the *Nea Estia*).

*Nea Estia, Ἀφιέρωμα στὸν Κάλβο*, vol. 40 (Christmas 1946) (Reprint, 1960).

Palamàs, K., *Κάλβος ὁ Ζακύνθιος* (1888) (now in *Ἅπαντα*, vol. 2, pp. 28–59).

—— *Ἀριστοτέλης Βαλαωρίτης (1824–1924)*. *Ἄρθρα, γράμματα, ὁμιλίες*, Athens, 1924 (now in *Ἅπαντα*, vol. 8, pp. 161–275).

—— *Ἰούλιος Τυπάλδος*, in *Διαλέξεις περὶ Ἑλλήνων ποιητῶν*, vol. 2, Athens, 2nd edn., 1925 (now in *Ἅπαντα*, vol. 8, pp. 285–310).

Seferis, G., *Ἀπορίες διαβάζοντας τὸν Κάλβο. Πρόλογος γιὰ μιὰ ἔκδοση τῶν "Ὠδῶν". Κάλβος, 1960*. In *Δοκιμές*, Athens, 2nd edn., 1962, pp. 21–8, 145–72, 369–89.

Sofroniou, S. A., *Ἀνδρέας Κάλβος, Κριτικὴ μελέτη, Πρόλογος* R. J. H. Jenkins, Athens, 1960.

Vitti, M., *Πηγὲς γιὰ τὴ βιογραφία τοῦ Κάλβου (Ἐπιστολὲς 1813–1820)*, Thessaloniki, 1963.

CHAPTER IX

(a) TEXTS

Dimaràs, K., *Ποιηταὶ τοῦ ΙΘ' αἰῶνα*, Athens, 1954 [*Βασικὴ Βιβλιοθήκη*, 12].

Makrygiannis, General, *Ἀπομνημονεύματα. Κείμενον, εἰσαγωγή, σημειώσεις Γιάννη Βλαχογιάννη*, 2 vols., 2nd edn., Athens, 1947.

—— *The Memoirs of General Makriyannis, 1794–1864*, edited and translated by H. A. Lidderdale, foreword by C. M. Woodhouse, London, 1966.

(b) STUDIES

Michaïlidis, M. I., *Βίος καὶ ἔργα Δημητρίου Ν. Βερναρδάκη*, Mytilene, 1909.

Palamàs, K., *Ἕνας λεοπαρδικὸς ποιητής*, in *Πεζοὶ δρόμοι*, Athens, 1934 (now in *Ἅπαντα*, vol. 10, pp. 267–82 (D. Paparrigopoulos)).

Politis, L., ʿΕλληνικὸς ρομαντισμὸς (*1830–1880*), in ʾΟργανισμὸς ʾΕθνικοῦ Θεάτρου, Δώδεκα διαλέξεις, Σειρὰ Β΄, Athens, 1962, pp. 158–80.

Seferis, G., ῎Ενας ῎Ελληνας, ὁ Μακρυγιάννης, in Δοκιμές, Athens, 2nd edn., 1962, pp. 173–203.

Vlachos, A., Ἀνάλεκτα, 2 vols., Athens, 1901 (P. Soutsos, A. Soutsos, J. Karasoutsas, G. Zalokostas, G. Tertsetis).

## CHAPTER X

(*a*) TEXTS

Palamàs, K., Ἄπαντα, 16 vols., Athens, 1960– (in progress) (edited by the Palamàs Foundation under the direction of G. K. Katsimbalis).

—— *Life Immovable*, first part, translated by Ar. Phoutrides, with Introduction and Notes, Cambridge, 1919.

—— *A Hundred Voices, and Other Poems, from the Second Part of 'Life Immovable'*, translated by Ar. Phoutrides, with an Introduction, Cambridge, 1921.

—— *Royal Blossom or Trisevyene*, translated by Ar. Phoutrides, with an Introduction, New Haven, Conn., 1922.

—— *Poems*, selected and rendered into English by Th. Stephanides and G. Katsimbalis, London, 1925.

—— *Three Poems*, translated by Th. Stephanides and G. Katsimbalis, London, 1969 ('The Palm Tree', 'The Chains', 'The Satyr').

—— *The Grave*, rendered into English Verse by A. D. Michalaros, with an Introduction by Prof. Louis Roussel, Chicago, Ill., 1930.

—— *A Man's Death*, translated by Ar. Phoutrides, with a Foreword by D. C. Hesseling, Athens, 1934.

—— *The Twelve Words of the Gypsy*, translated by Frederic Will, New York, 1964.

—— *The Twelve Lays of the Gipsy*, translated, with an Introduction by G. Thomson, London, 1969.

Roidis, Em., *Pope Joan, an Historical Study*, translated from the Greek, with a Preface by Ch. Hastings Colette, London, 1888.

—— *Pope Joan, an Historical Romance*, translated (and abridged) by J. H. Freese, 1900.

—— *Pope Joan, a Romantic Biography*, translated from the Greek by Lawrence Durell, London, 1954.

(*b*) STUDIES

Chourmouzios, E., ʿΟ Παλαμᾶς καὶ ἡ ἐποχή του, 3 vols., Athens, 1943–60.

Dimaràs, K., Κωστὴς Παλαμᾶς, ʽΗ πορεία του πρὸς τὴν τέχνη, Athens, [1947].

Jenkins, R., *Palamas, An Inaugural Lecture delivered at King's College,* London, 1947.

Karantonis, A., Γύρω στὸν Παλαμᾶ, 2 vols., Athens, 1959, 1971.

Katsimbalis, G. K., Βιβλιογραφία Κωστῆ Παλαμᾶ, Athens, 1943 (and many Supplements in the following years).

Paraschos, K., Ἐμμανουὴλ Ροΐδης, 2 vols., Athens, 1942–50.

—— Ἐμμανουὴλ Ροΐδης, Athens, 1952 [Βασικὴ Βιβλιοθήκη, 20].

Tsatsos, K., Παλαμᾶς, 2nd edn., Athens, 1949.

## CHAPTER XI

(*a*) TEXTS

Eftaliotis, A., *Die Olivensammlerin, Neugriechische Erzählungen,* aus dem Neugriechischen übersetzt und herausgegeben von Alexander Steinmetz, Kassel, 1955.

Papadiamantis, A., Τὰ Ἅπαντα, Ἐπιμέλεια Γ. Βαλέτα, 5 vols., Athens, 1954–5.

—— *Skiathos, île grecque,* Nouvelles traduites et publiées par Octave Merlier, Paris, 1934.

—— *Nouvelles,* traduites du grec et présentées par Octave Merlier, Athens, 1965.

Psycharis, Τὸ ταξίδι μου, Ἐπιμέλεια Ἄλκης Ἀγγέλου, Athens, 1971 [Ἑρμῆς, Νέα Ἑλληνικὴ Βιβλιοθήκη, 11].

Xenopoulos, Gr., Ἅπαντα, 9 vols., Athens, 1958–9.

—— Ἅπαντα, Θέατρον, 4 vols., Athens, 1913–22, 1945.

—— *Red Rock, from Ecstasy to Tragedy,* translated by W. Spanos, New York, 1955.

(*b*) STUDIES

Bastiàs, K., ʽΟ Παπαδιαμάντης, δοκίμιο, Athens, 1962.

Chalvatzakis, M., ʽΟ Παπαδιαμάντης μέσα ἀπὸ τὸ ἔργο του, Alexandria, 1960.

Kriaràs, E., Ψυχάρης, Thessaloniki, 1959.

Panagiotopoulos, J. M., Γ. Βιζυηνός, Athens, 1954 [Βασικὴ Βιβλιοθήκη, 18].

Rouillard, G., *Notice biographique et bibliographique de J. Psichari,* Melun, 1930.

Sideridou-Thomopoulou, N., Ἀντρέας Καρκαβίτσας, μελέτη, Athens, 1959.

Triantafyllidis, M., Μνημόσυνα: Ψυχάρης – Πάλλης – Ἐφταλιώτης, Athens, 1939–46 (now in Ἅπαντα, vol. 5, pp. 366–452).

Valetas, G., Παπαδιαμάντης, Mytilene, 1940 (= Άπαντα, vol. 6, Athens, 1955).

CHAPTER XIII

(*a*) TEXTS

Karyotakis, K. G., Άπαντα τα ευρισκόμενα, Φιλολογική επιμέλεια Γ. Π. Σαββίδη, 2 vols., Athens, 1965–6.

Kavafis, K. P., Ποιήματα, Athens, Ikaros, 1949 (4th edn., 1958).

—— Ποιήματα. Πρώτη τυποποιημένη έκδοση, Θιλολογική επιμέλεια Γ. Π. Σαββίδη, 2 vols., Athens, Ikaros, 1963 (2nd edn., 1965).

—— Ανέκδοτα ποιήματα (1882–1923), Φιλολογική επιμέλεια Γ. Π. Σαββίδη, Athens, Ikaros, 1968.

—— Αυτόγραφα ποιήματα (1896–1910), Athens, 1968 (facsimile edn. of an autograph copy-book, presented by G. P. Savvidis).

—— Ανέκδοτα πεζά κείμενα, Εισαγωγή και μετάφραση Μιχάλη Περίδη, Athens, Fexis, 1963.

—— Πεζά. Παρουσίαση, σχόλια Γ. Δ. Παπουτσάκη, Athens, Fexis, 1963.

—— *The Poems of C. Cavafy*, tranlated into English with a few Notes by John Mavrogordato, with an Introduction by Rex Warner, London, 1951.

—— *The Complete Poems of Cavafy*, translated by Rae Dalven, Introduction by W. H. Auden, London, 1961 (new edn., A Harvest Book).

—— *Passions and Ancient Days*, New Poems translated and introduced by E. Keeley and G. Savidis, New York, The Dial Press, 1971.

—— *Gedichte*, aus dem Neugriechischen übertragen und herausgegeben von Helmut von den Steinen, Frankfurt a. M., Suhrkamp, 1953.

—— *Présentation critique de Constantin Cavafy, 1863–1933*, par Marguerite Yourcenar, suivie d'une traduction intégrale de ses poèmes par M. Yourcenar et C. Dimaras, Paris, 1958.

—— *Poèmes*, traduits par G. Papoutsakis, Préface de A. Mirambel, Paris, 1958.

—— *Poesie*, a cura di Filippo Maria Pontani, Mondadori, 1961 (Greek text, Italian translation, and notes).

Sikelianòs, A., Λυρικός Βίος, 3 vols., Athens, 1946–7.

—— Άπαντα, Φιλολογική επιμέλεια Γ. Π. Σαββίδη, Athens, Ikaros, 1965– (in progress, 8 vols. up to 1972).

—— *Mater Dei*, Texte grec avec traduction et introduction de Robert Levesque, Athens, 1944.

Sikelianòs, A., *Sikelianos*, ed. by Robert Levesque, Introduction, Choix de poèmes. Avant-propos de Paul Eluard, Athens, Ikaros, 1946.
—— *Poèmes akritiques*. *La mort de Digénis, tragédie*, Adaptation française par Octave Merlier, Athens, 1960.

(*b*) STUDIES

Bowra, C. M., *The Creative Experiment*, London, 1949.
Forster, E. M., *Pharos and Pharillon*, London, 1926 (pp. 91–7: 'The poetry of C. P. Cavafy').
—— *Two Cheers for Democracy*, London, 1951 (pp. 246–50: 'The Complete Poems of C. P. Cavafy').
*Lessico di Kavafis*, a cura di Gina Lorando, Lucia Marcheselli, Anna Gentilini, Padua, 1970 [Università di Padova, Studi bizantini e neogreci, 2] (A word-index).
Malanos, T., ῾Ο ποιητὴς Κ. Π. Καβάφης. ῾Ο ἄνθρωπος καὶ τὸ ἔργο του, Athens, 1957 (1st edn., 1933).
Papanoutsos, E., Παλαμᾶς, Καβάφης, Σικελιανός, 2nd edn., Athens, 1955.
Peridis, M., ῾Ο βίος καὶ τὸ ἔργο τοῦ Κ. Καβάφη, Athens, Ikaros, 1948.
Sarigiannis, J. A., Σχόλια στὸν Καβάφη. Πρόλογος Γ. Σεφέρη, Εἰσαγωγὴ καὶ φροντίδα Ζ. Λορεντζάτου, Athens, Ikaros, 1964.
Seferis, G., Κ. Π. Καβάφης–Θ. Σ. ῎Ελιοτ, παράλληλοι, and Ἀκόμα λίγα γιὰ τὸν Ἀλεξανδρινό, in Δοκιμές, Athens, 2nd edn., 1962, pp. 250–60.
Stergiopoulos, K., ῾Ο Τέλλος Ἄγρας καὶ τὸ πνεῦμα τῆς παρακμῆς, Athens, 1962.
Tsirkas, St., ῾Ο Καβάφης καὶ ἡ ἐποχή του, Athens, 1958 (2nd edn., 1971).
—— ῾Ο πολιτικὸς Καβάφης, Athens, Kedros, 1971 (collected essays).

CHAPTER XIV

(*a*) TEXTS

Kazantzakis, N., *The Odyssey; A Modern Sequel*, translation into English Verse, Introduction, Synopsis, and Notes by Kimon Friar, New York, 1958.
—— *The Savior of God; Spiritual Exercises*, translated with an Introduction by Kimon Friar, New York, 1960.

English Translations of the Novels:

*Christ Recrucified*, by Jonathan Griffin, London, 1954.
*The Fratricides*, by Ath. Dallas, 1964.
*Freedom or Death*, by Jonathan Griffin, New York, 1956.

English Translations of the Novels (*cont.*):

*God's Pauper Saint Francis of Assisi*, by P. A. Bien, New York, 1962.
*The Greek Passion*, by Jonathan Griffin, New York, 1954.
*The Last Temptation*, by P. A. Bien, Oxford, 1961.
*The Rock Garden*, by Richard Howard, New York, 1963.
*Toda Raba*, by Amy Mims, New York, 1964.
*Zorba the Greek*, by Carl Wildmann, New York, 1953.

(*b*) STUDIES

Chourmouzios, E., *Κωνσταντῖνος Θεοτόκης*, Athens, 1946.
Delta, P. S., *Ἀλληλογραφία, 1906–1940*, 'Επιμέλεια Ξ. Λευκοπαρίδη, [Athens, n.d.].
Izzet, A., *Nikos Kazantzaki, biographie*, avec un tableau chronologique établi par P. Prévélaki, Paris, 1965.
Paraschos, K., *"Ιων Δραγούμης*, Athens, 1936.
Prevelakis, P., *'Ο ποιητὴς καὶ τὸ ποίημα τῆς 'Οδύσσειας*, Athens, 1958.
—— *Nikos Kazantzakis and his Odyssey*. A study of the Poet and the Poem, translated from the Greek by Philip Sherrard, with a Preface by Kimon Friar, New York, 1966.
(——) *Τετρακόσια γράμματα τοῦ Καζαντζάκη στὸν Πρεβελάκη*, Athens, 1965 (with a biographical essay by P. Prevelakis, notes, and chronological data).
Stanford, W. B., *The Ulysses Theme: A Study in the Adaptability of a Traditional Hero*, Oxford, 1954.
Terzakis, A., *Κωνσταντῖνος Θεοτόκης*, Athens, 1955 [*Βασικὴ Βιβλιοθήκη*, 31].
Zografou, Lilì, *N. Καζαντζάκης, ἕνας τραγικός*, Athens, Kedros, 1960.

CHAPTER XV

(*a*) TEXTS

Elytis, Od., *Poèmes*, texte avec traduction par Robert Levesque, Athens, 1945.
—— *Poesie, precedute dal Canto eroico e funebre per il sottotenente caduto in Albania*, traduzione e nota di Mario Vitti, Roma, Il Presente, 1952.
—— *21 Poesie*, tradotte da Vincenzo Rotolo, Palermo, 1968 [Istituto Siciliano di Studi bizantini e neoellenici, Quaderni di Poesia neogreca, 3].
Seferis, G., *Ποιήματα*, Athens, Ikaros, 5th edn., 1964.
—— *Collected Poems, 1924–1955*, translated, edited, and introduced by Edmund Keeley and Philip Sherrard, Princeton, N.J., 1967.
—— *Poems*, translated from the Greek by Rex Warner, London, 1960.

Seferis, G., *Six Poems from the Greek of Sikelianos and Seferis*, translated
by L. Durell, Rhodes, 1946.
—— *The King of Asine and Other Poems*, translated from the Greek by
B. Spencer, N. Valaoritis, L. Durrell, London, 1948.
—— *Three Secret Poems*, translated from the Greek by Walter
Kaiser, Cambridge, Mass., 1969.
—— *On the Greek Style*, Selected Essays in Poetry and Hellenism,
translated by Rex Warner and Th. D. Frangopoulos, with an
Introduction by Rex Warner, London, 1967.
—— *Séféris. Choix de poèmes*, traduits et accompagnés du texte grec,
avec une Préface, par R. Levesque, Athens, 1945.
—— *Poèmes, 1933–1955*, traduits du grec par Jacques Lacarrière et
Égérie Mavraki, Paris, 1963.
—— *Poesie*, a cura di Filippo Maria Pontani, Mondadori, 1963
(Greek text and Italian translation).
—— *Tre poesie segrete*, a cura di Filippo Maria Pontani, Mondadori,
1968 [Lo Specchio].

(*b*) STUDIES

Karantonis, A., *Ὁ ποιητὴς Γιῶργος Σεφέρης*, Athens, 1957.
Kokolis, X. A., *Πίνακας λέξεων τῶν ποιημάτων τοῦ Γιώργου Σεφέρη*,
Thessaloniki, 1970.
Mirambel, A., *Georges Séféris, prix Nobel 1963*, Paris, 1964.
Pontani, F. M. (ed.), *Ommagio a Seferis*, Padua, 1970 (various essays
on Seferis) [Università di Padova, Studi bizantini e neo-
greci, 1].
Savvidis, G. P. (ed.), *Γιὰ τὸν Σεφέρη. Τιμητικὸ ἀφιέρωμα στὰ τριάντα
χρόνια τῆς Στροφῆς*, Athens, 1961 (essays on Seferis by various
authors).

CHAPTER XVI

(*a*) TEXTS

Myrivilis, S., *The Mermaid Madonna*, translated from the Greek by
A. Rick, New York, 1959.
—— *The Schoolmistress with the Golden Eyes*, translated by Philip
Sherrard, London, 1964.
Theotokàs, G., *Argo*, translated by Margaret Brooke and Ar. Tsatso-
poulos, London, 1951.
—— *Le Démon*, traduction de Marie Colombos, Préface de Thr.
Castanakis, Paris, 1946.
Venezis, E., *Aeolia*, translated from the Greek by E. D. Scott-Kilvert,
London, 1949.

Venezis, E., *Beyond the Aegean*, translated from the Greek by E. D. Scott-Kilvert, New York, 1956.

—— *La Grande Pitié*, Paris, 1946 (= *Number 31328*).

—— *Terre Éolienne*, traduit par Pierre et Loulou Amandry, Préface de A. Sikelianos, Paris, 1946.

(*b*) STUDIES

Chatzinis, J., *Προτιμήσεις*, Athens, 1963 (Karagatzis, Terzakis, Theotokàs, Xefloudas, Petsalis, Giannopoulos, Venezis, *et al.*).

Karantonis, A., *Πεζογράφοι καὶ πεζογραφήματα τῆς γενιᾶς τοῦ '30*, Athens, 1962.

Sachinis, A., *Πεζογράφοι τοῦ καιροῦ μας*, Athens, 1967 (K. Politis, Kazantzakis, Myrivilis, Venezis, Karagatsis, Terzakis, Theotokàs, Petsalis, Beratis, Athanasiadis, *et al.*).


EXCURSUS

*Les Lettres Nouvelles*, Numéro spécial: *Écrivains grecs d'aujourd'hui*, [Paris], mars–avril 1969 (Translations; Introduction; Jacques Lacarrière, 'Le défi' [On the prose-writers]; Nanos Valaoritis, 'La poésie grecque').

Meraklìs, M., *Ἡ σύγχρονη ἑλληνικὴ λογοτεχνία (1945–1970)*, *I.*, *Ποίηση*; *II.*, *Πεζογραφία* [Thessaloniki, 1971].

Raftopoulos, D., *Οἱ ἰδέες καὶ τὰ ἔργα, δοκίμια*, Athens, 1965 (Critical essays, mainly about prose-writers: Kazantzakis, Karagatsis, and others of the post-war generation).

Sachinis, A., *Νέοι πεζογράφοι. Εἴκοσι χρόνια νεοελληνικῆς πεζογραφίας: 1945–1965*, Athens, 1965 (A. Giannopoulos, D. Chatzìs, Sp. Plaskovitis, V. Vasilikòs).

Stergiopoulos, K., *Ἀπὸ τὸν συμβολισμὸ στὴ "νέα ποίηση"*, Athens, 1967 (Vafopoulos, Geralis, Dimakis, Varvitsiotis, Themelis).

Thasitis, P., *Γύρος στὴν ποίηση*, Thessaloniki, 1966.

Themelis, G., *Ἡ νεώτερη ποίησή μας*, Athens, 1963.

# Index

The original titles of books are given in brackets after the English entry, but titles of single poems or short stories are not included. Main references are given in italics. The index covers neither the Chronological Tables nor the Selected Bibliography.

# 336 Index